CATCHING THE BAG

Catching the Bag
Who'd be a Woman Diplomat?

by

Margaret West

Fare well, fellow Ruskinites!
Margaret West.

The Pentland Press Limited
Edinburgh · Cambridge · Durham · USA

Mrs. Margaret West
Luntley House, Pembridge
Leominster
Hereford HR6 9EH
Tel: 01544-388376

First published in 2000 by
The Pentland Press Ltd.
1 Hutton Close
South Church
Bishop Auckland
Durham

British Library Cataloguing in Publication Data.
A catalogue record for this book is available
from the British Library.

ISBN 1 85821 750 4

Typeset by George Wishart & Associates, Whitley Bay.
Printed and bound by Bookcraft (Bath) Ltd.

For Roger, and in loving memory
of my mother, Molly Archer
(Mary Robertson Auchterlonie)

Illustrations

My very grateful thanks to Joan Hughes and Bridget Bufton for the daunting task of deciphering and typing my letters in the first place.

Prelude

Roger has always called me his Old Bag as I am eleven years older than he is. But I could at least put 'diplomatic' in front of it by the time I met him.

I never set out to be a diplomat. I like to think that my way there was unprecedented. I took my first step in the shoes of the lowest grade of the civil service, that of female labourer, temporary and unestablished. The Ministry of Supply had appointed me in 1943 as an assistant welfare officer in the Telecommunications Research Establishment in Malvern. They had not made this appointment before and they had no idea how I would shape, so they wisely put me in my place at the beginning. I was certainly female, I was prepared to labour, and I remained temporary and unestablished for the next nine years.

At the end of the war I was tipped to go to London for an interview at the Ministry of Education. The Ministry had expanded rapidly after the passing of the Butler Act in 1944 and wanted a welfare officer to help with the problems of that time. As I had no expectations of success, particularly on seeing the formidable bevy of competent career women awaiting their turn, I treated my interview as a happy lark. The solemn board – I can see them now – must have forgiven me my youthful brashness, for they gave me the job. I was thunderstruck.

I stayed at the Ministry for four years and then got itchy feet. A useful grapevine whispered in my ear about a possible job in India. Sir Archibald Nye, High Commissioner in the newly independent India, was in London seeking, among more important issues, a welfare officer for his Mission. I bought a smart suit for £20, a fortune for me in those days, went for my interview with Sir Archibald, and got the job. Within a few weeks I was on my way to India.

I should explain the background to my book. Unlike me, my mother was born in the wrong century. One of four children of a blind and penniless Congregational minister in Edinburgh, she had to leave school at fifteen and earn her living. She became so skilled a shorthand writer that her reputation reached Lord Minto, Viceroy of India from 1905 to 1910, who asked her to go to India as his secretary. Her Victorian parents refused to let her go.

When I went to work in India some forty years later than she would have done, I determined to try to compensate for this injustice. So I wrote to her every week during my three years in India, and subsequently from my three years in Africa, some three hundred letters in all. She kept them until she died, when I put them under our stairs for twenty-five years. They form the substance of this book. I have taken out irrelevant material, and most of the headings and tails, but what is there is exactly what I wrote at the time – grammatical errors, family clichés and all.

A word to any young who may read this. Do record the more interesting things that happen to you. They may be boring to other people but they will amuse you no end when you come to read them in your old age. I have no recollection of many of the antics recorded in my letters, and often feel that I am reading about somebody else's life. The rest have been good joggers of the memory.

In October 1949 I sailed for Bombay in the splendid port-out-starboard-home *Strathmore*. For me, who had never been out of Europe, it was a stunning experience. The sights, sounds and smells were all new to me. I had a shipboard romance with a Cambridge blue (more about this later) and arrived in Bombay ready for anything.

The letters begin with the excitement of embarking at Tilbury. I hope that you will want to read on.

India
1949-1953

1949

Strathmore

26 October 1949

Dearest Mother

It is 8.15 and I've just consumed a large meal. To face a seven course menu is quite beyond my capacity and I shall try to approximate more to the utility three! The journey down to Tilbury was very quick and comfortable. The priests read their bibles studiously, silently moving their lips, and I read Donald McCulloch and roared loudly. At Tilbury we sat in the train for some considerable time and very wisely I fell sound asleep! Soon after three I was on board with customs formalities over and all my luggage safely with me. My trunk had forestalled me and was securely lying in wait under my bunk. Mrs Lethbridge, my cabin companion, was also installed by then. She is the wife of the Legal Adviser in the High Commissioner's office in Delhi. She has spent years of her life rushing backwards and forwards to India, so I shall be very safe in her hands. I had tea with her, collected my mail (five telegrams and a letter), discovered a beautiful cyclamen from Vera, roses from the Youngs and roses and some lovely red flowers, genus unknown, from the Bryans and, recovering from my intense surprise, started my unpacking amid my floral bower! Of course, we are still lying securely in port. The headlines in the evening papers show 'Worst October storms for years – wind reaches hurricane force' etc, etc. It will only be with luck that we shall get away on the next tide – at 2.30 tomorrow morning! Evidently Tilbury is impossible to navigate when gales are blowing. The *Strathmore* really is lovely. I still get hopelessly lost, but have already been on several voyages of exploration round her. I can see I am going to have a magnificent holiday. It seems rather ridiculous to be sending you an air letter from Tilbury, but it is the only form of communication with the outside world at the moment, and I believe is taken off by the pilot boat when we eventually sail. The next chance of writing to you will be from Port Said, so don't be optimistic for at least another fortnight.

A thousand thanks again for all your help. I could not have managed without you.

Strathmore
Mid-Mediterranean

1 November 1949

Dearest Mother

You must come on a long sea voyage sometime, swimmer or no swimmer! Never have I spent such a luxuriously wonderful week as this first one at sea. To glide on, day and night through tranquil seas, with miraculous menus and sunshine and no need to do anything but please oneself, is a fabulous and gloriously unreal experience. Tonight there is a sudden Mediterranean squall, but the *Strathmore* is riding it in solid stability. But the weather has been perfect. All day I sprawl on the deck reading or snoozing and occasionally shaking off lethargy with a vigorous game of deck tennis or quoits. The food is as manna from the gods. I'm just working off a dinner of fresh salmon, guinea fowl, raspberry sundae, cheese straws and melon, and then I left a couple of courses untouched!

I've successfully tamed a most handsome Cambridge Blue (unmarried, six foot three and twenty-eight!), who rowed in the last Boat Race, and we treat each other as refugees from the large quantities of elderly passengers who hold numerical superiority on this ship.

We sailed out of Tilbury at 2.30 on Thursday morning and I never even heard us go. Gibraltar we passed at 4 a.m., but I got up to see the lights, and this morning I hauled myself out of bed at 6.15 a.m. to see Malta lying sunlit on the horizon. For the past two days we have hugged the coast of Africa. To see the giant mountains of Algeria rising from the blue Mediterranean is a sight long to be remembered. All sorts of odd craft go by – steamers and liners and fishing vessels. Yesterday a whole factory ship crossed our path with a retinue of ten tiny whaling vessels. They looked too fragile to hunt such monsters of the sea.

We arrive at Port Said tomorrow and will have four hours ashore. David and I have planned to look after each other in the wicked city and restrain each other from spending too much at Simon Arzt!

We have a couple of maharajahs on board who are disgustingly wealthy. One is quite old and comes on frequent trips to Europe to whisk off white women as so-called wives. This time he has got a fascinating young French woman. She rarely appears. The rest of the time she is under guard in her cabin and is even escorted when she goes to the bathroom! Anthea Askey stalks around in loud checks and plays bad deck tennis with hair flying. Every other night there is a dance. Dancing on a slightly swaying deck gives one a most peculiar sensation of drunkenness. The other night David and I wandered into the tourists and found ourselves being hearty with the British Speedway Team bound for test matches in Australia – a strange collection of people these are here, without doubt. Next epistle from Aden. How I wish you were enjoying the fun here too.

Strathmore
Aden

7 November 1949

Dearest Leslie [*my Eighth Army brother*],

Now that Aden approaches I must write and tell you about Port Said and the Canal and get it posted. I was so very glad that you had drawn your maps, as I was easily able to follow them. As I said in my card, de Lesseps is still standing magnificently at the entrance to the Canal. When we had had our tea in Simon Arzt we wandered around the wall to have a look at him. The light was fading, but I have never seen such a beautiful dusk. Perhaps you will remember it – a velvety, almost purple sky reflected in the sea and the deep, warm russet colour of the nets of the fishing smacks moored along the wall. A number of ships were also moored in the harbour aglow with light, and as night came, the moon rose grandly, putting out the stars near to it.

We had to be on board again by 10 p.m. but did not sail until 1 a.m. Long after the pontoon bridge to the ship had been removed, the little green boats remained piled high with leather poofs and zipper bags and brightly woven baskets. I wonder if they were there in your time? Bargaining went on to the very last minute with a thin rope and aged basket as the means of communication. As the time of sailing drew near prices dropped lower and lower until the most beautiful leather bags were going for £1! We had a gilly-gilly man on board in the evening who did the most fantastic conjuring tricks. He was uncanny. I think he must have sold his soul to the devil. We were appalled at the squalor of the back streets of Port Said. The only solid building going on seems to be of mosques. We were amused to see one nearby completed with the washing hanging out to dry between two of its walls.

We had to creep through the Canal. We watched the ferry plying its trade and I saw the Officers' Club; and luckily we didn't enter Lake Temsah until mid-morning on Friday. I saw your very diving board. What a heavenly spot it looks. There was a British family standing there as we passed, and they hailed us nostalgically as we steamed by. The banks of the Canal are strewn with the corpses of ships that had got stuck at some time and been blown up. Evidently they are only given a short time to free themselves if they are to avoid destruction – pathetic sights they were.

Strathmore
Aden

7 November 1949

By this evening we shall be in Aden and therefore have a chance to send off more mail. We have been lucky with our weather in the Red Sea. We crept through the Suez Canal incredibly slowly, taking nearly fifteen hours over it. It is an amazing experience. We entered it at 1 a.m. and stayed up until 3.45, sitting in moonlight and heavenly warmth, gazing out over vast expanses of arid desert. We entered the Lake Temsah later in daylight and I was able to see the very spot where Leslie and Tess [*his dog*] used to dive in and swim across the Canal. The temperature rises rapidly as soon as you enter the Red Sea. This is the cool season, but believe me it is fantastically hot. Mercifully we have had a head wind all the way through the Red Sea, so really it has been heavenly. Sometimes with a following wind the ship has to be stopped and reversed in order to change the stifling air. But we have been able to strew ourselves on the boat deck, with the sun beating down and a strong wind to keep the surface of the skin cool. I am getting a superb tan by being very careful and not exposing myself for long at a time.

We are deep in the throes of games competitions at the moment – all very exhausting. I am still in the table tennis and bucket quoits, but to my relief have been eliminated from everything else! It is so much pleasanter to laze in the sun or flop into the swimming pool. I now leap out of my bunk at 7.15 and swim for half an hour before breakfast and then have another dip before changing for dinner in the evening. David is still very devoted, and we have now got to the stage where I wash his socks for him!

Strathmore
300 miles from Bombay

11 November 1949

We shall be in Bombay tomorrow. I couldn't be sadder that the voyage is over, but alas working woman must come out of the clouds sometime!

It was lovely to get your letter at Aden. We had a marvellous time there. We arrived in the early evening: it was a magnificent sight to see the lights of Aden across the bay, framed in a circle of stark volcanic rocks. A friend of David's met us at the ship. He is working in Aden and showed us the sights. He took us out to his flat which consists of three huge rooms and a verandah all round. We sat on the verandah which overlooked the bay, and the evening air was like velvet. At such a time you know what is meant by the magic of the east.

The weather since we left Aden has been superb – just a little cooler than in the Red Sea but with glorious sunshine and cool evenings. We have finished off all the competitions and I have won the women's table-tennis singles – 25 shillings to be spent in the ship's shop. I am just waiting to be 'presented' with a very utilitarian aertex blouse and a jar of cream!

I have no idea yet how soon I shall be whisked from Bombay to Delhi. I shall be met by a member of the Bombay office, but as the ship is so late I may have to stay a day or so. I rather hope I shall, for David will be in Bombay for a day or two and the affair progresses by leaps and bounds! No doubt however this is mid-ocean madness, so don't start imagining things.

Hotel Majestic
Bombay

13 November 1949

We had a most uproarious fancy dress party on our last night but one aboard. I dressed David up as an artist, put a palette and brushes in his hand, and went as his easel, carrying a canvas on which I had painted a face. Then on our last night there was a concert, the star turn being Arthur Askey. David was asked to be compère – no doubt because he speaks so beautifully and looks so handsome – which was very good for him for he is also so shy. By midnight it was over and the lights of Bombay were already on the horizon. We stayed up until we drew alongside, snatched three hours sleep and were up at 6.30 a.m. to begin disembarkation. Mrs Lethbridge and I were met by a security officer who whisked us through customs as if by magic. As we do not leave for Delhi until tonight I was taken to a hotel after being introduced to the folk in the Bombay office. David's train to Calcutta did not leave until yesterday evening, so we spent the afternoon together in the Hanging Gardens, then had tea with friends of his a couple of miles out of town. At the station where I saw him off I was hailed by a most friendly middle-aged Scot whom I had met aboard and who, when he realised I would be alone in Bombay for the evening, invited me to dinner at the famous Taj Mahal Hotel. His train did not leave for Calcutta until 11 p.m. so I had a very pleasant evening with him and one of his friends.

It is now 11 o'clock on Sunday morning and I am quietly recovering from a rather sleepless night, spent in this most peculiar hotel. The temperature even at this time of year is well over 90 degrees. I love it and it doesn't worry me in the least, but it makes one very lazy, particularly after the freshness of the sea.

I am going out now to see a few sights. I am being collected at 6 p.m. Mercifully we have got an air-conditioned coupé in which to travel to Delhi, so I ought to be very comfortable. Then – WORK!

Delhi

16 November 1949

Dearest Mother

By now I am certain that the office will have sent you the usual communication that I have put in an appearance at Delhi – safely and well. Yes, I really and truly am here and at last I'm beginning to believe it. And I've got so much to tell you that I'm determined to stop the social whirl into which I can see I shall be ensnared – for at least an hour or two to get off the first instalment to you.

Well, now, where did I get to in my last letter? I do hope that my various communications have reached you by now. I should be interested to know. Apart from the first air letter, I sent you air letters from Port Said, Aden and I think two from Bombay. Incidentally the bag for London leaves only on Thursdays and Saturdays from Delhi and therefore it is sometimes quicker to post through the ordinary mail. But I believe it's quite a gamble, so I shall probably stick to the bag. Also, if you are sending letters through the bag to me would you write on air mail paper? We are all requested to do this as the air freight charges are gigantic, and if everyone's private mail is on air mail paper a considerable saving is made.

Now then, back to Bombay. Mrs Lethbridge and I were duly escorted to our beautiful air-conditioned coupé on the Delhi train and left at 7 p.m. on Sunday evening. The coupés really are marvellous. The air conditioning not only keeps the temperature down but prevents dust coming in and reduces noise to a minimum. And as one is sealed in there is no chance of a thief's hand creeping round one's luggage in the dark.

We had a two-berth coupé with hand-basin, table and lots of small, minor comforts. We were bang next door to the restaurant car, and if we didn't want to go along to it we merely rang a bell and had food brought in. I must admit that I spent a large proportion of the twenty-six hours journey sleeping. I was still feeling the cumulative effects of staying up late, sauntering round 'A' deck in the moonlight romantically with my honey of a Cambridge Blue!!

Most of the country through which we passed was very flat and sparsely populated. But the little stations at which we stopped fascinated me with monkeys running wild and odd clusters of ramshackle yet picturesque huts. And some of the country Indians are fine-looking people – far better types than those who scratch out a living in the towns. Of course, one of the most distressing sights in the towns is the host of maimed children who have often been mutilated at birth in order to turn them into professional beggars. And you hardly dare fling them an anna in case you become completely surrounded by all the cripples in the neighbourhood.

We arrived at New Delhi at about 8 p.m. on Monday. We bundled out all our possessions to find there was nobody there to meet us, so we decided to split up. I left Mrs Lethbridge to find her own way and went on to Old Delhi, where of course I fell into the arms of her agitated husband and a man from the office who had been sent to greet me.

As by a miracle my trunk appeared from some obscure place lightly carried on a coolie's head, and I counted my other baggage and found it to my astonishment all there. Baggage is a constant source of worry. You never dare take your eyes off it for a moment. Soon we were bowling back to New Delhi in a sumptuous car and I was driven to my new home, Eastern House. This is a large block of flats mostly occupied by single girls and I really can't imagine how anyone could ever dare to grumble (though of course they do!). The High Commissioner wanted me put immediately into the best flat in the place as my grade is higher than any of the girls here, but this would have meant moving somebody, and mercifully one of the men in Establishments used his brains and quietly put me temporarily into a flat already empty. I should certainly have started off on the wrong footing if I had been shown any favouritism. Anyway, I'm in my present flat for a month or two and will move over to another better one when the present occupant finishes her tour of duty.

But even my present flat is a comparative palace. I have a sitting-room and bedroom, both large, square rooms with lofty ceilings. A wide verandah runs along the outside of the building so I have a fair chunk of this. Then I share a bathroom with one other girl. The amount of space really is a joy.

I have fireplaces in both rooms – very much on Claygate lines – and when I arrived on Monday evening a heavenly coal fire in my sitting room gave me a blazing welcome. And jolly glad I was to see it for the evenings now are really chilly. The temperature at this time of year rushes from about 46 degrees in the night up to 80 degrees during the day – quite a fantastic change and one which needs getting used to.

Furniture is plain but pleasant. In my sitting room I have a writing desk, an attractive round table, a couple of small tables, two easy chairs and a bookcase. Of course the thing to do is to buy lots of oddments to give the rooms an individual character, and there are such beautiful things to buy everywhere that the temptation to spend is quite irresistible.

I have engaged a bearer, one Masharrif Hussein, whom I share with one other girl. He wakens me at 7 a.m. with a tray of tea. Then I stroll down to breakfast at about 7.45 and consume large quantities of porridge, fried eggs, toast and marmalade and coffee. A car then takes us to Albuquerque Road which is about two miles away and the day's work starts at 8.30 a.m.

We work through until one o'clock when we return to a hearty lunch – soup, main course, sweet, biscuits and cheese and coffee.

We start again at 2.30 and end at 4.30. It's marvellous to have such an early ending to the day. Back we come to our flats and our tea is then brought up to us by our bearers. We then do what we like – this is when I'm writing to you. Dinner is any time between 8 p.m. and 9.30 p.m. and we proceed to consume a meal of even heartier dimensions than lunch. I can well see that I shall not limit my weight-putting on to pounds, but hundredweights!

The lack of chores is still quite dreamlike to me. I fling my dirty clothes on the floor and they come back in twenty-four hours washed and ironed – you can send as much washing as you like to the dhobi and he may not charge more than 12 rupees a month – roughly 18*s*. I don't make my bed – I don't even have to put my clothes in the wardrobe. Mother darling, I think you'd better save up all your chores for the next two years for my return or I shall be lost for ever in the embrace of idleness.

Oh dear, there's so much to tell you – I don't know when I shall get this letter finished.

Now, about the job. So far I have only had two days and those have been spent discreetly with my nose to the ground, sniffing through files and quietly meeting people and being as inconspicuous as possible. There's plenty for me to do here, my goodness. It's *not* a very happy office in many ways and I think I'll have my work cut out, but that's just as well. Mercifully my immediate colleagues in Estab. have been kindness itself to me and everyone has made me feel at home. Sir Archibald is on tour at the moment so I haven't yet had to face him; but I've been invited to a dinner given by the Deputy High Commissioner next Tuesday at which all the big noises will be present. I'm rather looking forward to it.

I've already been down to the famous Connaught Circus, which is the chief shopping centre of Delhi. One of the girls was being run down there by car yesterday evening by a man from the Ministry of Works and she very sweetly invited me to go too. The shops nearly all stay open in the evening, and, quite apart from the shops, every corner of pavement is littered with street traders selling the most bewildering assortment of wares – anything from Gibbons' *Decline and Fall of the Roman Empire* to *Modern Sex Life*, and from contraceptives to incense sticks and incredibly lovely silks. Watches and cosmetics and sandals and shoes and beads and underwear and knitting wool and dusters and mouse traps and stationery and brightly coloured combs and cases and fur coats and oh – a thousand things are there for sale before your dazzled eyes.

When we had done our shopping we were invited along to the flat of the Ministry of Works man who was joined by a colleague (they live in another block known as Wenger's Flats) and there we had some pleasant drinks and were invited down to their restaurant for dinner – and *what* a dinner! Beautiful soup, ham omelettes, partridge, a soufflé of feather-lightness, with real cream, biscuits and cheese, walnuts and preserved ginger and coffee and cherry brandy.

On Saturday these two men have invited us to go to a dance at the Gymkhana Club. It may be a month or two before I can become a member as there is a waiting list, but I can go as a visitor in the meantime. Then on Sunday I am invited to play a round of golf. I don't feel I've exactly stagnated so far.

Now I'm going off to have a drink with the girl whose flat I shall probably take over. I believe it looks out over the famous Delhi Vista, which means I shall have a view of trees which are green all the year round, and grass and expanses of water.

So perhaps this is a convenient time to end this letter. I could make it go on for several writing pads!

All my love
Margaret

25 November 1949

My dearest Family

The diplomatic bag leaves tomorrow and I must hurry to get something in it or you will think I am deserting you. But there seems to be so little time for letter writing and so much I want to tell you that I find it hard to equate the two! But here's half-an-hour clear anyway before bath and dinner so I'll make a start.

I've now been here eleven whole days – how quickly time is going already. Foolishly I didn't jot down when I last wrote so forgive me for any possible repetitions.

I suppose the most important events of this week have been my talks with Sir Archibald and his wife. Sir A. was very pleasant and barked at me in his bluff military fashion, and more or less told me he didn't really expect me to do anything for a month or two but absorb the atmosphere and get to know people. This I am doing with great rapidity and already have very firm views on what's wrong with the office, though I shan't be able to voice them for a bit yet! I'll tell you more later. Lady Nye was very charming and told me all sorts of things very confidentially (that I already knew of course!) and equally of course I appeared duly surprised. She has a son and daughter by her first marriage and a tiny daughter of four by her present marriage. This small morsel is very attractive but quite hopelessly spoilt by her adoring father and mother. How she will turn out I dread to think, but perhaps she will miraculously escape from what appear to be inevitable results at the moment.

They have the most charming house and Lady N. paints portraits – so we had some common ground immediately – except of course that her portraits really are extraordinarily good and she's never had a lesson in her life.

The dinner party on Tuesday at the Roberts (Deputy HC), was very formal and quite a useful introduction to the sort of etiquette of their dinners. It was an *excellent* dinner including all the right drinks with the right courses, but oh! how I longed to do something quite outrageous like belching or blowing on my soup! Etiquette and social status and precedence and heaven knows what still count enormously in India and I suppose have some very good uses, but they will take me some time to accept – meekly.

Did I tell you that two very nice friendly men from the M. of Works (of the architect and estate agent breed) and a girl from the office have more or less befriended me? One of the men has a car and we have all been out together on several occasions – including golf last Sunday, dancing at the Club and various meals. They have been most kind and have been good to me.

I can well see that life in Delhi is quite impossible without transport and I'm very seriously considering buying a car. I might get a second-hand one or alternatively borrow some money or cash some savings certificates to buy a new one. We can get something like £60 off a new car here and there is a very good secondhand market so it might be a good investment if I can only rake up enough cash. What do you think? The one I've got my eye on is a 1949 Morris 8 open tourer. It's a pet – a wee pet, Mother – and I've already driven it all round Delhi! But of course it would cost something like £400 odd, which is a lot of money. But I should certainly get it nearly all back when I sold it. So I'll first have to think about it very carefully.

There's a play on at the moment for which I'm doing the make-up. Tonight all the big-wigs are coming, including the HC and the Estab. mission so I must be specially skilled. Afterwards one of the M. of W. men is taking me to my first Indian cinema show – an English film, I mean, but an Indian audience mainly.

Soon I must rush off to that bath – I shall probably be packing up a Christmas parcel – the posts are much more reliable now so I shall risk it. It may be better to send *all* the presents to you in one big parcel and get you to distribute them from home. Anyway, I'll see. There are so many fascinating things to buy out here that aren't fiendishly expensive that one can't resist the temptation of putting hand in purse at every opportunity!

Now to my bath – really.

David still writes most adoringly and I may go up to Calcutta for Christmas if transport is possible. Anyway, I'm invited and I don't somehow think I shall turn down the offer if I can overcome material difficulties.

Please *all* of you write to me whenever you can – even if only short notes. We all simply long for letters.

27 November 1949

I was so pleased that my descriptions of Port Said and the Canal brought back so many memories, Leslie. In some ways it was better than I had imagined, but you can't possibly imagine the atmosphere and the smell and the colour. Yes, to watch the traffic at the beginning of the Canal from Simon Artz is a never-ending entertainment. I was thrilled by all the Canal. I could have stayed in it happily for days.

And now, Mother, thank you for all your news. It's very sweet of you to be so concerned about my little shipboard affair and know you will forgive me for smiling at the idea that after all these years of caution I might suddenly lose my head in the Red Sea! I rather wish I could. It would be such a delightful novelty. But I think I'm getting past the age when such a thing is even remotely possible.

I can't imagine that I didn't at some stage give you David's name and general history: David Valentine Lynch Odhams in full, of the Odhams Press family. For seven years he was in the Navy, then returned to Cambridge and a degree in engineering. He is of the solid and dependable type, rather shy, yet of a warm-hearted and open disposition. There I hope you have him in a nutshell – he is not a complicated creature needing deep analysis(!) and he's one of those people who want looking after and organising a bit – appealing perhaps more strongly to the maternal instinct than any other! I must say we did get on remarkably well, and we found so many odd coincidental parallels in our respective histories, including almost identical characteristics in our two mothers and two fathers. Also his mother was older than his father by two and a half years. They also were courting for seven years before marrying. David's father died when Daddy died. His was a happy family too. He has reached the age now when he longs to be married and have his own family – but well, I continue and shall continue to be cautious. We may loathe each other after Christmas . . .

29 November 1949

I started this letter at one of the performances of the play given at Delhi University. It is a very modern building with a magnificent hall and we were given the warmest of welcomes and a splendid buffet meal afterwards. It was a model of Anglo-Indian social relations. But having seen the play through twice before I thought I would keep quietly in the background, having made up my set of faces, and get on with my letters.

Tonight I have had my first evening in for ten days. I washed my hair and lit a fire and have been happily roasting in front of it, reading. I had intended to do so much in the sewing and writing line, but my book beguiled me away, and only now with the fire low have I forced myself to take up pen.

Raymond's Indian suddenly appeared at lunch time on Sunday. I was entertaining my two Ministry of Works men and had invited them to lunch in the Mess when this man turned up. Don't tell Raymond, but we simply couldn't get rid of him! He had lunched but knew we hadn't but made no attempt to terminate his unheralded visit, and it was 2.25 when he finally left! Oh dear, how incredibly boring he was. He never stopped talking tractors the whole of the time. The three of us might have been stuffed dolls capable of saying Yes and No if the necessary buttons were pressed!

I am slowly getting together my various Christmas presents but I fear they will be late. There is so little shopping time. They will just have to be New Year presents instead.

I have heard that there is open-air skating up at Simla in the winter. Whether or not I shall ever have the chance of getting up there I don't know, but if ever you have a free moment would you be an angel, Mother, and pack up my skates? And if you could squeeze in a jar of honey my joy would know no bounds. The marmalade here is the one thing I dislike and I do so miss my dear old honey at breakfast time. I hardly dare to make such a request when we are fed so well but I should so love some.

Do let me know if there's anything in particular that you want ever, for everything is available here, some admittedly at a price but many things reasonable. I'll certainly send some Darjeeling tea to Noey and Auntie Madge. I'm delighted to have an idea of *anything* they want.

I must awa' tae ma bed the noo. I haven't acclimatised myself to Delhi yet. I'm always sleepy. I gather everyone is for the first month or two.

8 December 1949

I'm just filling in half an hour after breakfast in my flat. The High Commissioner is coming on a tour of inspection of Eastern House this morning and I am to be his conductress, and it's not worth going up to the office and back again, so I'll get this note to you started in time for tomorrow's bag.

I'm getting very excited at the prospect of this coming weekend. Four of us are going by car to Agra. The moon will be waning but we shall get up at 3.30 a.m. to see the Taj Mahal by moonlight. We are taking Friday afternoon and Saturday as leave to make the weekend worthwhile.

Last Sunday Douglas, one of the Ministry of Works men who has been so kind to me, let me drive him all round the sights and sites of the numerous old Delhis which have been built and lived in and deserted throughout two thousand years. Some of the Mogul architecture round here is magnificent and in a wonderful state of preservation. Then we progressed to the Jumna, the river of Delhi, and watched Indian fishing methods. By the river a snake charmer was plying his weird trade – the first I have seen since coming here. On our way back a kind of fair was being held on the Vista, and a tight-rope walker was sending our hearts into our mouths by doing antics on his rope with four great pots, one on top of the other, on his head. His feet were just like a monkey's!

The job is progressing. I'm gradually finding lots to do – all sorts of odd, interesting things. Last week I took the wife of the Deputy High Commissioner's bearer to hospital. She is a Muslim and in strictest purdah and of course Muslims are not very popular in this Hindu part of the world. But I took her to this Indian hospital for an examination and had a fascinating morning. As she was a Muslim she would, of course, have been attended to the very last, whatever order she appeared in. But because a white face was with her we were suddenly ushered right to the head of the queue. I've never been more acutely embarrassed in my life – it seemed so grossly unfair to my western mind! And nobody resented it. In fact when my little woman was being examined an old, grey-haired Hindu woman got out of her seat and offered it to me and we indulged in a gentle battle of politeness which was only terminated by a little more room being made somewhere else and both sitting down together!

I had to walk right through the hospital to reach a telephone to ring for transport back and I nearly fell over two large cribs, each holding five very new-born babes and looking *exactly* alike!

Our transport was rather a long time in coming, so I had an interesting hour or so sitting at the entrance to the hospital watching the comings and goings. It's the appalling poverty and wretchedness of the mass of the Indians that is so difficult to stomach. Even New Delhi, which is a remarkably clean city, is flooded out with refugees. A hundred thousand people in Old and New Delhi alone were slaughtered in the risings of 1947. It is unbelievable somehow, and we at home I don't think had any idea of what was really going on here. Racial and religious prejudices are indeed the most terrifying of human madnesses.

The golf is progressing. I and two other girls have now become astonishingly energetic. Every other day we get up at 6.30 a.m. and cycle to the golf course. There we practise for an hour, get back, consume a large breakfast, change and start the real work of the day. The early mornings are very nippy but wonderfully fresh, and then up leaps the sun with its comforting warmth.

To be continued later. Now I must away to my duties.

Evening. It's been a very hectic day. After my do with the High Commissioner I was whisked off with Lady Nye to their house to help to make arrangements for various parties to be given at Christmas to Indian staff and their children. I can see I shan't be able to breathe until well after the New Year.

Mother dear, I've bought some lovely copper things. I wish you could see them because I know how much you love copper. I've got a very plain tray and a solid, bold pot, both very old and just battered enough to give them character.

By the way, if you or anyone else ever sees a Vogue or pattern book or even a cutting of a small design, would you send them out please to this pattern-starved land. Just a picture is enough to go on. Magazines come out by sea mail in about a month.

I mustn't start another page. A bag came in today and still no word from you, you *horrid people*. Do please write regularly, even if you only have time for one line. (I have written each week and twice one week.)

14 December 1949

After a fortnight's silence I've now had two letters from you in three days – lovely, lovely treats. I can't over-stress how much we all long for letters.

I don't think I have many questions of yours to answer this time except further queries about David. Yes, he has come out to work in Calcutta in a big engineering firm called Bird & Company. The idea is that he should turn the whole business inside out and do a lot of the liaison work. It's pretty certain that if he keeps his head he's all lined up for a directorship in about a couple of years. He loathes Calcutta at the moment as he hasn't yet got into any of the clubs which have long waiting lists and I think he's rather lonely, and of course he's gratifyingly miserable about the distance of Calcutta from Delhi . . . !

He now has only two sisters alive out of his family. His mother died just before he sailed and both his brothers were killed during the War, and I think both his brothers-in-law as well if I remember correctly. I know that the last few years have been full of sadness for his family.

It would be amusing to get hold of the *Illustrated News* for the boat race, but much more profitable if you would write to *Picture Post* instead, for I believe they printed about six pages on the race. In fact one Australian girl recognised David on board just from the photograph she had seen of him in *Picture Post*. If you do manage to get hold of a copy do send it on to me for of course David would simply scorn to carry one around with him, the wretch!! He's quite horribly vain about his modesty. There now, any more questions ma'am?!

To return to the car business. Of course I should never dream of tackling long journeys on my own out here. What I really need is something to get me round Delhi – which is a pretty safe place – just when I want. I promise to be very sensible but I still think I'll pursue the idea.

Now for my latest news. I've been to Agra of course since I last wrote. Douglas and Stanley (Ministry of Works), Jeanne Barwell and I set out on Friday afternoon for the 120 mile drive. Driving in India is quite fantastic. The asphalt fairway is only wide enough to take one line of traffic with ease, but on either side are wide dust tracks intended for the use of bullock carts. What happens is that the old bullock carts and all other strange vehicles as well, including the odd camel or two that suddenly lean their long necks over the roof of your car – stick firmly to the middle of the road and send you off into the dust to pass them. You blow your horn continuously at them from the second you first spy them in the far distance, and although they are supposed to give way to mechanical traffic very few do, and by the time you are bumping up in the dust the bullock driver is just awake enough to give his bullocks a gentle tap which he knows and you know and the bullocks know is far too late to take action on anyway. You would go off your head, Mother. Driving through villages too is one long excitement. The roads are often so narrow that you can shop out of both sides of the car at the same time without moving from your seat.

Children and dogs and camels and bullocks and goats and pigs and horses all wander about quite oblivious of the fact that you have a purpose in life! Which is to get past them in the minimum amount of time with the maximum safety. And the dust – by the time you've gone a hundred or so miles you are covered by a dear little grey powdery layer which slips into everything.

But Agra was worth all the discomfort in the world. We bathed and dined and had just enough to drink to tune us up for our moonlight pilgrimage to the Taj. The moon was waning, but it threw just enough light onto that incredible architectural unreality as was necessary to justify its reputation in our eyes. Then by lamp-light we were conducted through its chambers, the beauty and richness and simplicity of which are beyond my powers of description.

But it was nevertheless by sunlight that I found the Taj most impressive. The brilliance of the marble in the brilliant sunshine dazzles you so much that you simply can't look at it. It's gloriously blinding and quite, quite wonderful. No picture that I have ever seen of it does it justice. Some people I know are disappointed in the Taj – but I wasn't.

There were a number of other fascinating places we went to, including the great Fort at Agra, steeped in the history of India of the Princes. We looked through the tiny mirror, no bigger than your thumb-nail, where Shah Jahan, the builder of the Taj, was said to have watched the reflection of his beloved work of art three miles away, during the last years of his captivity; and we too, with difficulty but final success saw the reflection of the Taj in it also. Then we visited Akbar's tomb and Akbar's deserted city, Fatipur Sikri, built in his lifetime and then completely deserted because of lack of water.

These monuments of the India of the past simply grip my imagination and thrill me to the core. I wouldn't have missed coming here for the world!

I met again several of the men in the British Council (whose headquarters are in Agra) whom I had met on the *Strathmore* and later on the train to Delhi. They are a very friendly crowd and I have an open invitation to go there whenever I like.

Oh dear, I could just go on and on about life out here, but I must get down to some more letters. I'm now completely submerged in my work – running this and organising that and sorting out a hundred and one odd problems in this very odd place and loving every minute of it – but oh for more letter-writing time.

If this should be the last letter you get before Christmas all my very best greetings to you all – I hope my presents won't be too scandalously late in reaching you.

21 December 1949

Another letter from you now. They suddenly seem to be flowing in thick and fast which is *lovely*! I take back *all* the rude things I have ever said. I think the answer is that all letters sent through the CRO take a bit longer than the ordinary air mail, and some take much longer if they just miss a bag. So that if you ever wanted to write to me in a bit more of a hurry than usual you might feel it worthwhile to fork out the extra postage.

Well now, it's grand to hear all your latest news. I'm tickled to bits about your efforts to track down David's face! Trust you. When you can bear to be parted from him, do send the sheet on to me. And let me know if you have any luck with *Picture Post.*

To hear you talk of snow and rain makes me realize how incredibly far away you are. We're just getting down to our coldest time now and for the next month, with day temperatures well over 70 degrees and always, always brilliant sunshine. And we don't have mud naturally – we have to make it. Every day the roads round Eastern House and Albuquerque Road have to be hosed vigorously to keep down the dust!

Rest assured that I wasn't tied up in the riots in front of Parliament House. These things go on so regularly but we never seem to see them.

The purdah woman I took to hospital wasn't the DHC's bearer but the wife of his bearer. You never have women bearers anywhere in India, and the purdah woman almost never leaves her quarters unless on such business as going to hospital, which is unavoidable – ghastly existence. The only place she isn't veiled is in her own home – one room for the whole family in this case, and then only when no men except her husband and sons are around.

Lady Nye's parties aren't until the Wednesday and Thursday after Christmas by which time I shall be back from Calcutta. I shall have only three days there, unfortunately, but I shall make the most of them! Goodness knows how I shall spend Christmas Day. David hasn't let on what the plans are – but we shall probably go to one of the clubs or big hotels. I've put on seven pounds in weight in the seven weeks since I left London! Delhi in the winter certainly suits me with a vengeance.

On Saturday night we all went to a fancy dress party at the Club. Then on Sunday I had a lunch party at the Club, going on afterwards to a gymkhana given by the Riding Club. This was enormous fun and included a magnificent display of tent-pegging by members of the Body Guard – a crack regiment of Indians who are magnificent riders. Then in the evening there was a Bonfire Night at the golf club. The world's largest bonfire was lit and we sang carols round it and drank rum punch and had treasure hunts. Then later a hard core of singing enthusiasts – of which needless to say I was one – stayed on beside a roaring fire in the club-house and sang and sang and sang. Several of us then were invited to a charming house of a charming couple and we got round the piano and went on singing. Bed at – forget it!

Then last night we went on a carol-singing expedition proper. About twenty of us have been practising and we're not bad. I'd love to stop and tell you all about the evening but I mustn't now. But we ended up at a large and wonderful house where about twenty Americans were having a magnificent party; they had no idea we were coming and turned out *en masse* at the front door to listen to us, singing by lamplight, then we were invited inside to drinks and cheese and stuffed olives and rich cream cakes and real American coffee, and ended up the evening by being taught American square dancing. Their hospitality is terrific and they have a stupendous capacity for enjoying themselves.

22 December 1949

Another day gone – this must catch the last bag tomorrow. Last night I had to break off to go to a party and then afterwards I was helping with a Christmas party given by the Dramatic Society, in which again I sang carols and took part in a very frivolous but amusing One Act Play.

This afternoon I have been helping to run a children's party at the Nyes' given to all the children of the Commission between the ages of two and eight. I've rocked rocking horses and pushed swings and cut Christmas cake for two and a half solid hours.

I've just got back now from a quiet and pleasant dinner party and am off to bed earlyish, for tomorrow will be busy, with the Indian staff children's party in the afternoon, more carol singing and my departure for Calcutta.

And so to bed. Now I hope you will all have a wonderful Christmas. It is the very first one I shall ever have spent away from you, I have just realized.

27 December 1949

My little holiday in Calcutta is almost to an end. I'm just waiting for Jennifer, the wife of David's cousin, to appear at the hotel to take me on a shopping expedition, and I thought I'd fill in time by dropping you a note.

Well, I've had a most interesting and entertaining weekend. I didn't dare to tell you before but I expect you guessed that I flew to Calcutta and thrilled with the experience was I. Flying certainly is the way to travel out here – it's so incredibly quick and comfortable and much less frightening than a long train journey and certainly safer.

Friday was undoubtedly a hectic day. After helping to run the Indian staff children's party in the afternoon I did my packing, went carol-singing to the French Ambassador and the High Commissioner and was then run to the airport by two of my friends. At 11.15 p.m. I was taking off in the night mail plane. This is the way to travel as the cost is half that of the day fare. The plane was a Dakota and I had a comfortable tip-up seat in which I was able to snooze quite happily. First you fly to Nagpur, away down in Central India, where the mail planes from Calcutta, Bombay, Madras and Delhi all meet and exchange their mail. We arrived in Nagpur at about 2.30 a.m. and I had three quarters of an hour's stop before changing planes and proceeding again. It really is fascinating flying by night, soaring above cities lit from end to end.

From my comfortable seat I watched the dawn break – an unforgettable sight – then gradually we came lower and lower until Calcutta stretched smoky and busy below us. It must have been a perfect night for flying as the plane was as steady as a rock and not for a second did I experience any uneasiness or sickness.

David and I spent Saturday wandering round Calcutta. It is a most bewilderingly noisy, busy, dirty, vigorous city and I first went round with my mouth wide open all the time. In the evening we were met by David's cousin John and his wife Jennifer, a very charming couple, who took us to the famous Saturday Club where we danced until well after midnight.

Then we progressed to a much lower dive, the 300 Club where we stayed in a terrific crush of people until some exceedingly late hour. Our progression from the one club to the other was on foot, as only a couple of hundred yards separated them, and we were escorted by a peculiar band of Indians who played an odd assortment of bag-pipes and drums and whistles as we marched along. It's quite amazing how many devices the Indian finds for making a spot of cash.

We finally ended up in the most beautiful flat of a wealthy young business man who didn't let us go until 4 a.m.

The temperature in Calcutta of course is very much higher than in Delhi, so on Christmas morning there I was in a thin cotton dress, lapping up sunshine at 80 degrees.

John and Jennifer invited us to spend the morning at a most beautiful club outside Calcutta – a golf club really. We sat quietly in the sunshine and in the shade of the trees with the most beautiful stretch of golf course in front of us. I tried to imagine what the temperature at home could possibly be like and failed lamentably!

David was picking up an office car for the afternoon for us from an Anglo-Indian member of staff with whom we stayed for Christmas lunch. They were a kind and hospitable family, but it is rather pathetic how terribly anxious these 'poor whites' are to please a true-blooded European.

In the afternoon we went to the races. You never saw such a terrific crush of humanity. We had a little flutter on two races and David for the very first time in his life backed two winners running!

We had Christmas dinner very quietly together after the festivities of the night before. I kept on thinking of you all through the day and imagining what you were doing with yourselves. I do hope you had a lovely day.

Yesterday morning we went for a stroll and paid our respects to the Ochterlony statue, then we sauntered on down to the Hoogly River and found ourselves at one of the old club houses belonging to the Calcutta Rowing Club. Of course David is a highly respected member of any rowing circle and we were invited in for beer on the verandah looking out over the river. One of Calcutta's few peers of the realm was there, Lord Craigmile – a peculiar oddity with gingerish hair and beard and a mongrel dachshund-cum-spaniel dog – who has never been known to buy anyone a drink, as he considers the rest of the world only too delighted to treat him for the sake of his title – queer oddities of humanity you find out here.

We were invited out to lunch by David's boss and his wife – a Glasgow pair – and I was duly shown off to them. They have a beautiful flat and we had a first-class meal with them. Afterwards they took us out to the golf course again where we had tea. As dusk came, out crept a little fox who came right up to our table for food. Sometimes whole families will come, so very tame are they.

John and Jennifer came to dinner with us and we then spent the rest of the evening again in the Saturday Club. There I met again several acquaintances from the *Strathmore*.

Today David has had to go to the office, hence my shopping expedition with Jennifer. Then I catch the plane back again tonight at 11.15 p.m.

Yes, it has been a very pleasant weekend, and of course David wants me to marry him. The logical rightness of such a move is unanswerable. He is a dear lad and quite ridiculously eligible and pathetically devoted. I can think of no sound reason for not marrying him except that in the old heart of hearts I can't find the requisite amount of the grand passion! Sometimes I wish I had been a little more dumb and devoted!! But there you are. It was as well to come and find out a bit more about it, but Delhi's too far from Calcutta to provide the necessary environment for further investigation, so in the meantime put away the wedding veil again.

Later Jennifer and I have done our shopping and I have invested in some golf clubs, so now I really shall be able to take up my golfing seriously. David met me for lunch and we drove right down into the Chinese quarter for a Chinese lunch. It's hard to believe that you're in India down there, so different are the faces and the buildings. The streets are so narrow and tortuous that you can scarcely get a car along them, and if a bullock cart suddenly looms round a corner you are completely stumped. It's a fascinating place during the day, but I should be terrified out of my wits to go there at night.

Talking of nights, there always seem to be odd things going on here. Yesterday evening we suddenly heard the sound of bombs being thrown and the quick retort of police fire, but you just don't take any notice of it, it is such a regular occurrence. And the squabbles are always between Indians, all sides leaving the Europeans happily alone.

This letter seems to have wandered on and must I think be over air-mail weight. So I will take it back with me and put it in the bag I think.

I'm going to be very busy when I get back – tomorrow and Thursday are the Nyes' two parties – then on Friday, I'm singing and acting again and on Saturday some Scots have invited me out to a Hogmanay do, which I suspect will be *exceedingly* jolly. And then life should settle down soberly.

29 December 1949

Just as I popped my Calcutta letter into the bag today along came one from you in the opposite direction . . .

Well now, to my news. The PS on the back of my last envelope will have told you of my safe flight back to Delhi. I really was profoundly impressed by my introduction to flying. I should never have the least hesitation in going anywhere by 'plane, so excellent was the comfort and efficiency of the service I sampled. I just about saw the lights of Calcutta fade away below me and the next I knew was that we were at Nagpur. Then again we were airborne and in what seemed like three seconds the dawn and Delhi appeared. I just slept solidly all the way.

I've been ceaselessly busy since I returned. The Nyes had their first dance last night and I'm just waiting to go to their second one tonight. Last night certainly was an enormous success. The house was most beautifully decorated, and several verandahs were closed in with tarpaulins to make extra sitting rooms. Though Sir A. is a teetotaller drinks flowed most liberally, and the office let its hair down in no uncertain fashion. We danced in the largest room and didn't go home until nearly one a.m.

Tomorrow we are giving our party to the hundred children from the neighbouring refugee camp. Nearly all day I have been wrapping up parcels and counting sweets and sorting out lollipops and recruiting Father Christmas and a hundred and one other things. I shall be thankful when all these parties are over.

I've just done a most depressing thing. I've sorted out a pile of letters that have whirled in over the holiday period and find I have about twenty to answer. When shall I ever get them done? At the rate these weeks are hurtling by I shall be home before I know I've gone.

1950

9 January 1950

I've got such a lot of news to catch up on and several letters to thank you for. It was lovely to hear from my dear brother and sister-in-law.

It's good to hear that old Dobbin is still behaving and that he got himself out of his skid without mishap. And talking of cars, I really have bought one at last. It is a second hand (1935) 10 horse power Sunbeam Talbot that once belonged to Lady Shone, wife of the last High Commissioner. It really is a little beauty. I shall have to sink some of my savings to buy it but now that the import of new cars has been stopped I should get almost as much as I have paid for it when I come to sell it.

I'm taking delivery of the car probably tomorrow and will insure it locally through the office. Then I'll take a snap and show off my little beauty to you! I'm terribly thrilled and don't feel in Delhi that it's an extravagance at all. It will make all the difference in the world to my living here and will enable me to take some of the girls about who haven't got many friends with transport.

Now for some questions of yours, Mother. Daylight hours at the moment are from about 7 a.m. to 5.30 p.m. or 6 p.m. Once the sun sinks darkness comes very quickly. We don't get much chance of any exercise after office at this time of year as the light has gone soon after we have our tea. I understand that even in the summer darkness comes at about 8 p.m. Yes, I really do take my camera around with me but more often than not simply forget to take things. I'm still waiting to finish off my Taj roll. They should be interesting, I'm certain.

In the meantime here are a few snaps taken by one of my friends of our first party given to the children of our Indian staff. I had most of the preliminary work to do on it and much of the actual running. The party was held in the grounds at the back of Number 6 Albuquerque Road. You will see me – just – on three of them. I've put a cross on the back in case you've forgotten what I look like. You see from my hand how brilliant the sun is even at Christmas time. It may also interest you to see these snaps of the *Strathmore*, taken by an old boy from the Board of Trade who was asked by the CRO to look me up and has recently put in an appearance at Delhi armed with these. David and I are on one only. You can't mistake me. Just look for the large bottom! The others will help to give you an idea of the *Strathmore* and some of the sights we saw from her.

Heavens, the bag goes today and I've hardly started. I meant to write you a long birthday letter, Leslie, but it just hasn't got written. Second instalment promised this weekend.

Car just received – absolutely *wonderful*.

18 January 1950

Now for my news. Much of it centres round my dear little car. Life in Delhi is already transformed by it. It goes so perfectly and looks so good and never shall I regret the money I have spent on it.

The other bit of interesting news is that it is just possible that I shall be one of the running commentators for All India Radio on 26 January – Republic Day. It is to be a day of much ceremonial and processions, and about four commentators are needed to cover strategic spots. One of our men in the office has done quite a bit of radio work and was asked to produce a good voice or two for this job, and he produced me! Today I was sent to Broadcasting House, had a mike thrust into my hand on the verandah and made to describe the scene in front of me for what seemed hours and was probably only five or ten minutes. Then a recording was made – there were two of us being tested at the same time – and the recordings were played back at us. One's own voice sounds wildly unfamiliar. The various managers seemed satisfied, but the recordings will have to be played over to the big-wigs before a decision is made, so it may be several days before I know if I have been selected. If I have, the broadcast will be transmitted over the whole of Asia, and it's possible that odd bits of it might appear in your own Radio Newsreel. It's all very much of a gamble, but who knows, you might hear my voice yet over the radio! I refuse to get excited though until something is fixed. If nothing comes of it it will still have been an interesting might-have-been.

I hardly know what else I have done lately. The golf progresses tolerably well. I've been to more dinners and lunches and dances. And now I've got the car I've been able to visit quietly those of my friends who are lucky enough to have a bungalow – to sit quietly in such a place where there is a garden too is a great joy in this life of bustle.

Already the weather is beginning to heat up. The days now are as warm as our June days and the nights which have been so cold are beginning to be warmer. Soon the hot weather will be upon us in all its devastating vigour.

I always seem to be trying to beat the bag. Tomorrow morning it goes, so tonight I must stop this little epistle.

1 February 1950

What with all these celebrations and an overdose of work I think it must be a fortnight since I wrote and much has happened since then.

Well now, the Republic Day. In the end All India Radio decided to have male commentators only, but I did all the same broadcast that night and it was in a feature programme called 'A Republic is Born' which we rehearsed and recorded the day before. I was merely a voice with less than a dozen lines to say, but it was great fun and I listened in to myself at night when the broadcast was given. *How odd* one's own voice sounds – not a bit as one imagines.

I had a lovely day. Delhi was absolutely packed with people. The President's procession was really rather short and a bit of a disappointment, but to me it was the crowds which were the fascinating thing. I saw everything from the roof of the *Statesman* building. In the *Statesman* next day was a picture taken from the exact position where I was. I am sending a copy of the paper with one or two others by sea mail. I think you will find them interesting.

Because I was going out to a big party on Republic Night I wouldn't therefore be able to go round the illuminations and went the night before, with one of my friends in a jeep. Blackpool illuminations weren't in it. All the main buildings had rows and rows of coloured lights and forty trees on the Vista were a mass of fairy lights.

7 February 1950

Did I tell you that I am to become a regular broadcaster on All India Radio? I am to announce gramophone record concerts on three nights a week. For this I get paid the large sum of ten rupees a night, which is roughly 15*s*. This little bit of pin money will be useful, but quite apart from this minor consideration it should be an entertaining experience.

I made a funny discovery the other day. The girl who sits at my table in the mess was born in Altringham and knows John and Coral Archer very well. Her mother and Mrs Archer have always been great friends – talk about a small world!!

22 February 1950

I took myself off to bed a week ago with a slight touch of dysentery. It has been only the mildest attack – nothing worse than a bit of sickness and diarrhoea, and the doctor here is most terribly cautious, and whether you like it or not, keeps you in bed for ten days. Actually I have crept out into the sunshine on my verandah this afternoon but I'm not officially out of bed until Friday and today is Wednesday. I'm absolutely furious of course as I feel wonderful – never better in my life – but our doctor is not one to be argued with, so I'm having a gloriously lazy time, reading long novels and having hundreds of visitors who are always popping in and out to see how I am faring.

Tomorrow, doctor or no doctor, I am moving my flat. I'm still not going to the one I really want, but a very much better one than my present one with my bedroom overlooking the Vista, and a much larger sitting-room. As soon as I am in I shall try my hand at some exposures for you.

Talking of photography, here are my Taj snaps. I'm quite pleased with the camera as I think it has brought out some of the details of the inlaid work very well. As I get to know the camera better I hope for correspondingly better results. Anyway this is my first instalment.

I've postponed my radio job because of this spot of illness, but when I finally start I'll certainly find out about the wavelength and let you know.

I'm awfully sorry to hear about the things that need doing to the car. Your bus and mine must be about the same age. I'm hoping I shan't have to fork out any great sums for my car. The cost of living here is so prohibitive that I can see I shall be able to save only a little each month and that by going carefully – at least until I get my overdraft paid off. With Leslie's cheque for Dobbin the back of it should be broken anyway. Money, money, money, *what* a curse it is, or is if it isn't, if you get my meaning!

Parcels alas are quite untraceable but don't worry. I'll get down to sending off another one to you as soon as I'm on the old pins again.

I imagined that you must be having an awful time with the floods, because today I had a peep at a copy of the *Weekly Times* and in it was an amazing picture of floods at Tewkesbury, and I know if those Midland rivers are flooded there's a pretty good chance that you're fighting the waters too. It seems so infinitely remote here. The weather is now heating up rapidly and it is almost too hot to sit in the sun at mid-day unless there is a breeze blowing. Actually, since the New Year it has been phenomenally wet for Delhi – quite eight or ten prolonged showers of an hour or so!!

I've had bumper crops of mail recently – today, besides your letter, long epistles from Nancy Jones, who asks after you, Arthur Unwin, my man assistant at the Ministry of Education and dear old Robert Hyde, who still writes regularly and appears to continue to miss me! He has just had his 'dubbing' from the King – a private affair accompanied by much amusement on both sides and informal chats on election prospects. The King is evidently quite well and flourishing again.

Then to my astonishment the other day I had a letter from one Peter Lum whom I met in Czechoslovakia nearly three years ago. I had almost forgotten his existence but he evidently hadn't forgotten mine! He has escaped to Australia and is starting life all over again there. Odd how these old acquaintances can suddenly come to life.

I'm also sending you at last the page of pictures in the *Statesman* of Republic Day. The bottom left-hand photograph was taken immediately below where I was standing on top of the *Statesman* roof, and the figure I have marked 'Geoff Weeks' is the lad in our office who broadcast the running commentary and who introduced me to All India Radio.

My dear old bearer has looked after me like a mother while I have been ill, and he's just gone off now to get my dinner and bring it over to the flat. I still can't take for granted the wonder of being waited on hand and foot.

So before he re-appears I had better put my pen away.

Maggie

9 March 1950

I haven't really very much news. I've been helping to run garden parties, and next week I have my own house warming party in my new flat. We're starting off at the cocktail dance at the Club, then coming back to bacon and eggs cooked on little coke stoves on my verandah. Afterwards rum punch and beer!

This afternoon I've got a half holiday and I'm being taken to the finals of the Indian Army Athletic Sports – a magnificent display, I believe.

Last Sunday one of my friends – who incidentally recognised Leslie's photograph and remembers seeing him frequently in the Officers' Club at Port Said – took me on an all day picnic down to the river. There we sat and read and had a lazy time and watched the real India going about its daily task. We were beside a part of the river where all the animals from a nearby village were being brought down to water. Men and boys and animals all clamber in together and wallow around in the filthy water. No wonder typhoid is so prevalent!

14 March 1950

The old car does seem to have given you a lot of trouble lately and what an expense too. Thank goodness mine is running perfectly. I now have the hood perpetually down. I had to whisk it up yesterday for a sudden and quite unexpected shower but that is rare these days. The temperature is now 90 degrees at midday and at night I'm already sleeping under a sheet only. So far I haven't felt the heat a scrap and gather I probably won't so much during my first hot weather. It's the second that gets you down.

I'm in the throes of preparing for my house warming party. Nineteen people are coming tonight and it's going to be quite hard work. But I thought I must first sit down this lunch time and start a letter to you as the bag goes tomorrow. So the start is made and now I must whiz back to work.

16 March 1950

The party is over thank goodness and very rowdy it was too. We started off at the cocktail dance at the Club, then left there at about half past nine. We came back to my flat. My bearer had brought two of his *sigris* (charcoal stoves) and these we set up in my sitting-room, with one male guest frying sausages and eggs and another bacon and tomatoes! We heated the plates by turning on the hot tap and altogether had an excellent, if extremely unruly, meal! *Sigris* are wonderful as they fling out no smoke once they are going properly, so you can have them right inside without any danger.

We then had the odd noggin or two and sang low songs and played silly games and I packed them off at midnight. I daren't keep them any later because of the incredible row they were making.

Later this afternoon I'm going to see my first polo match. The famous Argentinian team is here and is giving a demonstration match. We are going to be allowed to skip the last half hour of work to go to watch.

Tomorrow night I'm going to a big charity ball at the Club where a few of us are doing a semi-demonstration eightsome reel in an effort to get all the assembled company doing likewise.

Then in the next fortnight there are two dances at Eastern House, one at the Golf Club, which I am helping to organise, and a Ladies Night at the Jasmine Lodge to which I have been invited, and a concert given by the choir of which I am a member.

This I hope will be the last round of activities before the hot weather finally engulfs us.

We've just had a bad rabies scare in Delhi. Yesterday I popped along to our Sick Bay with some papers and a workman was brought in with two horrid bites on both hands. We rushed him off to hospital for injections straight away. I see in the paper today that thirty people were bitten by this rabid dog before it was finally shot. Mercifully, injections are a complete antidote, but they are evidently horribly painful – they're thrust into the muscles of the stomach and you often have to have up to twenty. We also had a slight earthquake yesterday evening but I was too busy dancing to notice it!

But we all continue to thrive most happily.

Now the lunch hour is up and I must stop.

8 March 1950

I'm completely cured from my dysentery now and have been back at work for ten days. In fact I never felt better in my life. I think the starvation and rest did me all the good in the world. Evidently this is a particularly bad time of the year for illness, and a number of our staff have had dysentery, and some of the amoebic variety which is very difficult to cure. I sensibly indulged in the unimportant one only!

Since returning to the office I have been very busy. I've temporarily postponed my job with All India Radio as I have such a lot of evening activities to take part in and organise. I'm disappointed in a way but my job has to come first and I don't want to take on too much with the hot weather rapidly on the way.

The temperature at the moment is unbelievably wonderful. The days are up to about 86 degrees which, in this dry climate, is intoxicating. You wander around in summer dresses and no stockings and soak up sun but don't feel in the least bit over-heated. This will last for about another month before the real rigours of the summer are upon us.

I witnessed my first dust storm the other evening – horrible things. I had just washed my hair when quite suddenly a terrific gale blew up and in a few seconds the Vista looked as if it were in a thick fog. Afterwards every mortal thing I touched was gritty!

30 March 1950

As usual I seem to have left writing until just before the bag goes. Where time flies to here I simply can't imagine. There seem to have been so many parties and things lately and they still aren't over – I suppose they never are in Delhi. The weather has been so heavenly that I've been out a lot, walking and playing golf. I was even up at 6.15 a.m. today and did five holes before breakfast!

But our spell of cool is vanishing and the temperature has bounced up again these last few days.

The office has been in a pretty good flap lately, what with Cameron's murder and Liaquat Ali Khan's proposed visit to Delhi and the everlasting Kashmir problem. I've seen some of the behind-the-scenes telegrams about Cameron, including the one from our DHC in Calcutta who went out and found the body and brought it back; and sober reading they were too. Mercifully we see little of the tension here in New Delhi. The odd incident you wrote about was an isolated one and has had no repercussions. But everyone seems to think that there may be some real trouble in Calcutta. It's all terribly interesting but very tragic.

My lunch hour for writing this letter has just been completely interrupted by the manageress of Eastern House coming and pouring a whole tale of woe into my reluctant ear, so this letter is getting potentially shorter and shorter! – and scribblier and scribblier.

We've just heard that a cholera epidemic is likely to start in Delhi – what a country! So we've all got to be re-stabbed. If it isn't communal disorders it's diseases.

Mercifully, we haven't had another sand-storm since I wrote. The old car didn't seem to object, thank goodness. More and more I pour blessings on the head of my dear little bus. It's running superbly now and continues to turn Delhi into a pleasure ground!

Back in the office. Must stop. I am sending by sea mail copies of our High Commissioner's rag which may amuse you.

23 March 1950

We are having the most extraordinary weather at the moment. We thought the winter had really gone a fortnight ago when the temperature rose to over 92 degrees, and then suddenly we started to get thunderstorms and torrential rain. The rain never lasts for long and the sun is soon out again, but because of it the temperature is kept down miraculously. This is going to make the summer very much shorter, because usually at this time of year the thermometer has quietly crept up to the 100 degree mark. We're wondering how long our phenomenal luck will last.

The only thing we dread is that our open air supper dance at the Golf Club on Sunday, which I'm helping to run, will get flooded out, for when a thunder storm does come on here it comes with magnificent fury.

Tonight we are giving our concert in Eastern House. The wife of the Deputy High Commissioner, who is Egyptian, is singing and we are all very curious to hear her.

The polo match the other day was tremendously exciting. I wonder if Leslie ever played it or saw it played – I can't remember. The final match is this afternoon and I shall try to get along again if I can get away from the office.

Last night I had dinner at the Club and ten of us decided to go up to Mussoorie at Easter. This is one of the nearest hill stations, being about 170 miles from Delhi, and is, I believe, really lovely. It will be my first sight of mountains for months. The monotony of the plains of Delhi is wearying after a spell.

Life in the office is very noisy at the moment. Air-conditioning plant is being put in and my office is a victim. Yesterday about eight men spent the whole day crawling about on the ceiling and perching perilously on ladders. Just before lunch there was a terrific flash when two wires had met, and a Sikh right up on top of a ladder got a terrible electrical burn on his hand. I bound it up and whisked him straight off to hospital in my car. Believe it or not it took a quarter of an hour to find a doctor, then, when he was found, another twenty minutes to find the key of the medicine chest. That's India for you!

One of my friends has just completely overhauled my car and it's now running like a dream. It's good to have the odd engineer among one's nicer acquaintances as it's impossible to trust an Indian garage. Their favourite trick is to do the job well that you have asked them to do, then loosen or damage something else quietly that you won't notice for a week or so, so that you have to bring the car in again. What a country.

6 April 1950

I'm still so thrilled about Susan Margaret that I'm bouncing around boring everyone with the news that I'm an auntie! But I'm *dying* for more information. I want to know weight at birth, ugly or beautiful (the truth mind you!) fair or dark, large or small, good or naughty and everything you can think of. I know writing letters will become ever more difficult what with nappies to wash and feeds to give and cooings to be cooed, but I shall *always* love to hear about my niece. After all, she's only got one paternal aunt!

I'm awfully disappointed. We're not now going to Mussoorie for Easter. Three of the places on the way have been under curfew, and although they are quiet now we are all advised not to go. Many of the Commission with wives up there are risking it, but the men folk in our proposed party won't take the responsibility of us women on their shoulders which I suppose is very right and proper of them! So instead we shall play golf and swim at the Club and stay quietly in Delhi. A pity, but that is India.

We're quietly beginning to swelter now. Last Sunday the temperature suddenly bounced up to 100 degrees in the shade and I played nine holes of golf in it without ill effect. It's wonderful how well you can stand up to dry heat. But the hot nights are the things which get you down most as it's so difficult to sleep.

I've taken some more snaps of the car, and when I've had them developed will send you a flashlight photograph of me at a cocktail party – full of grin and looking very plump and well fed!

I am just recovering from the world's worst mosquito bites. Thank goodness the little blighters have lost the taste for me, but they gave me hell and brought on an attack of boils – at least that's what the doctor put them down to. They were only small ones but very unpleasant. However, they've almost gone too and I'm back to normal.

I'm off to hospital now to visit one of our staff who has had a very serious operation – a locally recruited Anglo-Indian. She's in an Indian hospital where conditions leave much to be desired, and I want to go and snoop and see for myself just what it is like to be an inmate.

12 April 1950

Well Easter is now over and very pleasant it was. I was terribly disappointed not to go to Mussoorrie but managed to have a lovely time all the same. On Friday I went out picnicking for the day. We all got a bit lost and found ourselves in the depths of a huge refugee camp and there my car broke down – the petrol pump stopped working. But after an hour of fiddling and drinking copious draughts of cool beer which we had taken with us we were able to proceed, much to our relief. Fortunately we stuck in a most interesting place – bang in the middle of a corn-threshing session. This is done by making a huge circle of corn and driving four bullocks round and round and round on it so that their hooves beat out the grain. It is infinitely slow and laborious and therefore typically Indian. I could happily have watched the scene all day.

You see some quite astonishing sights going through Indian villages. Everything goes on in front of the public eye. That day I even saw one man shaving another under the arms with a cut-throat razor – a crude and distinctly terrifying sight!

Picnicking in India is too simple. You just get the bearer to prepare everything – take a cooked chicken which costs only about 6*s*. or 7*s*. and away you go with a right royal feast.

It was perhaps as well that we didn't go to Mussoorie. Most people had uneventful journeys, but one husband and wife who went by bus were held up for an hour in a small town and witnessed an unpleasant incident and actually saw two Muslims stabbed.

The weather miraculously continues to be endurable. The temperature hovers between 93 and 100 but so far there has been none of the usual leaps over the 100 mark. I drink my early morning toddy of salt and water and almost like it now, and manage to keep very fit.

This week has been one of the official 'do's' – three cocktail parties in four days! The Deputy Commissioners are all up from the Outposts for their quarterly conference and this is always the signal for stuffy functions. I shall never want to look a cocktail party in the face again when I get home.

26 April 1950

We've been very busy lately with the Deputy High Commissioners' Conference on, but they've departed now and our own DHC Roberts goes off tomorrow on a two month holiday so we can perhaps relax a bit. The poor old High Commissioner is having his very first dose of illness ever in his life and is in bed with dysentery. Of course he has always stipulated in the past that staff must obey the Medical Adviser's instructions and stay in bed ten days, no matter how well they feel, and now the tables are turned on him and he's being forced to stay in bed himself though he feels wonderful! The other Deputy High Commissioners, knowing Archie, think it's a huge joke!!

Last night I went out to dinner with one of the Trade Commissioners and his wife. Another guest was a new Trade Commissioner in Calcutta who is spending a month in Delhi, named Brazendale. No sooner had I been introduced to him than he stared hard at me and without knowing what part of the world I hailed from said, 'Are you by any chance related to a girl named Coralie Archer who lives in a small place called Hale in Cheshire [where I was born]?' *Complete* collapse of me as you can imagine! Of course we were inseparable for the rest of the evening. He and his family live in Hale Road and have known the Archers for years. What Brazendale couldn't get over was that Coralie and I are *not* related – at least not so far as we know – for he says we are the spit image of each other, mannerisms and all. Wasn't it *very* odd? Incidentally, Coralie married her Lord whatever it was and within a few weeks the marriage completely collapsed – he turned out to have some form of paranoia – I'm not sure what type – isn't it awfully sad?

I've just been up to Government House for the first time. I was invited to a film show given by our British Information Services on juvenile delinquency at home. I shook hands with Dr Prasad, the President, who has one of those awful wet fish flabby handshakes, so I'm even less impressed with him than ever! I was also introduced to the Health Minister, Rajkumari Amrit Kaur, an interesting woman with whom the High Commission has crossed swords on more than one occasion.

The weather still stays quite possible – fantastic year – never much above 96 degrees or 98 degrees and the last few evenings have been most pleasantly cool. Did I tell you that I am sleeping out on my verandah with a little table fan beside me to keep me cool and the mosquitoes out of the way? – and very pleasant it is too.

11 May 1950

My news continues to be limited to work and heat and there sure is plenty of both. The temperature wavers between 104 and 107 degrees during the day but it is still fairly pleasant at night – round about 80 degrees. Life becomes one long shower-bath. But I'm feeling in marvellous health. I had another tiny dose of my dysentery again but managed to cure myself with starvation and sulphur and now I'm fine. I've had all my hair cut short and last night I gave myself another Toni – this time completely unaided. I feel very proud of myself and the result is most satisfactory. Cost 4 rupees 10 annas – i.e. about 7s. 6*d*. whereas the professional permers out here charge 40 rupees! Thank goodness I've got a Scot for a mother!

We had a terrific dust-storm last night – and I out on my verandah. I nearly got blown out of bed, the wind was so strong.

I still want lots more cotton dresses. Two a day are very often needed out here, so don't forget if ever you see a picture of an attractive dress please just cut it out and send it as that is quite enough for my *derzi* to go on.

I've more or less given up golf now for the summer. It's getting just a bit too hot. So I have transferred my affections to the swimming pool at the Club.

Back now to the office. We had a lengthy electricity failure this morning which meant no fans for an hour and a half – phew, was it hot!

I'm so sorry this is such a very dull little note but it comes as usual with all my love and the hope that you are all flourishing.

16 May 1950

I'm quite ashamed to say that I have next to no news to tell you about. In this very hot weather one's life is inevitably somewhat circumscribed. But so far I can't tell you how much I'm enjoying this summer. It *is* blazingly hot, but in most of the heat of the day one is indoors and the evenings are unbelievably lovely. Often I go swimming quite late on and the air is always warm and velvety. You simply never know what it's like to feel an evening shiver, and oddly enough it's a very healthy time of year. I haven't felt better all the time I have been in Delhi.

We have had a great exodus from the office during the last month and quite a largish intake from home, so I have been kept quite busy meeting newcomers and accommodating them and helping them to settle in. We're sending one of our bad lassies home in ten days' time. I'm sure half the trouble in the past out here has been that not a strong enough line has been taken with the odd girl or two who does go round the bend; I've been on this girl's track almost since the day I arrived, and although she's only done nine months of her two years – off she's going! Apart from her all the girls are a very pleasant lot and I don't expect to have much trouble from them. More and more I'm being drawn into administrative work and I certainly find it most absorbing.

We are in the throes of trying to find a new manager for the big block of flats which house our higher staff, and I've been going through over three hundred applications from all sorts of extraordinary candidates. Some of the letters are unbelievably funny and I've had free laugh after free laugh.

I've saved up a little money and bought one or two things for my flat lately – including a most beautiful nest of tables – four of them – with most delicate carving, from Kashmir – for the large sum of about £3 10*s*.0*d*. Really the Kashmir furniture out here is marvellous – such artistic and skilled work and only about one quarter of the price of things at home. If there is any wooden thing that you particularly want I could probably buy it and send it home. They pack furniture very beautifully and it can be dispatched at quite a small cost.

Well, I'm just going to have some tea, then I'm off for a swim before going to a cocktail party given by the nephew of that great friend of Granny Kate's at Hampton Court. He and his wife are dears – so natural and friendly and I like them very much indeed. Of course, my cocktail drinking is limited these days to about one small drink followed by lots of tomato juice! It is odd, but since my dose of dysentery I've completely gone off anything intoxicating, and pour quantities of fresh lime juice and suchlike innocuous drinks down my thirsty throat. It's wonderful for the pocket.

I still haven't got up to the hills yet. Did I tell you that I was to have gone a fortnight ago when I got my second bout of the old innards trouble so that was that? Now I've got to wait for my party of friends all to be available again at the same weekend.

I hope to get up to Kashmir in the autumn if finances allow. What a holiday that can be – living on a house-boat in the middle of some of the most wonderful scenery in the world!

Now – splash – into that swimming bath!

24 May 1950

You asked about my *derzi*. I have two actually – both men. No skilled work is ever done by the women out here, or very rarely; their place is very much in the home and *not* elsewhere.

And now for my news. Yes, I really have managed to get to Mussoorie for the weekend and it's been a most wonderful experience. The High

Commissioner's secretary and I got the chance of a lift up with Bill Worth, the Yorkshireman who recognised Leslie's photograph. Another car load of folks went with us and we set out at 5 a.m. on Saturday morning. It's 170 miles, 150 through the plains and the last twenty up the most incredible mountain road I have ever seen in all my life. You climb well over 7,000 feet in those twenty miles and go round the most hair-raising corkscrew and hairpin bends. Bill's car is a 1939 Morris 12 and he is an engineer and the most competent person as far as cars are concerned. He had the whole car overhauled so that we should have no trouble – anyway we took thirteen hours getting there. *Never* have I known such a journey. Trouble started with the water boiling every few miles, even along the flat. We tested everything that might have caused it but all seemed to be in order so we just had to creep on. Then of course the petrol pump got overheated, doubly so with the radiator trouble and the awful new petrol out here which contains 25 per cent pure alcohol and is playing havoc with all cars. Then to add to our trouble a number of trees had been blown right across the road by a hurricane the previous night and had not been removed, and in trying to get round one we caught the exhaust pipe and ripped it off so that for forty miles we roared along like an aeroplane until we reached a garage where it could be repaired. Finally, she lost nearly all her power on the terrific climb up, caused, as we later discovered, by a bit of fluff stuck in the jet of the carburettor! We simply crawled up the mountain, boiling away furiously and having to stop innumerable times to let her cool down and completely change the water. But of course I loved every minute of it – it was quite an adventure. In desperation we sent the other car on without us and they mercifully had an uneventful journey.

But my goodness was it worth it! The hill stations of India as an engineering feat are magnificent. Mussoorie is literally perched on the top of the first real ridge of the Himalayas – and really perched. We all stayed in a very good hotel and spent our two and a half days there in the most energetic of fashion. We were very lucky with the weather. Often the Himalayas proper are shrouded in mist, even in the height of the summer. But for us they were clear, and by climbing a little way up from Mussoorie we could see a vast expanse of snow-covered peaks a hundred and fifty miles from us and stretching across half the horizon. I can't begin to give you an idea of the grandeur of this highest mountain range of the world. To see those desolate peaks in the glare of an Indian sun and to sense their awful permanence is one of the great and certainly one of the humbling experiences of life.

On one of the days we dropped by foot right down into the valley – over 4,000 feet in about six miles where there is a beautiful waterfall dropping hundreds of feet down the mountain side. At the moment the volume of water is of course very small but even so the sight is impressive. Near the bottom we found a pool formed by the waterfall and completely enclosed by rocks and trees. It was one of the loveliest places I have ever seen – a fairy grotto come true. The pool was very deep but as clear as crystal and the sun shone through the trees right down into it. Dozens of small trout flashed unafraid in the clear water and touched our fingers as we dabbled them. We stayed there for hours, entranced, unwilling to drag ourselves back to reality. Had the water not been quite so icy we should have bathed, but India cures you of submerging yourself in any water that isn't reasonably warm!

At last we did move and started on the terrific climb back again.

Of course, one of the joys of walking in India is that you don't have to carry anything. For a rupee or two you hire a coolie for the day and he humps along your sandwiches and Thermos flask and change of socks and shoes. It is walking in luxury. Our coolie for the day was marvellous. His load was not heavy but where we went the long and easy way round both on the ascent and descent he took short cuts straight up and down the mountain side with both hands full, and was always sitting calmly waiting for us after one of these short cuts as we came puffing along.

The loads that these coolies carry with ease are unbelievable. One of the most interesting sights of Mussoorie is to see the charcoal carriers. They build up the charcoal first in a small sack and then out into a great bulge on top, and they carry it on their backs with the main weight taken by a strap around the brow or over the top of the head.

The load is so heavy that I had great difficulty in even tilting one that was parked on a wall while its bearer had a rest.

Another interesting little thing is that on the wider of these mountain tracks – that is those about six or eight feet wide – the really smooth part of the path worn by the feet of centuries is always on the side nearer to the drop. This is to give you just a split second more in which to see an animal should it leap upon you from the undergrowth or trees above!

At this time of year you see nothing but monkeys, though in the winter panther and bear and other wild beasties come down for shelter from the higher Himalayas. The monkeys are an entertainment in themselves. I could never keep away from them in the zoo and I kept on holding up the party whenever I spied a family of them. They are quite tame and indulge in the most fantastic play among the tall trees. They think nothing of leaping twenty or thirty feet from one tree to another, large ones and small ones, huge mothers with tiny babies clutching their fur. The way the mothers leap with babies attached is a sight, and how they don't crack the poor little nippers' skulls open remains a permanent mystery to me.

I could go on burbling about Mussoorie for hours but this letter is already reaching alarming dimensions. But I haven't quite finished my story.

Bill spent a large amount of the weekend along with all the drivers of Mussoorie attempting to solve the boiling water problems. Even I got interested and now know an enormous lot more about engines than I ever knew before. Finally we decided that there must be a partial block in the engine jacket. Soda removed some, but not all of it, so we decided to come down the mountain in the afternoon and have the cool of the evening in an attempt to keep the water from boiling too merrily. With careful driving the ruse worked tolerably well, and we were congratulating ourselves that we had done sixty miles without mishap when suddenly we stopped *absolutely* dead. This time we traced the trouble to ignition and for a solid hour were baffled. Then our friends came along behind and one of them by an incredible stroke of luck happened to see a flash in one of the leads into the distributor. By a chance in a million the wire had broken inside the rubber cover and by an even greater chance it happened to be spotted when the two ends touched for a second and shorted! Mercifully the break was at a spot where the wire could be cut and still be long enough to stretch.

So very weary we finally got back at 12.30 a.m.

The heat in Delhi was wicked after Mussoorie and I hardly got any sleep, but now I'm acclimatised again.

A new girl wandered into my flat at that point to have a natter, and now the bag is closing, so I must end very abruptly.

I haven't re-read this letter so please make allowances for all errors.

1 June 1950

Life is fairly static at the moment owing to the heat. I went to meet a girl, who oddly enough I used to know in London, at Palam aerodrome on Saturday and the temperature was 112 degrees in the shade! Poor girl, when she first stepped off the plane she thought she was standing in its exhaust and was horrified to discover it was merely Delhi!

We had a terrific thunderstorm yesterday with torrential rain – unheard of in May, and temperatures have dropped a good 8 degrees by day and 10 degrees by night, but of course the atmosphere is damp and you stream with sweat. Awful the way we talk and talk about the weather but it is very near to our hearts.

The High Commissioner is working up to a great reception which he is giving on 8 June in honour of the King's birthday. There are to be eight hundred guests including – most important – me, and provided we don't get another freak thunderstorm it should be a very grand occasion.

I've just heard of the existence in Old Delhi of a Mrs Coates who is returning to somewhere near Leominster in three weeks time. On learning that I was from those parts she wants to see me and have a natter, and no doubt she will come and look you up and give you all the Delhi gossip. I do hope she does as I shall feel it is a very close link with you.

9 June 1950

How awful the streams of traffic must have been with petrol derationing, but what a boon it must be to you. Petrol out here costs Rupees 2 Annas 11 per gallon which is exactly 4s. so you still beat us by a bob!

The High Commissioner had his terrific reception last night. The President was there and I was introduced to the three Tibetans whose visas to enter China on a mission have been cancelled: you may have seen something about the incident in the papers. They all had the most wonderful faces – full of character yet strangely remote and withdrawn and mysterious.

It was terribly hot even out in the garden. It has suddenly gone very damp and sticky now the monsoon is not far off and we all simply dripped with sweat; but everybody does it so nobody minds. The poor old High Commissioner came an awful cropper off his horse this morning and is now in bed with concussion. He only just got his reception in in time.

Incidentally a photograph was taken with me in it – on the lines of that engagement party – and I hear it is quite good. So I'll try to get a copy and send it to you. I was wearing Effie Ogilvie's old dress. I bet there wasn't an older one present!!

After the reception half a dozen of us were invited to Jeanne Barwell's birthday party. We went on to the Club to dance and at 12.15 a.m. donned bathing costumes and had a mad three-quarters of an hour in the swimming pool, with half the inhabitants of the Club watching us. One or two of the men had had the odd spot to drink and were causing no small amount of amusement to the assembled company. But I must say it was a glorious dip.

The heat though really is getting severe. Today has been about 108 degrees in the shade and horribly humid. You get so wet that you just drip and drip and drip. The thought of a cold grey English day fills me with unspeakable longing!!

You ask what blooms in our part of the world. Oddly enough, almost every English flower. That amazed me when I first came out here. We even have some roses, though their scent is very faint. In addition there are the most glorious flowering trees and shrubs, including the beautiful jacaranda which blooms for a day in wonderful mauve against a blue sky and vanishes as soon as it comes.

In the early summer flowers are wonderfully abundant, but at this time of year they fade so quickly in the heat.

I must stop and get to bed early after last night!

Don't forget – patterns, patterns, patterns (including evening dresses and particularly patterns that look half naked and therefore cool!).

15 June 1950

I must just pop this into the bag for you today. It was the picture taken at the High Commissioner's reception. The girl in the middle is Daphne Maines. The HC's secretary is the one who was born near Altrincham and who knows Coralie Archer very well. I can assure you the glint in my eye was the product of one whisky only! This was the beginning of the evening when we all ended up in the swimming pool.

It's simply too hot to write for long or your hand sticks to the paper. It looks as if the monsoon can't be far off as the atmosphere is already so terribly moist. We shall be quite glad now when it breaks.

Now to relax for half an hour to recover a bit of energy for the afternoon's work.

22 June 1950

My news continues to be of weather, weather, weather. This is about the most wicked time of year. The temperatures are still very high but this awful humidity has descended upon us. Sleep is almost impossible – you can't think of lying on a mattress and even a pillow is too hot. When you lie on one you have to keep on turning it over to find a dry patch! Most people are now suffering badly from prickly heat and even I, who thought I was avoiding it nicely, have become a victim. It comes suddenly and you find yourself with angry red patches of tiny pimples that prick and itch all at the same time. Some people are covered from head to foot in it but so far I've only got it on my face, neck and chest and a tiny patch in the middle of my tum.

Beauty is temporarily ruined and one takes more and more showers and goes about looking like a ghost, caked in talcum powder. Do you remember the mad dash we had in the rain to get some powder before I caught my train? Well, I'm glad we bothered for it gives more relief than anything else I have discovered out here.

Two nights ago we had a really magnificent storm. I had just got to sleep on my verandah – 1.30 a.m. – when without a second's warning a gigantic gale blew up and literally almost threw me out of bed. In another few seconds down came a solid wall of water. I had a pair of cotton pants only on so I grabbed a brassière and my transparent mack and hoping I wouldn't meet anybody, hauled myself downstairs and into my poor little bus that had its hood down, got it started and roared round the compound to some Ministry of Works huts where I found some shelter for it. By that time I didn't know whether I was wetter inside or out, so much had I sweated in the mack. And of course I bumped into several people in my strange attire and am still having my leg pulled!

I got back to my flat and tried to sleep. But gradually the hurricane increased and the rain was driving in on me. So I heaved my bed round the comer to another part of my verandah and got a little sleep. Then a second storm blew up – the wind changed and the rain started to drive in on my new spot. So back I heaved the bed again. When the third storm broke – in the old direction – I cursed and remained where I was and pulled the sheet well over my ears and wakened up in the morning a soggy, but cooler, mess.

These storms are magnificent while they last and cause the temperature to drop 15 to 20 degrees in no time. But once the sun gets up it becomes hellish – far, far worse than before the storm. *What* a climate.

I see I've got a question or two to answer. No, nobody ever wears stockings in the hot weather except on very public occasions. At night you wear the very minimum. For instance when I'm in evening dress I wear a brassière only and not even a slip if I can decently do without it and never any pants – surprising what a difference even one garment makes! Hats are unknown except at receptions and perhaps on the golf course. You see, normally you are never in the sun for more than a few seconds at a time – you just can't be as it's far too exhausting.

30 June 1950

Forgive the pencil but it is so much less trouble in the heat.

For the fiftieth time I seem to have no news – except the weather – and that's bloody. I'm just getting over a nasty bout of boils and septic prickly heat. My poor arms look like battlegrounds. However, I've had seven penicillin injections and the patches have cleared up like magic. So many people suffer in the same way in this damp heat so I have not been alone in my misery – and I've been allowed to sleep in the air-conditioned sick bay which is worth having boils for! Any moment now we expect the monsoon to break. We watch each cloud with hope and it evaporates into thin air, leaving us sweltering in exasperation!

Thank goodness the weekend is here again – how we enjoy them. It's quite a ritual with a group of us now. Beer Saturday lunch time, lunch at Eastern House, sleep, change, dance or sit quietly in the warm evening. Sunday up fantastically early, golf until the sun gets too hot, bags of beer, swim, a pink gin with onions, curry lunch at the club, sleep (very soundly), tea, read and off to the cinema. Back to work on Monday.

The Deputy High Commissioner returns today after nearly three months leave and the High Commissioner and Sheila Stevenson leave for the UK by air tomorrow.

4 July 1950

It's still two days to 'bag time' but for once I'm starting to write to you well in advance to save the last minute rush.

But despite the early start there's really very little to say. I'm wholly and completely recovered from my boils and prickly heat, thank goodness. Penicillin is miraculous stuff and has done wonders for me. Our poor Medical Adviser is now himself in the Sick Bay with the same sort of dysentery that I had so the tables are turned, and as Welfare Officer I have to go and visit *him*!

The monsoon is just about on top of us now. We had the first of the pre-monsoon showers last night and today has been blissfully cloudy and much cooler. Already from the thunderstorm a fortnight ago and from last night's showers green things are beginning to sprout with mushroom-speed growth, and the golf course, which had become a pathetic dust track, is already miraculously changed. It's a wonderful relief to drop even a few degrees in temperature for a day or two. Maximums are down to about 104 degrees at the moment but minimums are still uncomfortably near 90 degrees. However last night to my delight when the rain came I had to pull up my sheet – a great advance!

Nearly every evening and much of the weekends is spent on the golf course. It's surprising how much better you feel in the hot weather if you force yourself to take exercise. I have started to practise furiously, bashing off about eighteen balls at a time. It's exceedingly hard work and my hands and wrists and arms ache from it, but it's doing me a lot of good. One of my troubles is my stupid thin little wrists for an otherwise buxom wench, so on advice I have bought two little rubber balls which I carry around and squeeze hard in the palms of my hands whenever I have a moment – a great wrist-strengthening exercise!

10 July 1950

I think it was most plucky of you to go all that way in Dobbin, Leslie, and I am pleased to know that apart from minor renewals he isn't letting his former driver down! My poor bus doesn't like the monsoon which has broken now with a wild fury. It leaks lamentably and has to be festooned in macintoshes and umbrellas to keep its front seats dry – and very odd it looks in such garb.

But the monsoon is wonderful. We had a few preliminary showers last week and then on Sunday down it came. I have never seen quite such torrential outpourings from the heavens. Within a few minutes roads and gardens are flooded, and if you happen to get caught in it you are immediately soaked to the skin. But after the heat and dryness of the summer you gaze at it in wonder and revel in it and long for it to go on and on. It has rained on and off but mostly on for three days now and already the golf course, which was mostly a dust track, is covered with millions of soft little green shoots – as if someone had sown seed about everywhere. And the shoots seem to grow as you watch them and you feel you hardly dare tread on them.

But every joy out here has its detractions and this is also the time of insects and creepy-crawlies *ad nauseam*. Never have I seen such a collection of evil monstrosities in the insect line. The only pleasant ones are the red spiders that have popped up all over the golf course, that look for all the world like small moving pieces of brilliant scarlet velvet. They're lovely, but everything else is hideous. Huge grasshopper things are the ones I loathe most. They can jump yards and when they don't they fly. They leap at you and cling to you and you find them in your bath and on your pillow and in your shoes. Ugh – horrible!

Now just imagine sitting down on the old throne and seeing a giant cockroach crawling meaningfully round your toes (which was *my* first introduction to one). Flying ants are horrid too. They flutter madly round lights with two pairs of wings many sizes larger than their bodies which they eventually shed (wings I mean) so that they become earthbound but in no wise nicer acquaintances. It's amazing to watch the respectable form of ant – i.e. those we get at home – coping with these fallen wings, and indeed any other form of dead insect matter that you happen to leave around squashed under foot. They come in their thousands and march off with their prey. Their combined strength and perseverance is something marvellous to behold.

But of course the lizards love it all. They park themselves on walls near a light and just simply let the insects come to them. They gorge and gorge and gorge, flashing out their little tongues and gulping so that their whole bodies contract; and they get so full that flies can come within tongue-length with impunity. I approve of the lizards – they are friendly little souls and only give you a bit of a start sometimes if they fall off the ceiling onto your bed or drop from your clothes as you take them from the wardrobe.

I've just bought myself a set of golf clubs to make the most of the monsoon golfing. The few clubs I bought in Calcutta were very rag tag and bob-tail and I happened to light on this set – the only ones anywhere in Delhi – and they're just my weight. As golf is my one and only vice here I thought I would be extravagant. And I expect they will last me a lifetime.

Apart from golf – when it isn't raining too hard – this is the time for reading. I've just had my nose buried in two wonderful ones – do get hold of them if you can – *The Jacaranda Tree* by H.E. Bates and *The Jungle is Neutral* by Spencer Chapman. Chapman is an amazing man and is well-known by my old boss Hamilton and also by Barbara Bryan. I reckon if once you open *The Jungle is Neutral* it's goodbye to pot-washing and stock-feeding and garden-weeding. I lost more sleep over it than I've done over any parties recently!

I seem to have waffled on about nothing in particular for quite long enough. It's raining so hard at the moment that I'm completely deafened and find the lure of watching the storm more than I can resist.

26 July 1950

I'm back to pencil again! We have had *buckets* more rain, including three days ago – *five* inches in twenty-four hours and most of those fell in two hours only, and now the sun is shining mercilessly again with the result that humidity is about 100 degrees and you ooze at every pore. It's even stopped me playing golf. I did nine holes last Sunday with another girl and we both nearly passed out. Four men friends of ours struggled through eighteen holes, the idiots, and they were *all* ill afterwards. One was so bad that I thought I ought to take charge, particularly as he lived in a room on his own with no one to look after him. Trust old welfare Maggie to get tied up in such a situation! I got him home and he proceeded to have a recurrence of malaria in front of my eyes – probably coincidental with the golf in the sun but nevertheless aggravated by it. Was I scared! He refused to have a doctor as he had had bouts before and knew what to do and just gave instructions. It was really rather an interesting cycle to watch and I'd know what to do with a malaria case again. First he went icy cold and goose-fleshy despite the temperature of the day. He kept on calling for more and more clothes so I had to hunt around his quarters and see what I could find. He ended up with a sheet, two towels, two dressing gowns, two curtains and a blanket and a travelling rug on! I gave him two aspirins and after an hour he began to sweat. It soaked through everything I had put on him. His pulse started to race and he began to breathe quickly but he assured me it was all right and that I was to keep him covered up for a time. His temperature shot up and I got really scared. Then he became slightly delirious and started talking about things that had happened in the war – a queer jumble – then that passed and I was instructed gradually to remove the coverings. After this had gone on for about five hours his temperature was back to normal and though very weak he was quite recovered. But I don't want another dose of that in a hurry!

News from here is little, the weather sees to that. We are all of course mildly concerned about Korea as everyone is, but so far as my own skin out here is concerned I'm a complete fatalist. *Don't* worry about me anyway, Ma love. I can always be home in two days.

2 August 1950

No word from you yet this week but I think the bag is late and I hope to hear instead tomorrow.

We are still being washed out – this is a record monsoon for rain. I have had my car patched up and it is now very nearly proof against India's worst, though of course if you have to park your car even five yards from shelter you are soaked while you make a dash for it. Last night, after torrential rain, was the coolest we have had for months, and for at least two hours I had to go and dig out a blanket. But by 6 a.m. I was suffocating and had to fling it off again.

Four of my best friends are all leaving Delhi this week and next so as you can imagine there has been quite a round of farewell parties. Last Sunday two of them gave a beer party at lunch time so when we had all played golf we trooped round to quench our thirst. By three o'clock about eighteen of us were still going strong so off we set in a variety of vehicles (including mine) to Nirulas, one of the New Delhi restaurants which serves the most wonderful Chinese food imaginable. We had a whole small room to ourselves. All the men took it in turns to tell a story and then the girls had to follow suit, but as you can imagine Muggins was the only one who got on her feet! The noise was considerable until the food came along – at 4 p.m! Needless to say we were all in bed by 5 p.m. and sleeping solidly. Once in a while a party like that out here goes with a real swing and you thoroughly enjoy it, but you haven't the energy for many repetitions!

We are just in the throes of a change in management at Eastern House. Ma Christie, the old Scottish battleaxe, is moving on to our other block of flats, and we have engaged a retired Major and his wife to look after us at Eastern House. I went down the night before last to meet them at Old Delhi station. They arrived with seventeen pieces of luggage and three Scottie bitches! –

pedigree champions and absolutely irresistible. I shall have a lot of dealings with the new couple and am sure they are going to be very helpful and easy to get on with – unlike the Battleaxe!

Only a month on Sunday now until I go to Kashmir, and am going to live on a house-boat on a lake near Srinagar – if I didn't tell you before – with two married couples and a man and girl from the office – all of whom are very jolly. Kashmir I understand is one of the glories of the earth. Without exception everyone returns enthralled by the place. I hope to spend a little time trekking and I might even go on a bear-hunt. There are endless possibilities!

10 August 1950

I had a lovely birthday. It wasn't a public holiday here so I had to work, but in the evening I had five of my best friends along – three men and two girls. We had the odd noggin in my flat and then four of us piled into one car and two of the men, my bearer Lalla Kam, two *sigris*, charcoal, two pounds of bacon and a dozen eggs, a pound of tomatoes, cooking fat, a huge tin of peaches, a dozen cushions, rugs, beer and a bottle of Scotch all got into a jeep and away we went through the night down to the River Jumna at Okhla. Okhla is a fascinating spot where the river is damned for irrigation purposes. It is so high this year that when we went down it was only eighteen inches below the level when it would flood half Delhi – a most spectacular sight. Once there we got old Lalla cracking on his *sigris* and in no time we were devouring a wonderful meal. Then we sat and sang songs loudly to drown the roaring river. It was a very merry party and we were back by midnight, which in Delhi is early, so that we should be fighting fit for work the next day.

Talking of the jeep – I've fulfilled one of my ambitions by driving it – not on that occasion but another. They feel gloriously powerful and the temptation to drive them fast is strong to resist. The other ambition – to drive a double-decker bus – is, I hasten to add, still unfulfilled.

Later That was written at 7 a.m. today! I got up very early as I was supposed to meet the C-in-C – General Cariappa – at an SPCA (like our RSPCA) do at 8 *a.m.* but as I got my teeth into my breakfast a message came through that it was cancelled, so with much relief I turned letter-writer instead. Now it's lunch-time and I'll finish this off and put my feet up for half an hour.

18 August 1950

I hear from the bank that I now have a credit balance £4! So my overdraft is paid off and I've got a whole car to my credit that would realize £200 any day. I shall continue to go on saving as much as I can in case the world situation is stable enough to let me come home via the Far East and America. That's my next ambition.

Thank goodness the weather is beginning to get a little cooler, though day temperatures are still over 90 degrees and it's very sticky yet. But in a fortnight I shall be in the paradise of Kashmir and by the time I get back the worst of the summer will be at an end.

Did I tell you I am looking after a Siamese cat that belongs to one of our men who has had to go home for an operation? She is the sweetest little thing but terribly timid and has lived most of her life in 'flat' seclusion. I'm trying to toughen her up, and took her out in the car the other day to visit friends in a bungalow and give her a run in their garden. Bringing her back I had the hood up, but there's a bit of flap that doesn't join properly and suddenly out of the corner of my eye I saw her leap through the gap – and I was doing about 20 m.p.h. I had pictures of a variety of squashed cat, but after ten minutes frantic search in dirty darkness finally found her and drove all the way home with one hand, clutching her by the tail with the other! We haven't ventured on a car journey together since.

We had a holiday this week for Independence Day. I kept well clear of the main roads as the crowds were out in their millions.

Our sickness rates out here continue to be alarming at the moment, but I mercifully am still in admirable and enviable health and as brown as a berry.

I've got to be up at crack of dawn tomorrow to meet someone flying out on the Argonaut, so it must be bed reasonably early.

23 August 1950

The snap of Mother sitting in the garden grinning and Leslie characteristically lying on his back and the dog rolling made me feel quite homesick. So many little things took me right back to Alleymoor in a flash – Nonna's stool (how often have we sat on that together with our toes in the cinders, Mother?) and above all the wonderful collection of untidy junk that always seems to accompany Archer outings in the garden. I've just looked closely to see what on earth Leslie is using as a headrest and I've found Dora! It rather reminds me of the puzzle pictures on the children's page where in a scene of wild unreality you have to find the most number of objects beginning with the letter 'X'! And the two of Susan solo make me hoot with laughter – she looks so exactly like Auntie Madge!

I always love opening your paper cuttings, Mother, particularly those about

India. You should read the Indian papers *in toto* and realize just what weird and incredible things do go on here. But it is always interesting to see what our English papers think worth reproducing.

Well now, I think that just disposes of your letters – oh, one more thing – yes, I go to Kashmir on Sunday week, 3 September, and stay a fortnight. Our party has now grown to eight so I think it should be very jolly.

Now for a change I have got a small piece of news for you. We've had a FIRE at Eastern House – in the early hours of last Saturday morning. Vast and great excitement – and vast and great scandal!

I had gone to bed early (with the beginnings of a sore throat which has since developed into one of my beloved and endearing coughs), out on my verandah still when suddenly there was the most deafening roar like a blast furnace flaring up, and in a second I was out of bed and wide awake. I thought at least a plane had fallen on Eastern House. Although the next block hid the scene of action from me the whole of the Vista was lit up with what looked like a lurid orange flare. I flung myself into a dress and hurled myself downstairs to see what was up. What had happened was that the British Information Films store had gone up in one splendid blaze (though the building was quite fireproof); monsoon weather can cause spontaneous combustion and that is what has been suspected here. Anyway the blaze was just dying down but a car parked beside it was merrily roaring away as were some of the servants' quarters, so was a motor bicycle parked on the verandah of the BIS office nearby, together with innumerable packing cases. In the compound a number of charpois were alight where servants had been sleeping until the roar of flame sent them flying to safety.

Well, we rushed and grabbed all the fire-extinguishers in and around the place and a variety of bearers, *chokidar*, *chaprassis* and security guards and the odd resident or two wielded them with remarkable success. Believe it or not, the fire engine was only four minutes in arriving from the time we rang for them.

The things that could not be put out were the car and the cycle, both of which are now as totally wrecked as they could possibly be.

The scandal part of the story lies in the car. It was a BOAC one which was used by one of the BOAC staff, a married man who has been having a terrific affair with one of our supplies girls, who had been married at nineteen and subsequently divorced. The man used to park his car very obviously around Eastern House and go off with great noise about breakfast time. I quietly avoided the girl and things appeared much better, but the fire revealed that he was hiding the car away to be out of sight and then sleeping the night with his lady friend. Well, Vengeance is Mine saith the Lord and in this case he sure spoke a mouthful!

Had the girl not been on her way home in any case in ten days time, I should have done something drastic earlier for the poor car's sake. It's a pity I didn't. Can you imagine how livid the head of BOAC is!

Great excitement – your parcel has arrived in Bombay, Mother, but I have had an awful customs statement to complete and I'm having to bluff like mad as I can't remember all the contents and have destroyed your letter detailing them. Anyway, I hope to get away with it. Results reported soon I hope – and favourable.

This is one other thing you asked about – magazines, yes. We get quite a few out here, though English and American ones are very expensive. I'm getting a pile of Indian ones together to send to you. I had hoped to get them off via a friend but was too late so will send them sea mail.

Kashmir

10 September 1950

After two false starts on Sunday and Monday when cloud kept aircraft grounded, we finally left for Kashmir on Tuesday morning. Lovely trip – for the first time I looked down on fleecy clouds instead of up at them. There were about twenty-five of us on the plane. I still don't know how or why (unless it was my irresistible beauty!) but suddenly the steward was asking me if I would like to go forward to the flight deck. Would I! So I spent the last three quarters of an hour of the journey in the co-pilot's cockpit chatting to the very pleasant Indian pilot. Never in my life have I seen a more breathtaking panorama than when flying towards the mountains and over the Banihal Pass. For hundreds of miles snow-capped peaks dazzled in the sunshine. Eighty miles away was one of 27,000 feet, only 2,000 feet lower than Everest. Suddenly we were over the Pass and descending into this idyllic Vale of Kashmir. Our houseboat is on the edge of the clearest cleanest lake, and more snow-capped mountains form a backcloth to the lake. We spend our days in glorious idleness. The sun shines superbly all day, turning us the most enviable honey-colour. In our first three days we have had roast chicken twice, roast duck and green peas and roast goose! This is the land of exquisite fruits, of wonderful pears and peaches growing in open orchards. The lake is warm for swimming and I have had my first experience of surf riding behind a motor boat – marvellous fun and the nearest thing to ski-ing I have yet discovered.

Kashmir is a second Venice – all waterways and one travels miles by *shikara*, a punt-like boat of superb comfort paddled by boys of anything from six to sixty years old. In half an hour we are off to the world-famous Shalimar Gardens, then tomorrow we go up the mountains to Gulmang. Before

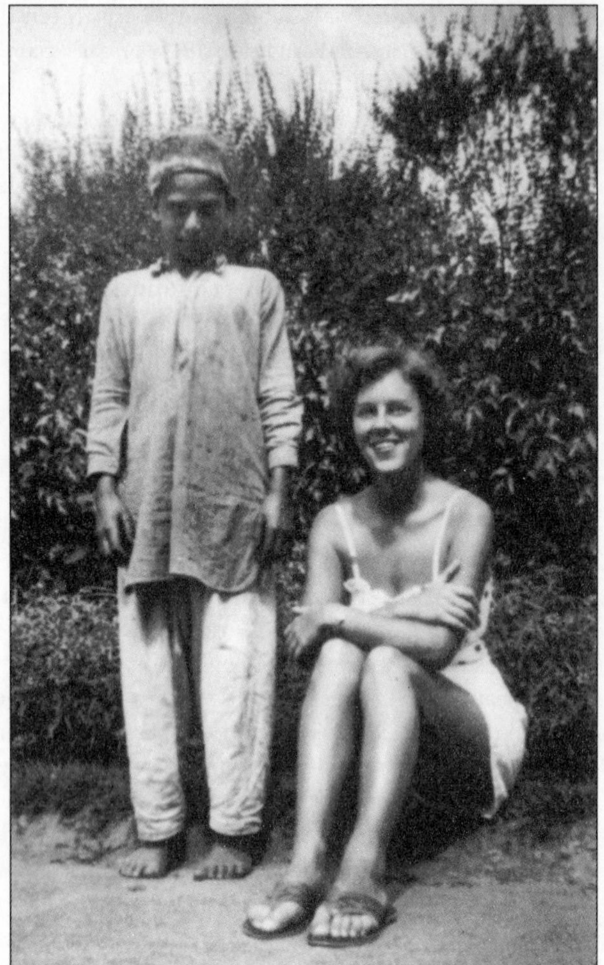

Myself with handsome Kashmiri youth.

breakfast we go riding for an hour for 1 rupee (1*s*.6*d*) and are just getting over our stiffness. Leslie would love the bird (feathered) life here. Believe it or not the kingfisher is the commonest. He is small and brilliant and completely unabashed by humans. Often he perches on the houseboat within a few yards of us. Masses of snaps coming up, but I'll wait for Delhi and security of diplomatic bag.

17 September 1950

Alas our wonderful holiday is almost at an end. We catch our plane back at mid-day tomorrow. But what a wonderful time we have had. I've never been so brown in my life before. We've had only half a day of rain and the rest of the time the sun has simply poured down onto us. I can't remember ever feeling better in my life.

24 September 1950

Somehow I never seem to be able to write a whole letter at one time. I got whisked off at that point to do something or other and now it's a whole week later. And what a week it has been. Believe it or not we are still in Srinagar! The very evening of the 17th it started to rain, and it rained and rained for three nights and two days. As a result Kashmir has had one of its very rare floods. The last one as bad as this was something like fifty years ago! We have been completely cut off from civilisation, and until yesterday hadn't seen a paper, heard any news or been able to get a letter or a telegram out of Kashmir. It's all been so amusing that I'll write you a long letter about it when I get back to Delhi. At the moment I'm squatting on the steps of a hotel in Srinagar waiting for the Indian Airways bus to pick us up and take us to the aerodrome. We really hope we shall get away at last today.

Much more news anon therefore.

24 September 1950

I've just put an air letter into the box for you and thought I would start another letter straight away while the wait to go to the airport continues. Well, I promised you further details of our funny holiday and here we go.

I can't remember just how much I told you of our first comparatively uneventful fortnight. The lake we were on – Nagin Lake – is about a mile long and half wide. Our party had two houseboats – *King's House* and *St James' Palace*. Other friends of ours had one alongside – *Buckingham Palace*! It amused me enormously to find such traitorous devotion to British Imperialism by allowing such names to remain. But that was only a tiny symbol of the Kashmir problem. Though under Indian rule, and with a Hindu Maharaja, 95 per cent of the population is Muslim and therefore of course violently pro-Pakistan, and considerably more pro-British than India and the Hindus, because of the holiday trade that Europeans have always brought them.

Our houseboat consisted of sitting-room, dining-room and three bedrooms.

Attached to each bedroom was a small bathroom with primitive furnishings – a wash bowl and water jug, two thunder-boxes (Indian duffies and very universally used and most aptly named) and a tin bath that came through the window at bath time. I must tell you more about the thunder-boxes. They are definitely reminiscent of parts of the Specialist. They are simply small lidded boxes with a detachable inner lid with the necessary hole and a very small sort of pudding basin in the middle. Visiting them is always a game of hide-and-seek with the sweeper who empties them. If you pop in after somebody else you usually find him there on duty and you're no sooner out yourself than there he is again. And if you make a morning of it with a book, your knitting or the newspaper, a foot will begin to appear through the window, thinking you can't still be there! And of course often the sweeper doesn't push down the inner wooden lid properly into the frame so this is done unthinkingly by your own seat, which proceeds to get nipped between lid and frame. I got completely trapped one day and had quite a job extricating myself, and most of us at some time or other have had quite unmistakable marks on the backs of our 'upper thighs'.

I can't tell you how marvellous the food was on our boat. Chicken, duck and goose are the most plentiful and cheap form of meat and occasionally as a treat instead you have a little mutton. Pears and peaches abound at this time of year and of course walnuts are about a hundred for sixpence.

All the cooking is done in the cookboat behind the houseboat on the most primitive fires – a brick construction which burns wood only and has four open holes above it. Believe it or not, for the last week fifteen of us were fed on food you would never see in the Dorchester, on that one primitive wood 'stove'. Then as eggs are so plentiful it is nothing to have a soufflé with a dozen of them beaten up as the main ingredient! Miraculously, none of us has put on much weight. I'm still only 8 stone 10 lbs. The lightest I've ever been – that's Delhi heat for you; you would never recognise my sylph-like figure these days.

Most mornings we went riding before breakfast – the ponies up here are rather poor things, usually throw-outs from the Army but mercifully fairly quiet. You know I've only been on a horse about three times, but I got the reputation of being 'the rider among us' so you can imagine what the others were like! These morning rides were not without their little side-lights of amusement. One day I was trotting happily along when my stirrup strap broke. Mercifully somebody was trotting beside me, and as I began to slither sideways I flung my arms around the neck of my companion's horse and by means of it came gracefully to the ground on my feet! Mercifully neither my companion nor my horse panicked at such undignified behaviour.

I think I told you we were going up to Gulmarg one day. Well, we went, and a splendid day it was. We went to the foot of the mountain by bus and there got on horse-back and proceeded up a very rough, steep and winding path until we got to about 9,500 feet. I had a peach of a horse, except that he refused to be anywhere except at the head of the procession, and lashed out with both hind legs at the same time at anyone who challenged his position as leader. I got a hell of a kick out of it – literally!

Gulmarg used to be one of the most popular mountain holiday places in Kashmir. Many Europeans had chalets up there. Miss Christie, who used to run Eastern House, owned a hotel there which she had run for over twenty-seven years.

During the troubles the whole place was completely wrecked. The damage was officially put down to raiders from the hills, but it is well-known that much of the looting was done by the inhabitants of the place who took the troubles as a suitable opportunity to rob the European dwellings. Miss Christie lost absolutely everything out of her hotel. What the raiders didn't loot or burn has been destroyed by avalanches, and what must once have been a beautiful spot is now a desolate shambles. It is very heart-breaking.

26 September 1950

Safely back in Delhi, you will be relieved to hear! Well now, to my story of the floods and our many abortive attempts to escape from Kashmir.

Evidently at this time of year it is very rare indeed to have business-like rain in Kashmir. September is usually a golden month of incessant sunshine and ripening fruit and rice ready for harvest. It is the month all the old stagers advise you to choose for a holiday. Our first fortnight was like that and then on the Saturday night before we were due to return, it started and did it rain! The old boy who owned and ran our houseboat, Salama, got more and more worried, knowing that the rain could only mean floods. Every day he got up at 4 a.m. and went to the Mosque to pray – 'for God is very angry with us this year,' he said. 'We all think far too much about money up here.' And in almost the next breath he would be asking us for some cash for some reason or another!

The rain continued for three nights and two days. We felt a bit like Noah in the Ark watching the waters rise, cooped up in our houseboat. The river Jhellum which runs through Srinagar rose over thirty feet. Much of the city is built on bunds or raised banks of earth. When the river rose to within a foot of the top of the main bund they decided to open one of the lock gates which shut off our lake and the Dal lake from the river. The waters swirled down, sinking some houseboats, flooding houses and destroying all the little market gardens which run down to the water's edge. In forty-eight hours our lake rose over six feet and we were quite cut off from the land and could only reach it by *shikara*. For seven days no planes left Kashmir, all telephone communications were cut and we had no news at all of the outside world. Some planes did get off on the Friday after the Sunday when we should have returned, but we couldn't get to the aerodrome. On Saturday however we packed up and left the houseboats, and not being able to travel by road to Srinagar went by water instead in a convoy of three *shikaras*. After an hour's wait we managed to commandeer a bus to take us the last seven miles to the drome. This was difficult as it was a Muslim festival day so no one was working. We waited five hours at the drome, only to be told that the one plane there was unserviceable and we would have to come again tomorrow morning. After an extra week of course funds were very low, but we trundled all our traps back to Srinagar and got the last two quarters in the one and only presentable hotel. We five women slept in one and the three men in the other. Far from getting off next day in the morning it was 5.45 p.m. before we were air-borne. We got the last flight of a shuttle service before darkness came. As you have to fly through a pass because the mountains are otherwise too high to get over, navigation has to be by daylight. Mercifully, since the very bad crash they had on this route a few weeks ago they are now taking the most elaborate care and I'm sure it must be one of the safest air journeys in the world in consequence. I can tell you these things now I'm safely back.

Lastly though – wonderful news – the parcel has arrived intact and the cake is as fresh as when it was made. Some of the oil had seeped out into the paper which formed a sort of wax covering. I'm absolutely thrilled. And honey for breakfast is an almost forgotten luxury. A thousand thanks to you all. I'm so delighted all your trouble wasn't in vain.

3 October 1950

You asked why all Indians seem to carry bedding rolls at stations. Well, most journeys in India are so long – many up to forty-eight hours in length – and unless you want to sit in great discomfort on wooden seats all that time you take a bedding roll. Even we always have one if travelling say to Bombay or Calcutta. And they are awfully useful for rolling other things up in.

I had my car decarbonised, thoroughly overhauled and a few new piston rings installed while I was away. It cost me £8 but that is the first money I have spent on it apart from servicing since I bought it and what a difference it has made. The engine is a beauty. You would never think it was thirteen years old.

Now let's see what's in your letter of 13 September. Just one question –

patterns. No love, I am *not* 36 inch bust and never have been. Only 34 and my hips have shrunk from 40 to 37!! You remember the taffeta evening dress with the two rows of velvet ribbon that I made for 18s when I was sixteen and which for years was a little tight? Well, I now wear it again with ease. It's started on its second tour of thirteen years!!

17 October 1950

I must get off to work. I was up at 5.45 this morning to try to finish a long job that I've spent most of the weekend at – there's never any peace in the office to get down to long drafting work, so I've been virtuous and spent my so-called leisure hours at it. I couldn't face any more after breakfast hence this letter to you. We don't start until 9 instead of 8.30 so it gives me time to do a few jobs before going to the office.

I'm hoping to go to Jaipur for a long weekend in November with all my Kashmir party. Jaipur is one of the most interesting cities round here – the capital of one of the old Princely States – and I haven't yet seen it so am looking forward to the jaunt.

23 October 1950

I wish you could be in Delhi at the moment – it's absolutely heavenly weather – gorgeous sunshine all day and nights not too cold yet, though getting nippier. I have started my early golf again – tea at 6.15 – on the course at 6.45 – play for an hour then bath, breakfast and off to work. It's a grand beginning to a day and I'm in tip-top health. There's an awful lot to be said for this life you know – it gets under your skin.

As usual I haven't much news – lovely and busy in the office and the new boss is proving to be very intelligent and go-ahead. Rehearsals for 'Hay Fever' progress well and we are looking forward to playing it at the end of November.

I've thought of two other things for Christmas – greedy pig that I am, but if any of the relatives ask you . . . ! One is a Tangee Natural lipstick – it's the only one I like and I can't get it any longer in India, and the other is an air mail edition of the *New Statesman* which can be posted weekly to anywhere in the world. That's rather an expensive request though, so therefore only terribly tentative.

I've just read a book which you must get hold of if you can, because it gives such wonderful descriptions of Kashmir and Srinagar (though they aren't called that). It is *The Rage of the Vulture* by Alan Moorhead, that excellent war correspondent, and it is about the troubles in 1947 after partition. The descriptions of the airfield, the main hotel where we stayed for our last night, the people, the houseboats, everything is wonderfully real. It will convey far more of Kashmir – and incidentally the Indian character and the pathetic dilemma of India – than anything I could ever hope to tell you. It is only a short novel but it's first class. Do read it if you can.

And now I must get ready to go out. One of our nicest officers is giving a farewell cocktail party tonight and I am invited to dine afterwards as well. Out is coming the old black velvet – it's just cool enough to be able to wear it again with comfort at last!

5 November 1950

It's 8 a.m. on Sunday morning and I've got an hour before I go to golf. Sunday is the one day I don't have to rise with the dawn to get my golf in. But so used am I to getting up at 6.15 now that I was wide awake at that time this morning so read for an hour before going in to breakfast.

Haven't missed my nine holes of golf before office for a fortnight now, and hope to keep it up throughout the winter. I'm still sleeping out on my verandah in my usual night garb (which you know well enough) and have just succumbed to a third blanket. Already the early mornings are very nippy and you feel it all the more after the blood-thinning furnace of the summer. But I'm convinced it's healthy to be spartan and certainly never felt better in my life. I find all this early morning exercise very conducive to sleep however, and if I don't have to go out you find old Maggie crawling happily to bed at 9 p.m., something I'm sure I've never done since I was ten!

Yesterday I went to the first day of the Test Match – the Commonwealth v. India. 18 runs were scored in the first forty-five minutes of our watching, but as we were in the R.25 seats for nothing (37*s*.6*d*. worth) we couldn't grumble. However, after tea play cheered up enormously and we had a final entertaining hour. This evening I shall meet four or five of them at a dinner party given by some very dear friends of mine, the husband being an Australian and a cricketer himself.

We are only three weeks off the play now. My greatest terror is that I have to sit down at a piano and sing a French song, accompanied by myself, and look glamorous and ogle a man all at the same time. May the saints in their infinite mercy preserve me!

I had my first tiny spot of trouble with my car yesterday, after ten months of running – not bad for thirteen years old. But as usual it happened where there was somebody at hand to help – in other words just driving out of Albuquerque Road – so the office transport section came to my rescue. All that was needed was a new diaphragm in my petrol pump and a bit of soldering to block up an air leak. I really have been lucky, you know, with that car. I think everyone in the office but me has had breakdowns this summer, particularly over the horrible alcohol petrol which we are forced to use, and until this very small spot of trouble I have emerged unscathed.

16 November 1950

What with going to Jaipur and the play and masses of work I just don't seem to have got down to writing to you. But there's ten minutes to spare of the lunch hour before the bag closes so here goes.

We had a wonderful weekend at Jaipur – all our Kashmir crowd. It's just two hundred miles and we came and went in six hours by Humber Hawk, starting at 5.30 in the morning. Jaipur is a thrilling place – a bit of real old princely India. Here are a few snaps I took. I've still got some to be developed. You bump into camels everywhere and we had a ride on an elephant!

The play is the next problem. I'm battling nobly with the French song I have to sing and accompany at the same time, but still have grave doubts as to whether my piping little voice will be heard beyond the second row of the stalls!

Heavens, time gone. Bye-bye.

20 November 1950

Here is one more Kashmir contribution. It's a companion photo to the one of the legs with the heads chopped off! I'm sending you a small one of an enlargement as I think it's rather an amusing one, and gives you a very good idea of the top of a houseboat and view across our lake. The trousers worn by Vera Hughes in the centre are real Nepalese ones and you will see we are all bedecked in Nepalese jewellery and hats. You can also see how brown my legs got!

Talking of Nepal, we have the fugitive king of that troubled land right on our doorstep. He has found asylum in Hyderabad House, a huge mansion right outside Eastern House, and the Delhi home of the Maharaja of Hyderabad. You mention Tibet and Nepal in your letters, but although they are on our doorstep their troubles seem a million miles away. The only tangible effects are a very much harder-worked office generally.

Did I tell you that three devoted swains spent all Saturday afternoon completely rewiring my car? It would have cost me Rs 50 (about £12) to have it done in a garage but they like mucking about with wire and hammers and

Jaipur, and Wing Commander Slee with elephant.

screw-drivers and were glad to have something to keep them occupied. What it is to have devoted friends!

I've been having a grand turn out of old letters and find I never answered a question about Ginger Dunn. Yes, he was reputed to be an absolute devil in the days of his giddy youth, but now he is married with two children he is the height of decorum and stability. His wife was equally a 'lass' before she married Ginger and everyone gave their marriage about six months. But it turned out to be one of those good things and after ten or twelve years they are still as devoted as ever.

Did I tell you about my 'success' with the Commonwealth cricket team!? One of them 'fell' quite devotedly and got up the next day, after meeting me at some unearthly hour, travelled all the way from Old Delhi and played nine holes of golf with me before breakfast! Needless to say he was as nit-witted as he was brilliant at cricket, which is saying something . . .

Now I must drag myself away from my fire and go to have some dinner. It's funny to hear you talking of rain. Our days continue to be blissfully sunny and hot but the nights really are fire-worthy. I'm the last stalwart at Eastern House to continue sleeping on my verandah. I'm hoping to keep it up throughout the winter but am making no rash promises to myself.

Don't expect much in the mail line now until the play is over! I'm still having fits nightly over the beastly French song.

1 December 1950

We are bang in the middle of the show and there just isn't a second to write letters. I thought you might like to see this, however. What do you think of your little daughter eh?!

Extract from the *Statesman*, Delhi, 1 December 1950 – 'Hay Fever'

> The story of the retired actress, who goes on dramatising her own life, and of the quarrelsome family around her (and who does not like to watch a good family quarrel on the stage?) has been presented by an able cast. By far the best player on the stage was Margaret Archer in the role of the ageing actress, who mixes up her own life with her performance.

The song mercifully was well received and I felt much better after it. Tonight the High Commissioner comes, so we must be at our best.

We have had some pictures of the show taken and will send them when they turn up.

4 December 1950

This past week has been one of my most hectic since I came to Delhi, what with dress rehearsals ending at midnight and three shows finishing only a little earlier. But the hard work was worth it and Delhi seems to have enjoyed our efforts enormously. Though I says it meself but shouldn't I seem to have made a great hit and have quite run out of original ways of making polite noises back at people who say complimentary things. And believe it or not, after all my terrors the song was the hit of the evening. But I am glad it is all over and now I can settle back into a slightly more ordered existence until the chaos of Christmas sets in.

'Hay Fever': I am playing Judith.

I have, in fact, very little real news to give you. The weather has now gone fantastically cold at night and for quite a bit of the day too, and I who never felt the cold go about like a starved misery, wailing and shivering in distress! How I shall ever face an English winter again I dread to think.

I seem to be in a fair way of dazzling one of our diplomats – one of the Wilfred Pickles family – bachelor in his thirties named Leo, very tall and scraggy and perfectly plain and very quiet and shy (I'm trying to 'develop' him!) but though a dear, not I fear the answer to this horrid maiden's prayer, so don't start thinking things – this is just a side-light on Delhi for your amusement. I'm afraid as a visitor I'm beyond hope. I had dinner with him in his flat last night and was so tired after all the play activities that I fell fast asleep on his hearth-rug in front of his fire – not awfully complimentary of me but he didn't seem to mind!

I must try to get down to some Christmas letters: already they are flowing in and I despair of ever catching up on my interminable arrears of correspondence.

13 December 1950

I'm still attempting to recover from my approximately bi-annual shock of receiving a letter from my brother, and I'm still tittering and sniggering over it. Of course, why he should neglect such superlative letter-writing powers is a source of wonder to me. Anyway, I was delighted and don't forget to repeat the performance before next Christmas. I was most interested in the Scottish trip, particularly as I remember Ayrshire well from my Butlin acting trip there.

And now your letter, Mother, which arrived at the same time. Yes, Lalla's Christmas card was his own idea. He produced it one day and asked me to send it on to you. I tell you what you could send him – and that's a portrait of 'Queen Mary'. If you can find one, be a dear and send it out and I will have it framed. He had one for years and it was destroyed – along with his treasures! – in an Eastern House fire. He would be thrilled to bits if he thought you had sent it.

Here are a few more snaps for you – self-explanatory. Leo and I took ourselves off on a picnic of our own on Saturday. He has a beautiful 1950 Standard Vanguard which I am allowed and encouraged to drive, so we did about a hundred mile round trip, I doing all the driving except for the last thirty miles, when, with my customary lack of ceremony, I promptly fell asleep. (This early morning golf is like a sedative to me!) The Vanguard is the first really modern car I have driven, with the gear lever on the steering column, and it just drives itself. It's an awful come-down when I return to my old bone-shaker.

Tonight and tomorrow are the two High Commissioner's Christmas dances for the staff and I have to be at both to help them out – an exhausting business. Then follows our choir concert and numerous Christmas parties. I still don't know what I shall do on Christmas Day, but I intend to enjoy it enormously.

28 December 1950

Christmas is over and at last I've found a moment to write to you.

Christmas has been lovely – I spent it remarkably quietly, and with almost nothing to drink. The day started with nine holes of golf with one of my very dear friends who returned from England on Christmas Eve – the one who brought you the packet of towels. Then fifteen of our little choir went to hospital to sing carols to one of the lads of the Ministry of Works who a short while ago had a heart attack and who is on his back for six weeks. It's terribly sad as he is only thirty-four and has just married and his wife is in England.

Christmas dinner we had at mid-day at Eastern House – turkey and Christmas pudding and then more golf in the afternoon and a quiet evening round the fire at night. I'm lucky to have friends in Delhi who, like me, prefer quiet evenings to noisy boozy parties.

On Boxing Day eighteen holes of golf and then out into the country and the sunshine for the rest of the day, picnicking and coming back as the sun went down – lovely. No hangovers for me!

Tonight we have an Eastern House Mess Party and I must run away and change for it now.

Here is yet one more Kashmir snap. I'm not nearly as fat as I look there, incidentally – just an unfortunate pose! I'm not much over 8 stone 8 now, but my friends are taking me seriously in hand and filling me full of butter and things.

Now I must away. Write and tell me all about Christmas.

1951

5 January 1951

Get out your atlas and find Mount Everest. By the time you read this I shall have seen it with my own eyes. Isn't it tremendously exciting? I'm off with the courier to Kathmandu – capital of Nepal. Don't ask me how I've wangled it, but I shall be the first High Commission girl (except the odd wife or two) to get up there. Full story later as I'm off tonight and have loads to do before I go.

We go by train tonight to Lucknow – have four hours there then spend the next 39 hours on another train to Raxaul. At Raxaul the fun begins and by a mixture of hiking, mules and station wagons one spends the next two days battling with the Himalayas until one descends to the Kathmandu valley. Everything is very quiet there now so no need to worry.

Shall spend three days in Kathmandu with the Ambassador and return to Delhi early on the morning of the 17th. Wonderful trip and one that few ever have the chance to go on.

Must dash away – don't expect to hear a word while I'm away as post from there I think slower than waiting to get back to Delhi.

Must fly.

All my love from your excited and lucky little

Maggie

The British Embassy
Kathmandu
Nepal

11 January 1951

Dearest Mama

I can't resist the headed paper – just to swank and prove to you that I really am in Kathmandu – and what an experience. I won't stop to tell you all about it now, as my three days here are so crammed with things to do, but I must get at least one little note off to you from this fascinating land.

This whole trip was planned and executed in two days – hence the impossibility of telling you anything about it earlier. The Lord fairly does look after me in letting me do odd things – I still find it hard to believe that I was allowed on the expedition. This is how it came about – we send a courier up here approximately every three months with the diplomatic bag. He's not allowed to go by air so he goes over land instead. This time Leo was chosen as courier. I gnashed my teeth in envy and before I knew what had happened, off his own bat he set the wheels in motion to take me with him. My own boss Pickard, who is an admirable soul, saw no objections, put up a good case to the High Commissioner who astoundingly saw no objections either – a telegram went to the ambassador, Sir George Falconer, and to everybody's intense surprise, he saw no objections either! In the past he has never allowed a single girl from the office up. So I packed in a hurry and off we set on the night of the 5th – Leo, a Security Officer named Max who has only one leg but managed splendidly on an artificial one and a Gurkha guard from the office.

The first night we slept most of the way and I woke up by falling nearly on the floor with all my bedding. We spent a pleasant few hours in Lucknow at La Martinière College and viewing the famous ruins of the Residency. Our next train, which was a shocker, took us with a minimum of speed and a maximum of bumping and swaying to Raxaul, just inside the Nepalese frontier. There we stayed the night in a guest house, barren of everything but three beds and a few chairs and tables. Of course we had to carry food for the whole journey, so we didn't starve (back to earth and air-mail paper). I was eaten alive by mosquitoes even at this time of the year, but apart from that slept well with Leo and Mac beside me and two Gurkhas across the door outside.

Next day we mounted the tiny Nepalese railway and went twenty five miles in about five hours. I forgot to say that at Raxaul we visited a Mission hospital run by an Irish doctor and his wife. They were saints if ever there were any. Many of the casualties of the troubles a few weeks ago were brought to them and they had some tragic stories to tell. A little way from Raxaul we stopped at Hergong, one of the chief centres of the disturbances. There we were met by a Nepalese Government Official who apologised that we had not had an armed escort from Raxaul, but that they had been frightened to come over to Raxaul! He offered compensation by a guard of 1 and 5 – all Gurkhas armed to the teeth and looking delightfully ferocious and picturesque. As the tiny train puffed its slow way through villages, and the jungle that forms one of Nepal's natural barriers against the world, the six men leapt to earth (I won't say platform in this part of the world), bayonets fixed, with the Sergeant in Charge wielding a Sten gun and loaded down by an ammunition belt. To me it was all delightfully Gilbert & Sullivanish because nothing could have been more peaceful than our journey. The puffing-billy stopped at Amlickgung, and there we piled into a station wagon and were driven along thirty miles of wild dust track into the foothills of the mountains. Our armed escort followed very usefully an hour and a half behind us in an aged bus which I still find it hard to believe ever negotiated the awful road. Our heavy luggage and our Gurkha and his brothers all rode perilously on the roof, much to the trepidation of all concerned.

In the wilds we were turfed out of our wagon and found three ponies waiting for us and a flock of coolies. We could see our destination – another Rest House, high above us in the mountains, so we upped into the saddle and started the ascent, our heavy cases astonishingly easily carried on the backs of coolies. We reached the Rest House, which belongs to the Maharaja and is infinitely superior to the one at Raxaul, just as the sun was sinking – and what a magnificent sunset it was. There seemed to be scores of Nepalese troops up there who came smartly to attention as our rag tag and bob-tail party trundled in. By 8 next morning we were picked up and off again on the last twenty-mile stretch – an arduous one too. The coolies are amazing. They carry enormous weights over the mountains and arrive at the other end looking as fresh as when they started – and most of them go bare-footed. We were able to go about three quarters of the way on pony-back, but some of it was so steep and rocky that there was nothing for it but foot slogging. Now, three days after, our legs are still so stiff that we can hardly move. I've never been so stiff in all my life before.

But that day's journey is quite unforgettable. You scale two great heights, descending after each into the valley. At the top of the first height you get your first glimpse of the everlasting snows of the Himalayas, with the Everest range far to the east. We were unable to say which peak was Everest but hope to be able to do so on the return. But the most magnificent moment of the whole day was when we had scaled the last height – quite the most strenuous 2,000 feet – and after toiling upwards with head well down and legs aching, the ground levelled and we lifted our eyes to see the almost unreal and wholly magnificent view of the valley ringed with the Himalayas.

Post just going so will continue on my return to Delhi – haven't re-read, so forgive any mistakes.

19 January 1951

The bag goes today and I must let you know that I am safely back from my Nepalese venture. I hope by now you have received my first instalment written and posted in Kathmandu. I hardly know where to begin as there is so much to tell you – inevitably I know I shall leave an awful lot out!

But first a million thanks for the three letters that were awaiting my return and (hurrah) the parcel! I had to pay 6s. on it as a matter of interest, but was it worth it! Unfortunately all the liquid had oozed out of the marmalade jar,

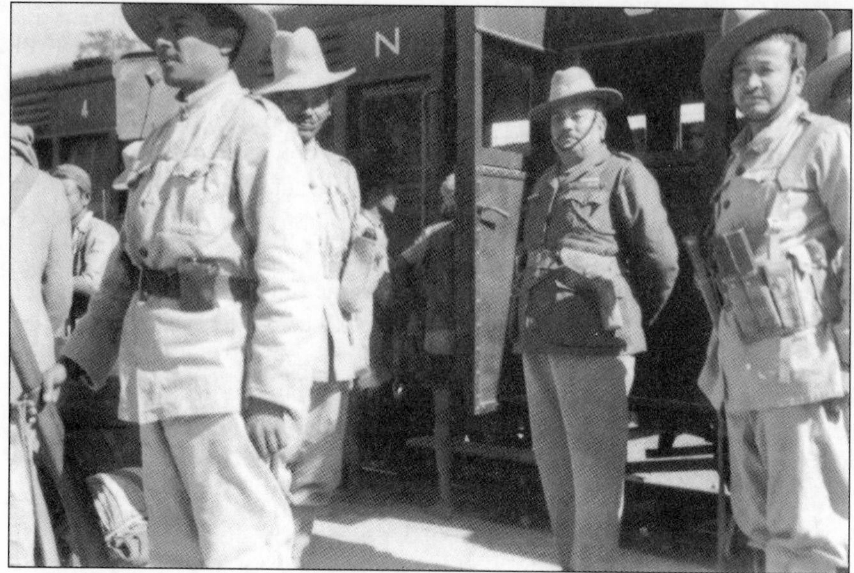

Gurkha guards on the way to Kathmandu.

leaving only dry peel but it hadn't caused any damage, and the honey and the cake and the talc were in excellent condition. Thank you again and again.

20 January 1951

I got interrupted there and have missed the bag after all, so will send this air mail instead.

Well now, a very quick word about Kathmandu. I think I was just crossing over the last mountain in my other letter. Once over the top we dropped down about 3,000 feet into the valley. It was too steep to ride except for the last bit and it was a sore treat to our muscles – incidentally Leo and I were still stiff four days after! Never have my poor muscles suffered so.

At the bottom of the mountain we were met by the Embassy shooting brake and travelled over a rough road – but to us in blissful comfort – for the last eight miles into Kathmandu. The sun was sinking and the snow-clad mountains towering over the valley gradually became red tipped until suddenly the sun was gone and all the colour fled from them and they became grey and austere in the dying light.

Our four nights and three days in Kathmandu were packed. The Foreign Minister of Nepal and son of the run-away King came and had cocktails, with a face a yard long and full of depression for his beloved country. The whole valley is a mass of aged temples, most of great antiquity and many of a most unbelievable obscenity: for a remote place, with so little contact with the outside world, religion and sex have become almost indistinguishable from one another, and it is nothing to find a temple dedicated to lust with the most astounding carvings festooning it.

As we wandered round all the strange squares and back alleys we were followed by hordes of people. Probably in the whole history of Nepal only a handful of English women have ever been seen and I was therefore the object of uncontrolled curiosity.

What intrigued them most were my shoes and nylon stockings and a few of them would come right up to me and bend down and have a jolly good peer! We've taken between us over a hundred snaps which are to be ready today so the best I will send by the next post.

It's time for work, so I'll send this now and continue yet again later.

Delhi

29 January 1951

I've been very naughty, I feel, about writing since I got back from Kathmandu, but I certainly have been busy. I was no sooner back than I was whisked off by my boss to Mussoorie to hunt for suitable places for wives and children in the hot weather. We had a good trip up in an official car – a Super Snipe, which purred along at an easy 60 m.p.h. I have found Delhi cold enough this winter but Mussoorie was like the North Pole to me, with snow still lying and the temperature down to freezing at night.

I got back just in time for Independence Day which by contrast I spent in the country, sun-bathing. After an hour in the sun I had to cover my shoulders in case I got too roasted!! Incredible country of contrasts this.

The golfing season is now in full swing. Yesterday I played my first competition match – the first round of the mixed 2-ball foursomes. I had dear old Bill Worth as my partner. Since he returned from the UK he is playing almost to scratch which gives me immense confidence. We were playing an American couple whose joint handicap was the same as ours and we beat them 8 and 7! Bill has been most patient in coaching me and I really am improving steadily. It's a wonderful game. I can forgive anybody becoming enamoured of it!

Incidentally, Bill said he had heard from you. He thought it so sweet of you to bother and would like me to thank you.

No, we never felt any earthquake tremors in Delhi, but yesterday we did experience a bit of nature's unleashed power. Just about noon the cry went up that a swarm of locusts was overhead. We all rushed out and saw the sight of a life-time. It was a terrifying and awe-inspiring spectacle. They were at tree top level and took nearly three quarters of an hour to pass. The whole of Delhi was covered at the same time. The swarm was estimated to be five miles long and two miles wide, and as they fly pretty well wing-tip to wing-tip, forming dense clouds that shut out much of the light, you can have a rough guess at how many there must have been – and still be trillions out! Numbers of course fall down exhausted all over the place but they don't make a scrap of difference. The Indians love them, and some of them just picked them up and like the birds, who had a red-letter day, ate them raw. At close quarters they are the most vilely evil-looking creatures. This was a rare sight in Delhi and certainly one I shall never forget. Just watching them made you feel pathetically powerless. They passed Old Delhi and vanished north over the river. I dread to think what damage they will do. They will probably devastate 100,000 acres at a time when they descend to eat. Poor old India – if she isn't indulging in communal riots she's suffering flood, or famine, earthquake or starvation – and now locusts.

I had another interesting sight on Sunday. I was at a picnic about ten miles out of Delhi. We had a good fire burning for brewing our tea and we were chatting quite loudly, but suddenly in the corner of my eye I saw something which for one sickening moment I thought was a tiger. It was only ten yards away and strolling along quite unconcerned. It was an enormous hyena, and a nasty piece of work with long snout, powerful shoulders and tapering haunches and short back legs. We kept quite still and it ambled on and we were able to watch it for quite five minutes. They won't normally tackle humans though they are known to run off with small children sometimes.

Did I tell you we have started our next play? 'You Never Can Tell!' Remember when we did it at Birmingham University? I am not the twin this time but the serious daughter. I find I remember whole chunks of the play though it's nearly ten years since I was last in it.

The office calls. Here are a few Kathmandu snaps – the best of my lot I think. Leo is having his reprinted and some of them I will send also.

7 February 1951

This is awful – what has Barbara been saying? Don't be disappointed, honey, but she must have completely misinterpreted what I said to her or she read much more into what I said than she should have. But the chances of my coming home this summer are infinitely remote. There was some talk a few months ago of changing our two-year tours into three-year ones, with a home leave after eighteen months. I may have mentioned this to Barbara, but I deliberately told you nothing of it in case nothing came of it. So darling Mumsiekins don't, don't, don't expect me this summer.

Just so that you won't be too disappointed I am going to tell you something that I was going to save up until I could be absolutely certain of dates etc. Last week the High Commissioner had me up and asked me if I was prepared to do a second tour of duty. I feel awfully bucked that he has asked me because I was honestly very dubious as to whether I should get the chance. Evidently the old boy is satisfied and wants me back. That means I shall complete my two years, come home for leave and return, probably for another eighteen months or two years. Now arises a problem, which may or may not be within my control. If it is, I want you to help me to choose what to do. Command and I shall obey!

I am quite honestly a little frightened of coming home in November and facing a winter and then returning to Delhi for a third hot weather in succession. If the office allows me, therefore, on the whole I would prefer to wait until March 1952, have the summer at home and miss the worst of the Delhi hot weather. It would also give us the chance of having some good weather for a holiday together on my return. But if I have this choice, I shall be guided by you. If you would like me to come home as soon as ever I can, despite all other considerations, of course I shall come. I leave it entirely to you, bless you, and what you wish will be what I shall wish.

But before you decide, I've got one more factor I want you to consider. I've got a lovely plan – for us! If I can save up enough money I want to buy a new car to be ready for me when I dock. I can get one on the export scheme provided I am returning to Delhi. I'm not thinking in terms of anything grander than a Morris 8 or an Austin A40 at the outside, but with serious saving and selling my old Sunbeam Talbot I should be able to manage. Now the reason for this is that I AM DETERMINED TO TAKE YOU ABROAD. If I don't get you across the Channel and into France and on to Italy and back through Switzerland my name's Gertrude Matilda Bloggins! Isn't that a lovely prospect? And do you think it's worth waiting for the summer of 1952 for?

Anyway that's the plan I wasn't going to tell you of for a bit, but I had to do something about any possible disappointment!

I see I've still got some questions about my leave to answer. I expect I shall return by sea and have about six to eight weeks at home – not more I don't think as I have had quite a bit of leave out here.

14 February 1951

Golf – I played shockingly in the semi-finals and we lost 1 down! But Bill and

I have played again in a match against bogey on handicap and so far are leading the field – it won't continue but it's pleasant to bask even in temporary sunshine.

Cough – yes, I've had the devil's own game with my wretched old complaint ever since last August. I was marvellous up to then, but the dampness of the rains finished me off completely. However, I've gone back to the aged old Famel syrup – remember? – in sheer desperation and after one and a half bottles of it really am nearly cured. It will quite go I know as soon as the hot weather comes up again.

Kathmandu – of course I was the guest of Sir George and Lady Falconer. Sir G. is very fierce externally and frightens most people but I thought him a dear old lamb. Lady F. is quite different though again with a reputation of dragonhood! But within an hour or two of my arriving and my meeting them for the first time they were calling me Margaret. Of course we dined and lunched and breakfasted with them. Dinner was always by candlelight – no electric bulb dare show its face above that table of superb silver and cut glass!! Yes, a costume was certainly necessary. Don't forget, in Nepal Valley you are still 4,500 feet up – a good deal higher than the top of Ben Nevis, with snows everlastingly all round.

This week is quite newsless. We continue to rehearse madly, and there seem to have been rather a number of parties that have demanded one's presence – but nothing exciting. The only amusing oddment is that I have been asked to teach the Persian Ambassador English! I shall do it if I'm allowed to go in office time, but otherwise life is quite full enough already.

22 February 1951

I couldn't help smiling at that nose of yours for ferreting out Delhi news, when I saw the tiny clock tower cutting. I know the tower well. It is at the end of a real bazaar street in Old Delhi called Chandni Chowk – a famous street. Ginger Dunn, whose offices are just beside the tower, actually saw it fall, and Bill Worth was on the scene ten minutes after it had happened and saw the body-rescuing. It caused quite a local stir.

I haven't anything of interest to tell you this week. The winter has quite suddenly departed and overnight we have found ourselves with noon temperatures of 85 degrees. There will be no looking back now until next autumn – but it doesn't appal me in the least.

Now I'm going to put my feet up for five minutes.

27 February 1951

Today I received your long letter and the locust cutting – your cuttings are always read out on receipt to whoever is in the office and usually cause smiles all round.

I'm delighted to hear that Leslie and Dora are doing so well with their chickens. What I wouldn't give now for a Hereford egg! Indian ones are small and tasteless and quite impossible unless well disguised in omelettes or scrambled form.

I never seem to have anything very exciting to tell you these days. The play is shocking and we are therefore rehearsing nearly every night. Heaven knows how it will turn out. I won my first round of the UK High Commission Golf Tournament last week and now have to play – of all people – the Deputy High Commissioner! In him, I know, I have met my doom. But Bill and I have tied for second place in the mixed 2-ball foursomes against bogey, so we are playing it off this weekend. If we win I shall get a silver spoon.

We are all looking forward to Easter now. I'm hoping to get up to one of the hill stations for a few days if I can – probably to Simla which I haven't yet seen.

How's your rain?! It's now almost 90 degrees here and simply glorious. If only it would stay like this. But it won't. Today for the first time I have shed my stockings. Soon the rest (almost!) will follow.

6 March 1951

One of my jobs as a Welfare Officer is to put all the new people straight on what to bring with them and a hundred and one other things about coming to India. CRO has a long document of mine on such matters and I write to most girls individually as well.

We are getting perilously near the dress rehearsal of 'You Never Can Tell'. The show is in a week's time. We give three performances and then we go quiet for the summer – thank heaven. The heat is really coming up now and the last shivers have gone out of the nights.

I played my golf match with the DHC on Saturday and took him as far as the 17th green where he beat me 3 and 1. But it was a grand match and seeing he played below his handicap and in fact produced his best round ever in Delhi, I feel quite satisfied with my performance. I really do absolutely love golf, and only wish I had taken it up much earlier.

9 March 1951

The Asian games are on at the moment and I had an afternoon there yesterday – most thrilling too. The cycling was the most fascinating. The Japs, of course, won hands down just by sheer brain work: in fact they are running away with most of the events. I shall spend quite a bit of this coming weekend at the stadium watching the finals.

On Monday I am lunching with the HC and Lady Nye. They are entertaining twenty-six Singapore athletes, many of whom don't speak English and I'm one of the victims to try to help the lunch party to go – heaven help me!

Temperatures are galloping up – we are now well in the nineties. Yesterday was 9 degrees above average, and all the weather prophets say we're in for a really stinking summer.

16 March 1951

I think I told you that I went to the Asian Games. They really were excellent to watch but the organisation was pathetic. I met twenty-six athletes from the Singapore delegation at the lunch party given by the High Commissioner. The Chinese members were very bitter about the Japanese competitors, and at the games themselves refused to stand up when any Japanese won a final and the Japanese anthem was played – all very embarrassing but quite understandable.

Well, I've won something in the winter golfing competitions! Whether it will be a silver spoon or a couple of golf balls I don't know. But Bill and I came second in the mixed 2-ball foursomes against bogey.

We have got the first night of the play over, thank goodness. Two more nights and then blessed peace – how relieved I shall be.

I'm off to the office now. This is very short, I fear, but once the play is over I promise not to be so brief.

20 March 1951

I don't think I have written to you since the morning of the first performance. Mercifully it really has gone off extremely well and the critics, without exception, think it the best play the UKCOM have ever put on. It nearly killed us as the curtain didn't go up until 9.15 each evening and the play runs for three hours, but we have survived. We had a party on the stage the last night and ended up in the Gym Club where we stayed until 3 a.m.

The next day was Captain's Day at the Golf Club – and believe it or not, I won the women's long driving competition! Wasn't it absolutely astounding? I've also got a beautiful little inscribed silver casket for being runner-up with Bill in the 2-ball foursomes against bogey. So altogether I'm feeling quite pleased with my first season of competitions.

Here are yet a few more snaps for your amusement. I'm now off to Simla for the weekend and hope to bring back some more pictorial entertainment for you!

By the way, Queen Mary has arrived, bless you. Mercifully, I opened it in case the glass had got broken, as it looked far too frailly packed for my liking, and alas it had. You have unfortunately to be super careful when dealing with a 6,000 mile journey. Anyway, I'm having a new glass put in and know Lalla will love it. Ever so many thanks, bless you.

And now I must proceed to last minute chores before leaving for the weekend.

27 March 1951

So dear old Leo did write to you. He asked for your address so that he could send you some photographs but I didn't know he was sending an accompanying missive! Poor old thing, I'm afraid he's got it very badly, despite the most sensible admonitions right from the beginning from practical me! And now proposals of marriage have come along, I have – I think very wisely – ceased to go around with him. Like so many men he just can't believe that I don't want to marry him and thinks I'm all wrong and stupid at my age to turn down such an offer! Can't men be incredibly vain on occasions – hence the 'faults' because his poor old vanity has been sat on. Anyway, it's just as well – he is being transferred to Bombay in a fortnight, so I trust he will find someone there. Heigh ho, what a life.

Our little party had a grand time in Simla but we got flooded out. When we got back to Delhi there had been nearly two inches of rain – absolutely unheard of in March. It's helped to stave off the hot weather and everywhere looks very green, but we expect to pay for it by an extra specially hot summer when the heat sets in in earnest.

I've just had an awful shock. A golfing friend of mine, an American woman, who played with her husband against Bill and me a week or two ago in one of the competitions, was killed two days ago. They were coming back from a party and her husband was driving. I think he had had too much to drink and hit an island, which here consists of tar barrels filled with sand. The door where his wife was sitting flew open and she fell out and when her husband picked her up she was dead. She leaves a four year-old child behind.

Isn't it absolutely ghastly. Thank goodness I never have, and never will, drive with anyone here under the influence of drink. Imagine what that wretched husband must be going through knowing that he is responsible for his own wife's death. And they were such an awfully happy couple.

8 April 1951

I seem to have missed all the bags this week. I've had a letter half-written to you for days and somehow haven't got it finished so I thought I had better post off this little reassurance that I am well. It's Sunday morning and I'm sitting on my verandah in the sun and nothing else except my curlers drying my hair! I was up at 5.30 a.m. to meet two new girls who were being flown out here. By the time the plane had arrived and I had got them settled into Eastern House and had breakfast, it was too late to get the best of the early morning for golf. So I've settled to a few chores instead.

The two girls have gone to bed for the day, not having really slept properly since Thursday night, so I shan't have to start worrying about them again until tomorrow morning.

The temperature is just beginning to bounce up again after a marvellous respite of three weeks due to these freak storms we have been having. Any moment now we expect to touch the 100 degree mark, but this is the time of year I like best.

14 April 1951

You asked about numdas. If you will look at the snaps of my flat I think you will see one on the floor. They are thin, neutral-coloured wool rugs with large, bold embroidered designs on them. They cost anything from about 25*s*. to 35*s*. and are a bit larger than the rug I sent you. They are most cheery and attractive and wear surprisingly well, and somehow don't show the dirt. And at that price you don't mind very much if they don't last for ever. We only have coconut matting in our flats and numdas are a cheap form of camouflage. They are made in Kashmir. I'm sure you will like them.

I've had a small dose of Delhi Belly this week – not dysentery, thank heaven, but I have to stay fairly near the wee house! I had my first summer shower this morning, and today's paper says the temperature will reach 100 degrees today for the first time this year. May the Lord be with us!

P.S. We are broadcasting today – making a recording of our choir concert on All India Radio.

26 April 1951

The famine in Bengal is terrible. It has been looming up for months, but alas catastrophe and India are always so closely linked that one almost becomes unaware or unheeding of the magnitude of the problems here. And if you could see the pathetic attempts at farming it would break your heart. Soil erosion is terrible and when you see the bits of wood that are used for ploughs and which only scratch at the surface of the soil, you would weep. I'm longing to set eyes again on a really luxuriant crop of Hereford wheat after the sparse, barren patches which are all you ever see out here.

Now – take a row! It is never a burden to write to my little Mamma, even if sometimes I don't write as much as at other times!

You asked about the two girls coming by air. Normally we never fly girls out, but we were so desperately short of stenographers that there was no alternative about these two. They arrived worn out on the Sunday morning and slept all that day and the night as well!

There is honestly nothing I want out here though honey continues to be an unmitigated joy. I'm spinning out the last pot as long as I can.

I can't really think what news I have for you. I can't even remember if I told you about the Civil Service exam I have taken. I'll tell you again in case I forgot. I took it last November. I kept quiet about it as there was some chance I would be flown home for an interview if I got through the written part. I have got through the written part – and quite astonishingly well, being 194th out of over 10,000! But alas, the interview is being held in Delhi next month, so no chance of a trip home. If I get through and accept establishment I probably won't be able to return to Delhi for a second tour. But everything is in such a state of chaos and uncertainty that I'm not planning anything. As far as I can see I shall be here until November at the earliest, and my return to Delhi will be dependent on my decision about establishment.

I just can't think what other news I have for you. I continue to work busily. So far the summer has been an odd one. We keep on having odd bouts of very high temperature and then suddenly we get a thunderstorm and a shower and bang goes the temperature below 100 degrees again. We came back for instance from a game of golf when suddenly I got drenched to the skin. It's unheard of to have rain here in April, but it's certainly helping to postpone the worst of the summer.

3 May 1951

Life seems to be quite newsless. Whitsun will soon be here, but I'm not going away. I shall play a lot of golf and sleep a lot and leave it at that. The Golf Club is hoping to organise a holiday to Gulmarg, Kashmir at the beginning of June. I think I described my visit to Gulmarg last year. Then it was a deserted and desolate place. But this year I believe great efforts are being made to revive it and the golf course is being put back into working order. So I shall probably end up with a golfing holiday – lovely!

Tonight we are having a big dance at Eastern House. It is an invitation one to the whole of the High Commission. The temperature is now absolutely perfect for a dance – or rather it's perfect for sitting outside. Just imagine the joy of being able to sit out until 3 in the morning in a flimsy dress and not feel even one tiny shudder.

On Saturday I go to a wedding. Do you remember my telling you about the woman who lost her father, mother and husband all within six months? Well, she is marrying again, just under a year after her husband's death. She is marrying an accountant who was a confirmed bachelor. I'm glad for her sake that she is remarrying though we all think it a somewhat odd combination! I'm in the awful throes of not having a clue on what to wear!! It will probably end up in being my old pre-fab television dress: remember?

And now for some tea. I was determined to get this note written first for tomorrow's bag. But now my thirst really demands quenching so off to the goodly brew.

10 May 1951

Last Saturday, after what seemed an age, came two letters from you which were naturally received with exclamations of great joy. They were written on the 25th and 27 April, and one contained the marvellous snaps of Susan. How incredibly quickly she is growing up. She no longer looks a baby but a little girl already. I am very thrilled with them.

Really, your weather appalls me – 100 degrees one day and fires the next! At least we always know what's coming here!

You ask about the other mat in my sitting-room. That was one of the ones on loan from Jack Hughes and has now been returned together with all his furniture. So my flat is looking a little prosaic again.

Yes, Joan Burbidge turned up about six weeks ago. She is extremely nice and I like her very much. She thought it most kind of you indeed to have written to her.

My Del. Bel. is back to normal thank heaven. The difference between it and dysentery is that it is just a bad attack of diarrhoea, caused either by a chill or fatty foods or some other dietary upset, whereas dysentery is a different bug, usually transmitted by flies. The latter is much more serious as the bug has to be killed.

You ask what vegetables we have here. We get nearly all the usual European ones, but on the whole they are very tasteless, and of course at this time of the year they tend to die off until the rains come.

I hope old Dobbin will still be around when I return. To think that he may fetch £90! Absolutely wonderful.

The Diplomatic Colony is US! And an enormous amount of work it's causing us. It's a Government of India idea to have all Embassies and High Commissions in one spot, together with their flats and bungalows. We are all rather appalled at the insularity of such a scheme, but as it is doubtful if the Government of India will allow Missions to stay in their present accommodation when they have been given the chance of building in the Dip. colony, most are coming into line. We are the first to buy a plot of land, and at the moment we have two very eminent architects out here now working on our plans. Unfortunately the older and more eminent of the two has suddenly become very ill and is suspected of having enteric fever. His wife has been alerted to be ready to fly to India at a moment's notice if he gets worse. It's all rather alarming.

I'm astounded at how far you have made your birthday present go – but of course, I forget – you are a Scot!

Life is too quiet with heat to have anything much in the way of news. I'm still managing to play some golf, but only very early and late in the evening.

This morning I had one of my rare patches of trouble with the car. I noticed the battery wasn't charging, so I drove quietly into our transport yard and opened up the bonnet. The fan belt had split and come off. The engine was very hot, but mercifully no damage was done. I left them to buy me a new fan belt and should have had the car back this evening, but guess what they have done – I asked them to top up my batteries while they were about it, and they topped them with kerosene oil. So they have had to drain them, refill them and recharge them on the bench. Trust Indian labour! So I'm still car-less.

24 May 1951

At last I can get down to a letter to you. I have just had a very exhausting three days, rushing up to Mussoorie to settle a few problems that had arisen over wives and children in the hills and rushing back again. It was simply glorious up there in the cool, and I evidently missed a couple of absolutely stinking days in Delhi. But coming back into the blazing dusty heat of the plains after such a very short break is not so pleasant. You need at least a fortnight up there to make the sweltering, dusty journey worthwhile. All the way you sit in a pool of sweat and your back sticks to the leather upholstery – not very pleasant However, the problems are sorted out so the trip was well worthwhile from that angle.

Alas, my golfing holiday in Gulmarg is off. One by one people had to drop out. So instead I shall wait until September, which I think is much the best time to go on leave as you come back into cool weather instead of hot. I'll just stay and grill in the meantime. It's been up to 113 degrees maximum shade temperature and the minimum night temperature is now 82 degrees – which is b— hot! But I've got no boils and no prickly heat, I've stopped losing weight and I'm as brown as a berry. Playing golf sees to that.

And now for some tea. My pen I think is beginning to run out – but then so is the sweat from my hand and arm and I keep sticking to this writing paper.

30 May 1951

I can't think what there is of interest to tell you this week! We are going through a most miserable spell of weather. A hurricane descended on Delhi at lunchtime yesterday and ripped down scores of trees and lamp-posts, blew in a number of windows and generally left chaos in its wake; then the heavens opened and we had over half an inch of rain, which is absolutely unheard of in May. My hood has broken, so you can imagine what a state my poor car was in. I thought I was safe for at least another five weeks until the monsoon breaks before having it repaired. Although the rain cooled the air temporarily it is now blazing sunshine again and wickedly humid and out is coming the prickly heat. I'm clear of it still, thank goodness, and am so brown this summer with playing golf in a sun top and shorts that I think there is very little danger of my becoming a victim.

Our poor old architect is still on the danger list and the other one has gone into hospital now with heat exhaustion and prickly heat. We are convinced that after their joint experience of Delhi weather they can't fail to plan a wonderland of a Diplomatic Colony for us!

I always seem to be talking about the weather when I write to you. How frantically bored you must get with it but somehow it is impossible to keep off it.

I am reading my leisure hours away at the moment. Here are a few first class books if you can get hold of them – forgive me if I have mentioned them before – *The Kon Tiki Expedition*, *Desperate Voyage* by John Caldwell (both these are impossible to put down once you start them), *The Wooden Horse* and

The Tunnel by Eric Williams, *The Great Escape* by – can't remember and *Nineteen Eighty Four* by George Orwell – and the rest of the time's your own!

Here is an awful picture of me – I look quite forty. But I've sent it to show off my lovely Nepalese necklace that I bought in Kathmandu. I have ear-rings and bracelet to match – and the dress is cut down from the one I had made for the play. You will recognise Stanley Bolton – the one between the Indian woman and me – from photos of the last two plays. The picture was taken at Stanley's farewell cocktail party before he left for home on leave.

The Indian woman is one of Delhi's principal photographers. She had just had her hair cut off so one of the lads shoved her in the middle of us, grabbed her camera and produced this. I've had to cut the picture down to get it in the envelope, but it's just as well, as the man I cut off was caught with his eyes half shut, and looked quite tight – though he wasn't.

Now to tea and a shower.

14 June 1951

I have been very naughty to keep you letterless for so long. We have had a really stinking fortnight – the hottest in my experience out here – and we have all just flopped about doing as little as possible. It is so terribly difficult to sleep in this heat and you feel quite useless at the end of the day's work. I have now vanished away to 8 stone 6 which is the lightest I have ever been. But mercifully, despite everything, I am very well – no boils or prickly heat, no heat exhaustion. Long may it last.

We spend a great deal of time at the moment in the cinema. All of them are air-conditioned, and when you have been in an air-conditioned office all day you feel the heat terribly at night. So off we troop to the cinema sanctuary. I have just been three times in four days – an absolute record in my experience.

I am still forcing myself to play golf at the weekends, but on a Sunday morning now it demands being on the links before 6 a.m. if you are to get eighteen holes in before the sun drives you away.

But enough of this perpetual weather talk. And yet I have almost no other news for you.

I was interested to hear you had met somebody who knew the Bullocks. I was quite friendly with them and they were dears. Humphrey the husband was quite a Delhi institution, and the great authority on all the ruins round these parts. He used to spend all his spare time digging about in peculiar patches of rubble and concocting wonderful theories about them. He has a bright red wig which he deliberately had as wiggish looking as possible so that nobody should think he was attempting to fool them. Most of the comic little articles and verses in the Outpost used to be written by him under a wild assortment of pen-names.

19 June 1951

There will be so many new things and people to see when I finally get home. What excitement.

I still haven't a clue when this will be. The results of the exam aren't out yet and when they are it will still probably be a month or so before CRO knows if it is getting me (that is if it wants me in the first place!). So I'm just sitting back and not worrying. What will be, will be.

We had a bit of amusement going into the office this afternoon. There, on the steps, was Gandhi! This is a little man who is the spit image of Gandhi: he has been 'discovered' by some film company and is being flown to Hollywood to make a film. He is quite a humble soul and comes from a village about fifty miles from Delhi. What a transformation of scene for the little man! He was in our office about a passport to the UK.

I've just emerged from a very long meeting with the SPCA of which I have been acting honorary secretary for the last two months. It has been a revelation to me to see how widespread corruption is in this country, even in a humane society. More and more I wonder what is going to happen to this poor country without our honest hand at the helm. It must be heartbreaking work for people of Nehru's integrity to realize this bitter truth.

And now for an early roast – in bed!

9 July 1951

I missed the bag last week as I had to dash up to Mussoorie for a couple of days to sort out a few more problems of families in the hills. It was a beastly hot journey which I didn't enjoy at all.

India is a strange place. Coming back there was a body right across the road at which the vultures were already getting busy with their hygienic work, and nobody had bothered to remove it. I suppose it had been knocked down by a car and the driver had simply proceeded on his way.

Good news of my exam. I came 44th out of the original 10,000! They finally established about 500. I was very tickled to see that I had the second highest mark of everybody for the interview – trust old Maggie's gift of the gab. It still remains to be seen what happens and whether I finally accept establishment.

I have just been playing golf with the Nawab of Pataudi, the famous cricketer. I'm going up in the social scale!!

17 July 1951

As usual I seem to have little news for you. Since the three inches of rain we had at the beginning of the month we have had no rain at all, and it really is vile. The monsoon seems to be just non-existent. Even up in the mountains in Mussoorie there has been almost none. The rainfall this July is 26 inches less than usual. I hope to goodness this isn't going to be another 1947 with no rain until September.

Life continues to be quietish because of the heat. I've still managed to keep my Sunday golf, but last Sunday was pretty gruelling. I had a swim afterwards at the Cecil Hotel in Old Delhi and then lunch with Ginger Dunn's successor as Lloyd's Bank Manager. The Cecil has a lovely open-air pool, which is a great joy in the hot weather.

Last night I gave a little dinner party for eight to introduce three New Zealand nurses to a few folks. They have come to teach in the University here and are rather lonely. They were on the *Strathmore* when she had that collision in Colombo Harbour. There was a gramophone record recital on in the lounge so I dragged my party to listen to it. Then we all sat outside drinking until well after midnight, discussing India. The three of them were open-mouthed at some of the things two old inhabitants of India had to tell!

Tomorrow night a party of us go to Tughlachabad, one of the ruined cities of Delhi about eight miles away, for a barbecue. Joan Burbidge is giving it as a farewell do to her boss, whose tour is ending shortly. One of my shooting friends shot a buck last Sunday and it is being roasted whole amid the ruins. I bet you anything the monsoon decides to break just as the fire is lit!

25 July 1951

I must admit that we are all interested in the war talk between India and Pakistan but are pretty sure most of it is hot air. Anyway, Sir Archie fixed his annual jaunt home long before these recent happenings, though I bet they are adding to his headaches in London.

We continue to puff and pant in this quite vile summer. Still not a vestige of a sign of the monsoon. I continue remarkably perky, while most of my friends are groaning under the discomforts of prickly heat and some of them from boils.

All that happens to me is that I get more and more sylph-like. I had to have the tailor in the other day to alter the skirt of that yellow linen suit I took out from home. His eyes popped out of his head when he saw he had to take in the waist a full two inches! I am now a graceful 26 inches in that part of my anatomy, which for me is nothing short of miraculous.

I'm writing this almost flat on my back on the old charpoi and the fan is playing havoc with the paper. I think I'll be lazy and not wander on to another sheet. This is only therefore a tiny note, but reassure you of my continued hail-&-heartiness and all my love as ever.

There are no letters between 25 July 1951 and 2 November 1951 as I was in England on mid-tour leave. Because I was flying home I did not tell my mother, for I knew she would be worried. I gave her the surprise of her life when I rang her from London. I spent the summer with her, then returned to India by sea.

S.S. *Chusan*

2 November 1951

Dearest Mother

Just a tiny scribble to say I'm safely installed in my cabin with a very nice girl of my own age who is going out to Singapore to be married. She has not been out before so I – the hardened traveller – am taking her under my wing.

I have hardly seen anything of the ship yet, as the post goes in a few minutes and I want to get this off to you.

4 November 1951

Tomorrow morning early we are landing for three hours at Ceuta where I hope to be able to procure some local stamps and get this note off to you. We are all hoping that by then the weather will have improved. Ever since we left the Thames estuary it has been horrid. I've been listening in to the 6 o'clock news and understand that there have been storms and ships in distress everywhere, so no wonder we have been sufferers too. I've just been talking to a man who has been going back and forwards to the East for twenty-three years and this is the first time he has been seasick. I'm feeling frightfully smug – I'm one of the few who has taken every meal with relish and retained it with equanimity!

The poor little stable mate is still cabin-bound after two whole days. I think she's beginning to wonder why on earth she ever decided to go to Singapore.

There haven't really been enough people about nor has the weather been smooth enough for anybody to get to know anybody very much. Apart from that American girl whose picture you may have seen in the daily rags, who is reputed to be secretly married to the Maharajah of Cooch-Behar, and who is now going out to marry him officially, everyone appears to be pretty quiet. I'm delighted, as I have already been allowed to read the whole of a 540 page book in peace.

The first night though I did bump into a couple who had gone out with me on the *Strathmore*. In the course of conversation it transpired that they were Hamiltons, and cousins of Sir Daniel and Lady Hamilton who used to own Duncraig Castle. They were trustees of the girls' school there which we saw round, and had been at the opening ceremony. I learnt a lot of interesting information about the school from them and they were interested to hear what I had to say about it as they had not been back to it for a year or two. But wasn't it strange to find this common topic of conversation?

The whole ship wreaks with Scots voices; there must be scores of them on board. The Armstrongs are among the passengers, but I haven't succeeded yet in tracking them down. Quite possibly they haven't yet made a public appearance in any case.

We're rolling about all over the place at the moment. All day mountainous seas have been hurling themselves against the bows and sheets of spray have drenched even the high upper decks. It's tremendously spectacular, and nothing pleases me more than to put on my mack and go out into the teeth of the storm with the spray in my face and the wind tossing me about like a feather. You will be pleased to know though, Mother, that there is no danger of being blown overboard – so that's one form of sudden death less for you to worry about.

Our stay in Ceuta is to be so short, as our ship is racing to catch one of the convoys through the Canal. I'm looking forward enormously to the sight. It should be an interesting one. I shan't forget to post you when we're through.

12 November 1951

I promised to let you know when I was safely through the Canal. Well, I am. Nothing could have been quieter and more sedate.

But to go back a little. Our three hours in Ceuta extended to eighteen because of the very severe gales. The harbour is tiny and the one tug available not strong enough to cope with a large liner. We went ashore for several hours and indulged in the usual bargaining pantomimes and drank wine in a funny little café and renewed our acquaintances with the flies and the smells and the sounds that seem inseparable from this part of the world. We had a superb view of Gibraltar from Ceuta. In the afternoon a terrific sand storm blew up from the desert, which not only obscured Gibraltar but the sun and the harbour and almost the end of the ship itself.

The Med. was comparatively calm though cold, and we passed de Lesseps' statue *just* as the sun was setting. Everything looks exactly the same, though of course no-one was allowed ashore. The inevitable gilly-gilly man – much to my surprise – was permitted to come aboard, but hardly anybody else. I went to bed at 8.30 p.m. that night being very tired and intended to get up again at midnight to see us entering the Canal. But it was 3.30 a.m. when I crawled out of bed and by that time we were well on our way at the head of the convoy, with not a sign of life either on board or on the land.

We were at anchor in the large Bitter Lake for nearly six hours, waiting for the convoy from Suez to pass. The bathing place is still there, Leslie, and a small and rather pathetic little group of Tommies was standing there waving their arms off as we went by.

We are almost at the end of the Red Sea now and arrive at Aden at 2 a.m. tomorrow. We don't know whether there will be anything to go ashore for, but we're hoping.

The temperature is now gloriously high and I'm turning the most glamorous colour. But for the Red Sea it is remarkably cool.

UK High Commission

19 November 1951

By now you should have heard from the office that I am safely back. I was thankful when the voyage came to an end.

We were able to go ashore at Aden though it was 2.30 a.m. All the shops opened and we were there until 5.30 a.m. when we returned exhausted to bed. We had hardly recovered when we went slap into the middle of a cyclone. I don't ever wish to encounter another. We had it for about thirty hours and I was horribly sick and felt terrible – along with most of the passengers. We only ran out of it as we approached Bombay, and we had to face all the formalities of disembarking with empty tummies and shaking knees.

Thank goodness the office met me. We landed at 2.30 p.m. and I discovered there was a lad in the transits also destined for our Delhi office. So I shot off and had tea with some friends in Bombay and then this lad and I were put on the train at 6.30 p.m. for Delhi. Twenty six hours later we were back, and thankful to have our journey at an end.

By Sunday morning I was trying out my beloved new golf clubs and am delighted with them. The Delhi weather has only just started to cool down, but I was still able to play in a cotton shirt and pants and feel hot! I can't tell you how wonderful it is to be back amid sunshine and warmth. It does more to me than all the medicines in the world!

This morning it was back to work with a vengeance. There seem to be a host of problems that have just been shelved for me to cope with. But I suppose it's just as well to be busy. My poor old boss certainly seems relieved to see me, which is gratifying.

Poor Leonore Storar – the girl whose luggage I brought with me – is still on her way by air. She was due in yesterday at 6 a.m. and isn't now arriving until 2.30 p.m. today. I dread to think how weary she will be.

In bed

27 November 1951

Your last letter arrived yesterday and cheered me up enormously as I lay in bed.

Yes, isn't it stupid. Here I am again. I dreaded I would catch a cold coming off the healthy sea and of course when I got to Delhi everyone had them because of the sudden change of temperature. So I thought – this is where I'm sensible – no pretending I haven't got a cold and a cough – and I've been in bed three days now. The cough alas is one of my better efforts, but I'm having a new form of penicillin injection which tackles lung bugs first, so I'm hoping I shall soon throw it off. It's maddening of course, as I was just getting back into my stride at work, but for once in my life I'm really coddling myself. I lie in state and lots of people come in and chat and sit on the edge of the bed. I've already read three substantial books and am about to start on the Churchill tomes. So I don't mind how long I stay here.

I'm glad you are safely home and that you enjoyed your trip up north. You may like to know that the glamour girl on the ship gave us all plenty to talk about for the whole voyage. She was quite unbelievable, with the most fantastic wardrobe you ever saw – talk about Jacques Fath! And when it came to the fancy dress dance she appeared in very high-heeled thick platform-soled silver evening slippers, men's white drainpipe-legged flannel trousers with a fly opening, a tie made entirely of red sequins, gold mounted sun specs, a long gold cigarette holder, and the most extravagant and ostentatious white fur cape on top of the lot. She flung herself round the room like somebody demented and it wasn't until the next day that we discovered what she had gone as – a film star – in other words herself!

She had a frightful female companion, whom Leslie would have described as 'all bum and belly'. Add to that a pretty formidable bust, a skin-tight white brocade cocktail dress with pencil skirt that just covered her knees and slits nearly up to her waist at the side, and a large diamond-shaped bare midriff, through which her (also large) diaphragm oozed, and you have a not inaccurate version of Female Companion.

I'm afraid, poor dears, they found the male population on the ship sadly disappointing, and all they got most of the time was derisive stares.

But so much for the cattiness!

I must finish this off and get Lalla to find someone who will put it in the bag for me this afternoon.

In the meantime, there is nothing for you to worry about. It's just that me and me old pal are having one of our regular renewals of acquaintance and hope this time he'll take himself off speedily.

3 December 1951

I'm now up and about again and feeling very much better, though of course my cough still lingers as I knew it would. I was allowed up last Friday and went back to work on Saturday. In the afternoon I played nine holes of golf with Gwen Worth, Bill's wife, and another eighteen with her yesterday morning, without feeling in the least tired. So you see I really am very much better.

It was the birthday of one of Bill and Gwen's children yesterday, so they invited me out to the birthday party, which was a picnic amid one of the ruined cities of Delhi. We are having magnificent weather, so a picnic is

My mother, Molly Archer.

certain of success. We played all sorts of mad games with a gang of children and thoroughly enjoyed ourselves, though we were all quite exhausted at the end of it.

You may be amused by the enclosed snaps. The one of you, Mother, in the broken deck-chair I'm wildly proud of. It's one of the best I've ever seen of you.

17 December 1951

Just a very hurried note to wish you all the best for Christmas time. I shall be thinking of you all day, knowing what fun you will have with all the children round you.

I hardly know where to turn at the moment, so busy are these days before Christmas. I have just emerged from our last choir practice before the concert on Wednesday, and you will be pleased to know that you will have the chance of listening to our dulcet tones in the world link-up on Christmas Day before the King's speech. There is to be 3½ minutes from India and we are singing 'Brother James Air' and a lovely, jolly carol called 'A Merry Christmas' which talks about us all loving figgy pudding, and we won't go till we've got some! We are recording it on Thursday, together with a half hour broadcast which will be given on All India Radio some time on Christmas Day. As I have quite the loudest soprano voice you might even hear something of me.

I have been the proud possessor of a car for the last week. Joan Burbidge has lent hers to me while she has been on tour. Alas, she returns in two days time, but it has been a great blessing. My own car arrived in Bombay on 14 December, so I'm hoping to have it up before the end of the year. Unfortunately it is impossible to get leave at this time so I am just risking it to the railway.

I had to get up at 3.30 this morning to meet one of our girls flying out from home. Usually this plane is late, but just because I had to meet it, it was on time. Was I livid! I didn't get back until 6.45 a.m. by which time it was too late to do anything but lie on the bed waiting to get up again.

I've just won my first raffle – a hand crocheted rug in a heavenly blue which is big enough to cover a bed. It was made by a sick girl who wanted a little pocket-money, so one of our nurses raffled it for her. The same day I won the first round of a women's golf competition, and over 15s. from Gwen and Bill at nap. They tried to get it back from me the other night, but I only won another 12s. from them! Never could I have believed that I could be so consistently lucky in picking up cards. It became quite farcical.

29 December 1951

The All India Radio broadcast went off very well. It was quite amusing hearing my own comic voice singing an unaccompanied solo.

Christmas Day was a very quiet and pleasant one for me. I played golf in the morning, had Christmas dinner at mid-day in Eastern House and went out on a real family picnic with Gwen and Bill and the two children, when we sailed boats and ate quantities of tea. And the evening I spent with Gwen and Bill playing silly games. We tuned in to the King's speech, heard the first few sentences and then in true Delhi fashion, the electricity in their hotel failed and was only restored in time to hear the National Anthem. We were livid.

1952

1 January 1952

A Very Happy New Year to you all. And may your weather improve.

Now congratulate me. I've just won my first golf competition – and probably my last. I'll send you the cutting out of the paper to frame. I'm the proud owner of a cup for a year and a duplicate for life. *And* my handicap has come down 6 strokes, which I'm much more proud of! It's early on New Year's morning. I've had only a very few hours in bed after a gay time at the club, but feel fine and am off to my beloved golf course again. We've got a holiday and are making the most of it.

8 January 1952

I was terribly disappointed, Mother, to hear about the broadcast – or rather lack of it – but was much tickled by your righteous indignation. I shall be much interested to hear if the BBC bother to produce any sort of reasonable explanation. Yours was the first news of the business to be received by any member of the choir and it certainly caused some gnashing of teeth, as I wasn't the only one to send a telegram home and raise the hopes of 'the Folks'. However, there we are. At least the Delhi broadcast was quite a pleasant little success.

Thank you all very, very much indeed for all your congratulations. I first knew about the possibility of my MBE before I left England but I honestly didn't take it seriously. It wasn't till a telegraph or two started coming Delhi-wards early in December followed by a letter from 10 Downing Street itself that I began to realize I wasn't dreaming. Actually if I could have got out of it gracefully I would have done, because the awful thing is that one can look around and see dozens of people who one knows have earned something far more than oneself. But there you are – they seem to like to dole out a few to women and my name must somehow have got in the way. How, I don't know, but I somehow seem to have hoodwinked the High Commissioner into thinking I'm not too bad a sort, and far be it for me to disillusion him! – and I had a sneaking feeling it might give you all a bit of fun. I can just see you, Mother, being given the news in advance and simply bursting to be out with it. The mental picture makes me cackle with glee. What an awful lot it must have cost you in postage, letting everybody know! Do please thank all those kind folks who rang you up or wrote to you. It was very sweet of them.

I've had all sorts of telegrams and letters from all sorts of people and am quite overwhelmed by the piles of correspondence that face me. Even Sir Percivale Lieching sent me a personal telegram, which I thought very kind of him.

I shall be most tickled to see what the Leominster paper makes of my face – if anything at all. I think a footnote should be added: 'Don't get excited, you lads, it's five years old and the real thing has deteriorated a bit since then.'

I haven't received anything official yet about the thing, so it's news to me that I can wait and get it at Buckingham Palace. Of course I'll wait, Ma, if you would like me to. I've no desire to have to give a speech which I certainly would if the High Commissioner gave it to me at a little function. I think it would be much more fun to go and have a squint at the curtains and the carpets and things at the Palace and see if we can get a few new inexpensive ideas for Alleymoor!

16 January 1952

I had made all arrangements yesterday to fly to Bombay and drive my car back in the company of one of our transport men who was going to drive a new office car back, when at the last moment I heard my car was on the train after all. So I hope to see it in another few days. How thankful I shall be to get it after this long time.

25 January 1952

Tomorrow is Independence Day and a great march-past is planned. We get a holiday and Gwen and I and the children have got tickets to admit us to seats on the Vista just below my flat. So we hope to have a good view.

The heat is already coming upon us. Day temperatures are up in the eighties – unheard of for January, and we are expecting an early and very hot summer. But you will be pleased to know *I'm still wearing my vests.* I shall hardly dare to shed them even at 110 degrees in case I have to 'take a row' from you!

28 January 1952

My car is now running beautifully and I'm so thrilled to have it. The garage here knocked out that little bump you put in it most beautifully and you simply can't tell it was ever there – and they never charged me as they presumed it happened in transit! If they had been a decent garage I would have told them, but they were so utterly inefficient and hopeless over the whole business of getting my car to Delhi and putting it on the road that I just kept my mouth shut and to hell with them.

Yesterday afternoon I was taking Mr and Mrs Grant, our managers of Eastern House, for a little Sunday afternoon drive and to give them some air, and passing along a country lane a small child suddenly picked up a brick and hurled it at us. It caught the rear wing and has made several nasty gashes right down to the metal. I could willingly have murdered the infant, but you daren't stop and make a scene in an Indian village.

You will be pleased to know my cough has completely gone and I'm looking and feeling better than I have for months. I'm almost looking my age again instead of ten years more!

On Saturday, Gwen and Bill and the kids and I went to see the Independence Day parade. With our white faces and our invitation card we calmly walked through police cordons and sat down within fifty yards of the saluting base and saw absolutely everything. It really was a magnificent spectacle and proved just what the Indians, with training and discipline, are capable of. Bill, with all his military background, said he had never seen better.

Tonight I go off to a terribly high-powered dinner at the High Commissioner's. Lady Nye has been very ill for a long time and is still far from better, so her daughter has had to do all the hostessing and I think she wants me to help her out. Formal dinner parties are quite a strain and I shall be thankful when it is all over.

8 February 1952

We are all terribly upset by the news of the King's death. We knew of it only twenty minutes after it had been announced in England. All social activities have of course ceased until further notice. Poor Elizabeth, what a burden she will have to carry.

20 February 1952

We have had Mr Hamilton here for the last ten days and only packed him off last night. So that has meant almost no spare time for any of us in Estabs. He came and lived very humbly with the junior staff here in Eastern House, which I thought was very decent of him. He says he is going to write to you and assure you how well I am looking. I shall be interested to know if he remembers.

I asked him if there were any chance of my staying out here until March

1953. Quite frankly, with my cough and dreadful feeling of the cold I was appalled by the idea of returning to an English winter. He has agreed, provided nothing crops up in the meantime for which it would be in my interests to return home.

I have just been granted diplomatic privilege (or rather am in the process) which will help my finances enormously as I shall now get cheap petrol and duty free drinks and cigarettes, and I am going to take over some consular work to give me some training for my future career in the office. So altogether I'm feeling really rather pleased with life.

I don't think I have thanked you yet for your letter of 31 January – oh yes, on rereading it I realize I have. But I know I haven't acknowledged your last one – of February. Now let's see what you say in it. The party at the High Commission. I'm trying to remember who was there – among others the Finnish Ambassador and his wife, Mrs B.K. Nehru and some frightfully important Monseigneur something from the Papacy, bedecked in the most wonderful garments. There were two other Catholic Monseigneurs and they were dears; I got on famously with them. Oh yes, then there was the new Air Marshal, a big white chief of all the Indian Air Force – Gibbes – and his wife. They are both golfers and he is a great wag, so I had no trouble there either. I really rather enjoyed myself. The meal was quite simple – can't even remember what we had, but everything is always perfectly cooked at 2 King George's Avenue.

I saw Gwen Worth and the two children off yesterday morning on their way home. I am sad to see them go. We have all had such a lot of fun together.

And that is really the end of my news. We are completely cut off from taking part in any social engagements because of court mourning. One of the few things we are being allowed to carry on with is our choir, though our concert in March will have to be limited to our own staff with no outsiders present. I'm delighted of course and shall have a little peace and quiet for a change.

And now off for a bath, and a chance to drink in the Sick Bay with the poor wretched man who shot half his foot off the other day. Did I tell you about him?

I've missed the bag again so in desperation have decided to spend the large sum of 12 annas on you!

22 February 1952

As it was only the day before yesterday that I wrote, this will just be a tiny letter. We have been having some blessed rain the last few days which has reduced the temperature and done wonders to the golf course. Incidentally, talking of golf, Bill and I lost our match last Sunday, on the last green. I played the best golf of my life and didn't have a dud shot all round, but never have I seen poor old Bill play worse – and his handicap is only 4! He must have been playing to 24 that day. Even he himself can't stop talking about it.

There is an International Film Festival starting in Delhi tonight. The leading countries of the world are all showing their best films, so I expect to go to the cinema every night for the next week. The fare is too good to miss in this town of little culture.

1 March 1952

News continues to be scarce from this part of the world. I am just enduring my first few days without smoking. I've started sucking sweets instead (a much more expensive occupation here I may tell you!) and I have every hope of putting on a bit of flesh before my penance ends.

I have started playing nine holes of golf every evening after office. This afternoon I play in the second round of our office Spring Cup and tomorrow in the President's Prize competition, which is a two-ball foursome against bogey – the competition that Bill and I got second prize for last year. This year I have drawn to play with an Anglo-Indian whom I know well and who has a long handicap – which is very useful in a competition against bogey. So I live in hopes.

6 March 1952

Tomorrow is Joan Burbidge's wedding. I shall wear my dear old stone-coloured gaberdine suit with the hat we bought in M & S, Mother – or was it C & A? It's still just about cool enough to be able to wear a suit without getting too hot. I'll try to take some snaps to send on to you.

We are preparing for a very big exodus from Delhi this month. Crowds of people go on leave and some vanish, never to return. The Nyes have had to cancel their passages by sea because of Lady Nye's continued illness, and they are all flying home instead in a fortnight – two days of horror only – and then Lady Nye will go straight into a nursing home on her return. It really is terribly bad luck for them.

I have been a little off colour this week with the beginnings of a boil. However, I am having penicillin injections and the beastly thing is fading away. I only hope I shan't get any more.

We had a freak storm in Delhi last weekend. I was as far away from the club house at the golf course as I could be when the heavens simply opened and poured down sheets of water. We tried to shelter but it was impossible. In ten minutes nearly the whole course was under water – quite astounding – then as we made our way back to the club house in the teeth of the storm we were caught in a barrage of hail-stones – the biggest I have ever seen. It was torture to have them pelting down on bare heads and arms and hands. I was thankful to reach shelter. The thick tweed skirt I was wearing I took off and wrung out – it was as wet as if it had been dipped in a tub. So I drove off home with a towel as a skirt only.

We have at last heard officially about our broadcast in Radio Newsreel. It *was* transmitted, but the BBC send out five different Radio Newsreel programmes. We went on on two of them – two overseas programmes – but we were definitely not on any of the home ones. The BBC made the mistake in not telling their representative in Delhi which wavelengths it was to be transmitted on. Isn't it maddening? One or two people at home did hear it, so presumably you could have tuned in, even if reception were not too marvellous.

11 March 1952

I'm so pleased my dear old boss did write to you. It was very kind of him to remember among all his multitudinous chores.

The story of the man shooting off part of his foot is a very sad one. He is one of our Second Secretaries out here – a man of about fifty who belongs to the Foreign Office. All his life he seems to have been unlucky with his health. He was invalided home from Moscow before coming out here, and has had all sorts of operations and accidents in his time. He's just born under an ill-fated star. Anyway, the week after I got back he went out shooting and got a cartridge stuck in the barrel of his gun. He took it back to his flat and without telling anyone, fiddled around with it for over an hour and a half, trying to get the cartridge out. Suddenly the thing went off – the cartridge went right through his foot, blew off his shoe and ricocheted off a glass cabinet. He didn't realize he had damaged himself for some seconds until he looked down and saw he had no shoe on and little bits of bone sticking up through his sock.

Our doctor did a wonderful operation, but he has lost his big toe and the next one and a huge bite out of his foot, so that it looks like this –

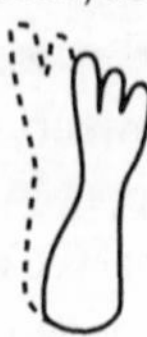

Dotted line shows what should be there and isn't. He blew such a lot of skin away that it still hasn't completely grown over again, so he is still in bed, after nearly four months.

We are all wondering if he will be able to balance on what is left of his foot and if he will be able to walk. If he can't, the rest of the foot will have to come off so that he can have an artificial one.

Joan's wedding went off very well. The High Commissioner gave her away, and he looked marvellous in his grey morning suit and topper. Joan was wearing a broderie anglaise dress which was very charming and will make an excellent evening dress afterwards.

19 March 1952

Isn't it awful to think of petrol at 4*s*.3*d*. a gallon? That's up to the Delhi price now and twice as much as my petrol is at diplomatic rates. Who'd live in England . . . !

We are doing another choir recording on Saturday for relaying on several European services. This time we are determined to pin them down to accurate facts so if you get an obscure cable saying – 4 April 35.5 metre band – or whatever the official jargon is, you will know what I'm referring to and you can get Bobby or Leslie to decipher. We are also giving another concert in April, and one of the items is five songs by Henry Purcell sung by a quartet. I'm the soprano voice and I must say quartets are enormous fun, and excellent practice for sight-reading.

Sunday is Captain's Day at the Golf Club, when I won the long driving competition last year. My driving's 'off' at the moment so I'm not in the least optimistic *this* year! But it should be a jolly day. When all the competitions and prize distributions are over, we knock back the odd beer or two, then have a buffet lunch out on the lawn. In the evening, the Captain, who is a most impressive-looking Major General, invites all the Committee, of which I am a member, to dine with him, and there is an out-of-doors dance to round off the day.

The High Commissioner and his family leave tomorrow. The Old Boy is coming round the office to say 'farewell' to everybody today and we are giving him a presentation this afternoon. Lady Nye is still very ill and is being driven to the aerodrome tomorrow in an ambulance, put in bed on the plane, and pushed straight into hospital on her return to London. Isn't it a sad way to say 'goodbye' to a country you have lived in for so long?

28 March 1952

Well, we have had a wonderful musical treat in Delhi these last two days. Yehudi Menuhin has been giving charity concerts in India during the past month. He gave two in Delhi a week or two ago but I simply couldn't get hold of any seats, to my bitter disappointment. He returned the night before last and I still couldn't get seats, but to my joy dear old Bill got two marvellous ones which were really for the editor of the *Statesman*, and bless his heart, he asked me to go with him.

As we were standing in the foyer while Bill finished his cigarette before we entered the hall, I found myself colliding with Mrs Indira Gandhi, Nehru's daughter, and in a second there was Nehru with Lady Mountbatten! Not one official whisper of Lady M.'s presence in Delhi had been heard, but there she certainly was, as large as life, and at close quarters pretty ravaged-looking. See her a few yards away however and she is marvellous for her age. She and Nehru and the President, Dr Prasad, all sat together in the front row of the stalls, and as we were in the front row of the balcony we had a fine view.

There were two very amusing incidents. Just as Menuhin had his bow poised to start his concert, a couple of dozen people were still rustling about finding their seats. Nehru leapt to his feet and stormed up to them, gesticulating wildly and making them sit down. He was absolutely livid. Menuhin watched from the platform with a wide grin on his benign face.

The same thing happened again after the interval, but this time his daughter jumped up after her father and laid a restraining hand on his shoulder and propelled him back to his seat. You could just hear her saying, 'Now Pa, for goodness sake don't make an exhibition of yourself in front of all these people!'

The following night Menuhin's accompanist, Daniel Gazelle, gave a piano recital, and as tickets were easier to get for this I treated Bill in return. It was another exceedingly pleasant concert, with the same exalted company, but no gymnastics on the part of the PM.

I also had the honour of giving one of the Everest Expedition – Dr Pugh – a lift in my car. He has been staying in Eastern House, prior to leaving for Nepal – definitely one of the absent-minded scientific types.

April 1952

May I remind you that it is a *leopard* that never changes its spots, and not a leper!!

Now about my health. You will be delighted to know that I now weigh

8 stone 12 pounds, which is only two pounds less than I weighed when I left for India the first time. I really am delighted with myself and can bear to look at myself in the mirror again. How I love the hot weather!

I keep on forgetting just what I have told you in previous letters. I know though that I have not written since Lord Reading came to Delhi. He gave us a talk yesterday in the office on foreign affairs and most instructive it was. He also told us about a few things at home, among them being his eye-witness account of the funeral of the King: it really was most touching. He said what impressed him most was seeing that forlorn group of women, so many of whom had their men folk no longer beside them. He also said that it was significant that among the mountains of flowers that were sent to the Chapel, more than half were anonymous and came from people who obviously wanted no official recognition.

We are not now doing our broadcast recording until next Saturday 5 April, so I won't know for a day or two when the recording is likely to be retransmitted to England. But I will tell you as soon as I have news.

We are giving another concert next Monday. I can't remember if I told you that I was singing in a quartet but I am, and feel very dubious about the whole thing. To my horror I am now singing one verse of a song solo, and it is one of those songs that demands a tremendous amount of breath, which quite frankly I wonder if I have. Don't get too excited though, as there is almost no chance that this concert will be recorded at a later date.

I have been very busy in the last few days making up that dress length of cotton that I bought at home – the one incidentally that you were not awfully keen on. To my glee it is turning out just as pretty as I thought it might, despite your discouragement!

9 April 1952

My car is going in for servicing today as tomorrow I am off to Raniket for the weekend with some of my golfing pals. Thank goodness dear old Bill is in the party, so if anything goes wrong with any of the cars he will be able to put it right. I am looking forward to playing on another golf course, and to getting away for a little while from the heat. Yesterday it was up to 99 degrees – any minute now we shall reach the 100 degrees mark.

16 April 1952

Here is my news of the weekend from which I have just returned.

We really have had a marvellous time – five hundred miles in all and my little bus has gone like a bird. We started off on Thursday afternoon bound only for Rampur, about 120 miles away. There are seldom any hotels in these smaller towns but usually government rest houses, where a bed only is supplied and you take your bedding and your food. I had written a day or two before to the District Magistrate for permission to stay in the Circuit House at Rampur which is the rest house of the place, and there had not been time to get a reply.

As we trundled into Rampur dusk was falling. We had all sorts of varying directions as to how to reach the Circuit House, got hopelessly lost and finally found ourselves in the middle of the bazaar area, with thousands of people swarming around. Bill was driving my car at the time and we were leading. In desperation – for it was now quite dark – he said to me – ask this man in the blue shirt and see if he knows the way. The blue shirt looked slightly less tatty than the thousands around. I hailed him, and almost had to be revived with smelling salts when he said in reply, 'You must be Miss Margaret'! He worked in the District Magistrates Office and had been deputed to arrange our accommodation. The Circuit House had been closed and apartments in the fabulous Palace had been set aside instead. So he squeezed in beside us in order to direct us through the labyrinth to the Palace. Only in such a country as this could so strange an occurrence occur. He had thought we were coming by train and had been to the station. Not finding us he had wandered into the bazaar to do some shopping.

We found ourselves in the most opulent building. Nearly all the furniture had been removed except a bed and a chair or two in each room, but the rooms themselves were magnificent with marble floors and gold leaf paint. Talk about shades of the past! The whole place wreaked of the opulence and splendour of days that are gone. My bathroom was twice the size of our old sitting room at Nowhere, again with marble floors. You could shower fifty people at a time quite happily. Of course, in true Indian fashion, the bath and wash-basin had been ripped out and only the taps remained!

It was a very hot night, and although I had the fan on I got bitten to death by mosquitoes. When we all compared notes next morning we found we had all suffered the same fate, and we were like a lot of monkeys at breakfast time.

Before we left the next morning we were taken over the Palace proper by the old electrician in charge of all the buildings. This is fairly modern – built about forty or fifty years ago by one of the last Rampur princes – and at the same time as our luxurious quarters. We were tickled by the prince's bathroom, where you mounted three marble steps before you could sit down on the 'throne'. In many ways, inside it was hideously ornate though the outside was lovely, but we were appalled by the amount of money that must have been poured into its construction. There were dozens of the most gigantic chandeliers I have ever seen. The whole place has of course been empty since Partition, and again we felt the ghosts around, particularly in the huge Durbar Hall, and under the coronation umbrella of embroidered red velvet and silk.

The old electrician had been in the Navy and fought at the Dardanelles. He had been to Liverpool and Manchester, but never up the hill to Naini Tal or Ranikhet, less than a hundred miles away whither we were bound! He had lost one son in an aeroplane crash, a daughter and another son from typhoid and he had only one thirteen year-old boy left, on whom all his hopes were fixed, and whom he was determined also to put into the Navy in a year or two.

I forgot to say that *all* the way to Rampur a dust storm was blowing which at times was as thick as a good old pea-souper. We were thankful when the sun set and the wind dropped.

The next day we ambled up the hill comfortably. Ranikhet is lovely, with the most glorious view of the Himalayan snow. We spent the next two days playing the most hilarious golf. It is a nine-hole course, of good mountain turf and with browns instead of greens – that is sand mixed with glue to make a hard surface. Two very small boys were our fore-caddies and their father one of our caddies. The golf club is also a place of ghosts. Hardly anybody ever plays there, and we never saw another soul on the course except our own party, though it was Easter. You can imagine how delighted the caddies and *aggewallahs* were to see us! When we paid our caddy for himself and his two little sons, he immediately handed his share over to the boys and asked them what they wanted to buy. Their little faces lit up and they both said '*Potatoes!*' So I popped them in the back of the car and drove them to the bazaar to buy some. They had a 3½ mile walk back but that is nothing to hill children. We had also taken some tinned beer with us, and the father handed them one empty tin and told them to buy some oil, but not to pay more than four annas for it. Again their little faces beamed, for the oil was for light, a very great treat to these almost penniless people. But though they are so poor, they were clean and well-dressed and obviously very happy and healthy – and you couldn't wish to see brighter or more intelligent faces in a couple of children.

The road up to Ranikhet is anything but dull. You have to pass over the river bed of the Ganges. At this time of year there is only a little water which is crossed by pontoon bridge, and three miles of sandy desert where there is no road, but only wooden or metal slats in two parallel lines just wide enough to take your wheels – and often these vanish under the sand. During the monsoon the whole of this area is flooded, and you have to do a terrific detour, put your car on the train and go over the railway bridge.

Another odd feature is the railway-cum-road idea. There are two terrific railway bridges. You wait for the train to go through, then the gates are opened and you run along the same track. There are also countless railway crossings and they are nearly always shut. The Indians are excessively 'precautious'. But a word with the gate keeper, and the gate is opened and you walk through, leaving strings of bullock carts and tongas quite happily waiting for another half hour.

At one railway crossing though we were not so lucky. The engine was actually halfway across the road and there it stuck, with a slight gradient in front of it and far too many carriages behind. Its wheels were spinning merrily round without gripping, and it took quite twenty minutes of men with shovels sprinkling dust in front of the wheels to get it, inch by inch, and its retinue of trucks, over the crossing. The passengers didn't seem in the least impatient or perturbed, but just hung out of the windows gazing interestedly at the operations!

When we got back to Delhi we found the temperature had bounced up to 105 degrees in our absence, and we longed again for the cool of the hills.

23 April 1952

We had quite an amusing day on Sunday when we had our office golf society competition. We played two-ball foursomes and I drew Joe Garner, the Acting High Commissioner, as my partner, and we played against his wife and Rowland Owen, the Senior Trade Commissioner. It was a fiendishly hot day and we all played so badly, and therefore so slowly, that we were out for 3½ hours, which pretty nearly finished us all off. But to my delight Joe Garner and I won the booby prize – which I had been deputed to buy – and I'd been fairly canny in my choice as I knew how badly Joe played, and I thought there was a good chance that we might head the list in reverse! So I'm now the proud possessor of a lovely Chinese bowl with spoon to match. We drank quantities of beer when we got in, and then had an excellent buffet lunch at the Club before we all staggered home to sleep soundly.

I've just been across the road from Eastern House to an art exhibition in Hyderabad House. This is one of the many palaces owned by the Nizam of Hyderabad, who is still, I believe, the richest man in the world. I went more to see the house than the exhibits and I was not disappointed. In one room which must be about 200 feet by 50 feet there is a Persian carpet woven in one piece. It is quite fantastic – and such beautiful colours and design. It alone must be worth tens of thousands of pounds. I didn't realize just what gigantic opulence I have lived opposite for so long.

26 April 1952

I have really no news since I wrote two days ago. The temperature continues to rise alarmingly and it is degrees hotter than the normal for this time of year. I went to a cocktail party in an upstairs flat at Eastern House last night. I only had on a short fine lawn waist-length petticoat and a cotton dress and *nothing* else, and still the sweat streamed down the backs of my legs and poured into the heels of my evening slippers.

I've just had a very sad letter from one of my pals in the Ministry of Education, telling me about one of the lads I knew well. He had two children of his own and an adopted child, and his wife was rather delicate. All the time I was there he was trying to emigrate to Australia, but somehow he never pulled it off. He was a fine athlete and the champion swimmer of the Civil Service. Anyway, he eventually resigned his established post and did go to Australia with his family. He had only been there a week or so when he contracted polio, and he is now permanently crippled in both legs and gets no paid sick leave or compensation. Really, this life does deal underhand blows to some people, doesn't it? And what a tragedy that Australia isn't a bit further forward in its social services.

I definitely start my consular work on 1 May. To begin with I am going to take over some of the Assisted Passage work. This is a scheme which advances money to destitute Europeans and Anglo-Indians in order that they can get home to start a new life. It is work essentially dealing with people and their problems so I look forward to it immensely.

28 April 1952

This is such stinkingly hot hot weather that I have plucked up courage to ask to be allowed to leave Eastern House, which is one of the hottest holes in Delhi. To my delight Garner has made no objections, as I have got Eastern House well organised now and never have very much trouble there. I have found myself a very pleasant room with a large verandah in a bungalow owned by a high official in the Government of India. They have a beautiful garden, which means more than anything during the hot weather, and I move in later this week. I haven't yet met the owner and his wife, but I have been recommended to them by a man in the British Council and they are prepared to take me on spec. Poor old Lalla Ram is very upset about being parted from all his crony pals with whom he gossips all day in Eastern House, but it will be jolly good for him to have to do a spot of hard work for a change.

I start on my consular duties on Thursday. The need for me there has suddenly become much more urgent as one of the men in Consular Division – one of the few – had an accident last night after a cocktail party, on his motor cycle, and is in hospital with a suspected broken skull.

6 May 1952

Well, my two main items of news this week are that I have started my consular work, which I'm certain I'm going to find fascinating, and I've moved house, which delights me. I have a large room and enclosed verandah, facing north, which is miraculously cool. It's funny how a north elevation is the best in this part of the world! I sleep right out in the garden and it's heavenly. It's quite twenty degrees cooler than inside at Eastern House. I wake up at about half past five, my tea and the paper arrive at six, and then I lie for three quarters of an hour in the early morning sunshine reading the paper and watching the tremendous early-morning activity of the bird life in the garden. Yesterday I even saw two golden owls. I can't tell you what a joy it is to be right away from all the people I work with, and to have somewhere really cool for a change. Lalla cooks me my breakfast, I lunch still at Eastern House to keep an eye on the place, and I dine wherever I feel like it.

14 May 1952

I'm just getting bedded down into my Consular work. You ask how I am coping – well I'm still primarily Welfare Officer and fit in what Consular work I can when I have time. I have shed as many as possible of my more routine establishment jobs, and a lot of my welfare work is all buttoned up now so I'm finding quite a bit of time for my new tasks. I must say they really are fascinating, though it is astounding to find such a multiplicity of problems still remaining among the British and Anglo-Indian community in India. Quite a lot of the hardship caused is because of the enmity and bloody-mindedness between India and Pakistan.

If a person has worked all his life, say on the railways, in a part of the country which is now India, but has retired to another part which is in Pakistan, the Government of India has probably not paid him a penny of his Provident Fund since Partition – and the same goes for teachers with their tiny pensions and so on. And we have to act as mediators. This is just one small aspect of one of the problems we have to tackle.

The new quarter is grand. I've just hired a sofa as it is a bit sparsely furnished, and am going to get myself some new curtains; then I shall be all fixed. Sleeping out is heavenly. I expect the garden is full of snakes and creepy-crawlies, but so is India in general, so I don't bother to speculate.

Soon we shall be out of Court Mourning and the parties will start up again. I'm *not* looking forward to it!

Mother, be a darling and send me that lovely recipe for salad dressing where the base is a tin of sweetened, condensed milk. I shall have a lot of salady meals in my new quarters and dressing is very difficult to buy here.

21 May 1952

My memory must be melting in the heat for I can't remember your query on who the people are in whose bungalow I live. As you have asked me a second time I presume I must have forgotten. They are an Indian couple named Banerji. They have one son in England reading law at Oxford – whose room I have – and a smaller one in school here in India. I have not yet met Mr B but his wife is very sweet. Of course, I see little of them as I have a separate entrance.

Today and for three weeks I have to face most of the work of Consular Division alone as the man with the fractured skull, who miraculously returned to work a week after his accident, has departed on three weeks' leave. So I'm shaking a bit in my shoes.

One more query to answer. No, I don't bother to sleep under a net at the moment as this period of great dry heat kills off most of the insects. and they don't start flourishing again until the monsoon.

29 May 1952

Your long, long letter from Manchester of 22 May has just arrived and I'm ashamed to say I'm replying to it in the office. We are enduring a heatwave at the moment, and it's absolutely impossible to attempt to do anything out of an air-conditioned room. Maximum day *shade* temperatures are between 112 and 115 degrees and minimum night between 85 and 92 degrees, which is as hot as it ever is with you during the day. This has lasted four days and we are praying for a dust storm to cool down the air – what a grim alternative.

Now a word more about my accommodation. All Government of India officials are given furnished accommodation, and the Public Works Department are pretty stingy. They have to be with India as poor as it is. So in these Government of India bungalows you never get any furniture except the stereotyped stuff. Even high Government of India officials are not terribly well paid, so if they have a spare room going they are only too glad to have a tenant. I don't mix with the household at all, as I have my own entrance and the most lovely bathroom to myself with marble chip floors.

As usual I haven't much news. We are out of purdah on Sunday and are celebrating it with an informal dance at the Golf Club. Then on the 5th we have the big UK do of the year – the reception at 2 King George's Avenue to celebrate the Queen's birthday. I'm treating myself to a new evening dress for it – a lovely soft billowy blue chiffon one.

Joan Burbidge – now Macintosh – has just had a smash on her motor cycle, resulting in a stitch in her hand and the most awfully grazed leg. She's the third person in Consular Division in a month to have a motor cycle smash – first the man about whom I told you, then a Passport girl on a pillion, who lost a finger-nail and most of the skin off one hand and a knee and now Joan. Nothing will persuade me to get on one ever again.

6 June 1952

The big party went off splendidly last night. Rain and dust storms were in the air but mercifully they held off until the party had just finished. I had a talk to Rajkumari Amrit Kaur and introduced her to one of our girls who had also been to Sherborne School.

My new evening dress – which has cost me under £4 – is absolutely lovely and was very much admired. I had a touch of a chill on the bladder yesterday, but nevertheless contrived to enjoy myself immensely.

There is really little news again. The worst of our heat wave has passed thank heaven, but it is still b— hot!

And now I think I'll pop off and have a 'cuppa'. After the holiday yesterday, today has been completely crazy with work, and I've left about thirty files that I haven't even looked at yet – but why worry.

20 June 1952

I expect you will have seen that our new boss has been announced. As so often happens in this country, somebody in the Government of India must have let the cat out of the bag, for the first we of the staff knew of it was a little announcement in the *Hindustan Times*. There has been a hell of a rumpus about it, but there we are. It was supposed to be announced at the same time as the change in the Indian High Commissioner in London. This was not divulged – trust the British! There was a very unfortunate misprint in the *Statesman* about Clutterbuck. It said he was married in 1929 and has a daughter of twenty-three, which set us all doing an inevitable bit of mental arithmetic! It wasn't the *Statesman*'s fault either. That was the information given to them by the British Information Service. Actually he was married in the same year that I was born. Joe Garner gave us a little talk yesterday on our new boss. Evidently he, his wife and daughter are all over six feet. Mustn't they be a grand looking family?

The weather is still unspeakable. Humidity is now up to 50 per cent, and together with the high temperature it means that we are constantly streaming with sweat. It pours down one's face and nose and neck and glistens on arms and hands and gives one soaking shoes where it gallivants down the legs. It is the worst spell I ever remember in Delhi, and nobody has any other topic of conversation but the horrors of it. I now spend my lunch hour either back in the air-conditioned office or lying in the bath with a book propped up just above the water line! It doesn't stop me from playing golf, however. I really am getting very much better and am horribly pleased with myself. The trouble is that I shall probably never get the chance of playing regularly when I get home and I shall forget all I have ever learnt.

Incidentally, talking of coming home, I expect to hear something definite about the date during the next month. The most likely time is about January or February next year, though I have said that I am prepared to stay on longer if they want me to. I don't think I shall be allowed to though, for Mr Hamilton says very firmly that it is not in my interests to be away from the main office for too long. Anyway, don't get excited one way or the other yet. I shall be glad to know definitely so that if necessary I can get cracking on finding accommodation in London.

I shan't have time to start another sheet, so will only apologise for sending you this tiny note. I have been consulting the girls in this office as to what to tell parents in the hot weather when there is really nothing but the heat to talk about, but they are confronted weekly with the same problem they say.

23 June 1952

Don't get excited. I really haven't much news since I wrote a few days ago, but I went to a rather beery curry lunch party yesterday and heard one or two good jokes, and before I forget them I thought I'd pass them on to you!

The first is about the two Red Indians who were great fishermen. Every day they went to the river, and one sat on one bank and the other on the other, and every day one said to the other in greeting, 'How,' and the other replied, 'How,' and then they both fished like mad for the rest of the day. This went on for weeks until one day one of the Red Indians suddenly had a bite. He hauled away and finally brought up a beautiful mermaid. He unhooked her and turned her this way and that, and scratched his head and turned her that way and this, and after a very long time he threw her back into the river. This was too much for the Red Indian on the other side of the river who therefore shouted across to the first Red Indian, 'Why?' Whereupon the first Red Indian sadly responded, 'How?'

The next one is about the mother who was asking her four year old daughter what she wanted for Christmas. She said, 'Last year you asked for a baby brother and we gave you one, but this year I'm afraid we can't manage that again. Now what would you like, dear?' The little girl put her head on one side and thought for a long time and finally she said, 'Well, Mummy, if it wouldn't spoil your figure too much I'd rather like a rocking horse.'

I daren't tell you the third!!!!!!

I must say it was a grand party. It was given by one of my golfing friends – the man who looked me up in London when I was at home. He has an incredible driver-cum-cook-cum-bearer who specialises in curry. He had boasted so much about this man's prowess that we demanded to be given first-hand proof of his worth. And yesterday we had it. Joan and Ian Macintosh and Bill were in the party and they are enough to make any party go. And the meal was wonderful – quite the best curry I have ever tasted. I shan't half miss that when I come home, so you had better take some lessons! I staggered back to my quarter at about three o'clock, fell fast asleep, wakened up for an hour or two to have a cup of tea and then collapsed again until morning. I've never known a better antidote to insomnia than beer and curry.

I've just thought of another that I dare tell you. It's the story of the vicar who had a parrot. This parrot indulged in the most frightful language, which really was most embarrassing for a vicar, and nothing would cure him. One day the vicar went visiting one of his parishioners, who, he discovered, also had a parrot – a lady one. To his amazement this parrot, unlike his own, did nothing but pray all day long. He decided therefore to confide in his parishioner, and told her about the awful trouble he was having with his parrot and his frightful language. The parishioner was most sympathetic and asked the vicar if he would like to bring his parrot along to see if he would be reformed by her own parrot's excellent example. So the next day the vicar took his parrot to his parishioner. The parrot was in the very worst of moods. His language was at its worst. Hopefully he took him into the room where the parishioner's lady parrot was. The vicar's parrot took one look at the praying lady parrot and shouted out to her, 'Come to my arms, you beauty, and let's have a bit of necking,' whereupon the lady parrot rushed at him shrieking gleefully, 'What the devil do you think I have been praying for all these years!'

28 June 1952

Joe Garner called me upstairs yesterday to give me some good news which is that I have been upgraded to Higher Executive Officer. This means that I shall not have to go back to CRO on my basic grade ever, not even for a few months. It doesn't mean anything more in my pocket at once as I am already acting HEO out here, but it will mean something to me when I get home. Heaven knows how I have got away with it with the Staff side of the Union, as I have jumped from the very bottom of the list of EOs and it is rarely in the Civil Service that one is upgraded very much out of turn (that is out of seniority in the grade turn). This is all the result of the Promotions Board that I had while I was at home, so I'm glad now that I had the chance of going through it.

There is still no news of the date of my return. Garner said that CRO are still thinking in terms of my returning in November of this year, but that in view of my old chest they (I mean Garner) had asked again if I can be left until at least January or February so that I shall miss the worst of the winter when I get back. In view of this promotion it may well be that they have some job in line for me at home which means I must go back before the end of the year, so I may have no choice at all.

30 June

Rain at last, and torrents of it. I was out on the 14th green, as far as I could be from the Club House, when it broke. By the time I got in I was scarcely decent as the two garments I was wearing were completely saturated and clinging lovingly to my poor torso! But I won my match 5 and 4 and yesterday won my two-ball foursome 2 up. Luckily the rains kept off during the morning so we were able to have some pleasant golf on soft ground for a change. By afternoon however the clouds rolled up and there was a terrific storm raging most of the rest of the day. The temperature has only dropped to a minimum of 80 degrees, but this is a vast improvement.

With the rains of course have come the trillions of insects again. By yesterday evening there was a positive fog of flying ants, which are large juicy creatures with two enormous sets of wings. They fly without any sense of direction and just biff straight into you. Their wings drop off at the slightest touch and then what's left of them – a horrid fat looking slug, which is the embryo ant, wriggles and squirms about all over the place. If you kill them their bodies are immediately whipped up and carted away by their fellow ants to provide good meals in their larder. I actually watched one ant methodically bite the wings off a fallen but alive flying ant, then throttle it and cart off the only just dead corpse. Nature is red in tooth and claw even among such small creatures.

Tomorrow is the big Nepalese reception. Did I tell you that I met the Nepalese Ambassador when I was up in Nepal? I don't suppose for a minute that he will remember me, but it is just possible he will as so few European girls ever go to Nepal. Anyway I shall try to have a word with him to tell him how much I enjoyed my stay in his country. It will probably pour with rain and we shall all be huddled indoors. It is a tricky business holding a large reception at this time of year.

1 July 1952

Your letter with the Norah Gregory cutting has just appeared. The Norah Gregory cutting has been all round Consular Division where it was greeted by various groans and scowls. Do we know Norah Gregory – *I should think we do*! For the last few weeks we have had nothing but trouble with her and so have our counterparts in Pakistan. She first soared into view somewhere near Lahore where she broke down. She had no money there, and was only let out of Pakistan with her bike to India by depositing £50 with us to cover her import duty of £30, which had to be paid and could be recovered provided she re-exported it in time. When she arrived here by train we had all sorts of complicated money dealings to do for her. After a lot of trouble she got her bike repaired and set off to Agra to have a look round. She broke down again and had to stay on in Delhi for several weeks waiting for spare parts. Finally she got them and proceeded on her travels to Calcutta. About forty miles out of Delhi a monkey jumped from a tree onto her, she had a bad crash, her bicycle was damaged once more, and she herself had to be rushed back to Delhi to be stitched up by our Medical Adviser. Eventually we got her off to Calcutta by train. She had just enough money for the fare and she hoped to be able to get a boat somehow in Calcutta. I must say we are thankful to see the back of her, though I suppose she will be a source of trouble to our Calcutta office next.

In the meantime we have had to indulge in much correspondence by telegraph with the Customs Authorities to try to persuade them not to retain the customs duty on the bike as her accidents have prevented her from re-exporting it in time. It's all very well for these people to set out on these stunts if they have enough money behind them, but God knows what they would do without their own representatives abroad to get them out of their difficulties. You will probably gather I'm *not* awfully sympathetic!!

But enough about our Norah. I have been dealing these last few days with another interesting case – getting a woman of forty-six who has been in a lunatic asylum out here for the last sixteen years back to England. She was a pathetic little thing – mother divorced, and one of twins. The other sister being very attractive and marrying young, this one couldn't understand why she wasn't married too. So quite early on she developed the most alarming super-erotic tendencies, and couldn't keep her skirt down whenever she saw a man. She is much more amenable now she is older, and speaks quite intelligibly. I'm sure if she had had good parents who had sent her back to England when the trouble started and had her properly treated, she might have been cured. As it was they shoved her in a mental home and forgot about her, the line of least resistance. I got her off last night on a plane accompanied by an assisted passage case – an Anglo-Indian sister who had polio two years ago and is no longer able to find employment out here. It really distressed me to see these poor things setting out for England with no more than 20 lbs of baggage each – their entire worldly possessions.

The rains alas have come and gone and it has become terribly hot and sticky again. I think the rains of last weekend were only very severe – pre-monsoon showers, but not the monsoon proper after all.

The Nepalese party had alas to be held indoors because of the threat of rain. A big *shamiana* (coloured tent roof) had been put up over an open court-yard and it was quite unbelievably hot. It was such a pity as the garden had been beautifully decorated with fairy lights and we only saw them as we went in and out. I had quite a little chat with the Ambassador who swore he remembered me in Kathmandu but I expect he was a good liar!

10 July 1952

I don't think I told you that I had dinner with a very new German Ambassador and his wife and the Swedish Ambassador last Saturday night. Joe Garner was short of a woman, so I had to fill in at the last minute. Rather a grim way of having to spend a Saturday night, but it was quite interesting. Mrs German Ambassador is very charming and never stuck for something to say. The Ambassador is also very chatty for a German, but makes life a little trying by never getting away from the subject of Germany's shame and how apologetic he is for Hitler. Such a subject is far better left alone, as nothing he says can possibly make any difference to what people think about Hitler, and only causes embarrassment in the conversation. The Swedish Ambassador is a pet. We talked solidly about gardens most of dinner time, which I thought was pretty clever of me as I know nothing (as you well know!) about this subject. Anyway, I've learnt an awful lot about the habits of petunias.

The trouble with these typed letters is that the quantity looks so little. If I had written this in my large florid hand you would think that you had had your money's worth. As it is, if I stop now you will think me an awful measly creature. I really have very little news as usual, and have definitely got to the padding stage.

Oh, I have got one piece of news for you, Mother, and that is that Joan Burbidge is going to have a baby. We are all tickled to death as they were both so adamant about 'not starting yet', when in fact she must have set about it a month after she got married.

14 July 1952

We are all feeling thoroughly down and depressed. The monsoon continues to by-pass us, and it is unbearably hot and humid. We trail about feeling thoroughly languid and bad-tempered and life really is a tremendous effort. Everybody seems to be feeling it particularly badly this year. It looks very much as if we may have another monsoon failure like last year. Clouds are all around but there just isn't any rain in them. It will be catastrophic for the farmers if they have another year of drought.

I have had some good news that I shall in all probability get the import duty on my car back. There have been terrific arguments going on with the Government of India about the whole question, and it looks as if my category is going to be all right. If I do get my import duty back it means I shall be able to face the purchase tax. If anything goes wrong and I don't get it back I shall be forced to sell it out here and buy a second-hand one at home. I do want to avoid this if I possibly can.

I've just got hold of three marvellous books written by an Englishman who lived most of his life out here. His name is Jim Corben and the three books – *The Man-Eater of Mumaon*, the *Man-Eating Leopard of Rudraprayag*, and *My India*. The first two sound rather bloodthirsty but they are absolutely fascinating, as indeed is the last one, which is a collection of anecdotes about the people living in the foothills of the Himalayas, among whom Jim Corben spent so much of his life. Try to get them if you can.

18 July 1952

Since putting the letter into the bag yesterday to you I have had a personal note from Mr Hamilton to say that I shall have to be back working in the CRO by the middle of January. He hoped to be able to allow me to stay out in India until after the winter, but the staff posting programme is such that this will not be possible. It looks therefore as if I shall be getting on a boat some time at the end of the year. I think I shall put off my return as long as possible in order to miss the worst of the winter at home, but I shall certainly be home some time in January. I'm glad to know something definite at last as I can now get down to accommodation and other problems. I think I shall drop a line to Dolphin Square just on the off chance of their having something going, though I am not very optimistic.

Bill Worth and Peter Mote, the friend of the man who met Bobbie and Jessie, have just moved for six months into a very nice flat at the back of the golf course. They are having a lunchtime housewarming party on Sunday, and I have been asked by them to spare old Lalla Ram and myself to help to make the thing go. They sent out such a silly invitation to '"The Motworth Arms" – R.S.V.P. quite unnecessary – we know you'll come!' They really are a couple of idiots and I'm sure it will be a crazy party, but I am looking forward to it.

Our Civil Air Adviser has just come back from a three week conference in London. When he got there he said the temperature was 95 degrees and he longed for India once more with its light clothing, fans and showers. But then he said the weather suddenly broke and it turned into one of the coldest spells imaginable in England. How on earth am I ever going to survive such terrific changes in climate? You had better start knitting me some thick woolly combs! (That looks like the thing you put through your hair – how do you spell what I mean? 'Comms' or what?)

22 July 1952

Your letter of 15 July has just arrived and I'm most intrigued by all your news about cars. What excitement in the family. I can just imagine Leslie giving you lessons in double declutching. Do you remember my efforts to teach you to revv up when changing down? I wonder if that has stood you in good stead?! I shall await further news now with very great interest and if you do sell your Morris I shall be more than interested to hear how much you get for it.

By now you will have got my letter telling you about my car plans. I am still waiting for absolute confirmation that I am to get my import duty back, but I'm pretty certain that all will be well. While you are thinking in terms of cars, you might like to know of a very far-off plan that I have about mine. If I bring it home I can't sell it for two years, but then it looks very much as if it will be two years before I shall be on my way abroad again. If so, and you want my car, it might be a very good plan to sell it to you and buy a new one for taking to my next overseas post. As long as I could find enough money to pay for the new car, I shouldn't mind how little you gave me for my Austin. It should still be in very good condition as I really have looked after it like a Ma, and shall continue to do so for the rest of its natural days! Anyway it is just a thought for two and a half years hence.

Yes, we are all very thrilled with Garner's promotion. He was just about due for it, but nevertheless it is a very great honour for a man of his age. Yes, he will be senior to Hamilton by one pip when he returns to take up his new appointment, unless of course Hamilton gets promotion as well in the meantime. When he was here in Delhi he, Hamilton, didn't expect to stay much longer in the CRO, as the reorganisation job for which he was appointed is now completed, and he will probably be shot off to tidy up some other untidy office.

I roared with laughter about your comments on that Indian film. No, I haven't seen it and nothing would induce me to do so. I have sat through so many trailers of Indian films since I came to India that I have no desire ever to sit through a whole one. They all run on precisely the same pattern, always much song and dance, always a great love affair, always scenes of brutality, always buffoonery and always tears. And unless the film runs for three hours or more the Indians don't feel that they have had their money's worth. I shall never forget the ecstatic intake of breath from the large Indian audience that went to see 'Gone with the Wind', when at the beginning it showed that the film ran for 20,000 feet when most European films don't reach the 10,000 mark. Anyway, go by all means to 'Aan' but don't say I haven't warned you!

Peter and Bill's party went off very well on Sunday. About thirty people turned up from midday onwards and the last left at 2.40. Another girl and I kept an eye on things generally and therefore stuck it out to the end, and by that time it was far too late to have the usual Sunday curry lunch, so we just picnicked on the floor of the flat on meat sandwiches and then staggered home to bed. I hardly stirred for the rest of the day.

One of my very dear friends in Delhi, the manager of Grindlays's Bank, who is a bachelor in his early fifties and a complete 'gent' has been transferred to Lahore, much to his sorrow as he has so many good friends in Delhi. This week is devoted to farewell parties to him, for he is a very popular soul. The best one will be on Saturday night, given by Joan and Ian Macintosh, who live with Gordon Read, the bank manager, in his bungalow. Saturday is the very famous Hunt Ball at Meerut, about forty miles from Delhi, and Joan and Ian are taking a party to it. I am insisting on driving my own car, as I would rather be in charge of myself than in any other person's hands after a party that will last far into the morning. After that is over I intend to go back into my shell and spend a very quiet month to make up for it. All except for my birthday, when I am taking a small party of my best friends down to the river where once more we shall fry bacon and eggs by the light of the moon, with old Lalla in his element with his *sigri*.

My new boss and his wife arrive on Saturday, and we are all very interested to see what he is like. New faces in this small world are always welcome – at the beginning anyway, until we have made up our minds if they are acceptable!

I've just been reading another excellent book – one of the best war books ever. It is called *The Cruel Sea*. If anybody feels like giving you an unbirthday present, ask for it. It is the story of one of the first corvettes to do convoy work in the Atlantic, and it is quite enthralling.

25 July 1952

Now at last I have definite news about the date of my return. I have to be back working in CRO by 2 February at the very latest. Boats are very difficult, but the office is trying to get me on the *Stratheden* which sails on 8 January and arrives at Tilbury on 25 January. This will give me a good week in which to find accommodation and settle down.

I hope you won't think it awful of me not to have a longer time at home before starting work in the CRO, but I don't want to face any more of the winter at home than I can help. I have about six weeks leave to come before the end of April. I shall take three of them out here before I depart, then have one before starting work, and still have a fortnight to take after I have started work. With a bit of luck I shall be able to take some or all of this, if not altogether, at least in odd days at the weekends when I shall be able to come home. With the car, there is no reason why I should not come home very frequently, if you can put up with me! If I leave London at about 1 o'clock there is no doubt that I shall be back in time to enjoy one of your home made teas, Mamma. Then during the summer months I need not leave again until about 5 p.m. on Sunday evening. So I hope these plans will compensate you for not seeing much of me after I first return. Of course, what I really want to do is to try and get myself fixed up at once with a flat, so that you can come and meet me and stay with me for as long as you like when I get back. But perhaps that is too much like wishful thinking.

I am writing off to Dolphin Square straight away to see if by any chance they are likely to be able to put me up. I'm not at all optimistic, but there is no harm in trying. I shall also write to Overseas League House and see how long I would be able to live there in case of emergency. I am a member of the Overseas League, which entitles me to accommodation for a time anyway.

Well love, that's my bit of excitement for the moment. There is always the possibility that I can't get on that ship, or that because of some staff crisis I shall have to stay on longer here, but these are very remote and I think you can bank pretty firmly on seeing me on 25 January. I am hoping to get the car on the same ship, so that I can get it cleared myself and have it from the moment of landing. But that again is in the lap of the gods.

As soon as I have any more news about all these plans I will of course let you know post haste.

Tonight we are off to that Hunt Ball at Meerut that I told you of in my last letter. The skies are a bit clouded and it would be just our luck if we had a terrific monsoon shower after all this patient waiting, that would prevent us from being able to reach our destination. I have an awful feeling that we shan't be home till morning. Thank heaven it's Sunday tomorrow and we can all sleep it off.

31 July 1952

Joan Macintosh is going to have her baby out here. Her husband was due for leave just at the time when the baby was due to be born, so he has put off his leave until March when the baby will be two months old. India is a good place for small babies. They seem to thrive out here and don't begin to feel the hot weather until they are at the toddling stage. And of course for the mother it is ideal, with ayahs to do all the dirty work and the dhobi to do all the nappy washing.

Now a little bit more news about my homecoming. I have just heard today that I have got a berth all right on the *Stratheden*, and have I been lucky. There were none left at £105, which is the maximum normally payable for a person of my grade, so they have had to give me one at £111, which is a single berth cabin, and one of the best on the ship, outside the stateroom class. So after two very poor berths I shall travel in luxury at last.

There is also every hope that my car will be booked on the same ship, so I shall be able to clear it myself and drive it away. I'm wondering what on earth to do with all my luggage if I haven't got some accommodation all lined up. I shall have to pack very carefully so that if necessary the things I don't need immediately can be put in store. I can't quite see my little bus coping with three large trunks and the odd packing case or two.

My new boss has arrived, and both he and his wife are grand. We have all 'passed' them as fit.

I have left this letter very late for post I'm afraid and had better shut up shop early if I am to catch the bag. In any case there are only fragments of news and these can wait. Poor old Lalla Ram is ill at the moment with a fever and a fluttery heart. He is getting too old to do much work and I'm not surprised that he is under the weather. Anybody would be.

19 August 1952

The bags have been so haywire this last week or two that I can't remember how long it is since I wrote to you, but it seems a hell of a long time. If so, my humble apologies. Anyway, I know that I haven't yet thanked you for your letter of 4 August with the grand lot of snaps and the little cutting about David and his engagement.

Yes, that must *my* David! There couldn't be two of that name and the announcement also appeared in the *Statesman* out here. I have asked Bill if he knows the girl as she comes from Bridlington, and he is pretty certain he does. If it is the one he thinks it is he says she is very lovely. So David has obviously patched up his broken heart at last, and that is a great weight off my conscience!

We are all appalled at the terrible news of the floods in Devon. If it is as bad as that there I'm quite sure that you have had your fair share of rain also, and I can well imagine that you are cut off once more from Leominster as you so often are when there is a lot of rain about the place. All I hope is that you are not having serious floods. We are now having a lot of rain ourselves. This is the best monsoon of the three that I have lived through. Every day we have some rain. Usually it is a good, honest downpour which is the best rain to fall, and only occasionally have we had torrential showers that wash the soil away and are therefore bad. Everywhere is looking wonderful: brilliant green wherever you look, and magnificent skies all the time. Never have I seen such sunsets as we have had in the last few weeks.

My replacement on the Welfare side has just arrived. She is a pleasant lass and I think will settle down well. Unfortunately she has only been here two days and has developed a bad tummy. All I hope is that it will not turn out to be dysentery.

I had a bad scare last week. I started to get a sore throat which I assumed would turn into a head cold as usual and then into my dreaded bronchitis. As soon as I began to feel a bit of pricking in my tonsil area I went straight to the Sick Bay and had a shot of penicillin in my bot. I had a second one the next day and my throat got worse. The sister took one look at it and said she had never seen one just like that and sent me off to the doctor. He told me I had a streptococcal (or whatever it is) infection and that I must have further injections and my throat painted. To my amazement however, the very next day the penicillin took its delayed action and my throat was miraculously better. In another two days you could hardly see that anything had been wrong with it – and I have had no sign of my bronchitis. With luck now I may get through August, and if I do I'm determined to have no cough for the rest of my tour here.

Simla

7 September 1952

I did my damnedest to get a letter off to you by the last bag but somehow I was as busy as ever. This trip to Simla was planned so much at the last minute that I had a hell of a time finishing off all my work before leaving. My welfare successor is now over her dysentery, and we have had to have some very concentrated sessions to get her initiated before leaving her to it.

This is the most lovely spot imaginable. It is about ten miles beyond Simla in the wilds and right at the top of the highest of the foothills surrounding the town. This dak bungalow is the old United Services Club of the old days. It is therefore well built and well furnished, and despite its remote position boasts flush sanitation – a very rare thing in the remoter parts of the hill stations. All around us are pine trees which really do smell as they should do. I've come up here with some of my golfing pals of the Ranikhet trip. We left Delhi on Friday afternoon and stayed the night at a rest house on the edge of the river crossing about a hundred and fifty miles from Delhi.

I think I have told you about these rest houses and dak bungalows before. They supply you with the bare necessities of living and you supply the rest. This one was one of the barer efforts, but we lugged the beds out into the garden looking out over the river and there we slept under the moon and the stars for the night.

The river crossing is really a ford and is just navigable again by car after the rains. The very first vehicle we watched going over it went too fast, nosedived into a pot hole, and just managed to reach the shore before it stalled. It was quite dark and we watched this by moonlight. It was a quarter of an hour before its plugs were dried again and it was able to move on, and in the meantime it held up a lorry stuck on a sandy patch between two lots of water as the road – if such you can call it – is only wide enough for one car at a time. After that we watched many buses and lorries that obviously knew the ropes very well and went through at a reasonable speed and therefore didn't stall. Needless to say we went through at a very reasonable speed too – and didn't stall.

As we lay on our beds I saw a sight I have never seen before in my life – a host of fireflies all around us and in and out of the trees above our heads. They are a sight full of magic. They flash their lights on and off at will and you can follow the flight of them by their lanterns. I slept rather fitfully, and every time I wakened I looked to see if they were still shining, and they were, almost up to the time of dawn breaking. They are one of the things about India that I shall never forget. Lest you think that this all sounds too wonderful for words I must hasten to be fair and admit that fireflies were not the only occupants of the air around us. They were rivalled in number and activity by the ubiquitous mosquitoes, which also left their mark on us – of a less favourable nature!

We were off and away early next morning and stopped for breakfast at the railway station at Kalka, the foot of the mountains. The railways are the only places that boast reasonable restaurants in India these days. They are quite clean and still have good crockery and cutlery and linen left over from the time of the British Raj.

On the way we saw one funny sight that I must remember to tell you of. These long roads in India are nearly all one way traffic, so if you catch up a vehicle going in the same direction as yourself, at a slower speed, you have to honk like hell to get the creature to move over into the rough in order for you to get past. On one such occasion there was a large and decrepit lorry in front of us whose engine was so noisy that he obviously couldn't rely on hearing a horn behind. So he had a little lad up on the top of his load, and as we came along he pulled a rope very vigorously, and this rang a bell above the head of the driver. Imagine seeing that in England.

We did a lot of shopping in Simla before settling down in the wilds. Going round the bazaars of these hill stations is an education. The slums are quite unbelievable now. They would never have been allowed to exist in British times, but my goodness they are there now. The filth and squalor are appalling. One rather pathetic sight caught my eye – a rather dirty little girl doing her arithmetic sums with a piece of chalk on the road. She obviously did go to school, which is quite surprising, but she had neither slate nor paper – just a piece of chalk and the roadway.

More details of the trip in my next letter.

10 September 1952

Here is the second instalment of my holiday story. I can't quite remember how far I got in the last one before I found myself at the end of the air letter, so forgive me if I repeat myself. We are now well broken in to this high mountain air. I think we must be over eight thousand feet up. Simla is over seven and we have to do a devil of a lot of climbing from there. My car was the first up the hill, and you can tell how terribly steep it is in the last few yards up to the bungalow, because even in first gear the poor little thing couldn't manage it with a load on. And I must admit I had quite a load on as I was carrying all my stores and forty-eight bottles of beer to keep the party happy!

The first afternoon we decided to go for a gentle stroll and finally found ourselves making for a golf course which was over four miles away down the steepest of hills. Once we got started somehow we couldn't turn back. The result was that next day we could hardly move because we were so stiff. This road to the golf course must be one of the most spectacular in the world. You would die a thousand deaths round every bend, Mother. It is only wide enough for one vehicle, and turns and twists like something demented. It runs along the ridge of a mountain so that at one moment there is a terrific drop and the most wonderful view on one side of the road, then you go round a bend and there is another wonderful view on the other side of the road. You look down valleys which are a sheer three or four thousand foot drop, and away in the distance are the everlasting snows of the high Himalayas.

There is a bus which goes along the road twice a day, and usually at the time when we are on our way to the golf course. The horn does overtime and we all hold our breath until we have passed it. It is a journey not without spice.

The golf course is enormous fun. It is virtually a nine hole course, with a little variation for the second nine by having slightly differently placed tees. I shattered the party by having a forty one on the very first nine that I played. (Bogey is thirty six). But alas I have never done so well again. You need to be very fit to cope with the ups and downs. I've never seen such golf holes in my life. You have to drive over thousand foot chasms and up sloping mountain sides. The last hole of all is wonderful. You stand on one side of the road and look upwards. There two hundred feet above you is the green which is literally on a tiny platform wedged between two enormous curtains of rock. So you drive over the road and over a small pond and heave the ball as high into the air as possible to get it up. Of course the trouble with me is that I can't hit a ball high and far so what usually happens is that I hit the mountain side somewhere short of the green, and the ball simply ricochets off in any direction. Mercifully the fore-caddies are like mountain goats, and think nothing of tearing hundreds of feet down the *khud* side to retrieve an errant ball.

There is no club house, and we have only ever seen one other couple besides ourselves playing. I think it is too remote to attract many people, but we think it is marvellous. From any part of the course you look out over some of the most spectacular views I have ever seen, so if you make a frightful hash of a shot you just raise your eyes and there is all the consolation in the world before you.

We are just about broken in now to this rarefied air and our legs are losing the worst of their stiffness – which was considerable after their life in the flat plains – so today we are taking ourselves down to the reservoir that supplies Simla with water. We dread to think how far down it is. We cannot see it from our high peak and therefore suppose that it is tucked away right at the foot of the mountain. It will obviously be at the very lowest spot to catch the maximum amount of water. Pity us on the return journey! Mercifully this is a country where many things are made easy.

As we are not playing golf we have ordered a caddy or two to act as coolies, so all our lunch, beer, bathing things etc. will be carried by them and not by us. That's what I call hiking in heavenly peace!

Any minute now I expect to hear the breakfast up call. Bacon, eggs, sausages; tomatoes, fried bread, fried spuds – can you wonder I don't think India a bad place.

13 September 1952

I think I got up to the stage when we were about to descend to the water works that supply Simla. We started off the day before yesterday with our lunch carried by the caddies, and proceeded along the most lovely road imaginable. In and out it wound with the most glorious views of the mountains below and before us all the way. Then the track began to go tremendously steeply down hill. Down and down we jogged, not daring to think what a climb it would be on the way back. We reckoned that the drop must be about five thousand feet. The lower we went the hotter it got, so by the time we dropped three thousand feet we began to use our discretion. We had thought that there would be a beautiful reservoir at the bottom in which we could cool our aching bodies, but as we rounded a bend in the path we saw the water works below us – and they proved to be large tanks only – not in the last glamorous. So being canny we considered our curiosity satisfied and turned up the hill again.

We cut across a mountain path because I wanted to follow the monkeys. These foothills are a paradise for monkeys – the small brown ones and, my favourites, the large grey ones with black faces. These were only the brown ones, but they see so few humans and they are so curious that they are a real pantomime to watch. They retire to a safe distance and then peep at you from behind trees and through the leaves of the branches.

We got back to find that the coolies had arrived from Simla.

This is an amazing spot. We went and had a talk to some of our friends of friends in Grindlays Bank in Simla, who practically run the place. They made arrangements for all we needed to be brought by coolie every other day to the bungalow. Now Simla is ten miles away, and a very stiff ten miles at that. Up comes the coolie regularly, carrying anything up to twenty or thirty pounds of stores. He walks all the way, though there is a bus service, and the stock charge is Rs 2; in other words three shillings for a whole day's arduous labour. But so poor are these people in the hills that this is quite a fortune to them. We had ordered a chicken for roasting to be brought up by him. Imagine my astonishment when the coolie took the cover off his basket to find a live chicken underneath. I somehow couldn't bear the thought of the little thing coming all that way to be killed, but when we sat down to a lovely roast chicken supper the night after I was able to get over my distress.

From this rest house we can see various places that we are determined to reach. One we are going to today – a little place called Kufri, which appears to be perched on the edge of a mountain ridge. We can get the cars there so we hear, so we shall be lazy in getting there and then start walking after we have arrived. What we would love to do is to take the road all the way to Tibet. The signposts at the bottom of our road say tantalisingly – Tibet, 183 miles; or some such distance. It makes the wanderlust leap and bound within me, but luckily my friends are suitably discouraged.

I am now chocolate coloured all over except for a strip from bosom to beam to show that I am not a halfcaste after all. It is funny in this country. All, or most of, the European girls spend as much time as possible getting brown, and all the Anglo-Indian girls spend as much time and money as possible on getting white. The papers are full of miraculous bleach advertisements, which obviously have a roaring sale. It is such a pity, for if an Anglo-Indian girl attempts to bleach her face or put white powder on it, she looks so bizarre, and her arms and legs just don't match.

24 September 1952

The rest of our holiday from the time I last wrote was just as good as the beginning. We continued to play golf with great vigour, and went off on two or three more journeys into the blue. At the golf course we met one of the few British judges left in India, and his wife. They were a very pleasant pair, and to cut a long story short, invited us to spend the last few days of our holiday with them. We therefore packed up at the bungalow on the Thursday and trundled into Simla. They live in the most glorious house imaginable in part of the old Vice Regal Simla Estate, which is now the holiday home of the President.

The Falshaws have spent most of their life in India, and have wonderful tales to tell of Mountbatten and his wife in Simla, and the incredible parties which they used to throw. But to go back to the Falshaws' house, it is built right on the top of a little peak and had to be specially designed to fit onto the pinnacle. Not one room was square. They were all an exciting shape and most wonderfully furnished. All the contents are still as they were in the old days, as the original furnishings have been allowed to remain, and only Europeans have stayed in the house and therefore it has been well looked after.

Falshaw is a great book collector, and I could have spent months browsing through his wonderful collection. They kept a marvellous table, and I stodged myself unashamedly. In my fortnight in Simla I put on three pounds and am now back to the weight I was when I left England. And I couldn't look or feel fitter. When I came back into the office everyone gaped at me in horror and said it just wasn't fair for anyone to look so flourishing! I'm naturally delighted with myself.

I have now had a letter from Notting Hill Gate confirming that a large bedsitter facing south is booked for me. I am much relieved as I did not relish the thought of having to spend all that week before starting work house-hunting. I have also had a letter from Dolphin Square saying that as a great concession they have put my name on their waiting list. This is the final result of some very acrimonious correspondence from me, and though it is a long story I have finally outwitted them. They say it may be as much as two years before I am allocated a flat, but that is better than nothing, and I'll just have to see if I can use my influence when I get home. I'm still determined to try to get something unfurnished, as I now have the beginnings of a few possessions, and without an awful lot of expense could manage to get enough sticks together fairly quickly. But we shall see.

29 September 1952

I'm starting this well in time for the next bag, which doesn't go for three days, but as I've got something to talk about I might as well put it down while I have a minute.

This has been a very energetic few days. I can't remember if I told you that we have had a team of golfers from Kanpor in Delhi this weekend. It is the festival of Dussehra, which means everybody has had some holiday – anything from the half day that we got in the High Commission to the ten days that a lot of Indians have. We managed to trounce the visitors all right.

I have had the job of helping to act as hostess to the wives. On Saturday I went first of all to the wedding of one of our girls: you may remember my speaking of her. She is the fair girl who went to Kashmir with me in 1950, and who appears on my Kashmir snaps. The reception was held afterwards in Eastern House, where I had to have something to toast the bride. Then it was on to the Golf Club where the acting Captain, an Indian who must be more than a millionaire, gave a cocktail party. After that was over we all went to the Maidens Hotel in Old Delhi where we had dinner and danced until two in the morning. I'm such an early bird these days that I had to keep on drinking cups and cups of black coffee to keep me awake.

The next morning I was playing golf with one of the wives at 9 a.m. I retired to sleep for an hour or so after lunch and then went on to a football match. This was a semi-final in a very keenly contested competition in India. The two opposing teams were an East Bengal one and a Bangalore, or Southern Indian, one. The East Bengalis are notorious for their bad sportsmanship and dirty play, and you really should have seen them. The arguments with the referee were wonderful, and at times it looked as if some of them might come to blows. And there were several skirmishes among the spectators. Certainly an Indian football match has more than the ordinary number of thrills.

Tonight is the final between the East Bengalis and the Gurkhas. I have never seen this Gurkha team play before and they are absolutely fearless. They simply hurl themselves at their opponents without thought of life and limb, and there is certainly going to be some blood and hair flying before the day is through.

After the match we crossed over the road to witness the climax of the Dussehra celebrations. I am enclosing a picture of the effigies that are burnt every year traditionally. By the time we got on the scene the celebrations had officially been on for an hour and a half, but like all Indian organisation something went wrong, and a mile and a half procession got lost in the mêlées of Old Delhi and never got as far as the Ramlila grounds. So two hundred thousand people had waited ninety minutes for nothing.

Because of the football match we missed all the waiting and were in time for all the fun. Getting the car through the crowds was quite a feat, but I had an official invitation and a special car park notice, and somehow I made it. We were then passed from hand to hand until finally we found ourselves right at the very front of the celebrations, though we must have been the last to arrive! Anyway, as soon as we arrived up went the first fireworks and scores of hot air balloons. Finally came the climax when the enormous effigies that you can see in the picture were lit up from below. After a breathless few seconds the flames crept upwards, and suddenly hell was let loose and all the fireworks on the effigies exploded at once, and the great creatures became a burning mass that quickly crumbled and fell to the ground.

Our miserable Guy Fawkes is nothing in comparison, though we can beat the Indians hollow at fireworks.

30 September 1952

Tonight I go to the wedding reception of an Indian lad who is a member of the Golf Club and also a member of the Ministry of External Affairs, which is the department with which we have most to do officially in the Government of India. These Indian wedding 'dos' are usually very slap-up affairs, and it should be quite amusing.

Then on Friday the Garners are giving a cocktail party for the whole of the staff to meet the Clutterbucks. They arrived in Bombay yesterday, and should just be putting in an appearance at New Delhi station as I am writing to you. I'm dying to have a look at them.

To one and all my very best love

Margaret (Archer)

How daft of me – I've been signing so many official letters the 'Archer' just slipped out automatically!

3 October 1952

I have just got back from the cocktail party given by the Garners to all members of the staff to introduce the new High Commissioner and his family to them. The party was held in the garden of 6 Albuquerque Road and thank heaven it wasn't too hot. Well, the new High Commissioner seems a grand chap – not as ostensibly forceful of character as Archie Nye, but a much more human creature I suspect. There is no doubt about the size of the family, especially the daughter. She is the tallest of the three. Only one – no two – people topped her. One, our new Brigadier, who is about six foot three, and the other one of our British Information officers, who is six foot five! One rather amusing thing Sir Alexander reported as coming from Nye when he first heard of his appointment to Canada from India – 'Good heavens, out of the frying pan into the fridge' – which I thought rather witty of old Archie.

You may be amused by the enclosed cutting of a car smash. It happened within about half a mile of my bungalow. This is a very dangerous crossing which I go over every day and treat with the utmost respect. I have always expected an accident here and last Sunday it happened, just before I went over the crossing. This poor old car, which is much more badly damaged even than the photograph shows, collided with a Delhi Transport bus. Day after day the car remained, blocking the road, though the bus was removed within forty-eight hours. On the fourth day I could contain myself no longer, so I gave Bill a ring and told him the story. He got a reporter out and had this snap taken.

As a result the car was removed to the side of the road within half a day. But this is typical of India. Presumably the car was only insured for third party as it is an old one, it didn't pay the owner to get it removed, so nobody else bothered. There it stayed therefore, blocking the rest of the traffic. What is more, the little van which is parked on the side of the road further down is also a wreck – obviously it had crashed into the first wreck, which was not illuminated at night, and became itself a wreck. This also was removed after this picture appeared in the *Statesman*!

I've got a rather nice story for you, Mother. This was told at the swimming pool the other day by the Air Marshal – the head of the whole of the Indian Air Force, who is a pet and a great pal of mine. (Needless to say he is a golfer!) It's the story of Winston and Herbert Morrison in the House one day. Winston was leaning back and displaying his very large tummy for all the world to see. Morrison came up to him and said, 'Hello, Winston. Congratulations. I see you're in the family way. What are you going to call it?' Whereupon Winston replied: 'Well, if it's a boy, I shall call it Winston after me, and if it's a girl I shall call it Elizabeth after the Queen, but if, as I strongly suspect, it's only wind, I shall call it Herbert.'

If you will promise not to show this letter to anybody I'll tell you another story, told this evening by a very sedate Scot, who is the head of the Ministry of Works, to Miss Christie, the elderly and very Scots secretary of one of our messes. And of course it's a Scots story, and a golfing story too! It's the story of the Prince of Wales who was playing golf with a real old Scottish professional. He put his ball well into the rough, and he turned to the professional and asked for his advice as to how to play it. The answer came: 'Weel, yer Heeness, if I were you, I'd just pee on it and ca' it casual waaer.'

Now I'm sure you will give me the sack after that one, so I shall hasten to get this ready for the bag tomorrow.

8 October 1952

Many thanks for your letter of 1 October. You are an angel to offer to come up to London and help me to settle in my flat. What I should like to do if I may is to write to Mrs Lummus, the woman who owns the house, and ask her if it would be possible to put in an extra bed for you, or whether there would be a sofa or something that I could sleep on for a few nights. Then if you would, I should get your arrival to coincide with mine and we could put our house in order together. This sounds rather like more hard work for you, but I should do my best to make you sit around ornamentally while I did the unpacking. Then once we have got everything all right I could run you back home and I could have a day or so there before reporting for duty. What do you think of that? Do say if you think I'm being too greedy!

I must say I would like to feel that everything is in order before I come home, so that I have no hard work to do at the time that I am starting a new job.

It doesn't seem like a year ago since I was driving you into Hereford with the cider fruit, but it is. How quickly the time seems to rush by. I hope there is a good crop to make up for the awful price of the damsons.

The Clutterbucks have duly arrived and seem to have made a great hit already. I haven't seen much of them yet or had any *tête-à-tête* but expect to do so any time now. The old boy presented his credentials yesterday and so is now officially in the office and is no longer merely 'designate'.

Actually I'm very sorry for myself today. On Sunday I had lunch with some friends of mine who have a pet monkey. She is a dear little thing and quite harmless, but she has one failing: she loves beads, and I had a very bright string on. Because I didn't know this vagary, I took no precautions. She suddenly leapt onto my back and started to scrabble at my beads to tear them off my neck. In her excitement she took rather a large chunk out of my ear. I didn't think much about it, but the next day the Sister got to hear about it and before I knew where I was I was whisked off to the hospital where they insisted on my having a course of anti-rabies injections. Although the animal is perfectly healthy it is a golden rule in this country that you always have these filthy injections if any animal breaks your skin, especially if the injury is anywhere on the head. Well, I have had to have three of these brutes. I had my last today, thank heaven, but they have just about laid me out. I've been asleep all afternoon and am only just beginning to feel human again. You are given them in the stomach. The needle is about 6 inches long and very coarse as the fluid is horribly thick. They had quite a job getting the needle through my hard tummy muscles, and they are absolute torture. I've now got three great bruises on my tum, of varying hues according to which day they were done. I am forbidden to take any exercise or any alcoholic liquor for a week – so that means no golf and no beer. What a life! And there are such a lot of parties coming off this next week and one gets so tired of tomato juice and lemonade.

Now I have got to get ready to go out to a quiet dinner party with Joan and Ian Macintosh. I shall be able to come home whenever I want to so I am not too perturbed.

16 October 1952

This really is a stinker of a week – far, far too many things to do. I am just getting over the night before last when we had the big UK fête of the year. This is run annually by the UK Citizens Association in aid of their benevolent fund to help indigent UK citizens in India. It was held this year in the garden of a friend of mine only two doors away from where I live. And it certainly was a great success. Joan Macintosh did a lot of the organising, and did marvels. It took the form of an English Michaelmas Fair. There was a maypole in the centre of the village green, all sorts of stalls and side shows, a fish and chip shop, with *News of the World* carefully hoarded cver a period of months especially for the occasion, and, best of the lot, a real English pub. Our Ministry of Works built it in their spare time, and it was terrific. It even had a thatched roof!

I was running a golfing competition, chipping balls into lighted buckets. I did this solidly for five and a half hours, with only a ten minute break, and now I am so stiff I can hardly move. If you spend five and a half hours doing nothing but picking up six balls that have gone in all directions, something awfully queer happens to your thighs and calves. I closed my stall down at about a quarter past two, and then started to enjoy myself. I finally left at a quarter to four, but once in bed couldn't sleep as there was still so much brawly singing going on at the 'Queen's Head' only two gardens away!

My most spectacular achievement, however, was guessing how much in rupees there was in a glass jar. In one rupee there are sixteen annas, and in one anna there are twelve pice. So there are one hundred and ninety two pice in one rupee. The jar was full of pice and I guessed there to be seven rupees, two annas worth. There was seven rupees, one anna, ten pice, so in all that lot I was only two pice out. So I got the jar as a prize. The Manager of Lloyds Bank who was standing beside me guessed there to be seventy odd rupees in the jar. He will never hear the end of it. Luckily he wanted the pies, which are scarce, so I sold them to him for ten rupees, to put in my SPCA box.

18 October 1952

Another day over, and what a shocker. We had the farewell party last night to the Senior Trade Commissioner, who has also been choir master and producer of the Dramatic Society. For his entertainment, and that of the other members of the Society, we put on extracts from his last two plays, both of which I was in. We had lost some of the original casts, but managed to find others to learn up the necessary bits. A crisis arose two hours before the party when one of the old stagers was whisked into bed with an acute attack of dysentery. I wildly rang up the husband of an 'acting' wife just before office closed and asked him to send his wife along early to learn up the part. He told her the wrong part, so we had to start all over again when she arrived. We had just twenty minutes to put her through her paces before the guests arrived – and thank heaven she went through with only one tiny mistake that we were able to cover up.

After this party I picked up the Falshaws from their hotel and took them to the Divali dance at the Golf Club. The whole club was lit up with the little Divali oil lamps, and a great mercy it was, as there was a big fire at Jaipur House, about a mile away, which put paid to the electricity for the night. So the whole dance proceeded by oil and candlelight with one big tilly for the band to be able to see its music.

This morning we are on holiday, and I am just off to see the third day of the Test between India and Pakistan. The Falshaws will be there, for the match is their main reason for coming to Delhi, and I'm also taking my welfare successor, Connie Stimpson. We are going to take a picnic lunch and stay there most of the day – at least until I depart to play a golf match.

19 October 1952

This poor letter does seem to have been written in dribs and drabs. Well, we spent our day at the Test, going at 10.30 and leaving at 2.45 p.m. And during that time, believe it or not, we saw thirteen wickets fall. The famous Mankad was bowling like a demon, and the whole of the Pakistan side seemed completely demoralised. An hour and a half after we left the whole match was over, with one day still in hand. Rajkumari Amrit Kaur was there, and Gandhi's son, and quite a large number of other Indian celebrities.

It is good to be able to play golf again, though I still have lumps the size of walnuts under the skin of my tummy. It seems to take ages for these wretched injections to disperse.

21 October 1952

All the bags have gone haywire again recently, as we are changing over to the Comet service. I missed the last one as I forgot when it went, and now I find there is not another for several days. I have written you quite a long screed which I shall put in the next bag, but here is a little pot-boiler in the meantime.

Now for the Prince of Wales joke. Mother – and you a Scot!! How would you write 'water' phonetically if you were trying to put a Scottish accent into the word? And if you don't know what casual water is on a golf course, you can always ask Uncle Geordie!

I've been up since six this morning doing various odd chores. I had a very early night last night, and as a result was wide awake at crack of dawn. It has suddenly got very cold at night and in the early morning now. The day temperatures, believe it or not, are still in the nineties, and on Sunday last it went up to 97. But at night I find that I have to have three blankets on my bed, and even then I'm not over-warm. It is a very tricky time of the year, and you will be pleased to know that I am wrapping up well. I haven't got down to my woolly pants yet but they will be back in circulation any time now!! And please tell Auntie Madge that I possess two *woolly vests*.

I can hear the bacon sizzling in the pan, and I can feel the shout of breakfast up trembling on the air any minute now, so I'll end this pot-boiler.

29 October 1952

Now what news have I for you? I had a very successful weekend of golf last weekend. I got through the first round of our little office competition. I drew to play against the man who knocked me out in the first round of a similar competition soon after I got back from leave. This time I got my revenge. On the strength of a recent card or two my handicap has now been reduced to 23, and I therefore feel a golfer at last.

Did I tell you that I had had a letter from a girl who I used to know in the Ministry of Education? She was a temporary Administrative Officer, and her job has only just now come to an end. She was left a small legacy, and very sensibly decided to fulfil a lifetime's ambition by coming out to India and seeing the Himalayas. She arrived last Sunday and I took the afternoon off yesterday to show her some of the sights of Delhi. Then I took her to a cocktail party given by one of my friends, and we were both invited on to the Club for dinner by a man and his wife, who both found they had several mutual acquaintances of this girl in London and Cambridge. The lass has now departed on a tour of India, but is coming back to Delhi later on. I must say I do admire her pluck for setting out on this venture entirely on her own.

4 November 1952

My landlord, Mrs Banerji, invited me to lunch on Sunday to have a real Indian curry. Her husband has just returned from a tour of Canada, and it was the first time that I had met him. There were about twenty high-ranking officers of the Government of India present with their wives, and I thoroughly enjoyed myself, and the curry! It was interesting to see that even these most senior Indians, and particularly the wives, nearly all ate their food with their fingers. And curry is such a messy thing to eat. The only other European there was a Dr White, who I had not met before. He was working with FAO and believe it or not came from Herefordshire.

11 November 1952

I got through the next round of our office golf competition by beating our captain by 10 and 8, which is the biggest beating you can give to anybody at golf. Then the next day I played in a game against bogey, and came fourth out of thirty three entrants, being all square against bogey. On the strength of that my handicap has been reduced again, this time to 21. My great ambition is to get down to 18 before I leave for home. I'm sure I shall find golf much harder in England, as the course out here is very dry at this time of year, and provided you can keep tolerably straight you can get a fair distance even if you are not a very hard hitter. Anyway, I am feeling quite pleased with myself, as you can imagine.

Tonight I am going to have a wild duck dinner. One of the men in the office went shooting last weekend and this is part of the result. I'm looking forward to it immensely, as you get very tired of the meat out here; it is most tasteless. Beef you can only get on the quiet, and then it is usually buffalo, and mutton is more often than not merely goat. So the duck should be a welcome change.

We are now singing hard for Christmas, and as usual I have the odd little bit of solo work to do. We are doing a grand arrangement of a negro spiritual by Hugh S. Roberton and I have to sing the loud soprano bits above the rest of the choir. Much to our interest who should turn up at the practice last night but Roberton's son. He is evidently on some British Council racket. Once more we are going to sing over All India Radio.

17 November 1952

Alas, I am out of our office golf competition. I met a 12 handicap man who went round in a gross 80, and that put paid to my ambitions. I don't think there will be any more competitions now before I come home, so my trophy winning is probably over for a lifetime.

As the office is fairly quiet at the moment I am taking a fortnight's leave as from the day after tomorrow. I shall stay in Delhi and play masses of golf. It may be my only chance for a long time. I shall also break the back of my packing and do the last of my shopping. I am looking forward to it. The weather is so absolutely heavenly at this time of the year, and I have no desire to go anywhere else. The Simla do is looking a bit doubtful at the moment, as there are so many things on in Delhi at Christmas time that I ought to be at. So I may have to postpone that skating until I come home.

A whole crowd of us went to watch two football matches yesterday in one of the big Indian tournaments. The second match was between East Bengalis, who always cause trouble, and the Indian Air Force. After the referee had given one or two decisions against the East Bengalis, some of their supporters started kicking up a shindy and throwing stones at the referee. The referee had to have a message sent out over the loudspeaker that if they didn't behave they would be cleared out by the Police. Things quietened down a bit until the very end, when, to cut a long story short, the referee disallowed a penalty kick because the goalkeeper had moved before the striker had hit the ball. He had failed to score as the goalie had in fact caught the ball and prevented a goal which would have squared the match which the East Bengalis would otherwise have won! The same thing happened again, and again the referee called for a penalty kick. This was too much for the Bengali supporters, who swarmed on to the field and threatened the ref. So scared was he that he reversed his decision. Time followed immediately afterwards and I and my party got out as quickly as we always do to avoid the crush.

I heard this morning that just after we left the row really began, and the police had to conduct a *lathi* charge to prevent serious trouble developing. Can you imagine that in England? Incidentally, a *lathi*, in case you don't know, is a long wooden pole which all the police out here carry. They swing them wildly round their heads if there is trouble, and heaven help your skull if you happen to be in the way. These *lathis* are also very useful in keeping crowds back. The police make a wooden barrier of them and it's surprising what a weight of people can be kept back by a few police this way. I'm sorry now I didn't wait to see the fun.

24 November 1952

This poor letter seems to have been neglected. I'm having a fortnight's leave here in Delhi and enjoying it so much that I just haven't got down to letters. I'm glad I have managed to get this leave as I shall probably have to forfeit nearly a month when I get home, so I might just as well have some of it out here.

Now I come to think of it, I believe I have told you this already! I have been playing a lot of golf in the glorious sunshine, and one morning last week joined a painting group in the Lodi Gardens, which are one of the beauty spots of Delhi, boasting wonderful old tombs and lovely trees. I shall have the chance of going to three more of these groups.

Yesterday I started on some of my farewell entertaining by having a beer party in the garden of the bungalow. Beer parties are pleasant at this time of the year if you are lucky enough to have a garden to have them in. The temperature is such now that provided you have a big tree under which you can place your party, you are all right. It is still too hot at mid-day to stand about in the sun: it is possible if you are moving about on a golf course, but not to stand drinking. I had about thirty people yesterday, and I think they thoroughly enjoyed themselves. They were a real mixture, ranging from some of our junior typists to an Indian millionaire and his wife – golfers I need hardly say, for I certainly shouldn't have met them in any other walk of life. Afterwards about eight of us went on to one of the restaurants in Delhi and had a jolly good meal, and then we went to the final of a football tournament.

I'm afraid that one or two of the men in the party had a little difficulty in seeing only one ball for the first half hour, though the football was so good that they became very sober again in a very short space of time.

Now I am off to return all my borrowed property, such as glasses and trays, from Eastern House, and pop this into the office for the bag tomorrow.

28 November 1952

Well, my leave is fast rushing away but I am enjoying it so much. I have been out on three painting expeditions now, and still have one more before I have to return to work.

The day before yesterday I had a real treat, being shown round Delhi Cloth Mills. These must be the largest mills in India, and are owned and almost completely run by the Ram family – one of whom was the Indian millionaire at my beer party. I must say it was a most fascinating expedition. What struck me most was the complete absence of female labour – such a contrast to our mills at home. Working conditions on the whole were quite good, though the temperature in the weaving sheds was appallingly high, and the humidity even greater. After being in there for about five minutes I was soaked from head to foot. Imagine working an eight hour shift there!

One of the interesting factors – and a very serious one for Britain – is that all the machinery, or very nearly all of it, installed after the beginning of the war, is of Japanese manufacture. As Bharat Ram himself said, they can get this machinery in a few months at half the cost of British machinery, which in any case they have to wait anything from one to two years for! The Jap machines are not as good as the British, but are perfectly adequate for the cheap mass-produced work that these mills go in for.

They are just opening a new weaving shed, and I should think there were at least two hundred new machines installed and every one was Japanese. The mills are also manufacturing their own machines here in Delhi, which is a great innovation. Several have been working for a number of years without any trouble. It is significant that these mills are run without a single European on the staff, and they are going from strength to strength. They now also have sugar and oil mills, to say nothing of Insurance Companies and all sorts of other odd activities. It shows what India is capable of if she only tries.

Joan Falshaw has been down from Simla this week and I have been taking her round a bit. She always stays with the Iraqi Plenipotentiary and his wife, and the other day I was invited round to lunch. It was a strange meal, consisting of mountains of green spaghetti. It had been dyed in a spinach sauce, and was very tasty. But I was very tickled to go and spend a penny in the lavatory attached to Joan's bathroom. I thought how typical it was of the Middle East and its hygiene. It was exactly like the sort of outside lavatory that you have in England, which is never used unless you have a maid or the painters are in. The walls are damp, and the whitewash is peeling and you look at the broken-surfaced floor and think – well, really I must get that seen to one of these days, but in the meantime I suppose I had better wash the worst of the dirt and cobwebs away. *That* was the guest's lavatory, one of the senior members of the Diplomatic Corps.

I have just been this morning to an exhibition of children's art in the famous *Shankar's Weekly* competition. The exhibits are by children ranging from three to fifteen years of age. It makes me hesitate ever to pick up a pen, brush or pencil again. It's interesting to see that the most original and inspired pictures come from children up to the age of about nine or ten. Then as they enter adolescence they lose so much of their spontaneity and become far more self-conscious. Then as they get older again it is only the born artists that survive.

4 December 1952

Well, my leave is over and I have returned into the middle of a lot of trouble. It has been discovered that one of our locally engaged staff working in accounts has been cooking the books, and we are having to do an enormous amount of checking and detective work. So I have been put straight on to it. It's a sordid business. The man is a youngish Anglo-Indian clerk, who has obviously been drinking more than he can afford. He has a harmless little wife who is obviously quite innocent of what has been going on. I hope we don't have to prosecute as there is no doubt that we have him on three charges, and in India would get at least five years imprisonment. We are waiting for London to say what we are to do. I think the answer will be no prosecution, as it would reflect badly on the High Commission's name.

I went to a very amusing party last night given by the Rootes Group, to meet one of their big shots. Despite the fact that I was only one of the three European women present it was a most hilarious do. Indian women are terribly sticky at cocktail parties, and get themselves into a huddle together and won't be broken up by anybody. But their husbands can be very entertaining, and are only too happy to leave their wives to their own devices. Afterwards I went on with two of the men, an English one and an American, to the Gym Club for dinner, and ran slap into Ann Clutterbuck having dinner with one of her boy friends. So we joined forces and a most interesting argument developed between Ann and the American – who is a dear and most Anglicised – about the respective merits of Americans and British in the social sphere. Having lived for six years in Canada and met crowds of Americans, Ann has little love for her contemporaries in those countries. She says she has already made more real friends among the British and Indians here than she ever made all the time she was in the New World. I must say the American took it very well. But it was 11.15 when we finally went into dinner and 1 o'clock before I got home, which is too late for me. I'm getting an awful old stick-in-the-mud. And there was Ann longing to go on to one of the big hotels in Delhi to dance; such is the exuberance of youth. And she probably did for all I know, as I just skipped quietly out of the party and came home when we had had dinner.

After lunch. I have had another morning checking the wickednesses of the lad in accounts, and the situation gets blacker and blacker. If we reveal much more I don't see how we can escape from prosecuting. And the awful thing is that he might well have got away with it if he hadn't been too greedy. What a mercy not to be born with any inclination to thieve.

Lalla Ram has just given me a Christmas card for you which I will pop into an envelope nearer Christmas time. The poor old boy is getting more and more upset at the thought of my leaving. He has got to the stage now when all of a sudden he will say – 'Only four weeks and five days now, miss sahib.' He's as bad as you only the other way round.

And now I must get back to my beastly checking.

10 December 1952

The office is putting on a play next week. This is the one I should have been in, but I went on strike about rehearsals when I am so near to coming home.

Instead I have been commissioned to paint a backcloth of a garden scene. I have never tackled anything like this before and am decidedly apprehensive! However, I have just been having a Session with one of the Army Officers here who has done quite a lot of this sort of thing, and he has promised to help me. So next Sunday afternoon is to be devoted to painting the wretched thing.

In the meantime I have to persuade the Ministry of Works to build the necessary flat. Then I have to get some cotton material, sew it and pin it over the wooden frame; this then has to be painted first with a coating of size and whitening and then we start the real fun. Well, there is nothing like trying something new.

I went to a very interesting Indian cocktail party last night given by a golfing friend and his wife. The husband is the son of a Sikh, called Sir Sober Singh. He is a rare old character, and owns quite half the buildings in New Delhi. I daren't think how immensely wealthy he must be. They live in a most glorious home very near to 6 Albuquerque Road, with solid marble pillars and wonderful marble floors. Never in my life again shall I see such opulence as there is to be seen in India, even today.

I was very amused when in the middle of the party hot soup was served. I thought it was a marvellous idea, and had a cup of it myself. It was very hot, both in temperature and in spiciness. I had a quiet word with the wife later about it and said what a good idea it was at this time of the year when it really is so very cold in the evening, particularly when so many people drink soft drinks and don't therefore get any warmth from alcohol. She was delighted to hear what I said, as there had evidently been a terrific argument between her husband and his father about this blessed soup. The son had said that it just wasn't done – which is true – but the old father had insisted that his guests' comfort was more important than custom, and of course he had prevailed. I find that through my golfing contacts I am often invited to Indian parties where there are few Europeans and almost nobody from the office, and this was no exception, and I always enjoy myself enormously. And as far as Indians were concerned this was a very high-powered party indeed.

You may be interested to hear a little sideline on the question of our office thief. To cut a long story short, my boss tried to get the culprit into the office to give him his notice, but he wouldn't come, being a coward. But his little Anglo-Indian wife did. My boss was so sorry for her that he offered her a hundred rupees for herself so that she could buy a few things for Christmas. She thanked him, but refused to accept, saying that they would manage somehow. I certainly admire her pride and her pluck. But isn't it tragic that a woman like that should have such a rotter of a husband.

12 December 1952

I'm now right in the swing of pre-Christmas activities. The Dramatic club has just put on a very successful play. Last night I went to a dinner and dance given by Lady Nye for her son who is here on leave. I nearly died of sleepiness as I go to bed so early these days, but it was quite an amusing evening. Now we have all sorts of children's and other parties to cope with. A day or so ago I went right into the heart of one of the real bazaar areas of Old Delhi for the first time, to buy children's presents wholesale by the dozen. It was an education, I can tell you!

A week today we have the carol concert and if my tubes allow, I am again to sing the solos. I shall probably croak at an inopportune moment!!

Christmas I am certain to spend on my beloved golf course, which is a joy in this superb weather.

16 December 1952

Just a very quick note to let you know the latest on the car. I have now finally committed myself to selling it in India. Already I have been offered Rs 8,600 for it, which is Rs 300 more than it has cost me to buy it, get it rubberised and pay the import duty. So even if I get no more I have still had a car for year and a half and £20 in my pocket at the end of it. So I am quite convinced that I am doing the right thing. The man who has made me this offer is a real old money-lender who has just bought another newer A40, from one of our UK based staff for Rs 10,700, which is only about £30 less than the price of a new one in Delhi. It is the UK assembly that fetches the price out here. Anyway, will you please get Leslie to start looking for a second-hand car for me. I am prepared to pay up to £400, or even £500 if something very good came along, but I should be quite happy with something much cheaper provided it won't let me down. I really would like something very soon after I get back, as I want to be able to come home just whenever I like. Anyway, that's the latest. It may well be that I shall get Rs 9,000, i.e. £675, before I am finished, though I shall be very happy with my Rs 8,600.

I daren't stop to write any more, as the bag goes in a few minutes and I am writing this in the office. And any moment now I have more potential customers coming to look at the car. I should think I have had about forty enquiries already.

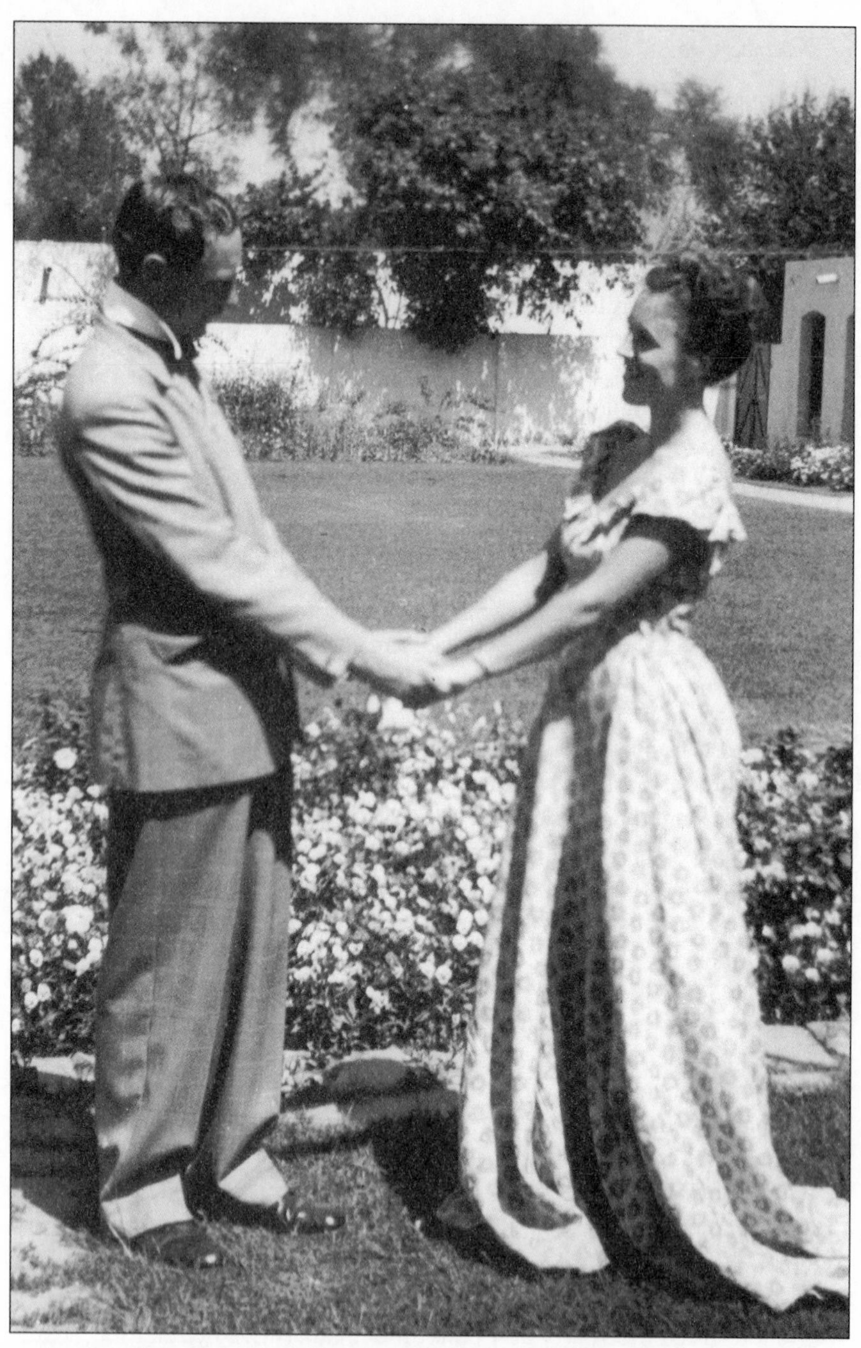

Amateur dramatic rehearsal in the garden of the High Commission, New Delhi.

18 December 1952

I expect the car is the chief item. I am still getting heaps of enquiries, but so far Rs 8,600 is still the best. I gather the old *bunyah* who has made me this offer went and sought out Lalla Ram yesterday, and asked him what the miss sahib thought she would get, and Lalla calmly replied – knowing nothing about it – 'Oh, about 10,000 rupees.' I nearly had a fit as you can imagine.

Yesterday I went out and bought myself a really large tin trunk to take all my heavy stuff. You remember the one I bought at home: admittedly it was a very superior creature, but it cost me £13 10*s*.0*d*. This tin trunk, which is quite three times the size, was only 33*s*. It isn't nearly as well finished off, but is perfectly adequate. In the same shop I bought a lovely pair of fur-backed gloves for Leslie. I won't tell you the price but make you guess when I bring them home. If I can find two smaller pairs would you and Dora like some – not to buy, but as part of your Christmas present? There aren't many things which are cheaper here than in England but a few things really are incredibly inexpensive.

At lunch time today I have been giving my numdas a rub over with soap and ammonia to cheer them up a bit. They have lasted remarkably well and are not showing very much sign of wear. Tomorrow I must get down to packing in earnest as my heavy stuff has to be crated and ready for removal before Christmas.

And that's all again this time. Once more a very happy Christmas to you all. Who knows, next year I may be spending it with you.

24 December 1952

If the news has not already reached you you will be delighted to hear that I have got £652 10*s*.0*d*. for my car, and am being allowed to keep it right up to the time of my departure. That means I have had a car for a year and a half nearly, and £30 in my pocket at the end of it. I got another hundred rupees above the last sum I told you I had been offered. I might have got a bit more if I had hung on, but I didn't think it was worth it for the sake of a few rupees, and I wanted to get the whole business off my chest. I have now had a letter from Noey confirming that he thinks, just as I do, that purchase tax will be reduced, so I am more pleased than ever that I decided to sell.

Christmas preparations are at a height at the moment. Parties galore, and not an awful lot of work being done in the office in the last few hours. There is always a terrific office party at 4 p.m. on Christmas Eve by tradition, which tends to be a bad beginning to the Christmas festivities. As I have to go on to two parties afterwards I shall be very abstemious! Tomorrow, Christmas Day, is devoted almost entirely to golf. In the evening though, a party of us will be quietly around the radio listening to the Queen, and as usual I shall be picturing you all doing the same.

29 December 1952

What frightful floods you must have had. Let's hope you are getting all this weather out of the way before I come home and that it will subsequently improve. We had an earthquake the other night which wakened a lot of people up but I slept soundly through it. At least I think I did. I remember the door of my French window swinging open; and I wondered vaguely if a burglar was about to descend upon me, but I can't have worried much about it because I was asleep again in a second.

And now I must tell you about Christmas. It was a very quiet day as I had expected. I had a grand game of golf in the morning, and then met a number of my pals in the bar of the Gym Club where we drank everyone's health. I'm afraid we didn't go into lunch very early and none of us felt like golf again. So we all went home and slept it off, and then we met again in the evening to listen to the round-the-world programme and the Queen's speech. The first part of it came through very well, but the last part had to contend with an awful lot of atmospherics. I pictured you all sitting round the wireless at 3 p.m. It was 8.30, of course, with us.

31 December 1952

I have been shopping and now have your sheets. In the end I got two pairs of blue, two of green and two of yellow. The green ones looked so pretty that I couldn't resist them. I have also to my great delight managed to run one of those rosewood elephants from the south to earth. It is only a little one, but it is the genuine article and really is very sweet. I went into the Cottage Industries shop to try to find something for the DeThiers, and suddenly spotted the elephant. I had never thought of looking there before. I was thrilled as I did so want to bring you the one thing for which you had asked. I hope you will like him.

The night before last was the High Commissioner's big do for the staff. I must say it went down extraordinarily well. The Clutterbucks have the art of making everyone feel really at home – quite different from the Nyes – and Ann was marvellous as MC. She is a tremendous asset to her parents in running such a do.

Tonight I am going with three of my friends down to Maiden's Hotel to bring in the New Year. The Club, where we usually go, will be far too crowded, so we are breaking our habit and going where it will not be quite such a riot. Then tomorrow my boss is giving a buffet party for me. It will not be a rowdy evening – just silly games round the fire and lots to eat!

On making enquiries from people who have sailed into Tilbury, it would obviously be madness for you to come to Tilbury. There is nowhere for anybody to wait and it is sometimes three or four hours before luggage is cleared and the boat train moves off. So please be a good girl and not attempt to go there but wait at Chepstow Villas. I should be so much happier to think that you were not hanging around in the cold.

I definitely start work on Monday 2 February, so if you agree, I think the timing of my week at home should be about three days in London to unpack and generally get settled in, and then off home on say the 27th, and back to London on the 1st. On the other hand, if you feel you can spare time to have a nice long spell in London, we could stay and I could curb my enthusiasm to see the rest of the family for a fortnight and come back with you to Hereford one weekend, returning on the Sunday. Anyway, whatever you say will go with me.

I think that that is all the news for the moment. My next letter will probably be written from the boat. I arrive in Bombay on the night of Leslie's birthday – no, the morning, and have a full day and night there, and we embark early on the morning of the 7th. We should be in Aden on about the 11th and Port Said on about the 14th or 15th. I do hope the weather is kind and that we don't have to contend with another cyclone. I should hate to arrive at Tilbury as I arrived at Bombay on my way out.

1953

Bombay

6 January 1953

This is just a wee note to let you know that the first stage of my journey is successfully completed. After a great whirl of activity on my last day, which was a Sunday, and which included golf, a beer party, a lunch party, the remnants of my packing and final drinks with the Macintoshes, I eventually got away intact yesterday morning. Of course I ended up with very much more luggage than I ever thought I would have. So many people asked me to take 'just a small parcel for me' and my 'small parcels' soon mount up! Anyway, I have finally emerged with one enormous tin box, three cabin trunks, three beer crates (not full of beer), three suitcases, two little hand grips, a set of golf clubs and lastly a typewriter, for which there was no room anywhere and which therefore is carted religiously in one hand with my handbag in the other. The one great advantage of the lack of space for the typewriter is that you are getting a letter, which otherwise I'm sure I should never had had the energy to write.

Joan Falshaw and I managed to get an air-conditioned coupé together in the train to Bombay, which was very pleasant. It is a twenty-six hour journey, and can be very tedious, but I spent it with my nose in the book written by my old English mistress at King Edwards, Anne Treneer, and with twelve of the twenty-six hours spent in my bunk the time passed well enough. I was met by somebody from the office in Bombay and brought to this hotel, which is pleasant. From my verandah I can crane my neck round and see the sea.

I went into the office this morning to pay my respects, and then went on to look up Ginger Dunn, who used to be manager of Lloyds Bank in New Delhi and is now in Bombay. You may remember his name. Anyway, Ginger seemed very pleased to see me, offered me his car and driver for the rest of the day and invited me out to dinner. So I've had the car all day, or at least all afternoon, and I have spent a lovely few hours sitting in the sun in a sunsuit at the European Bathing place at Breach Candy. Bombay is 20 degrees warmer than Delhi at the moment and suits me admirably. I'm making the most of my last few days of heat and sunshine. Now I am back in the hotel, and filling in the time until Ginger appears.

We embark at 11 a.m. tomorrow and sail at 2. I hope to goodness that I'm not going to be seasick. I don't want to waste any meals when so soon I shall be cooking them and washing them up myself.

The car finally went on Saturday morning and I was very heartbroken to see her go. But my nice fat bank balance is some consolation, I suppose.

My next letter to you will be from Aden, though it is quite possible that you will get my Port Said one first. The post from Aden is always rather irregular.

Our meeting on the 24th creeps nearer. Hurrah. I do hope you decide to come up to London in the car. And if you do, do be brave and bring it to Notting Hill Gate. You won't have to face any of the real London traffic to get there, and it would be so very useful to us for the return journey. Mrs Lummas says there are one or two places where you can park a car not far from Chepstow Villas. Anyway, you will very rightly be guided by the weather. I only hope it will be kind to us.

And now for a bath. I haven't had one since I left Delhi and I dread to think what the water will be like after the very dirty journey of eight hundred miles.

Please give Leslie my very best birthday wishes. I didn't forget him, but somehow in all the flurry of packing I didn't get down to writing in time. Tell him I'll make up for it when I get home.

Stratheden Arabian Sea

10 January 1953

This is our third day at sea and I am feeling on top of the world. The ship is only half full, which in many ways is an advantage – lots of deck space and good service and not too many people to have to be polite to. Apart from a sudden and unexpected shower of rain as I was getting up this morning the weather has been at its most blessed – glorious sunshine, but not too hot – just perfect for lying out on deck and turning a golden hue in comfort. To know you have nothing you must do, and to watch the ship cleaving the blue sea, with sun above and breeze around you – life indeed has much to offer!

The passengers are a somewhat mixed bag – mostly Australian. There are the usual number of potential wolves who give me delightful practice in being rude nicely, but there are one or two oases in the desert of passengers – my particular buddies being an aged American who is wandering around the world, and a wild young Irish boy with green eyes. They both keep me entertained in their respective ways. Of Joan Falshaw I see almost nothing, as she sits indoors playing bridge, and daren't expose her very fair skin to the blistering sea sun.

I have been dragged of course into certain of the deck games. By a series of miracles I am now in the semi-final of the ladies' singles deck quoits – a dignified and leisurely game which does not tax my limited sea strength! I am also still battling in the table tennis. I don't expect to win either. Australian women go all out for these sports and these on board are not known to pick up a book.

So far we have had the usual variety of evening entertainments. Dancing, tombola and films. Tomorrow we arrive in Aden at 10 a.m. It will be the first time that I have arrived in Aden at a respectable hour. Before it has always been in the middle of the night. I shall go ashore and see what bargains I can pick up. If all goes well we hope to have about five hours there.

I was called to the Purser's office today to be informed that they had been instructed by cable to pay me five pounds. I can but imagine that it is that naughty Noey. Do you remember he sent me money on my last trip out, bless his generous heart? I was so very thrilled by the thought.

According to the schedule we are due to arrive at Tilbury at 10 a.m. on Saturday the 24th. With luck therefore I ought to be at Notting Hill Gate by early afternoon. But that will depend on the English weather. If a fog is produced heaven knows when I shall arrive.

And now I must away to my few chores. It is strange to be washing and ironing again after all this long time, but there is no bearer to wait on me any longer and I am breaking myself in gently again.

So for the moment God bless you all. I'm getting on for two thousand miles nearer home and it won't be long.

14 January 1953

Another stage of our journey is nearly completed as we approach Suez. Aden was great fun. Of all improbable things it rained there – really poured so that we had to take shelter. I was moderately abstemious in my buying, though it is a horribly fascinating shopping centre. For two days after Aden the weather was at its best – gloriously sunny without being too hot. I only hope my sunburn will last until I get home.

The night before last was fancy dress night, and the Irish boy and I went as Gin and It. You never saw such a couple of awful old topers. Paddy wore my old brick suit – you know, Mother, the one I bought for John Collins' wedding. It is still in very good repair and he really looked almost too smart in it. With that beige hat with the feather, my black boned bra (stuffed) and a pair of my nylon stockings with the feet cut out he looked a dream! It was the first time that the passengers really let their hair down. So far they have been extremely stodgy, but they certainly came to life that night.

I am now in the final of the women's deck quoits and I am off to play it in a few minutes. The woman I am playing is about six months pregnant, but that doesn't seem to have detracted from her skill. Then I am still in the table tennis. But we are not hurrying with it as we can play it off when the weather is impossible for deck sports.

This morning it is definitely cooler and the chill of the northern hemisphere is beginning to creep into my bones. How I hate the thought. We have been told to have all our mail ready for Suez, as there are evidently some restrictions on mail at Port Said. So I am rushing to get this done before I ascend to the decks, as the post box closes at noon.

And now I must thank you for your letter, Mother, which was duly awaiting me at Aden. I was thrilled to get it as Aden is a problematic port for post. Letters seem to take such a long time to get there. And it was clever of you to find out all the addresses at the various ports of call. I have been thinking an awful lot about the car business. It is very good of Leslie and Raymond to go to so much trouble. On the whole I think I ought to say no to the Ford. It is a car which I should love to have, but with petrol so expensive I think I ought to look seriously for an eight horse power one, if such things are available. And I think too I ought to settle down a bit and see just how much it is going to cost to live, and what garage space is available and how much it will be before making a final decision. However, if the car is not sold before I get home, perhaps I could discuss it then with you all. If the man on the other hand wants a decision right away then I think you had better turn it down.

Off Marseilles

18 January 1953

Since Port Said we have had such a thrilling journey. There was great excitement soon after we had sailed from Port Said. Evidently the Egyptian authorities had refused permission for a family of father, mother and two children to land. Why was not divulged. Anyway, after we had sailed they had evidently changed their minds, and radioed to one of their pilot ships which was ahead of us. As we approached it, it signalled to us to stop, but at first the captain wasn't having any. At last we were hailed over a megaphone, when the captain was asked to 'Please stop your machinery!' So we stopped our machinery, and after much parleying, all the family and twenty-two pieces of luggage were lowered by rope into a tiny craft and transferred to the pilot ship. My steward says that no other P & O captain would have stopped, and even ours was livid and said that he had never had such a request made of him before.

He is a grand captain altogether. He will always go out of his way to get as near to the shore as possible so that the passengers can see all there is to see. Two days ago we came under the formidable shadow of Crete as the evening wore on, and he took us right in to see the tiny harbour where our troops had been evacuated during the war. And we could see the desolate track over the mountains where they had had to march to reach the coast. Crete is incredibly desolate. Apart from the little town and harbour there was no sign of life on the coast, and inland were high mountains covered in snow. Last night we had an even better sight. In the middle of the afternoon we could see the toe of Italy appearing on our starboard side, and Sicily on our port side. On Sicily Etna was sending out great belches of smoke that soared right up and joined the clouds, and immediately behind Etna the sun went down in a positive furnace of fire, so that the smoke was black against it with a lining of scarlet. It was one of those sights which are never to be forgotten. We also passed Stromboli later on, but alas I was in a cinema show and missed it. I could have kicked myself afterwards. The coast of Italy looked like a fairy land, with thousands of lights shining, not only on the coast but right up into the mountains. The Italians must light their roads in these southern mountains, for we were able to follow the line of the roads for miles and miles by the string of fairy lights. Before I die I must go back to the south of Italy: it looks a land of inexhaustible enchantment.

Today again we have had a feast for our eyes when passing through the Straits of Bonafacia, with Corsica on our north and Sardinia on our south. Again the captain hugged the coast as close as he dared, and we were treated to a near view of the most fantastic little town I have ever clapped eyes on. It looked like a painted backcloth to a dream play. I can't begin to describe it to you. The little houses seemed to grow out of the golden-coloured rock on which they had been built, for they are golden themselves and their roofs are gold and red and brown. And somehow they are all crooked and look as if they have been struggling with each other to get up to the light. We all stood spellbound as we went by. Prosaically I took a snap of them but I am sure it will never do them justice.

We reach Marseilles tomorrow at break of day and have about six hours there. I am looking forward to some gentle shopping, but must keep a tight hold on myself, knowing how attractive and how expensive French goods are!

I can't remember if I told you that I lost the final of the deck quoits, but succeeded in winning the table tennis. Everybody was delighted with the latter success as I managed to defeat a most unpopular member of the table tennis playing set. She was out to win in no uncertain terms, and she damn nearly did so. Each of the three games went to 20 all. The first she won, and in the second she was leading 20-17 – but I managed to equalise and that so shook her that I proceeded to win that game and the next. So I shall have a pound to spend in the ship's shop.

That was the last letter to my mother at the end of my Indian experience. I came to love India and the Indians, and am deeply grateful to the fates that allowed me the privilege of getting to know a little of that remarkable country. I only wish that my letters reflected more of the fascination that it held for me nearly fifty years ago. I have never been back.

Interlude

New Zealand
1954-1956

Interlude

New Zealand

I returned to London in early 1953 and worked for a year in Downing Street organising placements for young people from the Commonwealth under the Colombo Plan. Then I was given six weeks' notice of a posting to New Zealand as a Second Secretary. I bought a new car and got it quickly on a ship, but I had to fly. It took a week in 1954. The best bit was the last – by flying boat from Sydney to Auckland. There I picked up the car and drove down to Wellington.

However humble one's position in the diplomatic service it is not easy to be single; one needs a wife or a househusband. I had neither, but I got permission for my mother to join me as my hostess. At sixty-seven she ventured alone halfway round the world and felt that she was living at last. When I collected her in Auckland after a six week's journey she was wearing lipstick for the first time in her life. She had been practising on the boat. Because she was with me there are of course no letters from New Zealand.

At that time New Zealand was not the most stimulating post for a Second Secretary. But I was fortunate in having an enlightened High Commissioner in Sir Geoffrey Scoones, who did not believe in letting his staff sit too long on their bottoms in Wellington. So I was despatched around the country, and by the time I left after two years I had given fifty talks to a wide range of captive audiences, sometimes to a small group of women, at the most daunting to some three or four hundred celebrating some anniversary. It was a splendid way to get to know the country and the people.

I must tell you my two favourite New Zealand anecdotes, both of which I think illustrate strong characteristics of New Zealanders in those days – superficial properness and the most generous hospitality.

Let me take the first. The occasion was the opening of the annual Wellington Art Exhibition. Everyone of note was there, clad in full evening dress with medals, long white gloves, tails and tiaras. Sir Charles Madden, head of the New Zealand Navy, had been invited to open the exhibition. He surveyed this formal gathering with, I suspect, some dismay, but he launched into his prepared speech with bravado.

'My Lords, Ladies and gentlemen. It is so kind of you to invite me here today particularly as, like my father, I know nothing at all about art. Years ago my father found himself in the same pen at Buckingham Palace as the artist Sir Wilson Steer. Neither had ever heard of the other, nor did either know why the other was being decorated. Then when Sir Wilson revealed that he was an artist my father politely enquired what he looked for in the landscape when he went painting. 'Shelter from the wind and proximity to a lavatory.'

A deadly silence followed, lasting seconds, and nobody wanted to be the one to break it. Then somebody could contain himself no longer, and the audience forgot that they were meant to behave impeccably, and burst into an ecstasy of laughter and clapping. The evening was made.

My other story is one of typical New Zealand hospitality. Late in the afternoon on one of my talking tours Mother and I thought that we had better start looking for beds for the night. In the fifties there were very few hotels outside the main towns, and rural pubs rarely offered accommodation. I tried three in succession without success. At the third a man accosted me.

'You want a bed for the night, don't you? I have been following you from pub to pub.'

Mildly dismayed, I admitted that I did.

'It's all right,' he continued, 'I've got my wife with me.'

'And I've got my mother.'

'So follow us and we'll put you both up for the night.'

He would not accept our diffident protests, and we were pretty desperate anyway, so off we set.

When we arrived at their modest bungalow some miles away I remembered that I had an unopened bottle of whisky in the car boot; I always carried one in case of emergency. This seemed a good occasion to produce it, so I put it on the kitchen table round which we all sat. Mother did not drink, and I think that I may have had a couple of pegs, but they drank the rest. At about 11 o'clock when the bottle was empty they suddenly realised that we had had no supper. They were too drunk to prepare any, but despite our protests that it didn't matter, they staggered next door and got their neighbour out of bed. In her dressing gown she cooked us the most delicious bacon and eggs. What a splendid neighbour!

We duly went to bed and wondered what state our kind hosts would be in next morning. We should have had more faith in New Zealanders' capacity to carry it. Tea in bed and a good breakfast to follow, and we were sent on our way. We never saw them again, but we remember them with gratitude and delight.

I have just remembered another incident that touched me deeply. I had given a talk to a large gathering in Palmerston North on Royal Commonwealth Day. For some reason I was very nervous beforehand, which is not always a bad thing. As it happened it was one of my better efforts, and a warm and uninhibited audience shouted for more whenever I stopped. They kept me at it for well over an hour. The organisers, Fred and Muriel Stuart, were so pleased with the success of the evening that when Mother and I went to the car the next morning we found it filled with flowers from their nursery. And by filled I mean filled. There were dozens of blooms, from the floor to the roof and in the boot. I could not see out of my rear window.

Muriel and I wrote to each other every Christmas until her death in the early nineties. In 1996 Roger and I visited Fred in Palmerston North. He had had a stroke and was very frail, but he just remembered me.

Mother and I left New Zealand in 1956. I had saved up some leave and we returned via the Pacific, America, Canada and the Atlantic. I went back to work in the CRO, and there I stayed for four long years in the Central Africa Department. By 1957 I had lived for fourteen years in other people's premises. I was thirty-six and wanted something of my own. I bought a minute terrace house in slummy Balham and spent the next three years trying to master do-it-yourself skills. When building a brick wall to replace a privet hedge a man stopped and said, 'I haf not seen zee woman lay zee bricks since I left Russia.' I was hugely flattered!

As I laboured in London I began to think that I had blotted my overseas copybook, when at last came my third posting – that of First Secretary in the High Commission in Salisbury, Southern Rhodesia. The African letters that follow will explain what happened to me in the next three years.

Africa
1960-1963

1960

Winchester Castle

18 June 1960

Dearest Ma

We reach Madeira tomorrow afternoon, Sunday, so I had better get a letter to you started. (I've already written four letters and four cards – not bad for me!)

Well love, thank you a thousand times again for all your valiant help during the last few weeks. I could never have battled without you. And apart from that it was such fun just to have you with me – as indeed it always is. Thursday afternoon seems ages away already. We ran out of the sun into thick mist about an hour out of Southampton. From then on right throughout the evening and night and early morning the ship's whistle (fog-horn for the landlubber!) went every sixty seconds. What with that and the rheumaticky creaks of this thirty year old old lady, sleep was fitful, tired though I was.

There are only ninety first class passengers, and over two hundred tourists (including five Archers – must go and look them up). The ship is just like a rather dignified Bournemouth hotel in the off season. There are a few people younger than I, but not many. That attractive girl has never appeared again, and I can't identify any of the nondescript men. The plump girl is *not* pregnant, just plump.

The dining saloon is half empty, and I was put at the Chief Engineer's table for the first two meals, with that odd woman with the bright red hair, who turns out to be a character and nice in small doses, an Austrian by birth; a teacher who has lived all his life in South Africa after being expelled by the Nazis; and a charming Dr Hemming of London University who is something to do with the teaching of English. All rather fun in their way.

Then I was whisked off to sit at the Captain's table, beside the Commissioner in Ottawa and Ambassador for South Africa in the USA and his wife, and a charming South African couple who have just been on their first trip to Europe. The Ambassador, du Plessis, and his wife are very charming, and we find from our different elevations that we have many acquaintances in common, from Archie Nye downwards.

Apart from a warm spell of sunshine yesterday afternoon the weather has continued to be calm but grey, with more mist, and we are several hours behind schedule. I crawl from one deep easy chair to another and wherever I sit I fall asleep. It is wonderful.

Last night there was a film show, and tonight we are invited to cocktails with the Captain. We lose half the passengers at Madeira and then we shall be quieter and stuffier than ever. It could not suit me better. I won't close this letter before Madeira but that is my news up-to-date.

Sunday 19 June 1960

Not very much news. The cocktail party went off happily, followed by that dreary game Tombola and a bit of a dance. I got into conversation with a delightful man from Cape Town, who knows Ian and Vaudine Grey very well. Small world indeed. [Ian was Trade Commissioner when we were in New Zealand.]

The weather is grey again today, but a little bit warmer. We are steaming flat out at 19 knots, with not a hope of catching up our hours lost in the fog. But aged though she is (she has only one more voyage after this one) I have never known a ship so steady or so free from vibration. Knowledgeable people love her the best of the Union Castle Line ships.

Next epistle from Cape Town. (I gather our mail gets put on the *Pretoria Castle* at Madeira tomorrow.) Multitudinous thanks again and all my love to you all.

Margaret

P.S. We are very honoured. We have Sir Julian Huxley plus wife aboard.

Winchester Castle

27 June 1960

Only three days to go now to Cape Town, so I must get started with my ship's letter to you.

I find it almost impossible to remember how much I knew about my fellow passengers when I wrote my Madeira letter, and how much I have discovered since. Suffice to say that it has been a splendid voyage in every way. But to go back to Madeira. Arrival there was rather like Port Said or Aden – scores of bum boats with local wares, and little boys to dive for coins. We went ashore on a small launch as there is no proper harbour for the anchorage of big ships. Five of us hired a huge car and were taken for a drive round. I have sent the children some cards of the island, so you should be able to get a fair idea of what some of it looks like from them. I have seldom seen such magnificent flowering shrubs. It is obviously a gardener's paradise with its moist climate and perpetual warm sunshine. The temperature reminded me strongly of Honolulu. The women do the most beautiful cut-away work – table cloths and blouses and mats and so forth. I bought a lovely set of dinner mats for £2, though my conscience told me it was wicked to accept so much fine work for so little remuneration. Then I bought the most fascinating straw hat for 5*s*.6*d*. It has a high crown and it is absolutely up to the minute in fashion.

I have brought my usual bad weather with me to this ship. We have had fairly steady seas, but nothing like the expected amount of heat and sunshine. And in the Doldrums, where glassy blue seas are always found at this time of the year, it was positively cool and choppy. But at least I have been able to keep my pinks alive over the Equator. They are on my dressing table in front of me now as I type.

I may have said that we were to drop over half our First Class passengers at Madeira. The ship has indeed been blissfully empty since; and what few of us have remained are without exception devotees of the Quiet Life. Miraculously there is not a single hearty one among us to destroy the atmosphere of leisurely calm. That is not to say that we haven't taken our quota of middle-aged exercise from time to time. We have even had some organised deck sports, but as a couple of rounds put one in the final, this did not involve huge amounts of labour. I have succeeded in winning the table-tennis and deck quoits (ladies) and the shuffle-board and deck tennis mixed doubles, so I hope to have a large amount of money to spend in the ship's shop. What is more I have taken part in the Crossing the Line ceremony, and now have my third certificate, but the only one I have really earned. It was evidently not easy to get enough volunteers, so the Captain asked me if I would be prepared to be a victim. How could I refuse? In the end a young boy and I were the only representatives of the First Class, and the other eight came from the Tourists. The Captain very sensibly held a briefing meeting beforehand as he has firm views about unnecessary hooliganism! This meant that the whole thing was perfectly planned and we knew exactly what to expect. All I got was a real egg broken and rubbed into my hair, together with an evil concoction of sugar and egg gaudied up with coch (heavens, haven't the faintest idea how you spell it – try again!) that pink stuff, and fluffed up into a rich cream, which was also smeared over various parts of my anatomy. Then I, like all the others in turn, was tipped back in the special ducking chair so that I fell head over heels into the bath. There one is received by three of Neptune's minions, and duly ducked when at last one comes up for breath. But as we were warned about the ducking too, we knew to take a quick breath as soon as we broke the surface. A friend tried to take a picture on my camera, but he was feeling pretty seasick at the time and he wasn't sure that he had been successful.

Now to the personalities on board. Dear Dr Hemming is undoubtedly my favourite. He looks exactly as I imagine Puck should look, and he has the appropriate sense of humour. I have discovered that he and his wife live bang next door to the Deweys at Teddington. Isn't it an odd coincidence? Of course I get completely out of my depth in the intellectual arguments in which he tries gently to lead me, but I get my own back by beating him at deck quoits.

Through James Hemming I have got on to chatting terms with Sir Julian and Lady Huxley, though I don't mind admitting that they both frighten me to death. They are absolutely sweet with one another and cause us all a great deal of happy amusement, but when it comes to conversation I am quite lost. They gave a cocktail party last night before dinner for a select number of passengers, including Professor Catlin and his wife, Vera Brittain, and to my astonishment I was invited too. Unfortunately I never got into the same part of the party as Vera Brittain, but from a distance I am quite fascinated by her. She and her husband bicker in public, and I can't reconcile myself to the fact that she is who she is.

And that I think is about the end of my news for the moment. There is not much more to do before the end of the voyage – one more film and one dinner dance to which we are inviting some of the tourists. This is the only ship I have been on where the Captain positively encourages comings and goings between the two classes. He is an absolute darling, being charming and friendly with everyone without losing a scrap of his dignity. He is obviously terribly concerned to know what is to happen to him when the *Winchester Castle* is withdrawn after the next voyage. I sense that there are tensions between the various captains of the fleet with the new ship about to be introduced.

We passed the *Pendennis Castle* going in the other direction. Our Captain was livid as he said he had to chase the *Pendennis* all over the ocean to ensure that we saw her. He feels strongly that passengers should always have the opportunity of seeing another ship of the fleet as this is such an unfrequented sea lane, and it is therefore the done thing for two captains to make every effort to meet in mid-ocean. The Captain of the *Pendennis* simply wasn't playing ball, and I suspect that our Captain thinks that the other one thinks the old *Winchester* beneath his dignity. Anyway, we had quite a game of hide and seek, and in the end our Captain more or less had to turn right into the path of the other ship in order that we could get anywhere near. As a result we and they did some erratic swoopings, and very improperly passed on the starboard side instead of the port.

I don't imagine that I shall have a moment to drop you a line once I have started on my drive up through Africa. So the next communication you get from me should be the cable to say that I am in one piece. I am simply dying for news and am hoping madly that there will be a long letter from you in Cape Town.

2 July 1960

Postcard from Beaufort West

My first port of call and a very comfortable one too. I didn't get away from Cape Town until 1.30 with nearly three hundred miles to do before dark at about 6 p.m.

I flew in with the last flicker of light at 6.15 p.m., fearfully pleased with self and car. Am I glad to have a real engine in this vast, empty country. Cruising at 80 is positively restful!

Pretoria

4 July 1960

Probably by the time you receive this you will have had a telegram announcing my arrival at Salisbury. But just in case the air mails work properly, this is to let you know beforehand that I am at least safely in Pretoria, and staying very comfortably with my colleague, Eleanor Emery.

I have now driven about a thousand miles and nothing could have been simpler. The National Road is quite splendid and so safe. Most of the time you can see miles ahead; and as the side roads are few and unsealed anyway, you always know from the dust raised if a car is likely to appear.

The car is a continuing source of delight. I have had it greased and the oil changed, and the ignition adjusted to take account of the altitude at which I am now driving, and it is bursting with enthusiasm.

Eleanor gave a small drinks and supper party for me this evening and guess who were there? Freddie (in the office in NZ) and Jane Rump! Jane is exactly the same – still wearing startling and rather tasty clothes and masses of makeup. They both enquired after you and sent you their love. They very much hope that you will come out here and that they will see you somehow *en route*.

You will be glad to know that I have a passenger from now on – a young man who was on the ship. I bumped into him at a filling station the second morning of my travels, being given a lift as far as Pretoria by another couple on the ship. I offered to transport him for the second leg. Selfishly I would rather be alone, but he is a nice cheerful, brawny, freckly young thing and should be pleasant company.

Salisbury

8 July 1960

These are positively the first words I am writing in my new office, and as I am unlikely to have more than five minutes peace before the cares of three years descend on me, I'm making the most of them.

Well, here I am at last. The journey from Cape Town really was chicken-feed. It is the easiest thing to average 60 m.p.h. and there is no fatigue in it. It is far less exhausting driving three hundred miles here than fifty in England. The car behaved superbly throughout, and is a source of admiration and interest wherever I go. I am thrilled with it.

My passenger from Pretoria proved to be a pleasant lad – born in India, parents came out to Rhodesia ten years ago. He took a degree in the Union, and has just had a year at Cambridge preparing for the Colonial Overseas Service.

I loved Louis Trichard, the first stop after Pretoria. The Mountain Inn was really in the mountains, and it was biting cold. Bulawayo was pleasant enough, and my passenger, John, took me round some of his friends (his family lived there before going to Salisbury).

I arrived at the office at 2.30 p.m. yesterday, and spent the next hour reading my mail – absolutely masses of it, which was great fun. Bill and Irene McIndoe are putting me up. They have a wonderful house with swimming-pool, tennis court and the lot! I was whisked home for tea, bath and a change, then out to the first cocktail party, followed by a quiet dinner given by my hosts just for me, and the Deputy High Commissioner and his wife, Godfrey and Monica Bass. I seem to be booked up for all sorts of things for the next few days – far too hectic, but then I expected it.

I have just had the usual visit from the press – chatty women's column stuff, plus photograph. I dread the result, but will send on to you if not too ghastly.

This afternoon I am being lugged round the house agents. Getting a suitable house is not going to be easy, but I shall just hope to be lucky. I'm dying to unpack and get settled in.

The office is a very new building and extremely pleasant. I have a bright office with a good view over Salisbury. Unfortunately it faces south and therefore doesn't get the sun, but that will undoubtedly be an advantage when it is hot. At the moment it is suit weather, with sunshine and quite chilly evenings. It has been very cold and miserable for some time, but is bucking up a bit now.

The McIndoes are having Richard Sinnett* and his wife to dinner on Monday, but I shall probably see Richard before then in the office.

Shall try and write again within the next week to let you know further first impressions.

17 July 1960

I am still waiting to hear that you have heard that I am safely in Salisbury. Your last letter, for which many thanks, was posted on the very day that I was due here. I am hoping there will be another letter from you in the office tomorrow.

At this moment I am basking in blessed sunshine, winter though it be, sitting on the McIndoes' lawn. This is the first really good day since I arrived. Everyone here has been complaining that this has been the worst winter that they can remember. Certainly there has been a lot of cloud around, and it has been cold at night. Huge log fires and hot water bottles are essential.

Well now, I hardly know where to start. I think I had survived my first day when I last wrote. The very next day I suddenly went down with the Salisbury bug of the moment, variously gastric flu and winter vomiting. My heavens, was I sick. Six solid hours of it, working up to a crescendo of about every ten minutes. But as suddenly as I was ill I was better again, and after a day of fasting and being shaky at the knees I was completely recovered. Which was as well, for as you can imagine the office has been in a state of chaos ever since the Congo business broke. Last Monday and Tuesday were supposed to be public holidays, but not many people got much of a holiday out of it. The High Commissioner and the Deputy and Bill McIndoe were all got out of bed every night to deal with some message or other, and virtually all work has been thrust aside to deal with the multitudinous problems that the Congo has thrust up. I am still far too new here to be of very much use, but I get dragged in on the side lines of it all. It is quite hugely absorbing but oh, so dreadfully depressing.

I have just come back from lunch with the High Commissioner and his wife. At the lunch were the Belgian Consul-General, who has had a terrible time, and two refugees from the Congo – both Englishmen who worked with Unilever in the Congo. They parted from their wives and children some days ago. Their families were making for Léopoldville and England, and they for the Federation. They have not yet heard anything about their families, and

*Richard Sinnett's father and mine went through the First World War together and kept in touch until my father's death in 1949. His mother and I met for the first time in many years, a week or two before my departure for Africa. Imagine our astonishment when I was told that Richard had been posted to the High Commissioner in Salisbury as Assistant Military Adviser! We arrived within a fortnight of each other. How about that for a coincidence?

are themselves going back into the Congo tomorrow. Unilevers stand to lose £40 million if the Congo finally goes up in smoke.

I have already been out to a number of parties. The High Commissioner gave a big reception for me on Friday night, and the DHC is giving another one for me next Tuesday. Everyone here is extremely friendly, and I am sure when I get to know them all I shall enjoy myself. But at the moment I am in the awful throes of battling with countless new names and faces. Various bits have appeared in the press, none very exciting, and I haven't bothered to take any cuttings yet, but will if I can find the papers again. I have also given a four minute broadcast, which I heard played back to me but not when it went out over the air. The man who interviewed me was gracious enough to say that it was a delight to find somebody who didn't shut up like a clam as soon as the microphone was thrust in front of them!

Alas, I still have nowhere to live. I have been to see several houses, but for one reason or another they have not been just the right thing. One I have seen is absolute heaven, but won't be available until next November. But at the price the office are prepared to pay I shall get something pretty good – there are some superb houses here – and I shall have not the slightest hesitation in persuading you to come out. Meanwhile the McIndoes couldn't be kinder to me and I am very happy staying with them.

I have just seen my first other Alpine in Salisbury – in fact in Africa – and am furious. But we waved very amiably to one another!

I'm very thrilled with the colour transparencies that have turned up so far. I hope the rest are as good. I may not have told you that I had my camera and light meter stolen on the ship. I shall get the insurance money I hope, but I am still seething with rage. This won't come under the SUN but the office insurance. I bought another cheap camera in South Africa and am waiting to see what the results from it are like. But I was so used to my old camera and am very sad about it.

I won't start another page. This is very interim, but I promise better fare when we return to more normal conditions.

24 July 1960

Well now, where do I start? Things happen so quickly and so often here that I can't remember from one letter to another where I have got to. I imagine that you have heard about our riots in Salisbury and got all sorts of queer ideas. Needless to say, or perhaps needful to say, the whole thing was very localised, and apart from not getting our evening paper one evening, we were quite unaffected. But it made a lot of extra work in the office coming bang on top of the Congo.

I continue to be whisked off to a lot of parties. What with the bits in the press and my broadcast I find that most people know about me, which is rather alarming. But I'm beginning to master quantities of names, and everyone is most friendly.

And at last I have a house – only for three months and I don't move in until 22nd August – but at least it will give me time to look around and find somewhere more permanent. And the people are leaving all their china and glass and pots and pans so I won't have to unpack and pack up again.

The house is quite new (eighteen months old) but is built in an old nursery and therefore has well-established trees. And 2,500 rose trees! House was inherited with the nursery, but the present owners have put many more in, and sell roses as a profitable side-line. They will arrange for the garden to be looked after while I am away, so I shan't have the worry or the expense. And I inherit their gorgeous Airedale dog, Peter, who has a voice like a lion. The owners were reluctantly going to put him in kennels, but when I said I should love to have him they were delighted.

The house is smallish by Salisbury standards, but quite big enough for me – not my taste in furniture, but quite bearable. Meanwhile, Bill and Irene are nobly keeping me in their house. They are the easiest people to live with and treat me completely as one of the family. Their children are three and eight months and are characters in their own way.

I have already met several MPs. They are a comic lot but one or two are interesting and intelligent! Of course, as I may have said before, everyone talks politics morning, noon and night. This is inevitable, as nobody knows what will happen in Africa in the next few years, except that it won't stay static!

I must say all my friends seem to have come up trumps with letters. I have had a mountain of mail since I arrived, which is wonderful, but takes a lot of keeping up with. A long letter from Gwen Hunt, sending her love to you, and lots from colleagues congratulating me on my promotion. Then I have had a series of press cuttings of the speeches made at the Durban Educational Conference by my fellow passengers in the *Winchester Castle*. My dear Dr Hemming undertook to keep me posted, and stuck to his word. He also informed me that the Huxleys had declared to him that they had liked me (!!), and that Vera Brittain had actually quoted me by name in one of the lectures as an example of woman emancipated. How about that for a good one?!

I really must stop and go to bed. We have all been gardening like mad this afternoon and I am quite weary.

After two days of real heat we have shrunk back into bitter winter. When the sun shines it is warm, but when it doesn't it is b— cold. I am sitting almost on top of a log fire and am still frozen on the other side.

25 July 1960

Nearly forgot to tell you. Seretse Khama and wife Ruth came to lunch last week on their way back to Bechuanaland. Both charming.

Bag just closing.

31 July 1960

It has just dawned on me that I never sent you a copy of this photograph, taken at the dinner dance that we had with the tourists. From left to right: half hidden, Lady Huxley; near camera the S.A. Ambassador; the Captain; near camera, wife of business man sitting next to me; hand to ear, Marie du Plessis, wife of S.A. Ambassador; far right, dear Sir Julian Huxley.

There doesn't seem to be a lot to report from here at the moment. All our local troubles have quietened down; but wherever one goes everyone talks about the future and what will happen in it. The Southern Rhodesian Europeans have clearly been completely shattered by this trouble in their midst, and an awful lot of heart-searching and rethinking is going on. It is an odd contrast with England to find that wherever you go, be it dance or cocktail party or tennis party or simply friends in for a chat – the one topic of conversation is politics. My head is a jumbled mass of it! I continue to be asked out a lot. Bill and Irene and I went on Friday night to a dance given in quite a small house. The floors here are beautiful – all wood block – so you just shove out the furniture and there you have your dance. They were an interesting crowd of people, including one of the MPs who lost his seat when Todd did. We got home at 3 a.m.

Rootes here have really done me proud. They knew all about my car troubles before I arrived, and indeed had the various spare parts including a new dashboard. They admitted disarmingly that they had never fitted a new dashboard before, but they have in fact done it perfectly. They had the car a day and a half, and in that time also gave it a big service and changed my number plates. So we are all friends again!

Now I must go back to helping Irene with the gardening. Their garden boy is a bit of a dope so all moderately intelligent jobs have to be done by someone other than him. But it is bliss not to have any other chore to do. I am getting thoroughly spoilt.

10 August 1960

Time for letter-writing is at the moment virtually non-existent. This is simply to let you know that I am very much flourishing and not to worry if you don't have a long screed. Your last magnificently long letter demands a magnificently long answer, and you will get it – soon!

The main item of news is that I go up to Lusaka on Monday to pay my introductory visit. This means making nice noises to the Governor and officials of the Territorial Government. I spend the night with the Chief Secretary – and his wife! – and come back again on Tuesday. It should be fun.

Please thank all the family for their cards and say I will thank them properly as soon as I can. But this is my programme.

Tonight	–	Cocktails given by the McIndoes.
Tomorrow	–	Cocktails with Americans
Friday	–	Cocktails – Air Adviser
		Dinner party somewhere else
Saturday	–	Dinner party
Sunday	–	Mid-day drinks and racing meeting
Monday	–	7 a.m. to Lusaka
Tuesday	–	Back
		Dinner party in evening
Wednesday	–	Dinner party
Thursday	–	NOTHING – so far!
Friday	–	Reception at High Commissioner's!!

And may the Lord have mercy on my soul – and stomach.

21 August 1960

I am afraid I have been a long time in fulfilling my promise to write you a long letter. I hope anyway that my last letter to the family will have brought you moderately up-to-date.

Since I wrote to the family I'm trying to think what I have been up to. Life has been a tiny bit quieter and I did get my one free evening in on Thursday. We had a fine party at the High Commissioner's on Friday. Fourteen men who are on a course at Imperial Defence College are touring Africa as part of the course. Most of the men are senior serving officers, but about half a dozen are civil servants from one country or another. To my delight I discovered that I knew two of them. One is in the Ministry of Education and I hadn't seen him for twelve years. The other was in the Canadian High Commission in Delhi.

Anyway, the HC gave a cocktail party for them and we all went along. It was one of the best I have been to. Our Information Officer, whose cook I am taking over, invited me and the Canadian home to dinner afterwards so that I could meet the cook. I brought the Canadian back to Salisbury afterwards and we ended up at Salisbury's very-nearly-one-and-only gay night spot dancing. I had a lucky break after I had dropped him back at his hotel. When I got home I found I was minus my evening bag. I hadn't any money in it but I had my cosmetics and cigarette lighter etc. I realised what had happened. Paul had put his coat in the back of my car and I had flung my bag in the back as I always do. As he pulled out his coat he must have taken out my bag also. Thank heavens it was so late. I rang up the hotel the minute I got home and found myself without it, and asked if they would go and look on the road outside the hotel. They found it. Imagine dropping your bag in one of the main streets of any other capital city, and finding it there twenty minutes later!

I am typing this in the McIndoes' garden. The wind keeps on blowing the paper over so that the hammers hit the back of it, but it is too lovely to be indoors. It is just about getting to the stage where it is too hot to sit in the sun in the middle of the day, but we are still jolly glad to put the fire on at night. As soon as the sun goes down it is quite chilly, and you feel it all the more when you have had the warmth of the day. In about another hour I shall be on my way to my new house. The people leave for Europe at midnight, so I am going along before they go to take over. My cook, the one I mention above, and whose name is Sixpence, joins me tomorrow.

I fear we are not likely to have much peace in the weeks to come. For your private ear we are about to have a descent from our new Secretary of State, and as far as we can gather he is a perfect B—. I can well imagine that we shall be on our toes and no nonsense. Then soon after he vanishes again I return to Northern Rhodesia, this time to see something of the Copperbelt. I have had an invitation from the Provincial Commissioner there to go and see the sights. This all came about as I mentioned to the Governor that I hoped I should be able to see the Copperbelt one day soon. Much to his credit he did something about it immediately, which I thought good of him.

Now I think I must go and do the last of my packing. My next letter will no doubt be full of the terrors of housekeeping in Africa. I must say I rather dread the responsibility after six weeks of having absolutely everything done for me. I don't remember being so free of chores ever, except for my time in India. I must say I am all for servants!

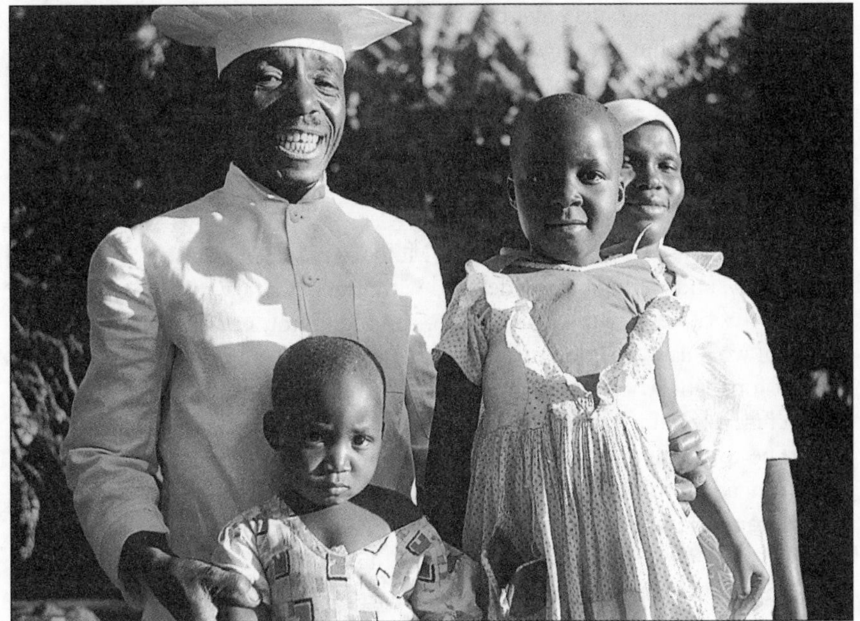

Sixpence with his family.

28 August 1960

I am safely installed in my house and really rather enjoying it. Sixpence is doing me proud, though African servants aren't anything like as self-reliant as Indian ones.

I have to do every bit of the shopping, not only for myself but also for him. This takes a bit of doing when you are busy, with the shops shutting at 5 p.m. and 12 on Saturday. (We are supposed to work only every other Saturday, but what with crises and the DHC being on leave I have only had one Saturday off so far). But he is a thumping good cook and washes and irons very well. In fact I am thoroughly spoilt for £6 15*s*.0*d* a month and his keep.

The roses are beginning to bloom and in another two or three weeks will be a terrific sight. This is my first full Sunday at home and I'm sitting on the stoop (veranda to you) sipping a gin and tonic while Sixpence is sweating away cooking me a chicken. He is a pastmaster at bread sauce, which endears him to me enormously. It is just getting to the stage where it is too hot to sit in the midday sun, though still we are having fires at night and three blankets on the bed.

Of course we are all in a tizzy about the imminent descent upon us of our new boss. I am OC his tour as far as our office is concerned, and already the headaches are legion. But as you can imagine, there is never a dull moment, and emergency telegrams have been whipping madly backwards and forwards. It hasn't helped that the news leaked in London before we were ready.

Won't stop to prattle any more at the moment. Gosh, that chicken smells good!!

12 September 1960

My news is almost entirely of work. Bill McIndoe has been away for ten days and is still away, and we have been deluged with crises, what with Stonehouse, the Secretary of State arriving, the Congo, the Monckton report arriving, and all the usual work as well. I don't think there have been more than two evenings in the last fortnight when I have not been rung up out of office hours about some emergency telegram. The best effort was when I was dragged out of bed at 3.45 am. to be told that the S of S was stranded in Accra after an airport man had had his head cut off by a propeller. I couldn't go back to bed, as there were so many arrangements to think about and make. And I had to give my first talk in Salisbury that very day to the Rotary Club. The previous few days had been so appallingly busy that I hadn't had a minute to think what I was going to say. Perhaps it was as well that I was dug out of bed so early, for it gave me the chance to collect my scattered wits. Thank heaven the talk went off well.

Saturday was pretty awful too. In at 8 a.m. The High Commissioner had to fly off to Bulawayo to meet the S of S, and the Deputy had to go and open some show. So I was left in charge. Telegrams poured in from all over the place, and the cypher clerk and I finally left the office at 7.30 p.m. Then I had to wait for a long distance call to come through from Wankie game reserve where the S of S had gone to start his tour. I had messages to give him and several to receive from him. His Private Secretary and I and Sir Henry Lintott and I spoke for half an hour on the most appalling line. We had to say everything about five times over before we could make ourselves understood. Then I had to ring up Zomba and Lusaka to pass on messages from Sandys to them! What a way to spend a Saturday.

Today is supposed to be a public holiday, but again I am in for the whole day. Sandys is supposed to have arrived in Salisbury an hour ago, but no news has come through yet. We are expecting him to have a pile of work for us. While I am waiting for this to descend, I thought I would get this started. At that very point the telephone rang and it was Godfrey Bass, the DHC, to say that the great man has actually arrived but was an hour late; and there is hell to pay all round, as Welensky and Whitehead were kept waiting a whole hour, and the Governor General had lunch for him and all the party, and because they were late they had all had it on the plane. I fear this whole trip has been bedevilled, and I dread to think what more can happen in the long fortnight that we have Sandys in our midst.

But apart from all this I am flourishing. In fact I seem to thrive on the chaos. It is infinitely more fun being a First Secretary than a Second, I can assure you! The weather is still quite cool, in fact I have taken my top off the car and almost regret it as it is mighty chilly at night. I still have three blankets and am not always warm enough at that. But I have braved the elements twice and had swims in private swimming pools – the first was at the High Commissioner's last Sunday, and the second yesterday at the home of the Clerk of the Southern Rhodesia Parliament. No house worthy of its name here is without its swimming pool.

Got stopped there yesterday. Haven't had second to read through.

18 September 1960

Life doesn't get very much easier for letter-writing, but I have an odd half hour this Sunday morning before I have to go out so I will at least try to get a letter started to you. An added complication is that I have a visitor at the moment – a colleague from the Colonial Office who is doing a month's tour of the Federation, most of it in the two northern territories. Bill and Irene put him up when he first came to Salisbury and I am coping with him now. He arrived on Friday morning and leaves again tomorrow morning. Luckily he is at this moment trying to catch up on all his bread and butter letters for the hospitality given to him in Northern Rhodesia, so I have taken the chance to write to you.

First of all, thank you for your letter of 7 September. No, I hadn't got in touch with the Pagets, simply looked them up in the telephone book. As soon as we get rid of the Secretary of State – not our 'bob' but our 'boss'!, I shall hope to have a minute to do something about the Pagets and the Campbells. Incidentally I have discovered that Evan Campbell is one of the most prominent farmers in the country!

You ask about the Sinnetts. There seems to be so much to tell you and so little time for the telling that I can't remember what I have said and what I have forgotten. No, I haven't seen much of them, but Ann has been in the last stages of pregnancy, and had a daughter about a fortnight ago. They invited me to dinner some weeks ago but I have not yet had them back. Richard is a dear and the spit image of John. Ann is incredibly young and wide-eyed!

You ask where the office is. It is in Baker Avenue, between Fourth and Third Streets, on the south side. It is a very new building and has a lovely little garden with a fountain at the front. I have taken one or two transparencies of it. I will certainly try to get a transparency of the house as well, but the sun is never really right to get the best picture of it. I have been trying for several days to get a good one, but decided to wait until the roses at the front are a bit further out.

I haven't a lot of news this week except for work. The S of S has been up in Northern Rhodesia and we have been bombarded with telephone calls and telegrams about the rest of his programme in Nyasaland and Salisbury. He is an incredibly fussy niggly-piggly man, and is forever changing his mind and being difficult. We have him in Salisbury from tomorrow morning until Thursday or Friday, and I can tell you we are not looking forward to it. Please don't expect any more letters until after he has gone! As far as the evenings were concerned last week was a great improvement – I think I had three clear nights. I gave a little dinner party for Ken Neale – the man who is staying with me – on Friday night, the first time I had tested old Sixpence out. It went off quite well. He cooks chicken and all the trimmings superbly, so I think I shall stick to that until I have to start the second round of having the same people for the second time.

No, I never have heard why you didn't hear about my arrival. I must have another word with the Chief Clerk. We have all been so busy that he may not have got round to making enquiries. But I will find out eventually.

Ken and I are just off to see the University college – at 10 a.m. Although it is a Sunday it was the only time that it could be fitted in. I must get out of my shorts and into something a bit more civilised.

Salisbury Airport

26 September 1960

It is a silly business having to be at an airport three quarters of an hour before a plane leaves. But at least it gives me a chance to write this, having missed the bag.

Well now to my news. Last week was *quite* frantic. I had Sandys' two private secretaries – one male one female – in my office and it was absolute *chaos*. Sandys himself is the most difficult man, but simply oozes charm when you meet him – even I melted, after all I had thought about him beforehand. He had a terribly exacting time here, but sailed through it splendidly. I went to his press conference on his last day, and was most impressed by the way he handled it. He was gracious enough anyway to thank me for all I had done over arranging his programme and apologised for being such a nuisance! Our next major excitement will be the publication of the Monckton Report – quite an anticlimax after all the speculation.

My two days in the Copperbelt are likely to be tremendously interesting. I'm going to Ndola and Kitwe, and if you want to look on the map I'm visiting a mine among other things and also speaking to a Rotary lunch. I come back on Wednesday evening so I shall only have two nights out of Salisbury. But it will be a welcome break.

Must dash now and spend a penny before I am called. Hope you are all looking forward to the winter as we approach the summer. We had a ten-minute shower on Saturday – the first rain I have seen since I arrived! *Wildly* exciting.

2 October 1960

It seems to be ages since I sat down and tried to write you a civilised letter. My private mail is in a constant state of chaos. Letters pour in from all parts of the world and I find them in handbags, shopping bags, in drawers and tucked away in corners, wherever I have put them on arrival. Every now and again I have a grand clearing-up, but I never seem to have time to get on top of them. However, today, Sunday, I'm having one of my few civilised clerking sessions. Bill and Irene McIndoe have gone away for a long weekend and I am back in my old bedroom in their house, keeping an eye on the children. This doesn't amount to very much as they have a good African nanny, but they felt they wanted somebody responsible on the spot just in case. It was as well. Earlier on today, Neil, aged ten months, was in his pram on the tennis court and he succeeded in tipping it up and hurling himself out onto the court. Nanny was far away from his cries coping with the other child. Luckily I heard the hullabaloo and rushed to the rescue. He was more frightened than hurt. Grace, the idiot, hadn't strapped him in, and he is at the very active stage. Thank heaven no harm seems to have been done.

Well now – I always seem to be saying that to you! I have about five letters of yours which I don't feel I have ever answered properly. I propose to read through them one by one and answer the bits that I haven't answered in earlier unsatisfactory scribbles to you. Ages ago you asked where servants lived and what they ate. They live in one-room quarters in an inconspicuous part of the garden, lit by candles or oil lamps. All very dreary I think, but the accepted practice. You supply them with rations – mealie meal, from which they make a sort of unleavened bread, meat, which they cook in a singularly unappetising way, jam, sugar and tea. You also supply them with uniforms. As you will gather, they are much less independent than Indian servants. I think I am particularly lucky with Sixpence, as he is one of the older type of servant, and very respectful and reliable. Thank heaven I don't have to lock up my grog as most people do. He never drinks.

Whatever you may say about not coming out here, I am still optimistic. I'm sure you wouldn't be lonely. Wherever I land up eventually, I hope to get home most days for lunch, and we usually leave the office at about 4.30. The residential areas here are quite lovely and life is really very civilised. I don't think the climate would be at all trying for you. The only major snag is that you get so sleepy so early if you aren't going out anywhere. I may have told you this before, but I can't help laughing at myself the way I toddle off to bed very happily at 9.30 if I haven't got to go out. Anyway, we shall see as soon as I have a permanent home. I'm determined not to be put off!

My visit to the Copperbelt was exceedingly hectic but enormously interesting. I stayed with the Senior Provincial Commissioner and his wife at Ndola, and spent one whole day in Ndola and the other in Kitwe. I was whisked off to the mining areas, but didn't actually have time to go down a mine. I saw a lot of African housing and welfare, hostels and schools and the like. It is an enormously prosperous part of the world. In fact the whole Federation virtually runs on Northern Rhodesian copper. But they are all desperately worried up there about the future, and I was subjected to one long ear-bashing from Colonial officials, mining magnates, ordinary citizens and heaven knows who. Their great proximity to the Congo doesn't do much to reassure them. I had tea in one simply gorgeous house belonging to one of the members of the Northern Rhodesian Legislative Assembly. The drawing room had a splendid view across open country and very near was a long line of hills – the Congo – only four miles away. It certainly makes you think when you can see that troubled territory so near that you can almost spit on it. It was blazingly hot in the Copperbelt and I was quite glad to get back to the cool of Salisbury. I was very tired at the end of it. It is quite hard work meeting a lot of people in a short time, though the only bit of official work I had to do was to give a talk to the local Rotary Club.

9 October 1960

For once in my life I am actually addressing a letter to you without owing you one. Chalk it up – it may never happen again! It is Sunday morning and Sixpence is busy upstairs making my bed and cleaning the bathroom and I am just about to embark on one of my very necessary clerking sessions.

Now to my news since last week. Most entertaining without doubt was dinner with Sir Roy Welensky. The High Commissioner was giving a small dinner party for Sir R. to meet Sir John Maud (of old M of E fame) and Lady Maud who were up from the Union for a couple of days. At the last minute Lady Welensky fell sick, so Rupert asked me if I would fill in as Lady W. There were just the six of us and it was absolutely fascinating. Needless to say, the two Sirs did most of the talking, for that was the point of the dinner. The timing couldn't have been more strategic. The results of the Referendum on the Republic had just come through, and J.M. was busy sounding out W. on what he thought the repercussions would be here. Also, as you may have gathered from press speculation, we have been having quite a to-do with W. over the Monckton Report, and just before the dinner Rupert had had a final session with the PM, and though unsatisfactory, at least there was an end of the argument. W. was therefore in a particularly relaxed and communicative mood. He is the gentlest and most charming man to meet socially, and despite his South African upbringing has a remarkably pleasant and quiet voice. He was regaling us with stories of how he walked the streets of Salisbury as a boy, bare-foot and hungry. He had some pretty caustic things to say about the British public and its emotional attitude of 'the Blacks are always right' and 'the Whites always wrong', but he tempers his outbursts with a merry twinkle of the eye.

As you probably know, he is a non-smoker and teetotaller, and much leg-pulling went on when Dorrie Metcalf by mistake gave him a Scotch and ginger ale, instead of a lime juice and ginger ale (his queer but favourite tipple!). He did not allow her to forget it.

I am feeling pretty depressed about the news of the shootings in Harare last night. I was having dinner with the Secretary for External Affairs and his wife when the news came through. Coming just before the publication of the Monckton Report, I fear there may be very unfortunate repercussions. It certainly isn't going to make any easier the mountainous task of trying to keep the Federation together.

I am going out to have a drink before lunch with a couple who represent the Tanganyika Government here. He is an ex-Colonel. They have just returned from two months' leave in the UK. I very nearly took on their house while they were away, but decided against it as it was so large. They left their two dogs and the house in the charge of their very reliable cookboy. The day before they got back, the house was discovered burgled, £400 of stuff missing, one dog dead and the other vanished. They think that the cook had been quietly taking things away during the two months, and when he heard that his master was coming back, staged a robbery. Needless to say, they are terribly sorry that I didn't take the house, as they are quite sure this would never have happened. I'm thankful I didn't take the house!! Am I thankful that Sixpence has a blameless record of years of service of Europeans.

I don't think there is much more news at the moment. We are still woefully busy in the office. Yesterday, Saturday, I finished my labours at 3.30 p.m. after an abortive attempt to track down some advance copies of our famous report, that were supposed to be on a plane from London and weren't. Heigh-ho. I long sometimes for the peace and quiet of slummy old Balham.

Talking of slums, tomorrow should decide whether or not I shall move into that perfectly enchanting house I saw soon after coming to Salisbury: I may have told you about it at the time. It was not to be vacant until the end of November. I thought I had better go back and have a second and sober look at it in the light of my experiences of the last three months. I am pretty sure I shall take it, if only the rent is within the limits set for me. If I do, nothing will stop me luring you out, as it is as far removed from a slum as anywhere I am likely to stay in my life, and has a huge garden – three acres I think. It will take a bit of keeping up, but I am quite prepared for that. Of course if the rent is sky high then I shall have to think again. But I am dying now to have something settled, as my lease here only has another six weeks to go, and time rushes by at such an alarming rate that I shall find myself out on the street if I don't look a bit slippy.

25 October 1960

You ask about Fyffe Robertson. No, I haven't met him though I have seen him. I did meet and have a long talk with John Roberts whom he interviewed in Lusaka. Roberts is the head of the UFP up there – Welensky's party – and quite a firebrand. I am sure that you know much more of what is going on from television than we do on the spot. But it is interesting to know that there is so much about Central Africa going out over the air at home.

We have just had the welcome break of a holiday weekend. I think I may have said that I hoped we should get this holiday, having missed the other two. Well, we did. We worked until pretty late on Saturday, but after that we were free. On Sunday I had people in for drinks before lunch, and in the afternoon went with some friends to some cross country riding trials. My goodness, was the course tough. The sort of point-to-point meetings in Herefordshire are absolute child's play in comparison. Then yesterday I went out for the day with Bill and Irene. There is not a lot to see round Salisbury, but we went on a 150 mile tour around, including Sinoia where there are some truly remarkable caves. Oddly enough on the way we were passed by a VW, the driver of which I was certain was the young man John Lawley whom I gave a lift to from Pretoria. He was travelling too fast for us; but later we caught him up when he stopped to give his dog a little run. It was John sure enough, so we had a grand pow-pow in the middle of the wilds. He had left Northern Rhodesia at midday on Saturday to come to visit his parents, and was on his way back again early on Monday morning. The round trip would be 1,000 miles. I rang up his parents tonight to tell them that I had met him again – and again in the wilds – and I have invited them to dinner next week.

With Sir Roy and Lady Welensky, Lady Dalhousie and Dr Bastos, Belgian diplomat.

We got back fairly early in the afternoon, with plenty of time for a shower and a rest before going off to the big reception of the year, given by Sir R. W. and Lady W. in honour of Federation Day. (This time I didn't have to deputise!) It was held at the RRAF Officers' Mess, which is a good fifteen miles away from where I live – rather a long way to go for a party, but one gets used to these long distances in Salisbury, which is so widespread. You ask about the weather. Well, it really is getting mighty hot now. It was stifling at the reception last night, though thank heaven everyone gradually drifted out into the gardens where there was a band playing. Oddly enough, I find the heat much more difficult to take here than I did in Delhi, where it was some 20 degrees hotter. After being out in the sun quite a bit on Sunday and Monday, by the time I got to the reception I had the world's most frightful headache, and all through the night my head kept on waking me up. It wasn't until halfway through today, with the aid of much aspirin, that it gradually returned to normal.

You ask what the temperatures are. The days are about 90 degrees in the shade, but the nights still get cool enough to want one blanket – I suppose the temperature goes down to the mid sixties. Certainly we have said goodbye to fires for a good long spell. Yes, we are in cotton frocks, though it is quite comfortable to wear silk or nylon at night, provided you aren't in too stuffy or over-crowded a room.

I had to lie to have this evening at home. The High Commissioner – sorry, name Rupert Metcalf, wife Dorrie – asked me just before we left if I would fill in at dinner as the wife of one of the guests had had to cry off. This was going to be my only evening at home this week, and I was determined to tackle some of my letters, which continue to be a frantic nightmare to me. I was also still feeling the after-effects of that shocking headache, so I wickedly said that I was already engaged. May I be forgiven! I spent all this afternoon in the Federal Assembly, listening to the opening speeches on the Monckton Report debate. I heard Welensky and the leader of the opposition, Winston Field. It was all pretty depressing. It was a wonderful opportunity for Welensky to make a really statesmanlike oration, but he just isn't a great enough man for it. A pity, for we all now believe that the Federation is doomed, hard though we shall work to try to keep it alive.

My trip to Nyasaland has been put off for a week or two, as it was going to coincide exactly with the return of the Governor after a long home leave, when everyone will be rushing around in circles. But there is so much going on in the office that I don't mind – any time away is a bit of a nuisance.

Now I must stagger off to bed before sleep overtakes me.

I have decided to take that lovely house if the owner will have me. He is overseas and doesn't return until the end of the month. Keep your fingers crossed for me.

Salisbury

I have come back early from lunch to write to you, and find myself locked out of my temporary office (my office furniture has at last arrived from London and is being installed) and away from my pen, hence pencil scratch. I seem to have got woefully behind again with my letters – I owe you two, but life doesn't get any easier.

Nothing of overwhelming excitement to report, except the continuing repercussions from Monckton and our latest lot of troubles in Salisbury. One of our locally-engaged girls has a husband who works in one of the townships. His car was completely burnt out and he had to dodge some stoning. Not a very pleasant experience.

I don't seem to have done anything dramatic since I last wrote. Work and more work, but not quite so many evening activities. I have been indulging in a few early nights, trying to get over my awful sleepiness.

We had two terrific thunderstorms with heavenly rain last weekend, and it has never really got hot again since – in fact the weather is just about perfect, though this is reportedly 'suicide month'. I had to put the soft-top of my car up in order to take my quite uncontrollable Airedale miles into the country to be stripped (I had to tie him down in the back, but feared he might get free and leap out if I had no lid on!) and with rain in the air I have just left it up. I really am having a battle with the dog. He is free all day and running round the fields (I am very countrified and I have cows within a hundred yards of me) and he comes back covered in ticks. Trying to keep him still while I de-tick him is some job. I shall be thankful to hand him safely back to his owners.

Monday is a public holiday and I am hoping desperately that we shall get it (the last two we have had to work). But I doubt if I shall bother to go away. It would be pleasant to have a rest.

Must go back to work now. Sorry this is such a wretched little note. Bag goes shortly.

30 October 1960

Apart from a lovely one and a half hour kip this afternoon I have spent the whole of the day at my private correspondence. I now have ten sealed envelopes to my credit and I am feeling bursting with virtue. Admittedly there is the odd bill paid and the odd thank you for an invitation thrown in, but the bulk of them are just long overdue letters to patient correspondents. The tips of my fingers are feeling quite tender as a result. But before they give up altogether I mustn't let the day go by without adding you to the list – the most important one of all. I have done a fair amount of lying this weekend in order to get some time to myself.

I had two invitations to dinner tonight and I knew I should be too tired to go out last night, as I had to give my postponed talk to the Business and Professional Women at lunchtime yesterday, on the United Nations. You will remember how I always used to be stupidly tired after speechifying. Well, the lunch went off very well and the Secretary asked me and four other women back to her house afterwards for tea to continue the discussion. They were very sweet, and one or two of them most interesting and entertaining – nearly all about my age. But I was jolly glad when I got back to sink into a bath and get into a dressing gown and go to bed at 9 p.m. Today I was quite determined that nothing should keep me from my letters, hence the lies.

Now, please don't worry about me. I'm quite sure everything sounds much worse from your papers than it is in reality. I can assure you that there is nothing to worry about. There is no doubt about it that it is a very unsettled time here, and heaven knows what the outcome will be, but I am miles from the African Townships and nothing could be more civilized. If I sounded a bit depressed in my last letter but one, just put it down to overwork and the heat. We all get like that at times, and then we perk up again. And you needn't worry about the tiredness.

If I haven't explained before I will now. It is undoubtedly the altitude. All good Rhodesians are in bed by nine o'clock at the latest if they have not got to go out. You see, life begins very early here – we are in the office by 8 a.m. and there is no doubt about it, the height does make you very drowsy. Some people never get acclimatized and are just reconciled to spending much more time in bed than they would at a lower level.

I have a not too bad week ahead of me next week. On Wednesday I am summoned to Government House to have dinner with the Governor General and Lady Dalhousie. As Bill McIndoe has never been to anything other than a reception there, I suspect that once more I am being used to fill in! If so I wonder who the odd man will be! Thank goodness I bought myself a short white evening dress to take up to Northern Rhodesia, so I shall be able to wear that. Otherwise I haven't anything suitable in my rather meagre wardrobe. I only hope I won't get invited again, as I shouldn't dare to turn up in it twice. Then on Friday I give a small dinner party – the mother and father of the lad I gave a lift to from Pretoria, the Clerk of the Southern Rhodesia Assembly and his wife and one odd man – haven't decided yet who – there are several to choose from, none very exciting! Must make up my mind tonight and do a spot of telephoning.

7 November 1960

Since I last wrote have dined with the Dalhousies and won five bob off Lady D. at bridge, and lunched with Sir John and Lady Kennedy (ex-Governor of Southern Rhodesia and chairman of the recent Indaba) and A.E.P. Robinson (HC Designate for the Federation in London, and a Monckton Commissioner). I'm going up in the world!

Painfully busy, but full of beans.

11 November 1960

This seems to be a worse spell than usual for the letter-writing front. We are in the throes of appraising the Monckton Report, which means an immense amount of reading of debates, and a lot of talk, and I am reduced to bringing work home whenever I don't have to go out. This is Sunday morning, and I have just done a four hour stint, and will have to press on this afternoon. But I thought I would take a few minutes off to write to you as a pleasant change.

Don't be too sorry for me. It is all intensely interesting, and quieter times I am sure are round the corner – at least I hope so.

The other awful thing hanging over my head is the talk I have to give next Friday to the Rhodesia National Affairs Association. I don't know whether I told you about this. I should have given it a month ago but it was put off to make way for Sir Charles Cumings, the instigator of the famous Indaba. Now I can't escape and I am terrified. Previous speakers at this forum have included Lord Home and Macmillan, so you can imagine the depths of my anguish. I have to speak on Women in Diplomacy, and there isn't an awful lot to say, so I am reduced to reading a lot about famous women of the past who have been diplomats in fact if not in name – and there is so little time for reading and digestion!

But quickly to my bits of news. I don't think I told you much about that dinner at Government House. It started off with rather nerve-racking preliminaries. As I was about to think of a leisurely bath and lots of time for hair and face the phone rang, and it was a visiting professor from Jamaica, whom we had been looking after for a bit, inviting himself to a drink. I could not say no, particularly as he is the most fascinating and intelligent of creatures, but I warned him I would have to chuck him out pretty speedily. He looks *quite* odd and is indeed of Portuguese extraction – immensely fat, huge grey beard, and the most beguiling Irish-sounding voice. He bowled up in short shorts, out of which his large belly bulged alarmingly! I finally got rid of him at 7.20 p.m. and I was due at Government House at 8, four miles away. Talk about a mad scamper. I tore out of the house with just enough time to get there, and suddenly discovered as I flew down the main road that one of my long gloves had flown away. (One of the hazards of having the roof off.) I had to take the instant decision of whether to risk being late by trying to find the glove, or being on time with only one glove. I decided on the first, did an alarming U turn in busy traffic, tore back up the road, and miraculously in the dark – no street lights – saw my glove floating in the air and dancing with each passing car. On with the brakes – up the road to retrieve, mercifully quite clean – another U-turn and off. I arrived not the last and with my two gloves firmly up and over my elbows!

It was an unexpectedly delightful evening. I sat on His Excellency Lord Dalhousie's left and had a rip-roaring and frivolous conversation with him. We got on to animals and after dinner he asked me if I would like to see his pet wild pig. So we all picked up our long skirts and tripped out across the garden to an enclosure where friend pig was – a dear little thing that His Excellency had found in the bush while hunting and had brought home for fun. We all admired it and scratched it behind the ears, and trooped off back to the grand drawing room – not, I hope, smelling too much of our unexpected introduction to the animal world. I then got into a bridge four with Lady Dalhousie, who is an absolute pet, and had the greatest glee in winning five bob off her! I hadn't played since New Zealand, and had the greatest difficulty in remembering the drill; but I needn't have worried for Lady D. was considerably worse than me.

Last Sunday I was once more summoned to fill in at Sunday lunch with the Metcalfs. They had Sir John and Lady Kennedy – he is an ex-Governor of Southern Rhodesia and came to chair the Indaba, and A.E.P. Robinson, HC elect for the Federation in London when Rennie goes next year, and also one of the Monckton Commissioners. As you know, the Commissioners have all agreed not to comment on the Report, but as this was a private gathering he was able to let his hair down. It was fascinating, and I understood for the first time just why they signed the Report with the controversial secession clause in it.

We had torrential rain on Friday, and several showers since, so we are obviously at the beginning of the rainy season. Although it is a bit humid it is certainly less oppressive than it was, and the grass has started to grow already. In my new garden I hope to manage with only one garden boy. It may mean having to buy a motor mower, but that would be cheaper and less of a worry than another boy. Can't wait now to get in, but am not quite sure what the date will be. Just at the very time when I think I should be moving I shall be in Nyasaland – what a life! I go up on 28th and return on 30th. It is purely an official trip and is not leave.

Must go now and cook some lunch. Sixpence has Sunday off when he has made the bed and cleaned the house and cooked breakfast and brought me a mid-morning cup of tea. Servants are wonderful, but it is good to have the house to oneself.

12 November 1960

Bag goes in a few minutes. Still very busy, but hope worst will soon be over.

Many thanks for letter of 27th received this morning. Christmas parcels arrived last week!! Amused about Lord Reith. You may remember he would have been my uncle-in-law if I had married dear David!

I move into my new house on Saturday. Hurrah!

Here is a cutting about my talk – very badly reported, but thank heaven it went down well. Had to speak for 35 minutes – without notes. Chairman kindly remarked it was the only time he had never seen anybody asleep. Had on nicest shoes and stockings and smartest rig. It all helps!

28 November 1960

Maddest weekend moving. I have left complete chaos behind, but can't tell you how thrilled I am with my new abode, particularly the garden. I should have spent yesterday putting the things I had unpacked (all my crates are empty now) away but I could not keep out of the garden. The lawns (they are numerous and enormous) hadn't been cut for three months and we have had a lot of rain recently. The mowing machine had been out of order and was only returned the evening I moved in, Saturday.

I have inherited a very good garden boy who has been with the house for years, but he can't possibly cope without help. So all day yesterday I mowed and mowed. The grass is six inches high in most places and you just have to go over the same bit time and time again. The sweat rolled off me in streams, my back turned mahogany and my hands got blistered. A terrific thunderstorm tried to prevent me, but the grass is so good you can cut it wet.

By the time darkness fell I was out for the count, and I did it all on one cheese sandwich and a handful of nuts and raisins – all I had to eat all day as it was Sixpence's day off and I didn't want to stop for anything. Feel marvellous today – have missed good physical exercise here but will certainly get it in my garden. Will take photos as soon as all grass cut.

Must fly – literally – now.

1 December 1960

The bag is again almost going, so here is another temporary note to assure you that I am safely back from Nyasaland after an intensely interesting trip. Zomba is enchanting – what a joy it was to see mountains again after the flatness of Salisbury. Met the Governor and Governor Designate and most of the heads of the departments and had a fascinating thirty miles jeep drive on a Milford Sound-like road round African villages, and went inside some of the pitiful little homes. One had not one *single* thing in it.

Now I face the task of getting the house straight. Have already started taking photographs to send you. I think you will be mildly surprised when you see them. Continue to be thrilled with it, particularly the garden. My garden boy is a treasure, and has worked like a stick while I have been away. I think he is encouraged by my active participation.

5 December 1960

I never got that letter to you written this weekend, so I have come back early from lunch to see what I can do on an office machine. The weekend simply fled by. I have had another great go at unpacking – nothing broken – a very late party twenty five miles out of Salisbury on Saturday night; yesterday of all mad things, to motor cycle and motor car racing – fearfully exciting – and bed at 8.15 p.m.

I don't know yet what rent will have to be paid for my house. The estimates allow up to £70 a month (doesn't that seem terrible), but I hope to get it for a bit less. I really am tickled pink with it. Being all on one floor it covers quite a lot of ground and I find I have to walk a long way between various parts of the house. I will try to get down to drawing you a ground plan one of these days. Together with the transparencies I am taking, you ought to have quite a good idea of what it is like.

I keep on finding new things about the garden. I now discover that I have oranges, lemons and grapefruit and bananas all growing happily, and a wonderful assortment of flowering shrubs. My garden boy, Seize or Sighs – I haven't discovered yet which, really is a treasure, and all I pay him is £3 15*s*.0*d*. a month, which he is very pleased with, as it is five bob more than he has been getting.

I haven't yet discovered where Reigate Road is, but will let you know when I do. Bilharzia is a foul disease. You get it from swimming in stagnant water. In fact you can't swim anywhere here except in private pools, where the water comes out of a tap. It makes you feel like death and is difficult to get rid of if you don't catch it in time.

Nyasaland really was very exciting. I went the rounds. Met the Governor and the Governor Designate – I think I may have told you this – and lots of officials. They are all quite charming and gave me a wonderful time. Thank heaven there had been some rain before I went up so it wasn't too hot. In fact it is much hotter in Salisbury at the moment, though we get the odd day still when it is positively cold. Did I tell you that one evening about ten days ago I went to a cocktail party and was so cold coming home that I had to put the heater on? And this is Africa in the middle of summer! Yesterday at the races a chilly wind blew up and I was far too cold in slacks and a tee shirt. Today it is as stuffy as anything, and the sweat is quietly trickling down my face.

We are hoping to be in for a quieter time in the next week or two, with everyone in London and battling away. What we are all wondering is what will happen to us if the Federation breaks wide open. I am sure we shan't have such a large staff here. But we must wait and see. There is no doubt that history is being made at this very moment.

One pretty nasty bit of history that hit me a few days ago was to pick up my morning paper and read of the murder of two more people in Katanga. One was a New Zealander. I met him and his wife and three children when they came off the plane fleeing from the Congo when the troubles first flared up. You may remember my telling you about them. I remember him particularly well because of my being in New Zealand. We had quite a chat. He was a funny little queer lost missionary type, and obviously at sea in Salisbury after years in the remote bush of Katanga. It certainly brings it home to you when you read of the murder of someone you have met.

Such is life in this strange continent.

12 December 1960

I was much relieved today to get your letter of 6th December with its many enclosures. The wife of one of our new members of staff has just arrived from England, with terrible tales of the floods in your part of the world and I was wondering when I might hear from you. The weather at home has been headline news here, and I can't tell you how thankful I am to be out of it. I only wish you weren't having such a miserable wet time. I know just how depressing England can be when the rain refuses to stop. I have had a letter from Margaret Hellings saying she would give anything to be back in Wellington or Salisbury at this very moment.

The office has gone deadly quiet and I actually got two days leave last week. I didn't do much with them but garden, but thoroughly enjoyed them. Seize and I have already planted about 150 square yards more of lawn – as if we haven't enough already. We have some rain every few days now so it is splendid planting time. You can't grow grass from seed successfully here, but you plant, in rows, runners of grass which you pinch from the edges of your existing lawns. I gather that half my present main lawn was only put in last March and most of it looks as if it had been there for ten years. And what a joy it is just to whip a lemon off the tree when you want one. They taste quite different that way.

I am now on Christian name terms with my other lot of neighbours – Bob Taylor, one of the Monckton Commissioners, and his wife. They are dears and I know I shall like them immensely. Bob and I were both up at a very early hour yesterday, mowing – he with a motor one and I with my hand one. At 10 a.m. he came across to put a new washer in Seize's tap – it had been dripping for months but he had not reported it, the idiot, and I only found it when I went on a tour of inspection. By that time, Bob and I had both put in a good two hours work, and I had lost gallons in sweat. So solemnly at 10 a.m., we replaced some of the lost liquid in beer. No sooner had he gone than more neighbours turned up, so more beer, and then I had to go to a pre-lunch party at Godfrey Bass's. I was still stone cold sober at the end of it.

I am hoping that all this gardening will get my weight down a bit again. I am thrilled to be a bit heavier but I can't get into some of my slinkier dresses, which is a bore. Although I still have to go to bed desperately early, I really am feeling and looking well, and think that at last I am getting a bit more acclimatized. It helps, of course, not being so busy in the office. Long may the quieter spell last – at least until I have got the house fully under control.

Had better get back to work again. Nipped smartly back from lunch today in order to get this written to you. The garden is just about the last straw in my hopeless battle to write letters in the evening. As soon as I get home, if I haven't got to go out, I garden until it is pitch dark – about 6.45 p.m. at the moment. After that all I want to do is eat and go to bed. Nine p.m. is getting late for me when I don't have to go out – but I am often up at 5.30 a.m.

27 December 1960

Before that wretched garden lures me out, I must at least start a letter to you. I am so terrified at the enormous pile of letters that I must write – Christmas has made it ten times worse – that I have decided I must have a little go at them every day, whatever else I have to do.

Well, this has been a funny sort of Christmas, it always is when one is away from home and family. I went in the morning to some young friends who have two small girls, and had mid-day Christmas dinner with them. Then at tea I went to the one colleague who has a television set. Most of the office were gathered there so that we could see the Queen. Afterwards we had a swim and sat about in the warmth of the early evening in our cotton dresses. Then in the evening I had my second Christmas dinner, this time with the Deputy High Commissioner and his family. We ended up by playing a very cunning game of whist – far more skilled than ordinary whist and really jolly good fun. We were accompanied by thousands of flying ants. As I left for the Basses, a terrific thunderstorm descended upon us with torrential rain, and this always brings the flying ants out in their hordes It was a question of be stifled and have no flying ants, or have the air and the ants too. We had the latter. By the end of the evening you could hardly see the carpet for discarded wings.

Yesterday I had lunch with some more good friends of mine who have three not so small children. Again we swam in their private pool, and sat around in the sun turning chocolate. (At least I did. I seem to be one of the few Europeans here who really keeps up a good tan. Most of the others turn pale and white again.) I was determined to have the rest of the day at home, so that

I could get at the garden. I had to lie like mad to get my wish, but I succeeded. Out with my fork and spade I went, and only came in as darkness fell and another thunderstorm descended. Then a battle with letters and bed early. Today we all go to Mirimba House, the High Commissioner's residence, for pre-lunch drinks, and this afternoon I have one of the locally engaged girls and her husband and child coming to tea and for a swim in one of the two pools that are at my disposal at the moment. Both owners have gone away to the Cape for several weeks, and they have invited me to swim whenever I feel like it. I am certainly living among the wealthy in this fashionable part of Salisbury.

Oh, I forgot to say, I spent Christmas Eve with my very nice next door neighbours who I may already have mentioned, Bob Taylor and his wife. They had a huge family-cum-close friends' party, and asked me to join them. It was a jolly do.

Now I must look back at your last two letters and see what wants answering. Oh yes, I haven't yet had my third polio injection, but I shall get round to it next week, when we expect to be fairly quiet. The thing is it doesn't matter very much when you have it, but you must not have it in under seven months from the second one. Many thanks all the same for reminding me. I did have it in my diary, but it is just as well to have a double check.

You say that we must be very disappointed at the outcome of the conference. Actually, we are not. It could so easily have ended in complete deadlock – indeed we very much feared it would – but the fact that it is to be resumed when the territorial talks are out of the way is quite an encouraging sign. It is still very doubtful, of course, just what will emerge, but there is no cause to despair completely yet. We must just go on keeping our fingers crossed.

I went to meet Rupert Metcalf when he got back from London – this is the usual drill for the office to turn up at the airport unless the plane comes in in the small hours. He arrived just after seven in the morning and it really was a treat to get up at that time – I mean to go out at that time; I am always up long before then. The plane was crammed with people returning from the Conference, and I happened to be standing among the Welensky family, and got a handshake from Sir Roy himself into the bargain.

Rupert was full of funny stories about the conference. One of the things that tickled him most was the astonishment of the Rhodesian contingent at the hours kept by London. As you know, out here we start work at 8 a.m. and with luck get away again at 4 p.m. The conference sessions didn't start until 3 in the afternoon, when all the Rhodesians were getting ready to stop work. It took them some time to become adjusted.

1961

8 January 1961

I have been counting up – this is my seventh Christmas overseas, and I don't become any more reconciled to them with the years. Never mind, here's to Christmas 1963 and a rollicking reunion.

Now I must go through your letters and see what wants answering. First of all your air letter, Ma. Yes, as you may have gathered from my last letter, we do have television here. It only started in November so is still very much of a novelty for Rhodesians. Nothing will persuade me to buy a set though. For one thing you can't get one for under about £100 and secondly, the bulk of the programmes are of the canned variety – lots of westerns and the like. I think only about ten per cent is live. This is understandable as the service only covers Salisbury and the surrounding districts, and of course the population is pretty sparse. So I expect it will be some time before they have enough income to make the programmes worthwhile.

My address – Klokkespel, Selous Road – is the first turn on the right. I am at the top of a hill and have the most lovely view out over the hills to the east. And, believe it or not, I have discovered that Reigate Road is a newish road off Ridgway North to the left, almost opposite Selous Road. Isn't that odd? I shall be looking up the Elliots' niece any day now – when I have got the garden straight and when I have got at least some of the thousands of letters I must write, written!

The garden at the moment is like a hydra-headed monster – at least the weeds are. We are having a terrific rainy season – lots of people think that it is the effect of Kariba, certainly the evaporation from it must be colossal and the moisture must come down somewhere. So we tend to have rain every day at some time, usually when we are leaving the office at lunch-time or just as we go home in the afternoon. And the weeds adore it.

In my shrubbery the hay is about two feet high and Seize is doing his best to mow it with the African version of a scythe – a bit of flat metal slightly curved at the end and sharpened up a bit at the edges. I take my turn at it and it is remarkably effective – light to handle and, manipulated with a flourish, quite devastating.

You wonder, Ma, how Mrs Wilkie* knew I was in Rhodesia. Evidently

*Mrs Wilkie was my landlady in Wellington.

someone in the Wellington Office thought I was still sufficiently newsworthy to tell the press and there was an article about me in the papers as a result. Such is fame. All sorts of people have written to say that they hear I am now in Salisbury. All I can say is that the Wellington papers must have been pretty short of news on that particular day.

Ma, before I go any further, I must tell you how absolutely enchanting I found your book. I enjoyed it so much I used to ration myself to a few pages, and then wouldn't let myself take it to bed, which would have been fatal. But when I was about two thirds of the way through, I had a free evening and it was no good, I just hogged the rest of it. If Dora hasn't read it, she must, though I am afraid she will be sorely tempted to add an otter to your already overloaded ark! It made me so interested in Gavin Maxwell as a writer that I have just got another of his books out of the library. It is about north west Sicily and quite shattering. It is impossible to believe that people can live in such sordid squalor in Europe in the middle of the twentieth century. Thank you a thousand times for introducing me to this very interesting author.

Now for my bits of news. I don't seem to have much since I last wrote except more parties of one sort or another. I brought in the New Year with a whole batch of the junior staff in the office. We played parlour games solidly from eight until midnight, but they were very sweet and it was good fun. New Year's Day I spent with my landlord and his wife who have a small farm about fifteen miles away out of Salisbury. It was a bitterly cold day and rainy and miserable. But this didn't deter their five year old son from having his usual dip in their private swimming pool. This child has been swimming since he was three, and I have never ever seen anything on two legs so completely at home in the water. Their other child is eight. I am fascinated how Rhodesians bring up their children here. Most of the ones I know give their children wine – just a little – from a very early age. The five year old had a good glass and a half of sherry and then a big glass of white wine! It doesn't seem to affect them and parents say that it gets them into reasonable drinking habits from the word go.

Expect to be frantically busy again soon, with Sandys nearly on the way. Say a little prayer!

16 January 1961

I don't think I can quite remember all the rules of that game of whist, but I will get Godfrey Bass to remind me and let you know.

The office is in a bit of a state at the moment. The High Commissioner, Rupert Metcalf, and Bill McIndoe are both across at Southern Rhodesia constitutional talks, so Godfrey and I are holding the fort. I may have told you that Rupert has Parkinson's disease. He is due to go home in May for good and is to have an operation. I gather that it is a tricky one, with only a fifty-fifty chance of success. That is bad enough, but his wife Dorrie has just been warned that she may have cancer. She is having a final examination today to see whether it is really true. If it is she is to be flown home tomorrow to London for an operation. Poor Rupert must be nearly demented, for there is no chance of his going with her as he has to be at these wretched talks. I do feel so desperately sorry for them, and they are the nicest pair.

Yesterday I had my first whole Sunday in for ages, and I meant to do so much in the garden. Instead it teemed with rain nearly all the day and I was only able to dash out in the few dry spells. It was just as well from my letter-writing point of view, as I was forced to get on with them. Not that I am getting any nearer success. As soon as I get a few off my chest the post brings another batch.

On Saturday I had one of the office families over for the day – mother and father and two girls. We took advantage of the offer of the swimming pool next door and all had a swim. It is a beautiful pool, but has no shallow end or rail to hang on to. The younger child couldn't swim, but spent all her time in an inner tube. I was scared to death that she would tip up in it, but all was well. They are a nice little family, but I was hearing from the mother the story of two years ago. They had a son as well as these two girls. Within twenty-four hours all three of them were in hospital with polio. The boy died; the two girls were very ill but pulled through, and now you would never know that anything had been wrong with them. But the poor father has never really got over the death of his only son.

This seems to be a pretty cheerless letter, so I had better stop. As far as I am concerned, I am flourishing. I haven't got any bathroom scales as I had in the other house, but I took my measurements the other day. I am two inches bigger in the bust and one inch bigger in the waist, but the same size in the hips – thank heaven. Salisbury can't be doing me any harm. I think it must be all the sleep. Yesterday for instance I had two hours sleep in the afternoon when the storm was at its height and I went to bed soon after nine and slept through very happily until 6 a.m. Incredible isn't it?

Now I must go back to work. I have to go over to External Affairs and discuss a tricky one this afternoon, and I must get some homework done before I go.

30 January 1961

I seem to have done nothing but miss bags, one after the other. If I get round to finishing this letter tonight, having missed yet another one, I do declare that for once in my life I shall have to spend 1*s*.3*d*. if you aren't to wait lots more days for news. As you will gather, life has been particularly hectic, as I warned you in my last letter.

Sandys and party arrived after various tribulations at 5 a.m. on Friday morning. I was the one to stay at home and keep a track of the aircraft, after the accident to the Comet at home. This meant putting my alarm clock on at hourly intervals throughout the early part of the night, and ringing up all and sundry to let them know what was happening. I would have been far better to stay awake all night. By the time I knew he was arriving I was past sleep and I felt like death the next day.

Sandys had telegraphed to say that he wanted to spend Sunday at the Victoria Falls. We hadn't been able to fit it in on his last visit. I was given the chance of going with him, as everyone else had seen the Falls at one time or another, and I don't think they relished the thought of starting off at 5 a.m. which was the original plan. Anyway, to cut a long story short, on arrival Sandys decided we should leave at midday on Saturday to avoid the very early morning effort. After the most frantic Saturday morning ever, when I must have put through at least fifty telephone calls, including one to the CRO, we eventually got off at 1.30 p.m.

The party consisted of the S of S, Shannon, one of my ex-bosses, Sir Ralph Hone, our Legal Adviser and Marjorie Maspero, representing the Federal Government – a nice lass of twenty-seven. The RRAF had laid on a Dakota for the journey. This is very well fitted up, with a particularly VIP bit at the front. Marjorie and I settled ourselves in the back with four RAF lads who had flown a Canberra out on a training flight from England. They had a free weekend in Salisbury, and the RRAF thought it might be a good idea to let them cadge a lift to the Falls, as a half empty plane was going anyway. Sandys had no objection – he couldn't have anyway as he was the guest of the RRAF.

By the time we reached the Falls, Marjorie and I and the four lads were all on hearty Christian name terms, and thankful we weren't in the front bit with the nobs. We also got onto the best of terms with the crew, and spent quite a bit of time in the co-pilot's cockpit. I must say it is enormous fun travelling in a plane fitted up with masses of space with no ordinary passengers to cope with. The pilot took us down really low over the Falls and flew us right round three times. It is the most miraculous sight from the air, and Sandys took a whole roll of films – 36 Kodachromes – simply circling round. I took a lot myself, but I am not over hopeful that they will come out, as the film had jammed in the middle and I am not sure whether I had got it clear without letting in the light. We shall see.

At the tiny airport we were ceremoniously met by the Mayor in his chain, and several other Livingstone bigwigs. On the way to the Victoria Falls hotel where we were all staying, we stopped for a good twenty minutes right on the bridge, so that we could gawp at the Falls. Stopping is not normally allowed, but of course we had a police escort, and everyone had to wait until it was our pleasure to move on – very gratifying, though I dread to think what the poor sufferers were thinking.

Now do tell me about this bridge. I am sure it is the one that you have often talked about that Uncle Jim helped to build. I am simply dying to know. I never had time to make more detailed enquiries than to discover that it had been built by a Scottish firm in 1901. A little further on we stopped again for a different view, well off the road, until we were forced to fly back to the car in a sudden thunderstorm. By then of course we were thoroughly drenched.

Marjorie and I steered clear of the Masters before dinner, and carefully kept out of range when we had a pre-dinner drink. There we were found by the four Canberra boys and the crew, and with them we danced until 1 a.m. As we were the only two girls among many, we weren't allowed to sit down for a single dance.

The S of S had earlier said that he was determined to get up before dawn to watch the sunrise over the Falls. Neither Shannon nor Hone showed any enthusiasm for the venture, and I thought someone ought to make the effort to get up at the same time, so I volunteered and the offer was accepted. Marjorie said she would be noble too. So we arranged for tea at 5.15., which was not the pleasantest prospect after our 1 a.m. effort.

Needless to say, I hardly slept, knowing that I had to get up so soon. But up we got, and by 5.45 the three of us were bowling along in the darkness, Marjorie and I wondering what we had let ourselves in for. As you will have gathered, the S of S is a fanatic when it comes to photography, and his idea was to try to get some slides of the dawn on the Falls. We left the car in the dim early light and started tramping along the side of the Falls, which is known as the rain forest, as the spray from the Falls boils up perpetually from the gorge and descends on you like a monsoon shower. The edges of the Falls are notoriously dangerous, particularly in the rainy season (now) since the rain and the spray drive in on the sides of the chasm, and if you stand on the edge it is likely to give way. There are well-defined paths which you are supposed to keep to. But would Sandys stick to them? Not a bit of it. If he thought there was likely to be a good vantage point, he suddenly struck off the track into three-foot high undergrowth, and when he got to the edge prodded ahead of him to see that the ground was firm and then stood on it. Marjorie gave up the struggle and left me to plod along as best I could in the tangle.

The thing is, as you may know, that Sandys is very lame, and it is quite miraculous how he forces himself on in the most improbable circumstances to overcome his disability. At that time of the morning the spray is at its worst, though it gets better when the sun is up to evaporate it before it reaches the top of the gorge. So there were Sandys and I, floundering along in a torrential downpour of spray, soaked to the skin, with the Falls appearing intermittently as the wind changed and for a moment or two gave us a view. I don't mind telling you that I was as scared as I have ever been when he insisted on getting right to the very edge. In my mind's eye I could see the headlines of the world recording that Sandys had gone over the edge with only Margaret A. and Marjorie M. as witnesses, and such questions as 'Who pushed him?'

Time and time again I pleaded with him to come further in, but he was quite oblivious. When on one occasion he grabbed me by the arm and said *I* frightened *him*, I assured him that he couldn't be half as frightened over me as I was over him! After an hour of this, he at last decided we should go home for breakfast. Never was I more thankful to see him safely back in the car. I should say that in the middle of our peregrinations he had had to stop to adjust his leather foot support which he wears in conjunction with a great calliper. His shoes were so full of water that the support, as he said, had swum around in his shoe and worked itself under his toes. This prompted him to tell me the story of his disability. During the war his driver had gone to sleep and driven him straight into a brick wall. One foot was completely shattered and most of his leg, and his other leg damaged too. When later in the day he shed shoes, socks, support and calliper to paddle in the Zambesi, the next part of my story, I was able to see how terribly injured he is. Anyway, when we got back into the car, absolutely saturated, he calmly took off his shoes and emptied them out of the window – all very homely!

After breakfast we all set forth again for different views of the Falls and were then driven up the river to get on a launch to look for hippo. We had a picnic lunch with us which we consumed before we found our target. The target turned out to be five hippos – one very naughty old bull, with his cows and a calf. We manoeuvred the boat on to an island beside the hippos, shed our shoes and stockings – that was when I saw Sandys' poor feet – and crawled over the edge onto the sand of the island. Our boatman dared not go too near the hippos as he hadn't got very good acceleration, and had nearly been overturned by the old bull a little time before. After we had been on the island a few minutes, a party joined us in a speedboat. Sandys immediately asked if he

Duncan Sandys at the Victoria Falls.

could requisition it to try to get nearer the hippos to take photographs. As I was the only other photographer of the party, the two of us got into this small boat, and spent an exciting twenty minutes stalking hippos. They are devils to photograph, as they only come up about once every three minutes for a quick breath and then vanish again. Anyway, there were the S of S and I perched perilously on this little boat, swinging our cameras in all directions and nearly falling into the water in the process. Huge fun.

I got one or two heavenly shots of Sandys standing in the Zambesi with his trousers rolled up trying to photograph hippos. I only hope they come out. I also got a good one of him with the Falls in the background, and he took one of me on my camera, also with the Falls in the background. I do hope this one comes out. I can never hope to be photographed by a Cabinet Minister and a son-in-law of Churchill again! By the time we got back on the plane I can assure you we were all pretty weary, and I didn't need much rocking last night. Altogether quite an experience – and all it cost me was my one night's lodging at the hotel!

One other interesting thing Sandys told me when we were on our early morning lark was the story of their accident near Rome.

It hasn't come out in the papers here yet, though it may have by the time you get this, that they had a quite miraculous escape. The pilot thought he was 2,000 feet up, according to his instruments. Suddenly, in a great rainstorm, he found he was almost into some trees. Three of the engines in fact collected the top branches. If they had been two or three feet lower, they could not have hoped to escape disaster. It was forty minutes before they were able to land, with three engines virtually out of commission. They went through all the emergency drill and had plenty of time to make their peace with their Maker. You know that the last time he came out here, his plane chopped a man's head off at Accra airport. I said to Sandys that he seems to be very unlucky in his trips to the Federation. 'No,' he replied, 'Very lucky!'

Now I really must go to bed after getting that lot off my chest. I am still feeling a bit weary after all the excitements, and it has been a pretty hectic day in the office. Thank heaven I had no appointments tonight. I still haven't got out your last letter, but I will write and thank you properly for it in my next epistle. When this will be I don't quite know, for Sandys is with us for over a week and anything can happen.

12 February 1961

I have a horrid feeling that it is a fortnight since I last wrote to you. If so, do forgive me. Each time a bag has been due out I have tried to scribble at least a small note, but there hasn't been time even for that. But before I tell you of my latest doings I really must look back over your last two letters, for which many thanks, and see what wants answering. I don't half smile to myself when you say how much less exciting your doings are than mine. It seems to me that you are always having excitements, albeit of a different kind from mine. Perhaps it is that you are such a thumping good letter-writer.

Now to your last letter. What an exciting one. I am thrilled to bits with the card of the Victoria Falls bridge.* I have proudly shown it to all my friends and they are tremendously intrigued. It really is a treasure. If I may I will keep it a

*This was a card sent to my mother in 1905 by her uncle, one of the Scottish engineers building the bridge. The card showed a gap in the middle of the bridge, still to be closed. The card took two months to reach Edinburgh from Livingstone.

bit longer, for I want to take it along to Archives, and see what they can tell me about the building of the bridge. But I will take great care of it. The other picture of the Malans' cottage in the flood was quite something too. Poor things, what a time they must have had. And I was most amused by that article by the Canadian on 'Us'. Not far off the mark.

Although we have got rid of the Secretary of State, we still have Shannon and Sir Ralph Hone in our midst. We are hoping to shed them sometime next week, but they have a lot of work to do on drafting the new Constitution and keep on delaying their departure.

Rupert Metcalf is now going home this month instead of in May. It is just as well. He is lost without Dorrie, and is not really in a fit state of mind or body to cope with the job. Dorrie had to have a major operation in the end, a hysterectomy. She had it a week ago and it is reported to have been successful, but I think it is really too early to be sure.

Alport comes at the beginning of March. I think he will be a thumping good High Commissioner, but I am not over-enthusiastic about him as a man. He is a cold fish, and I don't think the office will be the same very happy place under his command. Thank goodness anyway we are getting David Scott as our next DHC. You may have read about his appointment also in the paper. Godfrey Bass, our present DHC, is going to Cape Town, and David is coming in his place. I am absolutely delighted. David is a darling. You may remember he was my head of Department for a short while in London, until he was seconded as one of the secretaries of the Monckton Commission. He and his wife Vera were at Birmingham University a couple of years before me, and I have been down to stay with them at their home in Guildford. That was the occasion when I had to give all those VIPs a lift in my little car, remember?

Whatever Alport turns out to be like, David at least will be a splendid buffer state between him and the rest of the office. Needless to say, changing both HC and DHC within a fortnight of each other isn't going to make life any easier. I am trying desperately to get a bit of leave, for I haven't had any, except a couple of odd days in which to garden, since I came here. But I see no hope with all these changes for at least another month or two.

This may help to explain why I haven't got round to looking up any of the people whose addresses I have. I do find this an enormously exacting life. Not that I am grumbling in the least, but it takes me all my time to keep my head above water. It would be easier if the damned altitude didn't make me so sleepy. I don't believe I shall ever become completely acclimatized. And we really haven't had much of a break since I arrived. December was our only comparatively quiet month, and I was so busy then getting settled into my house that I just didn't feel able to get round to doing anything else. But one of these days we must have another quiet spell, and then I will get cracking.

This poor letter is getting written in dribs and drabs. We never seem to enjoy our weekend in peace these days. Yesterday morning I was the only one of the administrative staff in, until the HC put in a belated appearance, and there was a wild scuffle on with messages for Welensky from Macmillan coming through. Then this afternoon, Sunday, I had just got back from a curry lunch with some very interesting people, where the conversation was carried on in a splendid mixture of German, French and English, and I had gone to bed to sleep it off, when the damned phone went and it was Government House Lusaka, warning us that they were trying to telegraph an important message to us, but knowing what the cable office was like on a Sunday, would we be sure to listen to the eight o'clock news. My wireless has gone pfut, so I have been bobbing up and down alerting people to listen, and laying plans for whatever has to be done when we know what it is all about. No doubt a nine day wonder, and we have our shrewd suspicions, but not exactly a restful way of spending Sunday.

It is just about eight o'clock now, so any minute one of my colleagues will be ringing to tell me what it is all about, and then I may have to down tools. One thing about this life, we never have a chance to get bored. I can think of nothing more heavenly than a little bit of boredom.

One last thing and then I will shut up. I am about to inherit the Basses' cat Billy. I have resisted having a dog, as I think one would be too lonely. But a cat is different, and Billy is quite adorable, so I shall be happy. When the McIndoes go, either later this year or early next, I am also going to inherit their Willy-Willy (so called after Australian dust whirligigs, since as a kitten he used to rush round in circles after his tail).

Sorry, work calls. I have to go into town and collect two telegrams. What a life.

Office Monday. That was the end of that last night. Had to collect telegraphs and dash out with them to Rupert. Bag just closing. Many thanks for letter this morning.

20 February 1961

I really should have written yesterday, Sunday, but the garden claimed me. It is the only day free of office trouble for ages.

Got dragged out of a dinner party on Saturday night and ended up going to see Whitehead (couldn't help laughing. Me all dolled up in evening dress and the PM in shorts and a bush shirt!).

Now all today I'm at the Annual Congress, and all tomorrow, and heaven knows when I will get my own work done. Heigh ho, heigh ho.

Must dash back to the Congress. This is just a tiny assurance that I'm surviving. Rupert goes on Friday and we are likely to be furiously busy for at least another month.

27 February 1961

Dearest Ma

Still well, still busy.

Federation still in one piece, but only just!

Never a second to write, but will do soon I hope.

Bag closing.

Love

Margaret

2 March 1961

Sorry about the peculiar paper, but it happened to be the first bit to come out of the cupboard. In ten minutes I am off to the Federal Assembly to hear what Sir Roy has to say in winding up the debate on Northern Rhodesia, and the bag will have gone by the time I get back. So here goes in the few minutes I have.

To say we are still busy is putting it mildly. On top of everything I have been dragged out of bed on a number of occasions recently. I don't mind so much being got up at 4 a.m. for I have had a good sleep by then, but to be roused at one or two I find frightful. By the time I have got out the car and raced down into Salisbury and done whatever has to be done, I find it quite impossible to get to sleep again! Still, as I have so often said, it is just one of the penalties for having such an interesting job. Yes, I often look back on the incredible quietness of the office in Wellington and have a little smile.

I ought to be looking through your last letter to see what wants answering, but time is getting very short. Will save up for next time. One quick thing I do remember from it. Dorrie Metcalf is getting on very well. Her operation has evidently been successful so far, but of course only time will really tell. I had a letter from her this morning, and she sounds wonderfully cheerful. She has just come out of hospital.

Alport arrives tomorrow, so we are all on our toes. He wants all his senior staff to go to dinner with him on Saturday evening, without wives. So I shall be the only woman among eleven men. I'm not grumbling!!

Have been having quite a hectic social life recently, and gave my first black tie dinner on Monday, as a farewell to the Basses. Half the electric cooker fused in the middle of the afternoon, but Sixpence and I between us managed quite well. Soup, fish, meat and pudd. Was glad when it was over, particularly as two of my guests – a man and wife – are both reputedly millionaires in their own right. They rolled up in the most heavenly Bentley! They are all the same the most charming and unassuming people.

Here are a few of the transparencies. Will send a few more by the next letter.

Simply must fly.

Sunday 6 March 1961

Now to look a bit more closely at your last two letters and see what wants answering: not that even now I am likely to have much peace. In half an hour's time I have to go down to the office, though it is Sunday morning, and pick up a telegram that came in yesterday evening, do some homework on it, take it plus sensible ideas out to the new High Commissioner at Mirimba House and then go with him this afternoon to see a Federal Minister. (Shall do my damnedest to get out of the afternoon trip but am not very optimistic.) And the rest of my precious Sunday will be my own – with luck.

But now to your letters. I hope you saw 'Panorama' in the end. The very day after Welensky appeared – I mean recorded that programme – he gave me a very special wave in the street. I happened to be driving along outside the Federal Assembly just as Welensky emerged, having given one of his most outspoken anti-British tub-thumps. Although I was right on the other side of a wide road, he leant across his driver as soon as he saw my car and gave me the biggest grin and wave. At that moment of course I didn't know what he had been saying in the House, but as soon as I saw next day I thought, 'Yes, Welensky thought he had better give me a wave to show there is no personal ill-feeling towards us in the High Commission!'

Evening. There I got stuck and had to get off down to the office. I got back to Mirimba House by about 10.30. The next hour was spent trying to track down Federal Ministers and senior civil servants. This is some task at the weekend as they all vanish off fishing or to their farms. At last we got hold of the Secretary for Defence and along he came to do battle with us. I got to a farewell drinks party, at which I was due at 11.30, at 1.15. But it was interesting to see the new boy in action. Very smooth.

Don't worry about my grumbles of being so sleepy. I know what it says in the post report, that is quite a different thing from what I have. I am just plain sleepy with altitude, as nearly everyone else here is. And I must admit the life is hectic, as you will have gathered! I think I may have told you that on Monday I gave my first black tie dinner. It went off well. The next evening I actually had free. At 1.00 a.m. or so I was dragged into the office. I think I may have told you this already, in which case forgive. That meant not much sleep for the rest of the night.

Wednesday I went out with a party to a dinner dance in one of the few posh restaurants here. Thursday to another dinner party with some very nice colleagues in the office, but I was the first to leave at well after midnight. On Friday I was hopefully expecting to have another quiet evening.

During the day the phone rang, and it was a man who had been on the *Winchester Castle*, and with whom I developed the habit of having a drink most evenings before we went for our baths and change. He was an elderly Yorkshireman who had been in the Union for fifteen years. He is in Lavenda Wools. Out of the blue he rang. He had come up to Salisbury from the Cape on a farewell trip. He has two grown up sons and wants them to have some years in England, because of the grim situation in South Africa. If after that they want to come back to Africa that will be their lookout, but he feels he must force them to see what life in Europe is like, whether they like it or not. It will be an awful wrench for him, and a job for his wife, who is getting on and has become accustomed to servants. But they feel they must put their boys' future first. Anyway, not having had a squeak out of him since the voyage – not that there was any reason why I should – he rang up to ask if I would make a four with one of his colleagues and his wife. So it was out dining and dancing again. It was a splendid evening. The husband of the pair was a very jolly Scot, and the most wonderful dancer.

That brought me up to Saturday. I may have told you that Alport asked all his senior staff to dinner minus wives. That meant that eleven men and I sat down to dinner! There was hilarious discussion beforehand as to whether I was to be regarded as a man or a woman for the occasion. It was decided that the former would be preferable: in other words I stayed at the table until we all moved. All I insisted on was that I wouldn't go out into the garden to spend a penny. It is customary in Salisbury for the women to rise from the table and go to the various bathrooms. The men wait for them to remove themselves and then all troop out into the garden. Woe betide you if you choose this moment to arrive at a house with your lights full on. As it happened, at the very moment that the men were about to vanish the blessed phone went, and it was the telegram on which we had to take action this morning. So I was whisked to the telephone to battle and by the time I was through – and had tactfully taken the opportunity to vanish upstairs myself without so to speak having to leave the party – nature had duly been attended to. Alport is clearly going to be a terrific new broom and I can see us all working harder than ever.

But after the frantic business this morning of trying to get hold of anybody responsible in the Federal Government, Alport sat down there and then and sent a telegram home saying that it was useless London asking us to take emergency action on a Sunday and the sooner they realised it the better. We are enchanted. We have been trying to ram this lesson home for ages. Coming from Alport within forty-eight hours of his arrival, they may take some notice.

Although the day had been thoroughly mucked up I am delighted it has happened. He has been able to see for himself just what we have to contend with out of office hours. Alport said to me how sorry he was that my day had been mucked up. I assured him that this was normal business and that we were quite hardened to it. It was a miracle these days if we *weren't* interrupted out of office hours. When we were we just took it for granted. This was a bit of a line shoot, but not so far short of the truth.

That all arose from you worrying about my health. I really am fine, and everyone says how enormously much better I look than when I came out. I am sure this is just because I have put on weight and therefore am fatter in the face. But I do look well, thank heaven. (The only thing is I am getting greyer and greyer and will probably be nearly white by the time I get home.)

I had an hour and a half between getting back from my lunch party and going to pick up my new cat. During this time I had a wee snooze, lying in the sun, and then I put in three dozen sweet pea plants. Believe it or not, I put the seeds in boxes a fortnight ago today. They were through in under three days, and when I planted them out today they were about five to six inches high. The rate of growth is phenomenal. I am hoping to have a really good show. I got the garden boy to dig three feet down and two across. Then I myself returned the soil into the trench, mixing a lot of compost – home made – and bone meal with the soil. I got the very best seed from South Africa so now I have the highest hopes. The only trouble is that there are an awful lot of beastly insects that rejoice in seedlings. We shall see!

Now to tell you about my cat. He is Bhili (meaning cat in local language) and he was born at Mirimba House two years ago from a stray who simply walked in one day and was adopted by Dorrie. The Basses had him from a tiny kitten. He is an undoctored tom but has the sweetest nature. In fact as cats go he is an arrant coward and flies a mile if he sees another cat or dog. He is most handsome – a lovely soft grey colour with faint stripes. Anyway, I had a date to collect him this afternoon. He had never been in a car before, and as the Basses are up to their eyes in packing I didn't want to bother them to come with me. So Bhili and I had a little journey on our own. We gave up all idea of trying to put him in a basket or pillowcase. In fact he was wonderfully good, sitting on my knee most of the way. Only on one occasion did he get really upset, and then he crawled all over the steering wheel and kept on putting me in overdrive by standing on the lever. Anyway, after a lot of yowling we got home and I immediately fed him. He has a quarter of a pound of raw meat in a chunk, not cut up, so that he has to work hard for it. Within a few minutes he was purring away like mad, and of course I was down on the floor beside him trying to make him feel as much at home as possible. Now he is fast asleep under my spare bed and looking as if he had been here all his life. I am not going to let him out of doors though until tomorrow. I fear he might stray away in the night. So now at last I have fulfilled my ambition and have a cat all of my own. Needless to say he will be photographed as soon as I have a minute, and his portrait sent home for admiration. Don't worry, love. You are let out on that one. Dora can coo doubly to make up.

I was invited out by a charming Indian couple to dinner tonight, but after this really awful week of activities I told a white lie and said I was engaged – hence the fact that I am getting this letter written. All I hope is that the office doesn't come to life again. Alport was to see a Minister this evening but thank heaven he said he wouldn't want me. But one never knows what London will think up next these days. I never seem to have time to get round to telling you about the frantic complications of the situation here. It would take me weeks and I don't suppose you would be all that much wiser. We hardly really know what is happening ourselves, let alone try to explain to anyone else. But there is no doubt whatsoever that we are at a very critical stage in the history not only of the Federation, but of Africa. I never cease to bless the fates for letting me be in on it. But as time goes on I get more and more convinced that the Federation cannot possibly hold together. All I hope is that if it does break up it will do so peacefully.

I don't know what sort of impression you have in England of what the security situation is. People coming out in the last week or two have shattered us by saying that they expected to see Tommy guns at every corner! In fact it couldn't be quieter. The Territorials are being stood down and all is as peaceful as can be. Long may it last.

Now, love, I think I had better shut up. I am so sorry to have been such an awful letter writer recently. I feel thoroughly frustrated when I don't get at least one decent letter a week off to you. I fear you have had very short commons for far too long.

12 March 1961

I haven't really got a lot of news for you this week. Alport is keeping us pretty well on the go and there is masses of work around.

The Basses finally left on Friday, and as Alport goes up to the two Northern Territories for most of this coming week, Bill McIndoe and I will be left in sole charge. We hope as joint acting HC and DHC we shall have an opportunity to be rude to the Secretary of State! David Scott and his family arrive next weekend, and that will let us off once more. But as you can imagine, we don't expect the week to be exactly peaceful.

Bhili has settled down splendidly. He is just like a dog and always comes when called. And when I come home in the evening he always gardens with me. He really is the greatest fun and such good company. He insists on staying out all night, even if it is pouring with rain, and presented me this morning with his first offering – a mouse!

This is a miserable little bit of a note, but the sun is beginning to come out after rain all night and grey skies this morning. Before I stop resisting its lure, I must send out some invitations to a cocktail party for people to meet the Scotts. A deadly boring job, but it has to be done.

25 March 1961

Now at last I will get round to answering properly your last two letters of 12th and 19th March. It is Saturday evening, and I have lied to have an evening to myself to try to catch up with some of my letter debts. Alport goes back to England tomorrow, and I was invited to have dinner with him. But it has been such a hellish fortnight that the worm turned and I said I had a previous engagement. I have – with you!

Now back to all the questions in your two letters. How many rooms? Drawing room, dining room, large kitchen, one largish bedroom which I don't sleep in, one tiny room off it which I use as a study and odd job room, and one other bedroom at the far end of the house which I *do* sleep in. I decided on this bedroom though it isn't the bigger, because it is in fact like being upstairs. The ground falls away at the back of the house, and my bedroom is therefore a good height above the ground. Nobody therefore could look in. This is to me a great advantage, for though I have burglar bars throughout the whole house, it is rather comforting to think that no black face can actually peer through them at me. I also have a rather nasty bathroom and separate lavatory on this level. Then underneath my bedroom is another large room which the owners built on as a bedroom for their two children. It has off it a very nice bathroom, which as far as I am concerned is completely useless, as the little flat is down a long flight of stairs. I would hate to put any child of mine down in this room. I don't think it is damp, but it is a bit cut off from the rest of the house. I use it as a store for trunks, grog, hard top and gardening shoes. As you go out of the door from this room you are in the lean-to which holds two cars.

I have taken a lot more transparencies of the house for you, so I think you will be able to get the geography straight when you see them. I still have about ten more exposures to get through, but will try to finish the roll at Easter. The bit in the middle of the roof is just show. It is a window with virtually nothing behind it. The bushes you refer to are, if I can remember the transparency you are referring to, enormously tall fir trees. The people with me in the Christmas Day shot are not Basses, but Townsend-Coles – the family I had lunch with that day. No, you haven't got the name of the house right, but that isn't surprising in view of my writing. It is Klokkespel, meaning, I think, the ringing of bells.

Now at last to thank you enormously for the colour prints. I am enchanted with them and had quite forgotten that you had taken them. I couldn't help having a little smile when I compared my London home and my Salisbury one. Did I tell you that I have discovered that I have *seven* acres of land, not three? Thank heaven a good chunk of it is untamed, and will remain so as far as I am concerned. The large patch of new grass I have put in is the extent of my breaking of new ground. I reckon I have put pounds of value onto the estate already and the garden really is looking lovely.

Yes, Sandys is pretty tall, over six feet I should say. I can't remember who divorced whom, but I think he did her. Mind you, I bet he was a b— to live with.

Quite right about the hierarchy of the office. The McIndoes expect to go home in September, much to my sadness, but I shall just have to hope that we get someone as nice.

Bhili does not do anything so ungentlemanly as to jump up on tables for food. But he did give me a terrible fright the other evening. I was sitting quietly reading in my drawing room with the windows open but the curtains drawn. It was as quiet as the grave. Suddenly Bhili hurtled through the curtains in one bound right over my shoulder, hotly pursued by a belligerent ginger tom. Bhili is such an awful coward and he was panic-stricken. I managed to separate them and Bhili vanished out into the night again. I then made friends with Ginger, but have since dissuaded him because he is a bit smelly. But for a split second when the two of them pounded in my heart jumped sky high.

The last fortnight has been so hectic I hardly know where to begin. I got deeply involved in the aftermath of a terrible accident to the young son of Robin Turton, ex-Minister of Health and the leader of that group of Conservatives, ninety of them, who strongly criticised Macleod recently. Turton junior is a young barrister out here. He was knocked over by a car while crossing the street, and when I was rung by a colleague in the Bar Association, was not expected to live more than a few hours. We were asked whether we could try to track down Papa, as the telephone lines to London were closed because of sun spots. Anyway, to cut a long story short, Turton was found in Berlin, but not by us, but I had one hectic evening trying to get in touch with our embassy in Rome by telephone, to get them to hold up the Comet in the hope that the Turtons senior could get on it. I did get through to Rome eventually, but in the event the Turtons got held up somewhere, and didn't get through to Salisbury until the next day. The High Commissioner was away in the North when all this happened, but when he got back he wanted Turton to come and have a drink on the Saturday evening – last Saturday, before he caught the plane back to England on the Sunday morning. I had driven out to the airport on the Saturday afternoon to meet the Scotts and taken them back to Mirimba where they were staying with the High Commissioner.

As soon as I got to Mirimba I was detailed to go and collect Turton who was staying right the other side of town with Judge Briggs. The High Commissioner's driver had been sent away. So off I set and collected the men. I think he was a bit astonished when he found a woman and a Sunbeam Alpine there to collect him, but he took it in good part. Back to Mirimba, where he had the most wonderful arguments with Alport, then I got the job of driving him all the way back again. We proceeded to have a terrific argument ourselves in the car going back. All jolly good experience battling with ex-Ministers. All in all, I must have driven about eighty miles on these taxi-ing efforts.

Miraculously the young man is going to live. He had a fatty embolism which means that some of the marrow from a broken bone got into the blood stream, forming a clot. As luck would have it, he was taken to a doctor who I happen to know, who spotted in double quick time what was the matter, as he had a similar case a year ago when the man in question died within twenty-four hours. But from this calamity he knew the signs – mussiness and spots on the chest. The cure is to pour alcohol into the blood stream to dissolve the fat. This he did, and the man will live; but it will be six months before he is fully recovered.

I gave a small cocktail party for the Scotts a couple of days ago. One of the men I invited is a Scot. He and a girl from External Affairs stayed on when the others had gone and he ended up by taking us both out to dinner. We then proceeded to talk politics until a quarter to three in the morning. He was absolutely vitriolic about the British though he is one himself. There is no doubt about it, the British are just about as unpopular as they can be at the moment, and it is a daily job trying to convince people that we aren't downright monsters. I find it endlessly stimulating, but God knows where it will all end.

The night that it was announced that South Africa was leaving the Commonwealth I was out with fifty men and no women; in other words I was invited to a party given by the Ministry of Transport for a conference of technical experts in aviation from the Federation, East Africa, South Africa and the UK. As I am responsible for liaison between the the UK Government and the Federal Government on aviation matters, I was invited. The Minister of Transport was there – a poisonous little man of seventy, who spent three quarters of an hour telling me the story of his life, much to my embarrassment and to that of his officials, who wanted him to meet the boys. But I enjoyed the evening hugely – I always love being the only woman among a lot of men, they are all so charming and courteous to me and so astounded to find a woman in their midst on such an occasion. I discovered that one man in the UK delegation, whose face was vaguely familiar, had been at TRE at the same time that I had. And I made a great hit with the BOAC adviser who had come with the British delegation, who solemnly declared at the end of the evening that he had fallen in love with me. Fortunately he was flying home the next day. But what I really meant to say when I started this story was that when the South Africans, who oddly enough were all Afrikaaners, heard the news, they were so desperately upset that they all got blind drunk.

This particular technical organisation that were meeting are the friendliest lot and not a bit concerned with politics. And they were so depressed that South Africa's withdrawal would mean the end of their happy meetings, or rather they would only be able to meet again after complicated re-negotiation of the international agreement that had set them up in the first place.

It fell to my lot to go and see Alport off to Bulawayo the other evening. He is the sort of man that has to be seen off – not like dear Rupert Metcalf. His plane was due out at 6.45 p.m. He was of course given VIP treatment at the airport, and ushered onto the plane before the hoi polloi. As it happened it was a stinking hot night. The rest of the passengers didn't go aboard until a good ten minutes after him. Then the plane taxied to the edge of the runway and there it stopped. I had decided to stay and see him safely airborne, as I love airports at night. I couldn't think what was the cause of the delay. Then I realised. Out of the blackness came a delayed Boeing from Jo'burg. To see a

Boeing come down at night must be one of the sights of this age. I was enormously impressed. It was just like a train coming in. But I bet the High Commissioner wasn't much pleased. He was on the ground in his plane for twenty five minutes. And I know from experience just how damned uncomfortable it is to be buttoned up in a plane on the ground in hot weather.

Tomorrow, Sunday, we all go to the airport again to see him off home. It will be good to relax a bit. He has boundless energy, and has turned the office inside out. Mind you, I think he is going to be jolly good, and one splendid thing is that he is determined that we shall all go off regularly on tour. As you know, I have only had my two quick trips to Northern Rhodesia and one to Nyasaland since I came, and no leave. So I am delighted at the prospect. In fact I am already detailed to go to Umtali for several days in April, to talk to all and sundry and find out what they are thinking. On this trip I hope to look up the Ivan Campbells, as they have their farm in the Umtali area. Anyway, when I have fixed up with the mayor exactly when I am going and what I am going to do, I shall write to Mrs Campbell and ask her if I may call. I gather from Bill McIndoe that they only live in one of the show-pieces in Southern Rhodesia, to which royalty and visiting Prime Ministers are deflected!

I have an awful suspicion that this is a more erratically typed and constructed letter than usual. Please forgive. I find now that my typing prowess is in excess of the speed at which this very aged machine will work. (It is tied up with bits of Silko, which I am sure you as an expert would disapprove of.) I really must stop and go and cook myself a snack. I sent Sixpence off as he has had a lot of washing and ironing to do today and was looking pretty tired, so I said I would battle with my own supper. There seems to be so much odd gossip that I could happily go on for another fifty pages, but I must resist the temptation and think of your poor eyes.

2 April 1961

Here I am fulfilling my promise to get down to a letter to you during the Easter weekend. Alas, two days of the holiday are over already, and now it is Sunday morning and I am writing to you before I get out into that garden.

Having at last got Alport safely away, we seem to have sat back a bit in sheer exhaustion! I have been to a lot more parties, but not I think very interesting ones, and I have had odd batches of people in for dinner or drinks. Last night I met a rather interesting man, a bird artist. His main interest in life is falconry, and he is a bosom friend of James Robertson Justice. He is out here to do a bird-painting job for the Museum. I met him at dinner with some friends and gave him a lift back to the Museum as he has no transport. He invited me in to see his six hawks that are living in one of the rooms of the Museum. They were all on leather fetters, and one was tame enough to sit on your hand. The others he only caught last week and are still a bit wild. He showed me some of his paintings, which are exquisite. It is real precision work and must need endless patience. He also has an eagle which he is training, but it was out in a shed and I am to see it another time.

I must say I am loving this quiet weekend. Apart from the dinner date last night and having people in for pre-lunch drinks tomorrow I have lied my way into a peaceful time. Not that I have been idle. Far from it. It goes without saying that I have been gardening like mad, and I have also washed and ironed five loose covers for chairs and one for the sofa. They are in unbleached kaffir cotton, which is a coarse very heavy off-white stuff. They are getting pretty aged and I feared that they would not stand up to the cleaners. In any case I couldn't bear to be without them for any length of time when I saw what they were covering. Sixpence was obviously appalled at the prospect of washing them so I thought, to hell with you, I will do them myself. He is suitably impressed. The trouble is of course that they get dirty very quickly, but they are rather artistic. Bhili's dear little paws don't help, but I fear he will be chased off my clean covers after being allowed a bit too much latitude. Talking of Bhili, I had another fright a night or two ago. In the depths of night I suddenly heard all hell let loose in the house. I leapt out of bed and rushed through to see what was happening, and found Bhili and the ginger tom locked in mortal combat in my drawing-room. Ginger tom took one look at me and fled, and Bhili panted and blew and wouldn't be stilled. And my parquet floor was simply festooned with fur. I was glad to discover that there was far more ginger fluff than grey, so I think my little chap is getting braver in his old age. I went over him pretty carefully to see what damage was done but he seemed to be fairly intact.

My next minor excitement is to go down to Umtali. I think I may have told you this already. I have to go down to find out what people there are thinking of the political situation. Alport has all the right ideas about what his staff should do. There will be a lot of travelling and not nearly so much sitting around battling with paper in Salisbury. The Evan Campbells' farm is in the Umtali area, so I will make a point of looking them up.

Ma, would you be an angel and buy me and send off a pair of Sword rose pruning secateurs. I can't get them here. I have a rather hefty pair which I use for other pruning, but they are too coarse for my roses. Let me know the full cost. It is wonderful how quickly things get out here, anything from three weeks to about five, but never more. There is no desperate hurry, as pruning time is about July, but I thought I would mention it now before I forget.

6 April 1961

What do I have on the floors of my rooms and corridors? Virtually nothing. I may have told you that the floors in this part of the world are most handsome – nearly all are the most beautiful parquet. Mine are among the best I have seen anywhere. My landlord has subsequently given me only a few rugs, none very exciting, so I treated myself to a very attractive oval rug in a plain pinky heathery colour with an off white fringe, which I have at an angle across my drawing-room floor. This just takes off the bareness. I thought anyway that it would be useful when I get back home to have in my bedroom, in case my bedroom carpet is showing signs of wear, which it may well. I have actually taken a colour transparency of my drawing room by ordinary sunlight, but if it doesn't come out I will treat myself to a flash attachment and have a go with that. No, I have no real hedges as such. Along the road front I have a double line of fir trees which make a complete screen. Down one side is a wire fence grown over with a variety of greenery; on the other side nothing separates me from my neighbours – our two gardens simply merge into one, but they are far enough away for this to be no hardship – in fact we both like it as we get the benefit of each other's gardens! These are the neighbours I like so much – Bob Taylor and his wife. The fourth side is simply the end of the jungle at the bottom of the hill with a bit of a dip and stream on occasions. But though I have no hedges to cut, all my shrubs need keeping under control, and the bougainvillaea gallops all over the place like a mad thing. I can't tell you what a struggle it is to keep growing things within bounds during the rainy months of the year.

I sacked my second garden boy at the weekend. He was a lazy young bounder and got whipped in by the police a week or two ago for wandering about after midnight several miles from here. I felt he was too much of a liability, particularly as I am not on the spot during the day to keep an eye on him. I can't afford to have other than completely reliable servants and I am glad to be shot of him. Seize is such a marvellous and hardworking man, and I would far rather just have him and do a bit more myself.

You ask about Alport's peregrinations. Right from the word go it was arranged that he should fly out for a month to get all his introductions over and then go back to bring his family out by sea. This is not an unusual procedure, particularly if a High Commissioner has little notice of an appointment. In fact he and his family, wife and three children, are due to sail on 13 April, though we shan't be surprised if the poor man is after all forced to fly back to save time. He is reputedly a devoted family man, and one of the reasons he was so pleased to be posted here was to have a chance of seeing something of his children. Obviously he didn't have much time in the rat race of politics in London.

17 April 1961

I often think at the end of the week that no week could ever be worse until I find one that is. This time I really am convinced that I have endured the worst one ever. I may have told you in my last letter that the cat had gone lame following a terrible fight. Well, last Saturday week I took him to the vet, about three miles away. He has subsequently become a hardened car traveller. As long as he is on my knee he is as good as gold, and just sits with his head on my arm enduring it and having the odd peep at the outer world. I had to take him every morning for penicillin injections, then tear off to the office half an hour late – that precious first half hour when with luck one can get through work without being interrupted. Then no sooner had he got a little better than Sixpence went down with a frightful dose of tonsillitis. So he then had to have penicillin, and I had to do all the housework as well as look after him and the cat!

We have been as usual energetically in the throes. A lot has been blowing up over Katanga mercenaries and all the business in the UN, and on top of everything the man who usually handles this, Neil Ritchie, a Foreign Office chap who is now attached to us, was up in Northern Rhodesia, so all his work fell to me to do on top of my own. By Saturday I was just about out.

But one interesting thing happened during the week. My neighbours opposite gave a party – the enclosed cutting is about it – and there I recognised Evan Campbell. So I marched up to him and introduced myself and said I was just about to write to his wife and ask them if I could come and visit them. To cut a long story short, I am spending Saturday evening at their farm. I go to Umtali this afternoon (I meant to write this yesterday but never had time so am getting it bashed out before I go to the office for what I know will be a hellish morning). I leave at midday and take Sixpence with me as his home is in that direction, and I thought he might like the chance to see his family. I spend until Thursday in Umtali, then go up to Inyanga, which is supposed to be one of the loveliest parts of Southern Rhodesia. I spend Thursday and Friday there, then come back to spend the Saturday night with the Campbells and back to Salisbury on Sunday. I'm not looking forward to the Umtali bit of the week, since I am sure I am in for a terrible ear-bashing against the British Government, but I am longing for the rest of the week, when I am on leave.

Must fly now as I have so much to do. Will send you a postcard from Inyanga.

P.S. The Campbells are dears and gave me a terrible wigging for not getting in touch before.

Cecil Hotel Umtali

20 April 1961

Well, after a hectic morning in the office on Monday, I dashed home and picked up Sixpence. I may have told you that he comes from Inyanga, which is only about sixty miles from here and where I go tomorrow. It seemed very selfish not to let him have a chance of seeing his family after serving me for eight months without a break. I was appalled when I saw how much luggage he was taking, including his bedding roll and a tea set which I helped him to buy. But after a lot of juggling we fitted it and ourselves all in and set forth on over a 160 mile journey in blazing sun. Salisbury had suddenly gone as hot as I have ever known it. We happily did 120 miles in the first two hours, and then to my horror I realised that my red ignition light was on. I knew therefore that no charge was going into my battery. Fairly soon I came across a garage who pronounced that my armature had burnt out, but that I could probably reach Umtali safely, provided I didn't see clouds of smoke pouring out of the engine! We did, without smoke, and I was in fact the next day, yesterday, able to find a Lucas expert who repaired it by the end of the day. Great relief! I gave Sixpence his bus fare on to Inyanga, and in a fit of generosity an extra week's leave, so that I shall be on my own for a week when I get back (I feel so sorry for these men who see so little of their families, and I know that Sixpence sends very nearly every penny of his wages back to them).

Umtali was scorching that night and I tossed and turned for hours longing for a good old Indian fan to cool me off. Next morning my ordeal began and it finished three hours ago. Yesterday I had six hourly meetings, one after the other, with scarcely a minute between – the Town Clerk, the Civil Commissioner, the Executive Committees of the Chambers of Commerce and of Industry, and of the local Development and Publicity Association, and then a sundowner party given by the Deputy Mayor for Councillors of Heads of Departments that started at 6.15 and went on for jolly nearly two hours. Talk about an ear-bashing! All on politics, with terrific tirades against the British Government. Thank heaven I am now getting so hardened to this racket that I positively thrive on argument, and feel considerably better at the end of the day than I do at the beginning. Certainly no punches were pulled simply because I was a woman, which I appreciated; and at the end of each session we always finished in the best of good spirits, with lots of laughter and chaff all round. The Town Clerk and his Deputy, to whom I had written to arrange my programme, confessed, when they had had a few drinks at the Deputy Mayor's expense, that when they had first got my letter they had been filled with alarm and despondency, fearing that I would be a formidable career woman in horn-rimmed spectacles. The Town Clerk did in fact ring me three times in Salisbury to discuss my programme, and he admitted that he had done so the first time to see if my voice would dispel some of his gloom. He was gracious enough to admit that it had!

Today hasn't been quite so bad – only four sessions, but each considerably longer than an hour. Now I have had dinner and am about to go to bed. As soon as I have written my b. and b. letters tomorrow I shall be off to Inyanga to relax. I feel I've jolly well earned it.

My cheap Japanese camera has continued to give me trouble. The precious roll with Sandys on refused to be rewound. I got it done in a shop and only hope no light has got in. I have sent it off anyway with my fingers crossed. It is too much of a worry, so I have treated myself to another Kodak Retinette on which I got 33.3 per cent discount. I shall hope to try it out for the first time on my journey up into the mountains.

Will write to you again when I have stayed with the Campbells.

Salisbury

1 May 1961

I seem to have such a collection of letters from you that I hardly know where to begin. To keep the record straight, in case I have to acknowledge any of them, they are dated 1, 13 and 27 April and I feel there may be another one somewhere at home.

Questions. Polio injection. Really will make a special effort this week. Have got a doctor lined up, and it is just a question of time, which gets scarcer and scarcer to find. Alport and family came out by sea but flew up from the Cape. We all went to meet them. Lady Alport is very sweet and the children are quite unspoilt. There was to have been a big introductory party tonight for Lady Alport, but she has got a very nasty ear infection and it has had to be postponed. How I laughed at the idea that they might have gone to the airport in the airways bus! Lord Alport is far too superior for that – nothing less, I suspect, than the grandest car the Government could muster! No, I don't bother to shut my windows at night. We get remarkably few insects, except immediately after rain. Mosquitoes are the worst bugbear, but I have fly screens over my bedroom windows so I don't get bothered in bed. Yes, I left one key with the garden boy while I was away so that he could come in for his meat which I keep in my fridge, and feed the cat. I had meant to put the cat in kennels, but he had to have a cat flu injection and carefully absented himself on the Sunday when he was to have it. So I had to leave him with Seize after all. You can imagine my relief when I found him in fine condition. Seize had given him all his meat, plus most of Sixpence's as well.

Well now, back to my travels. It was simply lovely at Inyanga. Just like Scotland except for the sun! I had a very happy two days there, then set forth for the Campbells. I had to go an extra forty miles because of diversions where the road was being repaired, but I got there in time for lunch on Saturday. They have the most glorious house with a magnificent view. They were telling me how they started off in 1937 with £8 a month and a daub and wattle hut. They really have done splendidly. Their son seems to run the farm with Papa and Mamma returning at the weekends to see how things are going. They were great fun and gave me a wonderful time. Colin the son showed me all round the tobacco processing sheds. What a tricky and complicated crop it is, but what a lot of money you can make out of it if you are clever. Evan is building up a herd of Hereford-cross-Afrikander cattle. I have taken a photograph of one of the best examples of the cross to send home to you. The idea is to get the beef of the Hereford with the greater length of leg of the Afrikander, as they have to walk so much further for their food. If the progeny lean more towards one breed they cross it with a pure-bred bull of the other breed.

I have just finished my week on my own, and I must say I have thoroughly enjoyed it. Servants are all very well, but it is good to have the house to one's self. Sixpence turned up this morning and I think was quite surprised to find how well I had managed on my own. I was terribly busy last week trying to catch up on arrears of work, but with luck it should be a bit easier this coming week.

You will be pleased to know that my transparencies turned out very well after all my fears. I will send them on when I have had a chance of showing them to a few friends. One of the ones of Sandys is superb and the one he took of me is a winner, except for the fact that I don't think it looks a bit like me!

I haven't forgotten that I still have your postcard of the Falls bridge. I want to try to find a minute to take it in to Archives, if you don't mind my hanging on to it a bit longer. My pictures of the completed bridge have come out very well.

Remind me to tell you in my next about a letter from Donald Middleton.* Very interesting but mustn't embark on it now.

10 May 1961

I have been up to the eyes again. On Thursday, just when I was about to get round to writing to you, I was suddenly told that I had to go to Bulawayo on

*Married to my great friend Elizabeth, whom I met when we were eleven years old.

Saturday to help out at our pavilion at the Trade Fair. This was the first time that the UK had exhibited, and our pavilion won first prize. So I had to set to and work like stink to get my papers up-to-date, and soon after 5.30 a.m. I was on my way by road. I decided to go in the car rather than fly so that I would have the car at the other end. My goodness, it was cold at that time of the morning. I have got my hood down as the rains are virtually over, and I had to have my heater on all the way to keep my feet warm.

I got to Bulawayo at 10.30 without hurrying unduly; it is 285 miles. Most of the hard work had been done by some of my colleagues before I got there, so I had a lovely time, just wandering about the pavilion and answering questions, and taking myself off when I felt like it round the rest of the Fair. I also took the chance to dash up to the Matopos Hills to see where Rhodes is buried. It is one of the most impressive sights you can see. No wonder he chose it as the place where he wanted to be buried. I came hurtling back yesterday afternoon. I didn't get away until 3.15 but one thinks nothing of long distances in this country where the roads on the whole are good and where there is so little traffic. I got back by eight, having thoroughly enjoyed the break. The High Commissioner had been down for the opening of the Fair, and David Scott left today to do his stint.

Our pavilion really did deserve first prize. The theme was British steel and the actual construction of the pavilion was an example of the use of steel. It is a little jewel of a building and the exhibits were an exciting collection, ranging from a £4,000 model of Windsor Castle to a £12,000 turbo-jet engine to beautiful tableware. I have taken lots of photographs, which will make their way to you in due course.

When I got back today what should be awaiting me but the pruners. I do wish you would let me pay for them. They are exactly what I wanted and I have tried them out already when I got back this evening. They only took just over three weeks to put in an appearance. Isn't that good? A thousand thanks for sending them, but please do let me know how much I owe you or I shall feel that I can't ask you ever to send me anything else. And the longer I stay here the more I realise what a lot of money you can save by sending to England! Most things are enormously much more expensive, and of course I don't have to pay any import duty. I have even started writing to London for clothes that I have seen advertised, as I am a fairly stock figure.

We are just working up to a very busy time in the garden. The winter is the best time for flowers. You have to water like mad all the time, but as I have my own bore hole for the garden, this doesn't cost me very much. I have been growing a lot of stuff from seeds, and am having great fun planting them out. I am so pleased to discover that those I plant out do so much better than the ones the garden boy plants out, good though he is on most things! The grass has at last stopped growing at a furious rate, peas are growing like mushrooms. I am beginning to wonder if I have fed them too well, for they are making masses of greenery but so far no flower. But perhaps that is as well, for they are only about two feet high so far. They are comic things, as they don't like the heat here. They really begin to show their paces when the nights get cold.

You must tell Dora of one of the most exciting exhibits at the Trade Fair – the cheetah which one of the Regiments recently acquired as a mascot. He was being driven round the Fair in a jeep. Unfortunately when I saw him I hadn't got my camera with me, but I got right up close and he is the most gorgeous beasty. He is completely tame, and is simply on a lead. His handler is obliviously quite dotty about him and strokes him like a cat. On one occasion he was in the front seat of the jeep, and he is so long that his tail was out of one window and his head out of the other!

I think I told you in my last letter that I had had some interesting news from Donald Middleton. He told me not to tell you in case it got back to Mrs Ryder, but of course that is nonsense as I know you won't tell her if I warn you not to. He is very seriously thinking of coming into the CRO as an Information Officer. He has had an interview, and is waiting to hear whether the CRO will take him on. He has written to me for my views, and I must try to get round to writing to him tonight. Wouldn't it be the oddest business if Liz and I found ourselves in the same post? The ways of fate are very strange.

15 May 1961

I hardly dare admit that I haven't had that injection. Three times I have been on the verge of ringing up and each time something has happened at the last minute! Bulawayo didn't help, and I am only just now catching up on the arrears. But I am going to make a special effort this week.

No, I haven't played any golf at all apart from that nine holes with Bill McIndoe months ago. The garden is largely to blame, but I can't pretend that it is any hardship to have to work in it. I may start playing golf again when the rains are really over and there isn't so much to do. I thought we had had the last of them several weeks ago, but the last two Sundays have been very wet. I am delighted of course, for it means that everything will stay green that much longer.

On Saturday I went out to dinner with one of the Professors at the University College and his wife, and they took me afterwards to the Reps Theatre to see a grim but wonderful play about the brain-washing of a political prisoner. There is no professional theatre here, but the amateur shows are on the whole first class. The man who had the lead is one of my contacts in External Affairs, and he was simply wonderful.

The evening paper tonight carries a story of somebody being mauled by a leopard at Inyazura, where the Campbells have their farm. And incidentally, I don't think I told you that when Sixpence got back he told me that four of his eight cattle had been carried off by lions recently. I'm glad I didn't know this when I did my long solitary walk at Inyanga – not that there are any known man- or woman-eaters in this part of the world.

Now I think I had better go and eat. It is only a cottage pie, so I have sent Sixpence off, since I don't want to keep him just to take it out of the oven to serve it. Sorry this isn't a more newsy letter. No doubt something lively will happen in the next few days. It usually does.

23 May 1961

I had meant to get this written over the Bank holiday weekend, but unfortunately I had so many engagements that I never got round to it. One of the do's was a party given by Alport on Sunday evening for the Leicestershire Football team who are out here on a visit, straight from just losing the Cup. Then I also had a game of tennis on Sunday morning – only my third since I came out here, and boy am I stiff.

I seem to have been to a lot of rather dull parties lately. But one amusing one last week reintroduced me to the man I met on the ship, James Hemming, who is the next door neighbour of the Deweys in Teddington. He is out here for a month working on a course of English teaching books for Africans, and is staying with the Longman's representative Ben Gingell. Ben is quite delightfully mad, a bachelor, and as luck would have it is living just round the corner from me. He invited me to dinner to meet James again, and we had a hilarious evening, mainly listening to pipe bands on the gramophone. Ben is potty about the pipes, though he is an Englishman! He turned out all the lights and lit some incredible candelabra, and proceeded to take hold of the largest one and dance round the room with it in his hand to the skirl of the pipes! It was great fun to meet James again – quite one of the most interesting and intelligent people I have ever met, and simply full of good works for humanity, in a thoroughly unsentimental way. Ben has to chuck him out next weekend as he has some more people coming to descend on him, so if I can get Saturday morning off I may take James to Kariba or Inyanga to show him a little of the country.

You will be amused to know that I actually made an effort and went round to the Polio Clinic on Saturday morning, before coming to the office. As luck would have it, the doctor failed to turn up for the first time ever and I simply couldn't wait. So now I shall have to make another trip on another Saturday morning. But at least I have tried!

11 June 1961

I don't think I have ever gone for so long without writing to you and I am hugely contrite.

I think when I last wrote I was about to take James off to Inyanga. We left before dawn on Saturday morning with the lid off the car, and had a splendid run in the sun. On Bob Taylor's recommendation, we went to the Inyanga Mountains Hotel, and not back to Troutbeck where I had been the first time on my own. It was a less pretentious hotel, but I enjoyed it much more. It is in splendid scenery, and mine host was the most welcoming man. We had hot sun during the day and huge log fires at night. James is a very energetic person and dashed me off on long walks. We even climbed the highest mountain in Southern Rhodesia. This was not quite so arduous as it sounds, for you can get the car quite a long way up on a good track. But it was two hours of steady climbing in sunshine which frizzled us, and a superlative view at the top.

As soon as we got back James vanished off to Nyasaland and we were left to cope with the Secretary of State. I can't tell you what chaos there has been in the office since then, with all the constitutional pots boiling away like mad. Then when James got back Ben Gingell asked me if I could keep James as his Mum had come out from the UK for a three months' holiday. I have been delighted to do so. He is another Donald Middleton in the house, content with the simplest food, and happy to look after himself when I am out – which has been almost all the time, as it happens. I have asked James to let me know when next he is on television, knowing how you like to watch people that your daughter has met! So I will let you know; you have probably seen him already, as he has appeared a lot on educational panels and the like over the last year or two.

On top of everything, a week ago Alport suddenly said that he knew nothing of what the farmers in the north of Southern Rhodesia were thinking about the present situation, so he told me to organise a trip as soon as possible and report back not later than 10 June. By dint of using the Farmers' Union as an entrée, I organised a three day trip for Wednesday, Thursday and Friday of this last week. I had arranged to give a cocktail party on the Tuesday evening, and I had to leave at dawn the next day to start my tour. My guests went late, and I was too tired to do any packing. But somehow I was up and away next morning without feeling too ghastly. I left James and Sixpence and shot away.

I went up to Karoi first of all, which is about 140 miles north of Salisbury. It is an area which is only just being opened up for farming, and a lot of the farmers I met had only been on their land for less than a year. There is still a lot of virgin bush in the area, and it is hard work to get going. But it is good tobacco land, and a man starting up who knows something of tobacco growing can very quickly make a very good living for himself. I stayed with a delightful middle-aged couple, and they held a sundowner party for about twenty of the local farmers. I say local, but some of them had driven up to thirty miles on bad dirt roads to come to meet me. They represented every shade of opinion, and as in Umtali I had to have my wits about me. But it was huge fun and very stimulating. Of course they stayed on and on, and by the time the last had gone, and we had had a spot of supper, and then sat on chatting, it was pretty late and I was very tired. But I had to be up early the next day to move down to Banket and go through the whole palaver again. I should say that the palaver was to go round individual farms and gossip with the inmates, with odd meals at which I met groups.

My second lot of hosts were not a patch on my first. There was obviously some terrific strain between the husband and wife and the wife, throughout the dinner party, kept making the most cutting remarks about her husband. It was all terribly embarrassing, but even worse when everyone had gone but the three of us, and she launched forth in front of him into a diatribe about his drinking habits. I found it difficult to judge whether she had driven him, by a hard and selfish nature – which showed in her handsome face – to the bottle, or whether his going on the bottle had driven her to become a vixen. It was the most distressing relationship for an outsider to witness. Next morning they were much more relaxed with each other, so perhaps this is a game they play with each other. All very, very odd.

On the second day they took me really into the wilds to see another new area which has recently been opened up. There I faced a barrage from half a dozen tough farmers – and you have to be tough in that part of the world. Again all very stimulating, but exhausting.

I got back to Salisbury on Friday evening, and then had to turn out to a cocktail party and to go on from there to an Indian film on the life of Tagore. By the time I got that lot over I can assure you I was ready for my bed. Thank heaven yesterday was a holiday, for the Queen's Birthday. The Acting Governor General gave a huge reception in the morning, to which we were all bidden in our best bib and tucker. Margaret Archer was the only one to turn up in a sports car with the roof off! Keeping a smart hat on in such circumstances was quite something, but achieved without disaster. Then out to dinner last night.

This morning, Sunday, is, I think, the first moment of real quiet I have had in a fortnight. I indoctrinated James into our ritual of walking all round the garden after breakfast – quite a hike in this establishment – and now we are both getting down to our letters. We go round the corner for lunch with Ben and his Mum, and then they both come here tomorrow night for dinner. James leaves for London on Wednesday. Bless him, he has been very grateful for the peace and quiet of this house to get on with his work. The Gingell household is evidently a rather restless one, with ritual times for meals and tea and coffee and the like. To have the house entirely to himself, when not actually at meetings, has been a great joy to him, and he has poured blessings on Mrs Gingell's head for turning him out of the Gingell house!

18 June 1961

Just for once I don't seem to have any letter from you to answer. Or am I lying? Yes, I am! I haven't answered your letter of 7 June, which was waiting for me when I got back from my 'farming' trip. I am fascinated to know that Peggie and Rob lived in Baker Avenue.* Does Peggie still know the number? Although many of the houses have gone to make way for offices, a lot still remain. It would be fun to take a photograph of it if it is still in existence.

Funny your mentioning the Sinnetts. I do see quite a bit of them in the ordinary course of life, and am having dinner with them tomorrow evening. They are now living in a house quite near to me. They have just had their fifth wedding anniversary – and by the look of Ann, I wouldn't be a bit surprised if Sinnett number three weren't on the way. But I may be wrong.

I was very tickled to hear that you had been watching the Homemaker competition so eagerly, for James has been one of the prime movers in the programme, and has been one of the regional judges. I imagine therefore that you must have seen him. He finally left on Wednesday night. Ben Gingell and Mama Gingell and I went to see him off. He was having a few days in Nairobi on the way back, but asked for your address as he said he would like to write to you and tell you how I was getting on. I hope he does, but he obviously leads a terrifically busy life and time may be scarce. His wife is a headmistress and they must be a pretty brainy pair. I think they must have married rather late and they have no children.

I haven't very much news, beyond work. Everything is just about coming up to the biggest boil imaginable. Bill McIndoe couldn't have been away at a

*Rob was my uncle, who lived in Salisbury for many years.

worse time. Nearly all the work has been on his side, and I have had to battle with it. Thank heaven he comes back tomorrow. But when I have finished this letter I must get down to writing a long despatch on the chances for the referendum. I should have done it during the week, but there was never one free second of peace, so Sunday is the only hope. I think I have pinned my bosses down to letting me have some leave after the referendum, which will be on 26 July. I shall try to take off the first two weeks in August. I'm really getting to the stage where I need it.

Now I had better shut up and get on with that work. Next week will be as busy as ever. Among other things I am to go to a cocktail party given by Sir Edgar Whitehead. I expect it will be a large and impersonal affair, but it will be fun to see how Sir Edgar copes with the women. He is supposed to be frightened to death of them.

By the way, before you remind me, I have thought what I should like for my birthday – a woolly jumper, if you feel you can run to it. Plain, long sleeves and a V neck. Any colour, but if there is a choice, either that bright blue that is almost royal, or that pretty shade of darkish olive green. We are slap in the middle of winter, with log fires and bitter cold nights, and all my woollies are getting a bit tired. As I know they are rather expensive, perhaps it could be a joint effort from you all. I hope you won't think I am being too greedy.

I've just seen something in an earlier letter of yours that I haven't answered. You mention a picture of Jack Johnston but say I have never referred to him. I know him very well. He was a great pal of Gwen Hunt's and mine, and I had dinner with him in Pretoria on my way up here. He is one of the nicest people I know – very able, but also very human. Everyone adores him. He is a bachelor a few years older than me.

Had meant to get my polio injection yesterday (Saturday is the only day you can have them here), but I never had a busier day in the office and it was out of the question. Will make strenuous efforts next Saturday.

Office

26 June 1961

You will have gathered from the papers just what a time we have been having in the last week or two. The full story is really rather like an exciting melodrama, and it is by no means over.

Just time for a little bit of gossip. The cocktail party given by Whitehead went off well; and as I had been to hear him in the House that afternoon and had been enormously impressed, I could not refrain from telling him so. He went very pink – he is terrified of women – and could not do more than mumble in reply!

On Saturday night Bob Taylor and his wife took me to the annual dance of CAA of which Bob is now Chairman. It was one of those noisy 'servants' balls', and I didn't get to bed until 2 a.m. Heigh-ho, what a life!

I have to fly now and go to the opening of the new session of the Federal Assembly. We expect a few fireworks over the Northern Rhodesia business – but as we seem to live perpetually with crises these days we shall not be dismayed by anything we hear.

Must must fly.

Office

29 June 1961

Just a quick office lunch hour note to thank you for your letter written on your return from Nottingham. POLIO. Will make superhuman efforts on Saturday, but Saturdays tend to be more chaotic than other days of the week, and that is saying something! Am so glad James got round to writing. I still don't know where I shall go for my holiday, but it will probably be up to Lake Nyasa or across to Beira to see the sea. How I wish I could see a little of your wonderful summer. I listened to a bit of the Test, and was filled with nostalgia at the descriptions of the heat at Lords. We by contrast are glad of our woollies and big fires at night.

And talking of woollies, thank you so much for saying you will send me one, though you have already bought my present. I feel this is very greedy of me. 36 should be quite big enough. I seem to have lost a few of those pounds again, though I am still a healthy size.

I am almost without news. The climax of the N.R. business has now been reached and so we are a little less harassed. This doesn't mean that there is less work; we are just getting down to the things we had to neglect. The next real excitement will be the referendum on the Southern Rhodesia constitution. If it goes through we should be free of a lot of work on the S.R. side. But if it is lost we can expect months and perhaps years of continuing battles and uncertainty. We are therefore holding thumbs like mad.

I have on my desk my first picking of sweetpeas. I have picked the odd one or two, but this is the first bowlful and I am very pleased with myself! They haven't got as strong a scent as in England, but then few flowers have here.

What a dull letter this is. Shall try to do better next time. Seem to have a lot of parties coming up but I don't think any of them will be very inspiring. On Saturday I go to Canada's Dominion Day do, given by Mr and Mrs Glasse.

Do you remember them in Wellington? Very tame and dull. She used to get me in a corner and keep me there because she never seemed to be able to pluck up courage to circulate.

Back to work now.

Office

Sunday morning 9 July 1961

I am terribly sorry to have kept you so long without news. This has been a quite impossible week, and during the last seventy-two hours I have hardly stopped. Last night I was up nearly all the night. The trouble has been the South West Africa Committee. You may have been following its fortunes. We have got landed with them while the problem of whether they should be allowed to enter Bechuanaland is being thrashed out. I had the job of meeting them at the Airport on Friday, and even got myself onto television in the process, though I was far too busy at the time to see it. I can't stop to tell you all the excitements of these last few days, but it has been pure cloak and dagger and I have enjoyed it hugely. Professor Fabregat, the Chairman of the Committee, is an ageing Uruguayan, and an absolute charmer. I have been the intermediary for the office with him. As the HC has said, 'We always put our women in the Front Line.'! The whole exercise has been one of dodging the press, and I have popped the Professor alone in my little car and taken him for meetings with the HC. After two hours sleep I was out at crack of dawn this morning to take to the Professor our Government's answer to his last letter, and now I am taking advantage of a pause in proceedings to get this written to you. I know that in another hour I shall be hard at it again and I don't know when I shall have another chance to write. This is supposed to be a holiday weekend – Rhodes and Founders, when everyone is off for Monday and Tuesday. I see no prospect of having any peace at all, for I think we shall have the Committee on our hands for days yet.

Because of the holiday there will be no bag out until next Thursday, so I thought I would send this air letter to keep you in touch. Any minute now I may have to stop, but I'll go on as long as I can.

Next week I am supposed to be going for a tour of the Fort Victoria area to see what people down there are thinking. I rather dread having to face another of these do's when we have been so frantically busy, but I suppose I shall enjoy it if I ever get round to going. Then we have the Referendum, then the elections in Nyasaland and then – oh well, there is sure to be something!

Donald is definitely joining the CRO Information staff, and he and Liz leave for Kaduna in Nigeria in August. Isn't it odd to think that Liz and I are ending up in the same set-up nearly twenty years after leaving the University, and that at some time we may find ourselves at the same post! They haven't sent me many details yet, as they had only just heard when they wrote.

The Aikmans of Wellington are coming here in the next few months. They are on a long tour of America and Africa – or rather will be on a long tour. I have invited them to stay with me. I was flabbergasted at the terms of Colin's letter. New Zealand must have got the impression that we live in a police state here, and dare not be seen talking to an African or anyone who is suspected of having liberal sympathies. So much for the damage that the press can do!

Don't worry if you don't hear again in the next week. Although I am pretty tired I am feeling fine; and though grumbling at the fact that I have seen nothing of my garden for ages am really tickled pink with the recent round of activities. For the first time I have got quite far ben with the HC and find him more human on closer acquaintance.

Later. Our little crisis was first item on the news from London. We're going up in the world!

Tuesday 11 July 1961

I'm still bogged down in the South West Africa crisis, and seething with rage at having my holiday completely mucked up. I've forgotten where I got to when I last wrote, as so much has been going on one gets muddled. I was on the hop most of Sunday, but did have a whole night in bed. Except that hearing the telephone is so much on my mind that at one stage I must have had a vivid dream that it was ringing. I leapt out of bed only to find no phone ringing after all. I even went as far as ringing the office to see if anyone was in trying to ring me, before I was quite positive I had only been dreaming.

Yesterday, Monday, I was called by Fabregat at 12 noon to collect an answer to the last round of argument. To my fury I was greeted by apologies that the Committee had still not agreed on the terms of their message, and would I come back after lunch. United Nations Committee or not, I simply put my foot down and said I would see them only as and when they had a decision to give me, but that I was not going to hang around waiting on the offchance. Thank heaven, when I told the HC what I had said he heartily concurred! The answer came through at 5 p.m., but only a verbal one. This meant dashing up to Mirimba to tell HC, then back into the office to send off a long telegram. I must say the HC is jolly good. He leaves me to bash out these telegrams, which go straight to the Cabinet without casting an eye over them. He is very good at delegating responsibility, and doesn't fuss you if he thinks you know what you are at. It was as well I had to go into the office as I ran into two other minor crises – one a Parliamentary Question for today, on which we had to consult the Southern Rhodesia Government immediately – a difficult thing to do on a public holiday – and the other to try to get a message from Léopoldville to Elisabethville by telephone – in the end a fruitless task though I tried hard. Back home at 9.30. This morning the phone has already gone about half a dozen times, and I dare not move until we have final confirmation of the Committee's plans. And tomorrow we go back to work. It strikes me it will be a positive rest to get back, for all the staff will be there to cope, instead of just the HC and me!

Blast, the phone has just gone again and it was Professor Fabregat who wants to talk to me. I know that they are not changing their minds about what they propose to do next, so I have told him that I am not free to see him at present, and will he ring later. No harm in making the old devil sweat it out for a bit. I feel so bloodyminded about them it isn't true!

Have pruned my roses – always the job for Rhodes and Founders weekend – usually I got about half a tree done and then had to race in to answer the telephone. Your secateurs are bliss. I can't tell you how thrilled I am with them. They are lovely too for cutting flowers and thinning out sweetpeas (these are turning out well, and I have had some stalks 17 inches long!). A thousand thanks again for them.

17 July 1961

So hectic have the last few weeks been that I simply can't remember how much I have told you about what. I have a feeling I was bogged down with the South West Africa Committee when I last wrote. What a to-do that was. They kept me on the hop the whole of the Rhodes and Founders weekend. The HC left the whole thing more or less to me, which was intensely interesting but just about finished me off. But at least the old Professor and I got on like a house on fire; and when on the Tuesday afternoon he asked me to go down to the hotel to collect the Committee's latest Note to the UK Govt. – which I did in his bedroom so that we could both avoid the world's press! – we had an hour long talk in which he told me an incredible lot of things that the Chairman of a UN Committee should never really reveal to a representative of an individual government! And as I rose at last to go, he suddenly gave me a bearlike hug and a kiss and said, 'You are ze only beautiful thing to happen to me in Africa.' We then proceeded to stroll along the interminable corridors of the hotel, the Professor with his arm affectionately round my waist, and me having kittens lest some of the prowling press should see. My luck held! When I dashed to Mirimba House to discuss with the HC the next move in the game, I told him my story of the susceptible Professor. I have never heard Alport laugh so loudly and so long; and when next day he sent a personal letter to Lord Kilmuir, who is acting S of S while Sandys is away, to tell him the inside dirt of the Committee, he ended up by telling him of my little experience. He said in the last sentence, 'I conclude that neither the age of chivalry nor the resources of British diplomacy are at an end.' Alport is still chuckling about it and has told a number of his cronies who pull my leg like mad. And when we got a final message to pass on to the Professor in reply to the letter he had given me, and I put the letter before HC for signature, he asked me if he should put two kisses at the bottom from me. I have never known Alport so human. We had decided between us that I would not go to see the Committee off at the airport as their last letter had failed to give the assurances for which we had asked. Imagine my surprise when, ten minutes before the plane was due to leave, the Professor came on the telephone from the airport, where of course he was being besieged by the press, to say how heartbroken he was that I had not come to say goodbye, and that he would never forget me! Heigh-ho, the frolics of diplomacy. But HC, bless him, was very appreciative of what I had done, and paid me a handsome personal tribute in his letter to Kilmuir. So perhaps it was worth all the sweat and lack of sleep; and HC has insisted that I have today, Monday, off to compensate. At long last I hope we shall be in for a quieter spell, except that I have to go to Fort Victoria on Thursday to talk to the people in that area. But it should be child's play after last weekend! AND, I will have you know, I had my polio injection on Saturday morning!!!!

It has been bliss having a weekend without the telephone once going. I had to go out to a drinks party and lunch, and I had some folks in for tea, but the rest of the day was my own. I celebrated by sitting down and reading a book right through and going to bed at 1 a.m. Quite mad. I have no dates today or tomorrow and on Wednesday I dine with the Gov. Gen. Then early on Thursday, off to Fort Vic.

Will write again when I get back from Fort Vic. – in other words in a week from now I hope, and barring accidents.

25 July 1961

I am horrified to see that your last two letters are dated 12th and 17th July and ne'er a word from me. It has been one of those impossibly difficult spells for getting down to letter writing. I have missed bag after bag and in desperation am now whipping off this air letter between bags to let you know that I am flourishing.

We are on the very eve of the Referendum and therefore in a state of some tension. But to go back. I can't think what I was up to a week ago; mostly lots of paper work in the office if I remember correctly. Then on Wednesday night I went to dinner with the Governor General. It was a large party of some twenty-six guests, one of whom was Lord Malvern. After dinner we played a variation of 'What's my Line' with guests invited to think up their second or third line. Examples were 'Tired old man' and 'Shooting a line', to give you an indication of how things went. The party was considerably enlivened by dear Lord M. who is as deaf as a post and hadn't a clue what was going on, and who therefore produced the most splendid irrelevancies into the game!

Up at crack of dawn the next day to do my packing and to get off to Fort Victoria, some two hundred miles away. This only took about three and a half hours, and I got there in time to have a good lunch and a 45 minute sleep afterwards, before I had to go to my first appointment. Thank heaven for my infallible mental alarm clock, for I had no mechanical one with me. I had an interesting day and a half, very much on the lines of the Umtali visit. Most hilarious perhaps was the cocktail party given to me by the Mayor and the Council – wives not invited! They told me that the party was on the Municipality, and on the strength of it they all imbibed in no small measure. Needless to say, I stuck to two small Scotches!

I escaped late on Friday afternoon, and turned to the Zimbabwe ruins. I stayed at the hotel there, and went into the bar for a drink before dinner. Inevitably I got talking to the odd men, and mine hostess. Then dinner and straight to bed. I had not turned out my light more than a few minutes when a knock came at my door. It was mine hostess to say that the men had invited me to come and have another drink with them. I can assure you nothing would get me out of bed again! I spent the next morning at the ruins, which are intensely interesting; then in the afternoon went to the new Kyle Dam, which was officially opened only a month or two ago.

Kyle is a miniature Kariba, but much more lovely, The lake is beginning to form, and I was reminded very much of Scotland. I wandered around entirely on my own for a couple of hours, and then returned to the car to find I had a flat tyre. I couldn't believe my eyes, for I had put on four new tyres especially for the journey, as the old ones were getting a bit smooth, and on the pretty bad roads in this country it isn't safe to have bad tyres. A couple of girls arrived on the scene and we pumped the tyre up again hopefully. It got me back to the hotel but promptly went flat again. The next morning two South Africans, with whom I had played liar dice for hours the night before, changed the wheel for me, and I set off on the journey home. It was Sunday, and the day of the NDP unofficial referendum. None of us quite knew what was likely to happen, and as I had to drive back through one of the African townships I thought I had better try to find somebody who would mend the puncture, just in case I was very unlucky and got another one and got stuck with no spare wheel. I found a garage open at last, and they discovered a tiny corkscrew of metal shavings which was between my inner and outer tyre. Obviously the garage who put on the tyres had allowed this bit of metal to get in and it had eventually caused the puncture. Needless to say I am just waiting for a free moment to go and tell them what I think of them. I am going to refuse to pay for the putting on of the tyres and demand a new inner tube to replace the one that now has a patch. Thank heaven I saw no trouble on the way back, but there were a great number of police in evidence, and the office had anyway warned them that I was coming through, and I only had to ring them if I was worried. No more space. More in the next bag.

30 July 1961

I feel I have been treating you to very short commons recently. This last week we have suddenly become much quieter in the office, with the Referendum over and won, and we are hoping for a continuing peaceful spell for a few weeks. But we haven't really felt the effects yet as we are catching up on all our arrears. But it is wonderful to feel that you can go to bed at night and have a fair chance of not being wakened. The same thing at the weekends. It is Sunday morning now, and I have had my usual wander round the garden, which tends to degenerate into a gardening session unless I am very strong-willed. I have two guests coming for lunch – Ben Gingell and his lodger, Roger. I have got quite pally with them both, and we tend to pop in and out a bit. Roger is a young lawyer. He had polio as a child and still shows the effects. He is not exactly crippled, but can't co-ordinate all his movements; he gives the impression of being slightly spastic. We are all going to celebrate the winning of the Referendum. Roger is a Rhodesian, and has been working like mad to get the Referendum through, so he should be in jubilant mood. Having picked some flowers for the table I am being very firm with myself and not letting myself return to the garden until I have written to you.

The poor old cat has been in the wars again, and has a very bad wound on his front leg. Cats' teeth are evidently the most deadly weapons, particularly if they are eaters of dead rats. And the old ginger tom who does all the damage is I am sure a bit of a wild scrounger. Anyway Bhili has the most awful bad, really bad, smelly wound, and I have been lugging him backwards and forwards to the vet again. Thank heaven he is such a seasoned car traveller. When he gets over this I am going to have him neutered. The vet says if I don't I shall go on having this trouble. I didn't want to have him done as he is adult, but I have finally been persuaded.

I have at last decided on part of my leave. I am flying up to Fort Jameson and then going on to the Luangwa Reserve; this is one of the best game reserves in the Federation. The whole trip is organised by Central African Airways, and in the Reserve you have experienced guides to take you everywhere. The camps where one stays are right beside the river, so you can watch the game from your verandah. I decided to go to this reserve as it is one of the few where you are really safe walking about; in most of the others you have to be driven and are not allowed to have your own cars. And I am too weary to do a lot of driving, particularly as the roads leave a lot to be desired, and I don't want to bash my little car about too much.

On Friday I have another visitor, this time one of the men from Dulwich. I don't think you would ever have met him. He is coming out to lecture in South Africa and the Federation, and wrote and asked if he could look me up and tell me all the Dulwich gossip. As he was to be in Salisbury over a weekend, I thought it would be a bit miserable being stuck in a hotel, hence my invitation. He is an interesting man, and has a sister who is one of the most senior women in the Civil Service. I think she is in the Board of Trade.

I have a big African family on my hands at the moment. I have had to take on an extra garden boy to slash all the long grass on the jungly part of the garden, as it is a fire risk. Then my landlord has sent along a boy to paint the outside of the windows. This morning Sixpence's younger brother has turned up on his way to Bulawayo, and Sixpence's wife is supposed to be arriving at any moment. They all have to be fed and fussed over, and in many ways are more trouble than they are worth.

Think I had better go and make myself a bit respectable in case those boys turn up. Oh, by the way, one date last week was lunch at Mirimba with Lady Alport and five other women. Lady A. is a sweetie and it was a delightful party. I had Lady Hudson on one side and Lady Strachan on the other and Lady Chedwidden opposite. Felt I was almost in Debrett myself!

I haven't got round to telling you anything about the political situation. We are sick to death with it, but enormously relieved that the Referendum has gone through so decisively. The heat has certainly gone out of things for a bit, but it remains to be seen how well and quickly the Government are able to implement the new proposals, and the extent to which they can win the confidence of the Africans.

Office

4 August 1961

Two wonderfully long letters from you to answer, the 25th and 31st. If I have written you fifty-five letters I am sure you must have written me nearly a hundred! I always contend that there is no correspondent to hold a candle to you. And what a lot of news in these last two letters. Thank you so much for them and for all the manifold enclosures.

I must say I am always appalled at what gets into your papers about what goes on here. For every African who shouts, 'White man get out,' there are thousands who don't. I was very interested driving back from Fort Victoria on the very day of the African unofficial 'Referendum' to see how happy and good-natured all the Africans I passed were. I don't mind admitting now that I was a little bit worried about what I might see driving back through Harare, but throughout the nearly two hundred mile journey I got just as many waves from Africans as I usually do – they are a happy people and great wavers. In fact I got the impression that they were very much in holiday mood, not quite knowing what it was all about but sensing that it was a bit of an occasion. I was very tickled by one African. He was on a bicycle on the strip road in front of me. Strip in case I have never explained is two parallel strips of tar about eighteen inches wide, with dirt in between and on either side. You bash along on the strip until you see someone coming in the other direction. You then move over so that you have your offside wheels on one strip and your nearside ones on the dirt. The other chap does the same, so that you both have something to anchor yourself on. Cyclists are supposed to move off if they hear a car coming up behind them. On this occasion the African didn't hear me, so I gave him a very small toot on the horn. He moved off at once, and as I passed I put up my hand to say thank you. I was very tickled to see in my mirror that he was nearly falling off his bicycle in his effort to wave back. That is much more typical of the African than what you read in your disgusting old *Telegraph*! Why don't you buy a decent paper like *The Times*!

I think that hotel at the Grand Canyon looks quite monstrous. I can't help feeling that it will ruin the splendid wildness of the Canyon. There is a terrific battle going on here at the moment about developing the Victoria Falls. A Yank has come with plans for a stupendous hotel at the Falls and everyone is up in arms about it. And I am sure they are right. One of the most impressive things about the Falls is that they are unmarred by any sign of the hand of man – apart from the bridge. I should hate to see them spoilt.

There is very little news. We have suddenly gone wonderfully quiet in the office. The HC is away for three days, which always helps, and everyone seems to be taking a breather after the Referendum. Long may it last, so that I can get my leave in without being stopped. I had a good laugh the other day in the office. My electric iron had blown up the night before. I found that the flex had worn through, which meant taking the iron to pieces, getting new cord, levering off the little metal rings from the old cord and putting them on the new one as I can't get the little rings out here, and putting everything together again. I wanted the iron as soon as I got home from the office, so I put all my files to one side, and using my office knife as a screwdriver, got to work. Alport breezes into our offices unannounced about once a month. He chose to do so this very afternoon with all my iron in bits on my desk. I told him I would have made a much better mechanic than a civil servant, and with a broad grin on his face he said that if I went on like that I should probably have to earn my living that way anyway!

I have had a quiet week on the social side, and have been crawling into bed at about 9 p.m. and sleeping for nine hours. Tomorrow I have lunch *en famille* with the Scotts. They have all their children out here just at the moment. Their elder son has just arrived from home – aged seventeen and six foot three, and enormously broad to boot.* I am supposed to be playing tennis with them all tomorrow. Heaven help me. Nothing on Sunday, thank goodness, so I shall have a good old go at the garden. Did I tell you that I have had the whole of the outside of my house painted? I thought my landlord was only going to have the windows and doors done, but no, all the walls are in the process of being whitewashed. I'm beginning to look very smart. But oh, the paint splashes! Plants, paths, tiles, stones are plastered. He is such a messy worker, and of course I am not there to stand over him and make him put papers down.

Now I suppose I had better get back to work. When there isn't very much one is reluctant to do what little there is. It is far easier to work when one is really hard-pressed. Not that I am grumbling!

Thank you all again for your bounty for my birthday. Life begins for me, doesn't it, after Monday! Phew. If it hasn't begun for me already I don't know what I have been up to in the last year!!

13 August 1961

In one of your letters you were not clear where or when I was going on leave. It is on next Tuesday, 15th, by air to Fort Jameson in Northern Rhodesia, where I am met by a bus and taken to one of the game camps. CAA are running this as an all-in holiday. But I go on the ordinary scheduled flights, and not on a charter plane, so I may find that I am the only one. But there will

*Now Sir Robert Scott of Manchester Olympic bid fame.

of course be other people at the game reserve, which is reputedly the best in the Federation. It is only for a week and I come back the following Tuesday. It isn't much of a break, but David Scott goes away for the best part of a month on the day that I get back, and we can't be away together. I shall hope to get another spell a bit later.

Now where was I? Oh yes, not having much news. All I have is of my visitor, Josh Reynolds. He arrived on Friday evening, very weary after the most hectic time in South Africa. I had Saturday morning off and took him out for the day to Lake Macillwaine, about twenty-five miles out of Salisbury, that is in the process of establishing a small game park. We were greeted at the gates of the park by two very tame eland – large buck. They were most handsome and gentle, and took sweets out of our hands, and poked their heads through the car windows. We saw several other types of buck, wildebeest and baboons. There isn't much there yet, but it was fun, all the same, to see a few of Africa's better known animals. In the evening we went to dinner with the Salisbury manager of Josh's firm – British Insulated Callender Cables – and his wife who live very near me. They are an intelligent couple and Josh is bright, and we had the most stimulating discussion about Art with a capital A, and other such subjects until the small hours of the morning. Today the husband took us both out to his golf course, and I had my first full round of golf since I came to Africa and I immensely enjoyed it – though I fear I shall be stiff tomorrow. Josh has stayed with them for the evening to have a curry supper, but I excused myself as I wanted to get home and do a few chores, including writing this letter to you. Josh and Jack Emery leave very early tomorrow for Northern Rhodesia, then I have one evening to get ready for my holiday. I must say I am lucky with my visitors. Josh is another James Hemming – doesn't want anything but a boiled egg and is terribly grateful to get away for a short spell from the demands of his tour. He evidently hates lecturing and meeting masses of new people, and has to screw himself up beforehand. And of course I have thoroughly enjoyed hearing all the Dulwich gossip.

One potentially alarming thing is happening tomorrow – somebody is coming to view the house with the prospect of buying. My lease is up this month anyway, and is only renewable if the house is not sold over my head. I shall be bitterly disappointed if I have to clear out, but will just have to face it if it comes. I don't mind so much about the house, but I dread having to leave the garden, just when I have put so much into it. We shall see.

Now I had better stop. I won't be able to get a letter to you when I am in Luangwa – at least I don't think I shall, so don't be surprised if it is a little while before you hear. I shall write anyway the minute I get back.

Lion Camp
Luangwa Valley
Northern Rhodesia

17 August 1961

I am sitting at a table beside the Luangwa River, with the sun quietly going down, and a large bull elephant bang opposite me on the sandy edge of the river, spraying himself with sand. After three days in this game reserve I am getting positively blasé about elephant! But to go back to the beginning of my story.

The flight up on Tuesday was a pleasant pottery one: to Blantyre in one hop, then a long pause there waiting for the Dakota connection. At last airborne again and away up to Salima on the shores of Lake Nyasa. Salima is a funny little grass landing strip in the middle of nowhere. From Salima back to Lilongwe and another halt – rather like a country bus – and then at last to Fort Jameson. I there discovered the two other people who were on the same tour – a South African man and his wife. We were met by two men – Norman Carr, a retired game ranger who is now running these tours for CAA, and a CAA agent, Ron Kidson, who is a tobacco farmer and does this tour work in his 'spare' time. We all piled into a VW microbus specially constructed for game viewing. At about five we set out on an eighty mile journey through the bush on dirt roads. Highlight of the journey was when a rhino suddenly loomed up in our lights. Our brakes were jammed on to see what he would do, and Ron put the VW into reverse in a flash, just in case. But rhino took one look and ambled off and we proceeded.

We stayed for the night in a game camp right on the river – as all the game camps are here. We were the only people; and the African staff who had been out on a beer drink were rustled up and produced a splendid meal in no time, which we ate by lamplight.

Next morning early we were out of bed, and Ron ran us four miles through the bush until we came to an elephant which had been shot the day before as it had a broken leg. We then got out of the car. I, accompanied by an African game ranger with a rifle, started to walk through an enchanted glade of bush. In an hour we had seen a lion – obviously we had disturbed him at the dead elephant – warthog, impala, puku, water buck, eland, croc., elephant, hippo, rabbit!, and an unbelievable collection of birds. On the way back we also saw zebra.

According to Norman, this is about the best game reserve in the world, for it is completely unspoilt and difficult to get at. Back in camp we packed up and proceeded on our way to this camp, some two hours drive away. Here we shall stay for the rest of our week. We game-watched all the way along, and there is never a hundred yards without something to watch. Lying in bed last night I could hear lion calling, and elephant, and the strange throaty guffaw of hippo.

But today has been the best of the lot so far. I shall save up telling you about it for my next letter as I couldn't do justice to it now. I started writing, as you know, when the sun was setting. Almost immediately I got whipped away by Ron and Norman for a swim in the river to cool off. It isn't deep enough to swim, but we had a good splash until we saw a croc. sliding towards us and gracefully retired.

We have a camp fire going, and have just finished a huge dinner of fish caught in the river, and impala. The rest of the party are back round the fire and I am still at the dinner table, writing to you. Norman is going into Fort Jameson at 5 a.m. tomorrow and I am determined that he take this with him. Must rejoin them. More anon, *how* I wish you were all here.

Luangwa

18 August 1961

To continue where I left off last night. I said that yesterday had been a red letter day. The reason is that I have stroked, in the open, two lions. How about that? Four years ago Norman took charge of two lion cubs whose mother had been shot. They were only a few days old. It is a second Elsa story. He reared them on the bottle and gradually weaned them. They had the free run of the camp, and as they got older they started gradually to hunt for themselves. They always stayed together and they never went very far afield. Throughout their life Norman has supplemented their diet and occasionally locked them up at night to keep them civilized – much to their disgust. They are called Big Boy and Little Boy. Because they had the best of everything in cubhood, they are bigger than their completely wild companions, particularly Big Boy. I had heard about these lions, but never dreamt I should see them.

Well, yesterday Norman drove us round to the camp where they have their base. The African who is detailed to keep an eye on them reported that they had crossed over to the other side of the river the night before but had come back. Norman and Ron got out of the bus and shut us in, and the African was sent to find the Boys. Within a minute I heard Norman say, 'Come on, Little Boy,' and along a path bounded these two beautiful creatures, like a couple of great enthusiastic dogs greeting their master on his return. They nearly knocked Norman and Ron over as they were embraced and hugged, and we sat in the bus spellbound. When their initial bounce had died down we were let

Norman and the Boys.

out and formally introduced. This means standing with your back to a tree for anchorage and patting the great beasts as they come up to you. Little Boy can be a bit quick-tempered, but Big Boy from the word 'go' has always had the most wonderfully amiable temperament, and this shows in his benign face.

Very soon they went down to the river to drink and we with them. We all had great frolics on the sand with them. Then Big Boy walked and swam across to the other side, while Little Boy watched him. Little Boy was once caught by a croc. and has been wary of crossing the river since. Norman said they must have a kill across the river and Big Boy had gone to guard it. Anyway, after lots of shouting, Big Boy reluctantly came back again and we all scrambled up to the camp once more. There the two lions flopped down in the shade beside us and went fast asleep, for all the world again like two dogs. We stayed for another hour drinking tea, and when we left they were still peacefully lying in the shade of the hut and scarcely opened an eye to watch us go.

I can't tell you what a thrill this all was. To stand over those sleeping lions and examine them minutely at six inches really was something. I never had one moment's fear with them.

The reason the world hasn't heard much about these lions yet is that Norman is about to have a book published on them, and Collins, the publishers, don't want his thunder stolen in advance. The book should be out next spring.

Norman knows the Adamsons well, and in fact had offered to take Elsa just before she died. He has compared all his material with theirs and says that his is, in fact, much better. He is a *very* modest man and was just stating what he thought to be the truth. Elsa was mostly written up by a ghost writer, as Joy Adamson is a Scandinavian and her English is bad. Norman has done all his own writing, though Collins have suggested ways of improving it, and he is working now on revisions. I can't wait for the book to come out – and I can't believe my own good fortune at having actually *stroked* two animals who will certainly become world famous within a year. I couldn't help thinking of you, Dora, in particular while I was with them, for I know how immeasurably thrilled you would have been. I only hope my transparencies will come out well and give you a little vicarious pleasure.

We had a bit of fun on the way home. Ron was driving and it had become a joke that when we came to a tight bend he went hell for leather round it to prove how well the VW cornered. He hurtled round one of these corners when suddenly there was an elephant slap in the road. He had stopped and got into reverse gear in less time than it takes to write. But the elephant was just as startled and decided to beat it. You never drive past elephant close to the road without being very careful.

This morning Norman left at 5 a.m. to collect some more visitors from Fort Jameson, and Ron and an African game guard took us for a two hour walk before breakfast through the bush. We saw just about everything but lion, and best of all a rhino with her three months calf. What massive creatures they are. We dared not go nearer than about a hundred yards, but at that distance we had a splendid view through binoculars. We had an immense breakfast on return and now we are sitting quietly by the river, reading and writing. For once no elephant are in sight, but a croc. has just slithered up the river not twenty yards from us, and every now and then a hippo raises his head to see what we are up to.

Lunch is just coming up, so no more now.

Back in Salisbury

23 August

As I had no chance of posting the above until I got back here, I thought I would leave it open so that I could tell you the rest of the story. Now what were the other major excitements? A three hour walk before breakfast the following morning just with the game guard, Ron and one of the newcomers, a mining engineer. No elderly or timid people with us, so we were really able to stride out. Highlight of this walk another rhino, but very much closer this time. We got to within about thirty yards, and Ron crept even nearer to get a close-up for me, though he wouldn't let me do it. It is astonishing how completely safe you feel with these men who have lived close to the big game all their lives and know exactly what liberties they can take with them. Although I admit I was keyed up and breathless with excitement on these stalks, I was never for one moment really frightened.

On Sunday Norman and Ron took us far into the native area to meet one of the old chiefs who has sixty-three villages under his chieftainship. They were determined that I in particular, because of my job, should see something of the old type of African, untainted by political agitators. On our way back we bumped into a shooting party, two Americans on safari. The cost of a licence to shoot in the area is £300 a week, and then you are only allowed to shoot one of each animal. Of course there is no shooting in the Reserve on the one side of the river, and most of the big game learn that it is to their advantage to keep on the Reserve side of the river, particularly by day. The hunter who was conducting the Americans said he wished to goodness we would push a few of our Reserve game across the river as he was having quite a time tracking any down! And this reminds me of a wonderful sight we had on Monday morning. We were up at 4 a.m. to drive about thirty miles to a place where elephant regularly cross the river at dawn, getting back from the open country to the Reserve for the day. We reached the place as the first flicker of light began to appear, and sat still waiting. As the light grew, we began to see elephant appearing in great numbers on the other bank. They were led by a tuskless cow, and gradually they started warily to wade across, all the littler elephants holding the tails of the elephants in front of them with their trunks. At this stage we counted up to about fifty elephant in the river or on the bank. Suddenly the old cow paused in mid river, smelling the air with her trunk. She must have got our scent, for she sent up a great trumpet, and at the signal all the elephants turned round and fled for dear life back into the bush from whence they had come. Elephant have a miraculous sense of smell. We must have been two hundred yards away at least but the wind was a bit against us. And human smell anyway tends to hang about over water. The incredible thing is that it is only the smell of the white man that elephant fear. They take no notice of the black. They have learnt through the years that it is only the white man who has the power to be their enemy, and this knowledge seems to be transmitted from one generation to another.

We had one more exciting stalk of a rhino, this time one we spotted as we drove along. We had to send for an armed game guard, as it is against the rules for even an experienced hunter like Norman to take visitors on foot without a gun. Norman went with us this time, and I couldn't get over the nonchalance with which the guard treated the whole thing – smoking his old pipe the while! But what that man doesn't know about the bush, about the animals, the birds and the trees I have yet to discover. The bush is his life and he will obviously never leave it. He must be about sixty. In his time he has shot thousands of elephant, mostly on game conservation – they breed like mad in this part of the world. But he says now he cannot bring himself to shoot another one; he must leave it to somebody else. He says he has too much respect and affection for the elephant to take another life. After all the politics of the last year it was good to find someone so completely tranquil and free from the artificialities of civilization. A great man in his way, and I think that we all felt that it had been a privilege to meet him in his own world, and see a bit of it through his eyes.

Earlier on the morning when we got up at four to see the elephants, I had hardly any sleep. The bush around us was always full of noises and I couldn't bear to miss any of it. I was suddenly aware of the fact that there was some busy grazing going on right outside my window. I say window but there was no glass in our huts – just fly netting reinforced with strong wire. I looked out and in the moonlight saw a hippo grazing within feet of where I was sleeping. I got out of bed and ran my nails over the wire. The hippo came nearer to see what the sound was, and put his head over the little wall of my verandah. Our two faces cannot have been more than two yards apart. How I wished that I had had a flash for my camera. But it was a great experience all the same.

Norman ran the two South Africans and me back to the airport at Fort Jameson yesterday morning. We had to be up by 4.30 a.m. to get there in time. Then it was on the plane and away home, after the most wonderful holiday imaginable. My goodness, we felt we had had our money's worth. The whole venture, including about 1,300 miles of flying, and 800 miles of driving, and all our food had cost us just over £50.

I am having today off to get myself back into harness – hence this letter. I dread having to go back to the office tomorrow, but if it weren't for the office I shouldn't have had this chance of a lifetime, so I mustn't be ungrateful! I have taken about eighty transparencies, and will let you have them as soon as possible.

10 September 1961

I seem to be in a more hopeless state than ever over my correspondence with you. Since I got back from leave it has been one thing after another. As you know, David Scott went off the day I got back, and at the same time Bill McIndoe went sick, so we were two short. Then Bill got better and the third First Secretary – may not have told you about him but his name is Paul Thirsk, and he has been seconded from Northern Rhod. to help us – he was a District Commissioner there – went off and got married! So I have been doing somebody else's work all the time. Then Bernard Braine, our Parliamentary Under Secretary, came out for a few days, bringing his young private secretary with him – Brian Gilmore. Brian is quite brilliant and in the CRO was always one of my pals – he is nearly twenty years younger than me and fifty times as clever, but we always got on. Well, he decided to have a week's leave in Salisbury after his master flew home. Poor lad, he has had such a terrible six months in CRO that he was just about at the end of his tether. Brian Unwin, Alport's PS, put him up, but then Brian U. had to dash off to Lusaka, so I inherited Brian G., being the only other one in the Mission that really knew him. He was no bother at all, as I just left him in the house and went off to the office, and for two days he did nothing but sleep throughout the whole day. But of course by the time I got home he was feeling chirpy, and he is such good company that we sat up until all hours gossiping about the office. So by the time I got rid of him, I was jolly tired. Then we have been as usual, skipping from crisis to crisis in the office with only half the staff present. David Scott has had to cut short his leave and came back on Friday, so that should make a big difference to me.

So, as you will see, letter writing has not been easy. Oh yes, I nearly forgot, I have also given Seize a fortnight's leave, so I have been battling singlehanded with the garden. Watering and clearing up leaves are the two jobs, and full time they are too. If you don't water every inch of the garden at least twice a week, and seedlings every day, you are in trouble. I have been getting up early to do some of it, and then working until it is pitch dark, or I have to dash and get ready for guests or go out. Phew. Anyway, this is Sunday evening and I have it entirely to myself, and write to you I will before I am distracted. I have spent most of the day gardening, but I had to take three hours off in the middle of the day when the parents of the boy I gave a lift to from Pretoria came to lunch.

I am amused to hear you talk of Richard Williams. He is Dickie to me! I know him and his wife quite well, and am always colliding with them at parties. He is a funny little man – about five feet nothing – but has a very interesting and exciting life. He got arrested in Katanga some months ago and had quite a job getting out again. I am so glad you saw Mrs Campbell. She is a sweetie, isn't she? I haven't heard from her since she got back, but I expect I shall one of these days. I bumped into their son in Salisbury the other day. He was very full of himself, having just got engaged. When I saw the girl I wondered if he had done it deliberately while his parents were away.

I have just had back two rolls of transparencies taken on my holiday and I am absolutely thrilled with them. Some of the ones with the lions are too good to be true – at least I think they are but I may be biased. I hope you can bear to wait a little while for them, for I want to show them to a few people here. And I also want to keep them on the off chance that Norman Carr will be coming to Salisbury fairly soon, and I want to show them to him. I told Ben Gingell about Norman's book, and he nearly exploded with frustration that Collins had got it and not Longman's. But he persuaded me to write to Norman and ask him if he would write some other books in Longman's Educational series. I don't really think that Norman will, but at least I have written to him to put the idea into his head.

By the time you get this letter I shall probably have been up to Nairobi and back! Every fortnight now somebody from the office has to fly up there with secret papers as part of a courier service. Brian Unwin should have gone this time, but the HC is taking a week's leave, and he won't let Brian be away at the same time. So I have been asked if I will go at short notice: I shall know definitely tomorrow whether I have to or not. You fly up on a Tuesday, have the whole of Wednesday in Nairobi, then fly back on the Thursday. And if there is anything for Dar es Salaam you have to break your journey there. I have been dying to go on this trip, but haven't had a chance so far. Heaven help my plants if I have to but it will be worth it. If it falls through, I shall certainly go within the next month or so.

No word yet of the house being sold. I think they are asking too much. Did I tell you? They want £11,000, with only two acres of land.

Must now think about going to bed. If I have to go off to Nairobi on Tuesday tomorrow will be one long hell of a rush!

New Stanley Hotel
Nairobi

13 September 1961

My first hop in a Comet last night – what a civilized way of travelling. Less vibration than a train – superb dinner, and in Nairobi before I had time to go to sleep – which is fantastic considering planes always send me off. The journey took less than three flying hours. It will be double that crawling back via Dar in an old Argonaut.

And this hotel is the acme of civilisation too. My coffee pot, hot milk and cup were all removed after my first cup of coffee, and new pot, milk and clean cup brought for my second! I have the whole day now to myself. I'm being lazy and not attempting to make any polite noises at the Secretariat. I shall window shop, and then hope to have a run into the game park, which is only a few miles out of the town. Driving between the airport and Nairobi last night, there were half a dozen zebra quietly grazing on the verge and taking not a blind bit of notice of anybody. They skip out of the reserve at night because the grass is always greener on the other side of the road!

It is hard to believe you are almost bang on the equator here. At 6,000 feet it is cool, and today is positively cloudy and chilly. I was cold in bed last night with two blankets, and will demand an extra one tonight.

Must fly now and make the most of my time.

Salisbury

18 September 1961

What a bloomin' life this is. It is 1.15 a.m. and I have been in the office since six o'clock last night. With us bang in the middle of the Katanga crisis and the HC up in Ndola, we have had to man the office throughout the whole of Sunday. I had the day off, but was brought in at six to do my stint, and I'm still here. I have been trying to get down to writing to you but there has never been long without some interruption or other. We do seem to land ourselves in some larks, don't we? I am waiting for the HC to ring from Ndola any minute, and if I am to get this ready for the bag later today I must get cracking now.

To go back a bit. I can't remember when I last wrote to you in Nairobi. I think I was about to go into the game park. It was huge fun. The only other occupant of the coach was a sixty-six year old American spinster and ex-school ma'am, who only gave up piloting her own plane last year and now hires one if she wants to fly! We had a splendid three hours in the park and saw just about everything, except that there are no elephant. We found a pride of five lions lying fast asleep and not taking a blind bit of notice of us. And I hope I have some very good pictures of a mother giraffe and her little baby that was so young that it still had its umbilical cord hanging. I took myself off to the one theatre in the evening, and then left at ten the next morning for the return journey. This proved to be infinitely wearying as it involved eight flying hours in a noisy Argonaut. I had two incredibly heavy bags and one light one, my own case, handbag, camera and book, and all this lot I had to lug off at every stop. Mercifully a journalist who got off at Ndola, obviously bound for the Congo, came to my rescue and pulled my leg like mad, saying that he was the last person in the world to be trusted with a diplomatic bag. I came down at Dar first and had three-quarters of an hour with one of my colleagues from the CRO who is there in advance of Independence to get the office set up in embryo. We flew alongside Zanzibar, which was a lovely sight. Dar itself is attractive from the air, but of course I wasn't there long enough to leave the airport. On the way to Dar we also flew right past Mount Kilimanjaro, with its snow cap. I hope the picture of that will come out well too. I was very tired by the time I got to Salisbury and my poor old ears were fair humming. Give me Comets every time!

I had meant to spend this evening at home writing to you, and I came into the office in such a hurry that I left your letter behind. I am sure there were things to answer, but at this ungodly hour of the morning my brain is not at its best. We have just had news that Hammarskjöld's plane was approaching Ndola airport, about to land, and has simply vanished into thin air (that was since I started to write this letter). Now I have to stay put in the office until we have word of what has happened. It is all terribly worrying. While I am waiting I think I will get down on the stretcher that a kind colleague has brought in. I have about four diplomatic bags folded up and put inside a fifth diplomatic bag for a pillow. It's now 2 a.m. on Monday morning. Top of the morning to you! Will write again when the air has cleared a bit, but heaven knows when it will.

9 a.m. I got away at 3.15 a.m. and was in bed by 3.45. Up again at 7 a.m. and back in the office. Will put this in the bag while I think about it.

25 September 1961

It is lunch time on bag day and I have nipped back smartly from lunch to try to get a little note off to you. I have your two letters of 11th September and 18th, for which many thanks.

Now first of all, what to answer in them. No, no more news about the house being sold, but did I tell you that while I was in Nairobi somebody came back for the second time to look at it? I feel that is a bit ominous, but as my landlord is in England at present it may be difficult to get on with things. I just keep on keeping my fingers crossed and putting more plants in the garden in the hope that I shall still be there to enjoy them. The reason my landlord wants to sell is that five years ago he bought a small farm out at Ruwa, some fifteen miles away, which he farms in addition to his work in tobacco. He wants to sell my house so that he can have the capital to put into his farm. He certainly gets a worthwhile rent, but that is not his main consideration.

I gather that the 'African Now' programme which you saw caused quite a furore among Rhodesians as it was reputed to be a very biased programme. I only wish I could have seen it to judge whether this was a fair criticism.

Now to my activities since I last wrote. I think of all the crises that have hit us since I came here the latest Katanga one was the worst. I told you of my Sunday night vigil. Soon after I had put my last letter in the post we heard that Hammarskjöld's plane had crashed. It was a terrible shock. Brian Unwin, who was up in Ndola with the High Commissioner, actually heard the voice of the pilot a few minutes before the plane vanished, and I think I may have told you that he rang me to say the plane had been overhead but they did not know what had happened to it after that. Monday continued to be a hectic day, but I got away at about six and was very early in bed, as I was given the night off. The next day, Tuesday, I worked from eight in the morning right through until 12.30 the following morning, with a short spell off for lunch and two hours off in the evening for dinner. It was about the most hectic sixteen hours of my life, including long distance calls to London, and heaven knows how many to Ndola and Lusaka. Telegrams were pouring in from every side, and I had to take action on them one after the other, with the phone ringing incessantly. Bill McIndoe had the same sort of thing on Monday night, and took over again on Wednesday night. By Thursday the worst of the flap was over, but we were all pretty tired by then. If it weren't all so desperately depressing and worrying it would be enormously interesting. I can't begin to tell you the extraordinary things in which we as an office became involved. It is odd how Salisbury seems to get other people's crises in its lap quite apart from the ones of its own making. I suppose we are physically in the middle of such a lot of problems that we can't help but become involved. But if poor Hammarskjöld had to get killed somewhere, why did it have to be on Federal territory?

Thank goodness we have all had a fairly quiet weekend, and I spent as much time as possible in the garden, uncoiling from the excitements in the earthy business of planting seedlings. I think I should go mad sometimes if I didn't have the garden as an antidote to the extraordinary life we lead.

Joe Garner (Sir Saville to you!), ex-High Commissioner in Canada and my old DHC in Delhi, is out here at present. He is to be our new permanent head in the CRO, and he is on an indoctrination tour of the Commonwealth before taking up his duties. Unfortunately he arrived just at the end of the worst part of the flap. We wished that he had come earlier so that he could have seen for himself just what we had to battle with! The Scotts gave a supper party for him on Saturday night, to which all the senior staff were invited. It was great fun, but we were all pretty jaded, and thankful when Joe broke up the party fairly early and we were able to slink off to bed.

Here are a few more transparencies, two of Sandys in the Zambesi. In one of them is Freda Smith, Sandys' Private Secretary, Shannon and Sir Ralph Hone, Legal Adviser. The indoors one is taken with my back to my front door, with the drawing room on the left and the french window onto the back garden ahead. You can just see my reflection in the mirror, taking the picture. The garden one is taken from the upper lawn in front of the house looking over the lower lawn. The drive runs between the two, but you can't see it.

Back to work now. Pray for a little peace for us. I don't think we shall get it as Northern Rhodesia is about to rear its ugly head again. It never really lowered it, but was simply swamped by the Congo.

All my love

Margaret

28 September 1961

As usual, bag just going, but thought I would scratch a note to send these transparencies. The 'ducking' ones and Cape Town came to me from Marie du Plessis in Pretoria by hand of Brian Gilmore. I had forgotten she had promised to let me have them when she knew my camera had been stolen. One of me taken on stoep by James Hemming.

Have been asked by Chairman of Federal Power Board and his wife to go up to Kariba with them this week. Will see everything in style – and free, though in fact would have preferred a quiet weekend. But it is too good a chance to miss. Up on Saturday – by road – back on Monday.

Must go now. Pathologist who conducted Hammarskjöld's p.m. arriving any minute from Ndola.

9 October 1961

Battling against bag closing again, and have a suspicion I haven't written since before Kariba. *Very* interesting weekend. Saw all the works and the weed and caught my first fish – a 1.5 lb chesa (not good eating alas!).

Life in the office much quieter, but dreadful spell of social activities. Had Alport and Lady A. to cocktail party last week with as many nobs as I dare ask. Thank heaven it seemed to go off very well. Made most of the savouries myself, which helps.

Haven't thanked you yet for letter of 1st Oct. Hippo photos hardly worth sending – too far away. Best hippo ones in Luangwa very good and will come when I finish the round of showing them off here (am showing them at two parties next week, and that should be the end).

15 October 1961

It is Sunday morning, and I have just come in from an hour or two's gardening as it is really too hot even for me to stay out in the sun. This as you may remember from last year is what is known as Suicide Month, but after India I don't think it is likely to make me take MY life! The nights are always mercifully cool, but when the sun is high in the middle of the day it can be a bit much.

We really have been much quieter in the office this last week. What a relief. The High Commissioner even strolled into my office one day, sat in a chair and put his feet up on my desk and gossiped hard for nearly half an hour. What a change! When he is relaxed like that he can be most entertaining, and peals of laughter could be heard emanating from my office. But I have had a fearsome round of entertainments. Eleven days in a row, with only yesterday, Saturday, without some do or other. The eleven days ends next Thursday night – at least that is where it ends at the moment, but when the times comes it will probably be extended!

You ask about Donald and Elizabeth. They flew out to Lagos about a month ago. I had a letter from Liz which I will send on when I have answered it. They were to go to Kaduna originally, but are to have a few months first in Lagos, and in the end they may after all stay there. When Liz wrote they were still in a hotel, waiting to move into a house. Both Liz and Celia had fallen victims to gippy tummy, or whatever it is called there, but were otherwise all right, and very excited about their translation. I have also heard again from the Aikmans. They are definitely coming to stay with me at the beginning of next year.

Think I will make this a short one, and try hard to get a few long outstanding letters written while I am in the mood. The mood won't last long I fear in this heat.

24 October 1961

Sorry no time for a long letter. Maddening weekend with office interruptions throughout.

Weekend culminated with big Federation Day 'do'. Thought you might be amused by enclosed result. Hat thrown together by me from remnants of that big-brimmed black one I bought in N.Z. and a yard of feathery fluff – five minutes before party!

Also just received – candid snap taken at swimming party.

Enchanted you have seen 'my' lions! Transparencies follow.

Bag closing.

28 October 1961

I seem to have two letters to thank you for. One dated the 16th and the other 19th. Now through them for points. The Kariba weed. Great experiments are going on at this very minute, but there is a hope that when the lake is full the weed will automatically be controlled. While it is filling up there is so much decaying matter in the water to feed on, but once it is full this will get less and less. It certainly is a frightening thing to see, it is so vigorous.

I can't tell you how tickled I was to hear that you had seen 'my lions'. Did you write to Cliff Michelmore, and if so did you get a reply? No, I don't know that game ranger who got injured by the rhino, but I did hear the full story, which was that he sought protection behind a big tree. The rhino came for him, and to his dismay he found that the tree was riddled by white ant and was nothing more than dust. It only needed a bit of a shove to fall down, and with the whole weight of a rhino it just gave up and died. Not a very pleasant experience!

Now to my news. Although we haven't got a major crisis on our hands for once there still seems to be a lot of work around. I had an amusing experience yesterday. Something blew up which landed me in tearing round to Welensky's private house to show him something. I had never been to the private residence before, but the High Commissioner described where it was. It was as well that he did, for of course it had no name outside as nearly every house in Rhodesia sensibly has, and it looked so unpretentious, not to say scruffy, that I should have had doubts as to whether I had arrived or not! I couldn't see where the front door was, but there was a stoep with a large ridgeback dog lying on it. So I stopped and had a chat with the dog and then I heard W's voice inside a French window saying, 'Come on in, Miss Archer.' In I went and there was another big dog, two little white poodles and two Siamese cats lying with their backs to each other but touching on one of the easy chairs. Welensky himself was dressed in an open-necked shirt, a baggy old pair of flannels, and one shoe. He pointed to the other shoe lying on the carpet and said that he hoped I could bear the smell! The drawing room was the most homely clutter of the possessions of a lifetime. Bits and pieces everywhere, but obviously a very much lived in home.

The poor old boy is still suffering badly from gout, and is thoroughly aggrieved about it as he never drinks.

I don't think I have anything else of much interest to tell you. We are going through a very uncomfortable time with the weather. It is much hotter than it was last year, and although of course it never gets anywhere near as hot as Delhi it is much more difficult to contend with because of the altitude. It is just as if one were without any bones to support one, and bed or at least a horizontal position is all one longs for. I shall be glad when the rains come. They should not be far away. Today is stifling and sultry with quite a lot of cloud around, so I am beginning to be hopeful.

I have just been roused from an after lunch nap – much needed, since I was out to dinner last night and rather late home – by the four children across the way that I have just got to know. The father is an Edinburgh man – Campbell, who had polio in India eighteen years ago and is very crippled, and his wife is a South African. The children range from five up to fifteen and they seem to have taken a great fancy to me. They are always coming across trying to lure me into their swimming pool, or asking whether they can do anything to help me. I could have crowned them for waking me and told them so. But I shan't mind nipping across for a swim in a little while!

I have thought what I would like for my Christmas present. May I have a powder flap-jack. I have gone back to using loose powder and not the pancake type, and my old compact has just about had it. Could it please have not a gauze but an inner metal flap that opens. There, I hope that isn't too tall an order.

Must get on now with more of my Christmas cards. Some of my N.Z. ones have gone but there are more still to do. I hope they will be in time.

P.S. Kariba weed slide is optically illusive. It looks as if it was taken from a few yards away, but in fact it was from the top of the wall. The floating wood thing is a Heath Robinson effort to keep the weed from being sucked into the intake ducts.

2 November 1961

I have had three weekday evenings in a row at home, which has been bliss. I have gardened for an hour – until dark, had my supper, and been in bed by 9 p.m. each night – then up each morning at 5.15 a.m. for an hour and a half's clerking – Christmas cards in particular. I go out to dinner tonight, and next week I am out every single blessed evening!

Many thanks for your letter of 20 October. I tittered over your request for Donald and Elizabeth's address. Have a guess – c/o D. & M. Branch, CRO Downing St., 'By Bag to Lagos'!

The cutting about swimming. Yes, there is quite a hooha going on, both in S.R. and N.R. about multi-racial swimming, but it will die down. It is understandable, as Africans' habits are not yet quite as civilised as Europeans. There is incidentally no bilharzia in the Zambesi.

9 November 1961

Yesterday I took Lady Alport out to the only African Orphanage in the whole of the Federation. It is run by an African who was a Methodist Minister. He gave up his Ministry to start the home – though he had to give up his salary too. He now has twenty-six orphans, and has to rely on a minute government grant and voluntary help to keep it going. He is a wonderful man and deserves much more support than he gets. He showed us one little girl with a great scar over one eye. She was rescued in the nick of time by a policeman who found her parents in the throes of murdering her to sell her flesh to a witch-doctor. You hear plenty of these stories, but not until you actually see a near-victim with the scars does it *really* come home to you. How about getting the WI or Ivington fete to make a small donation?!! I am starting a collection in the office. It is almost unheard of here for an African to run his own charitable show. Usually they leave it to Europeans.

And while I remember, if Leslie has any of Noey's old suits that he has finished with, do you think I could have them for Sixpence? I would pay the postage. Out of his £90 a year income he has to find £38 next year for his eldest son's education. I will help him out, but clothes are quite a problem. It doesn't matter how old they are. Sixpence is a splendid patcher.

15 November 1961

From all reports you have been having a fair whack of my pal Sir Roy on TV, the radio and in the papers. We have had extracts of his various speeches and press conferences relayed over our radio here, and I must say, whatever you think of Welensky's ideas, you have to give it to him for personality. According to the papers here, he has made quite a hit in England. How does it strike you? Is this just the papers here boosting him up?

I do hope that the mistletoe gets through. What a lovely idea. What it is to have such an honest mother! If you had called it Christmas decorations you would not have been lying, and there would have been no trouble. Because I have dip. privilege my parcels are of course never opened. And that cookery book sounds heaven. Can't wait to get it. Thank you so much. After sending it off you shouldn't have taken any notice of my other request, you bad girl! I got your joint parcel off and only hope it arrives safely. It's a bit bulky but a lot of it is packing. Please tell Peter to be a bit careful when he opens his, or he may have to do some dentistry!

I won't forget to look up that friend of Winnie's. I'm afraid I am still finding it hard to do all the things I should do. Nothing would induce me to settle in

Salisbury. I find it the most trying place to live in. Something about the altitude just doesn't go with my particular form of metabolism. I need such a hell of a lot of sleep to keep going, and when I have a free moment from official duties and entertaining I just flop into bed. I was in bed last night at 8.30 – *me*, and slept through without waking until 5.30, when I got up to do my usual bout of clerking. It is quite maddening, but something I just have to live with. But this is not such a bad week at last. Only out Wednesday, tonight that is, Friday and Sunday.

Two nights ago I had a state visit from my landlord. He thinks that the woman who has been nibbling at buying the house won't buy it in the end. He puts the chances at about one in ten only. I hope to heaven he is right. The trouble is that she has just sold her other house for £20,000. Sorry, I may have told you this before – so you see there is no shortage of money. But the house is much too small, and difficult to add on to without spoiling the elevation. I can do nothing but sit back and pray.

Bath time now. No exciting news, just the usual grind without any startling crises just for the moment.

25 November 1961

I seem to have a lot of things to thank you for today. Your two letters of 15th and 19th November, the stamps, and your parcel of mistletoe. To my great sorrow, the mistletoe had virtually disintegrated with mould. The berries were still there, but the stalks had gone all soggy and the berries had fallen off them. It was a very noble effort on your part, and at least I had a little sniff of Hereford, for which many thanks. On reflection, I think it might have been better to send it dry as it had to be tied up wet for so long. But at least it did get through and was not stopped by the Customs. Many thanks for the stamps. They came in the nick of time.

I am thunderstruck by your great efforts over the Mission. What a one you are. I have written to Mr Rusike to tell him all about your efforts and am sure he will be thrilled. I have only just launched my appeal in the office, as I wanted to try to cash in on a bit of Christmas spirit. I will let you know how I fare.

Thank you also for your efforts over some of Leslie's clothes for Sixpence. When I told Sixpence he said with a broad grin that he didn't mind how old they were as he had a machine. Indeed he has an aged sewing machine and does the most wonderful patching. I have seen some of it on his own clothes and it is as good as you and I can do if not better. He is a very thrifty person, and as his wife lives away from him for so much of the time he has obviously learnt to be handy.

Since I last wrote we seem to have had every variation of weather. After being drowned and cold we had a spell of boiling humid weather which made us all feel lousy. Then last night just as I was preparing to go out to a party in stifling heat, the heavens opened and we had a terrific thunderstorm. It is dry again today and hotting up again and miserably humid. Oh for a bit of good old English temperate weather! Last week was rather a bad one, hence my lack of letters. I gave two dinner parties in a wild attempt to catch up on long-standing debts, and I had to go out on two other nights. Now it is the weekend and I have lied unashamedly to have the whole weekend without any dates. I just felt I couldn't face them.

Sorry, this is a very newsless letter! Will try to do better next time.

3 December 1961

Now to your letter. You really are wonderful to have collected such a magnificent sum. I asked Mr Rusike and his wife and daughter for the second time to a cocktail party I gave last week. I feel that the more people they can meet the greater the chance of getting help. I told him of your great collection and he was thrilled. I do think it is a truly wonderful effort.

You really mustn't worry about me. There is absolutely nothing wrong with me: everyone feels the altitude at this time of year and we are one and all going around moaning and groaning. Every now and again it gets on top of us. I am taking all the right sort of vitamins to counteract this, and I can assure you that I am really blooming, even if I can't resist a wail! The fact that I am heavier than I have been for a good fifteen years should reassure you. Greyer and more wrinkled than ever perhaps but otherwise a bonny bouncing babe. The worst of the hot, steamy weather is over now, so we should all be feeling a bit more cheerful.

Now what news? Nothing very exciting I don't think. Of course we have Maudling out here at the moment, but he hasn't caused me any bother. The only slight repercussion is that I am to have Ken Neal, the chap from the Colonial Office who came out here a year ago and stayed with me then, and who is now accompanying Maudling, to stay with me again for one night next week. He will be the beginning of a string of visitors. After him in January comes Eleanor Emery, the girl in our office with whom I stayed in Pretoria on my way up from the Cape. She is at the end of her tour, and as she doesn't want leave in England in January is going to spend some time wandering around our various posts in Africa and staying with all her old pals. Then the Aikmans come in early March, and James Hemming and his wife in April. I hope they will stay with me some of the time anyway.

I have just been out in my large estate gathering youngberries. I may have told you about the four children opposite who had adopted me. Well, they know more about my garden than I do myself, and asked me the other day if they could go and pick my youngberries. I hadn't a clue that I had any, but I find now that I have millions in one of the wilder parts of my jungle. They are enormous, and although they haven't got quite the flavour of our wild blackberries, it is difficult to tell the difference when they have been cooked. (I'm making them into a creamy kind of fool for a party I am giving next week.) Incidentally, the children were all in my garden a fortnight ago and Pat, the girl of eleven, was climbing her favourite tree, and I was mowing the lawn just below her. Suddenly there was an almighty crash and a branch gave way beneath her and she crashed to the ground, just missing the machine by inches. She fell at least nine feet and broke her arm into the bargain: I thought she probably had from the way she fell. I dashed her round to her own home in the car in a real muck sweat. I must say her mother was marvellous.

All she said was, 'Stupid child, it is her own silly fault for being so careless,' and got the doctor and packed her off to the hospital in no time. They have had so many broken bones in that family that to her it was no more than a cut finger! The eldest boy had only just got his arm out of plaster after a break some two months before. Pat can't have a plaster as the break is right at the top of the arm, but has to wear a sling for two months.

Still no news of the house being sold. A woman came to see it on Friday evening but declared at once that it was too small for her, so once more I breathed a sigh of relief. I have heard nothing more about the woman who had £20,000 to play about with and am hoping that has fallen through too.

Will go and do a little more gardening now in the last hour of daylight. The weeds are legion and everything is growing at an alarming pace.

10 December 1961

Six a.m. on a fine Sunday morning, and I am hastening to get this written to you lest the rest of the day proves as chaotic as I think it may. I have your two exciting letters with all their enclosures to thank you for, and best of all the cheque. I have sent it straight off to Rusike, and expect I shall hear from him in a day or two. I can't tell you what a wonderful effort I think it. You really are terrific!! And thank you so much for sending off the parcel of clothes. I will put a cheque for the postage in this letter. You should have seen Sixpence's grin when I told him the parcel contained five jackets. He has only had one for ages and it is very patched. What a lot of letters your appeal has prompted. I have read them with great pleasure, and will try when I have time to get round to thanking at least some of the donors.

But time is likely to be in short supply for a little while. With Christmas coming up there are of course the usual rounds of social activity. But much worse, we are quite back to old times so far as work is concerned. We seem to be past-masters in not having our crises singly. This weekend we have the demonstrations by Africans culminating in the banning of the NDP and the calling up of Territorials. Then we have had Maudling back from N.R. to hold his final talks with Alport before dashing off back to London, and on top of all that, all hell let loose again in the Congo, with our office the only means of getting messages from Elisabethville back to London. I had invited Roger West's mother and father, and a great friend of Mrs West, and Roger himself to come and have tea with me yesterday. (Roger is the young man who lives with Ben Gingell, and his Ma and Pa are visiting from Bulawayo while Ben is away.) They arrived slap in the middle of an enormously long telephone session on one of these wretched messages, and then the phone proceeded to ring at about ten minute intervals for the rest of the time they were with me. Luckily the worst of it was over by eight o'clock, and miraculously I wasn't called out in the night. But I'm not optimistic about the rest of the day – hence my getting this written while all is quiet.

You may have read about our office being visited by demonstrating women. We started off with about eighty on Tuesday morning. They just sat quite quietly in the foyer of our building and fed their babies and changed the babies' nappies and stared hard at everyone who went in and out of the building. After a lot of comings and goings by young Brian Unwin, they elected two of their number to come up and see the High Commissioner. After that they all moved off to the PM's office (Whitehead that is, not Welensky). The next day many more came and sat in the foyer, but the police soon moved them outside. There they squatted among the parked cars – I was thankful my car was a bit up the street – and the police simply could not move them any further. At last they brought along two Alsatian police dogs – and you have never seen women shift so quickly. Africans are terrified of dogs at the best of times, and trained Alsatians are just about the equivalent of a small atom bomb to us! In a way it was rather a horrid sight, for of course most of the women were completely clueless about what they were demonstrating over, and were simply obeying their husbands' instructions. I suppose I watched about a hundred of them being shepherded into Black Marias, and that was the end of them for that day. On Friday there were police on guard outside our building, so none of the women got near us. But I went slap into a big demonstration in Cecil Square at lunch time. All was quiet when I went to my lunch, and on the way back there were about eight hundred Africans in the square. As I wormed my way through them on the way to the Bank along came a lot of police in police vans and armoured cars, trained rifles on the crowd, and then dispersed them with tear gas. I did a Felix act, and just kept on walking until I was back in the office a few hundred yards away. The odd thing is the whole episode was very quiet. There was no shouting or singing – unlike some of the women – and a lot of the Africans had broad grins on their faces. Poor Roger had parked his car, as always, just outside the main police station, and there was some stone-throwing there on one of the days – I can't remember which. He had his windscreen and back window shattered and large dents made in the bodywork of his car. He is not insured for riot damage so has had to fork out £16 for the windows, and of course the bumps are in places where it would cost far too much to have them beaten out, so he feels his car has probably lost thirty or forty pounds in value. I wrote to the S.U.N. a month or two back to ask what the cost of including riot damage would be, and it was so expensive – can't remember what now – that I decided not to bother, particularly as most of the car damage happens in the African townships and not in Salisbury itself. But I'm beginning to think differently now. I think I had better look up the papers again.

Don't get alarmed by all this. It probably sounds so much worse to you than it does to us in the middle of it – always the way. The banning of the NDP seems to have gone off without any serious incident, so we may in fact have a quieter time with our African friends.

Now I think I had better get into the bath and think about breakfast. Thank you again for all your wonderful efforts, and please do pass on my thanks to those who are within hailing distance of you.

P.S *Monday*. As I guessed – it, Sunday, turned out to be an awful day – we took it in turns, I did 12-3 p.m., and was up twice in the night. Feeling sleepy today!

16 December 1961

It is more than your turn to have a letter from me. First of all thank you so very much for your Christmas greetings and the perfectly enchanting book. I say enchanting, not because I have read it yet – I am saving it up for after Christmas – but because I read such wonderful reviews of it and have coveted it ever since. You couldn't have chosen a book I wanted more and I am absolutely delighted. Thank you all so very much.

We are once more well and truly in the middle of trouble. I dashed back for a quick lunch today, Saturday, and flew back into the office to man it for the

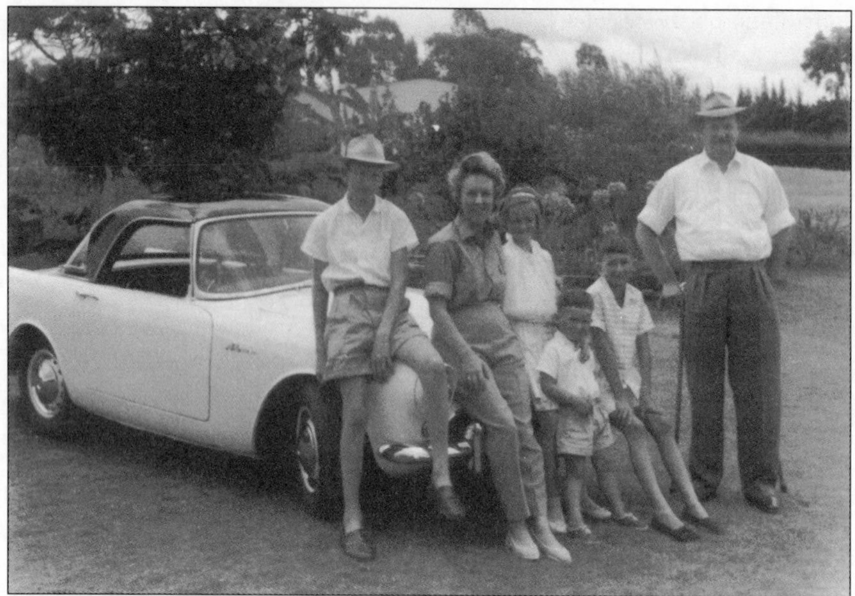

With the Campbell family

afternoon. I am trying to get a few letters written between dealing with emergency telegrams and long distance calls with Kitwe, who are doing their best to keep in touch with our poor beleaguered Consulate in Elisabethville. It is all very exciting but depressing too. And we are making arrangements to man the office throughout tomorrow, Sunday, as well. Who would be a civil servant? I am sure we work much harder than the business world!!

I haven't any really exciting news apart from work. It has been a pretty busy week and there has been little time to think of much else. I can't believe that Christmas is almost upon us. We haven't had a second to get into the spirit of Christmas. And of course it is a terrible time of year for parties, either to be gone to or to give.

Guess what. The children who often come and visit me from across the road saw two bush babies in the jungly part of my garden the other day. I hardly ever have the time to go down to that part of the garden, but I must now try to do so to see if I can spot them too. They make wonderful pets if you can catch them young enough, but I wouldn't have the heart to take them out of my gum trees. But it is exciting that they are on my premises. What I fear is that they won't be my premises much longer. One man came back no fewer than six times yesterday to look at the house. I can't help feeling that he wouldn't have done that if he hadn't been very interested in buying. I shall be spitting mad if I have to leave. The garden is looking lovely at the moment and I have a lot of seedlings on the way waiting to be planted out. I must just go on hoping for the best.

I don't suppose I shall be able to get another letter to you all before Christmas, so I will hope here that you have a wonderful time. I shall miss you all like hell as usual, and will be thinking about you.

27 December 1961

I am afraid that it is an age since I wrote to you and I have so many things to thank you for. I had better just plunge in and go through your last two pre-Christmas letters paragraph by paragraph to see what wants answering.

First letter. The Aikmans. No, they have left their children behind with, I think, Betty's mother. Imagine not seeing them for nine months. But it would obviously be impossible, if only from the financial point of view, to lug them all round the world. The Hemmings. James is writing a series of text books for the teaching of Africans. The Southern Rhodesia Government are changing over to his books and he has a collaborator in Salisbury, so he has to come out each year while they plan the next year's course. They find it easier to do it this way year by year, rather than write a whole series in one fell swoop. What James does is to go round a number of the schools using his books, and talk to the teachers and the children so that he can plan and adapt in the light of their experience. He is hoping this year to sell his books also to Northern Rhodesia and Nyasaland. If he does, Ben Gingell reckons that he will draw something like £2,000 a year in royalties alone from the Federation. Jolly nice eh! But he certainly works very hard and conscientiously for his money, and evidently his books are revolutionizing the teaching of English here.

I'm so sorry you have had a cold. It is quite miraculous, for colds and flu are fairly prevalent here and particularly in the office, and I haven't had a vestige of either in my eighteen months here. And not a sign of my old bronchitis. Obviously a completely smokeless, clear air suits me. And I have half a pint of orange juice every morning of my life – oranges are wonderfully cheap and I have Sixpence to squeeze them. I'm sure this helps to keep the bugs at bay.

Now to the orphanage. A thousand thanks for your second cheque. I haven't yet passed this on as I still haven't completed the office collection, and thought I would take the remnants of your money, the office money and a collection of clothes all along at the same time. We were so frantically busy before Christmas that I just didn't have time to chase the office list, which is circulating, and collect the money before the holiday. I have seen the list from time to time and I think I may collect about £30. Lady Alport has also made a separate effort, and took along an enormous pile of clothing and food and presents in time for Christmas. Meanwhile I have today received from Mr Rusike the enclosed letter and photograph. The letter took nine days to reach me – but that is not a bit surprising in this country, particularly at Christmas time. Isn't it wonderful to think that your effort will keep one child for a whole year? I also enclose the Christmas card he sent. Obviously to save money he uses old ones and cuts the bottoms off. A splendid idea! Please do thank everyone who has contributed – Mrs Edwards in particular. I shall try to get a little note to her written to put in this letter. You ask where the orphanage is. It is a few miles out of Salisbury – about twenty minutes run in a car. Yes, I took a picture of the Rusikes and all the children when I went to the home, but the film is still in the camera. It was rather a wet, dull day, so I am not very hopeful of its coming out well, but you shall have it anyway.

There now, I think that just about takes care of your letters, for which again many thanks. My news since I last wrote? I can't remember where I got to last. I think I wrote on last Sunday week, early in case the day got b—d up. It did! I worked from 8.30 a.m. until noon and from six until eleven at night. I had just got home and into bed when the phone rang. Luckily I didn't have to go back into the office, but I had to spend some time telephoning people. I had just got back into bed for the second time when the phone rang again. You can imagine my language! By then of course I was beyond sleep. But it was all very exciting and I had the thrill of talking on the phone direct to our Consulate in Elisabethville – the first direct contact we had had for a couple of days. The Congo really is the most awful business and we have completely lost all faith in the United Nations. Don't start me on it or I will go off pop!

The week up to Christmas was also busy on the social side. I had dinner with the BBC chap here, Dicky Williams and his wife. Dicky is still very lame from the wound he got in Katanga a month or two back. And you may have read about the FBC chap who was injured recently in Katanga – Jimmy Biddulph. I also know him well. We spent many an hour together in the Ambassador hotel when I was hanging around with that blessed South West Africa Committee. Thank goodness it looks as if he will recover, after a brain operation performed in E'ville by an Italian doctor.

Miraculously I was left in peace over the Christmas holiday. The HC and David Scott had a pretty thin time of it, but it was all so top level that we minions were left out. Was I glad! I had a lot of invitations, but lied my way into having quite a bit of time to myself: I spent most of it sleeping. On Christmas Eve I was lying out sunbathing in my bathing costume and thankful to have a bit of shade, and I heard the news over my portable radio that you were freezing in the coldest Christmas for seventy years. I mopped my brow with some satisfaction that I was where I was. It was the one tiny consolation for not being at home at Christmas. But it was fun to be with the McIndoes. There were seven small children altogether, the oldest being five, and to see them all running around in their birthday suits playing with the hosepipe – we all got a drenching into the bargain – really was rather sweet.

The best news I have is that I have persuaded the office to let me have three weeks leave in February. I am not quite sure what I shall do but I think I will go down into South Africa. Now that I can't be posted there I should like to see a bit more of it. Roger West and his brother are going down to the Cape at about the same time, and I might go down at least some of the way in convoy with them. The great thing is to get down to sea level, so whatever I don't do, I shall certainly do that. And I have a pressing invitation to call in at Mbabane in Swaziland, where a man who used to work in the CRO now is. Gwen Hunt used to work for him and she and I bullied him like mad. You may just remember about him. He is a bachelor – confirmed – and Gwen and I did our best to get him off. No luck! He is up here for Christmas staying with the Scotts, and has said I must pop in to see him at Mbabane on one or other of my journeys. Swaziland is said to be very beautiful and it would be fun to have a small peep.

I am so swamped by Christmas mail that I really must not write more. I am giving another cocktail party tomorrow and must do some preparations tonight. And I am out on Friday, Saturday and Sunday nights, so heaven knows when I shall get any more letters written. The important thing was to get this one done in time for tomorrow's bag.

Two quick postscripts. I had a Christmas card from Duncan Sandys, and hope to flog the autograph one of these days – he sent one to Bill and one to me – presumably as a way of saying how sorry he was to have been such a nuisance to us over the year! Secondly, the family opposite, with the four children, brought across for me a little Christmas tree all decorated. They had decided that I would never have time to do anything like that myself so they had done it for me. Wasn't that a charming thought?

Sorry this is so hard to read. I fear my aged typewriter is quietly dying on me and tends not to print the top part of letters. But as I was told by a London shop six years ago that it wasn't worth overhauling, I can't grumble if it departs this life now. It is still much more legible at least than my writing!!

All my love, and again so many thanks for so many things – particularly the collection.

1962

1 January 1962

That's the first time that I have written 1962 – in 1962. In fact it is 8.30 a.m. on New Year's Day, and I am writing to you before going off and playing with my new borrowed toy. The toy is a motor mower which the office have supplied for Bill McIndoe, as he is in a government-owned house. Bill is very kindly going to lend it to me from time to time, as it is almost impossible to cope with all my grass at this quick-growing time of year. Bill brought it round yesterday, and I had hours of fun in a sun top and a pair of shorts, battling with my meadows. Now I must complete the good work today and let Bill have the machine back.

I can't wait to get your next letter and hear how you are surviving the great freeze. I was listening to the news from London this morning and hearing that this is an unprecedentedly icy spell, and I must say I am a little relieved to think that I haven't got to battle with the journey between London and Herefordshire, though it would have been heaven to have got iced up in Hereford and unable to get back to work again! It really does sound awful though, and I only hope that you are all all right. The comparison with here is too funny. After some torrential rain on Boxing Day we are back in hot sunshine, and I am as coppery-coloured as they come in this part of the world.

Many thanks for your letter written just before Christmas. And while I remember, could you please let me know who it is that I am to thank for the collection in the village. In one letter you say Mrs Edwards, and in this last letter Mrs Davies. Trust you! Just as well I didn't get round to a little note in my last letter if indeed it is Mrs Davies!

And thank you so much for the trouble over Big Boy and me. It really has come out quite well hasn't it? I think that the easiest thing would be for us to have as many copies done as you want and then send on the negative to me. I can have prints run off in Salisbury in half a day. I could have had a negative made, but I don't think the technicians are as reliable here as they are at home, and I didn't want to run any risk with such a precious transparency. Incidentally I haven't sent you any more Luangwa ones yet as I have promised to show them to a girl in the office who I persuaded to go on the same trip. We simply haven't been able to fix a date, but hope to do so in the next fortnight.

I returned to the office after Christmas to mountains of work. The

Hammarskjöld crash is still causing me an immense amount of work; and now that the Federal Commission of Enquiry is about to sit, things are working up to a bit of a climax. But at least I haven't been called into the office over the weekend – we have today as a public holiday – and I am only hoping that my good luck will last over today. I had about a dozen phone calls yesterday, but none of them demanded going into the office. They just made me swear pretty roundly.

I had meant to go to bed instead of sitting up for the New Year. I had been out at a late dinner party at the very posh Salisbury Club the night before, and although I had an open invitation to go to a very gay party given by one of the City Councillors, I just felt too tired to be bothered being hearty. But Roger from round the corner ambled round at a loose end and stayed for a drink, saying he was determined to go to bed at nine p.m. Needless to say, we gossiped on and on, and in the end waited up to see the New Year in after all. If I hadn't done so it would be the first time since I was a child that I hadn't stayed up.

I can't remember whether I told you in my last letter that I had got three weeks leave. The only time I can have it is in Feb. because the Aikmans come in early March, Bill McIndoe goes back to England in March and his replacement doesn't arrive until July, so I shall have to stay put during the interregnum. I have almost certainly decided to go down to South Africa to get some sea air. Roger and his young brother Tim are both going down to Cape Town at that time and have invited me to go in convoy, though I shall have to come back long before them. I am just trying to work out whether this would be feasible. I must say it would be rather nice to have their company. I haven't yet met Tim who lives in Bulawayo, but he sounds a dear from Roger. The great thing is that barring accidents – i.e. more crises in the office – I have got my leave earmarked. I really am beginning to feel that I need it.

8 January 1962

I meant to write you a long letter over the weekend, but never got round to it. The weather is horribly enervating – small showers that do nothing to reduce the temperature but add to the humidity. Last week was so nerve-racking in the office that I spent most of the weekend sleeping.

And this morning there was a second letter from you with James' money. That's two letters I owe you. This is just a morsel on account.

I haven't heard from June myself for Christmas, but I sent her a real wigging just before for being such a rotten correspondent – including ignoring my little

Ma's appeal, which I said was a much more wicked crime than ignoring me! Perhaps that's what spurred her on to writing to you!!

I do hope that Leslie's lumbago is better. Poor lad, he does seem to have a lot of trouble with that blessed back. I wish I could send him some of our sunshine.

Bag closing.

14 January 1962

I've got such an enormous pile of letters to answer that I just don't know where to turn. They seem to have poured in from all corners of the world in the last few weeks, and after being miraculously nearly up-to-date before Christmas (i.e. only owing about fifteen!!) I now owe about fifty. But to hell with them all – you first!

Last week was a real stinker in every way. The Hammarskjöld enquiry is about to begin work, and all the toing and froing before involved me in endless bitty exercises. I got so bogged down with work that I had to get dear old Bill McIndoe to come to my rescue. Luckily he is having a very easy time on his front at the moment so he was able to step in without any difficulty. Eleanor Emery arrived four hours late on Friday night, at eleven p.m., and of course by the time we had had a good gossip it was well into the small hours – and I hadn't had much sleep all week anyway. The whole week culminated in a mad Saturday morning and a trip out to the airport to meet the famous Counsel Geoffrey Lawrence, two junior Counsel and a technical chap from the Ministry of Aviation. I had a tarmac pass to go right out to the aeroplane to greet them on arrival, and in my hand I had a large envelope of confidential information for them, and four air tickets for them to go on to Ndola at crack of dawn on Monday morning. I also had a telegram which had been thrust into my hand as I dashed out of the office inviting them to lunch with the Northern Rhodesian Attorney General on their way north. Just as I got up to them in my best bib and tucker and a bright smile, a huge gust of wind came and ripped all the papers out of my hand except, thank heaven, the confidential papers. Away went the tickets and the telegram, and we all scattered – Counsel and crew and Margaret in hot pursuit! Everything was gathered in, except the telegram, which I never saw again, but the contents of which I had fortunately memorised. So my introduction to Geoffrey Lawrence was somewhat unorthodox, since he held out his hand with some of my papers in it. I eventually got them all out of the airport – one of the Counsel from the Treasury Solicitors' Dept. I knew well by sight, and we subsequently worked it out that we had sat many a time opposite one another at lunch in the Treasury

Solicitors' canteen, and then in the same pub after the canteen had closed down. The rain poured down and I had to go back into the office and send off some telegrams, and finally got home for lunch at a quarter to three. I had just got to bed for a little snooze after lunch when the phone rang and this involved me in some hour and half's further work. Just as well I handed Eleanor over to the Scotts for the day, knowing I wasn't going to have a very peaceful one.

Monday morning 6 a.m. Can't remember now what I said overleaf: Eleanor and I must have got talking at that stage. She slept right through until 10.30 yesterday morning, had breakfast at 11 a.m. and was collected by friends at 12 to go out to lunch. It simply poured all the morning, and I was dashing about with bowls and towels trying to catch all the drips – I have two leaks in this house that are particularly bad and always defeat me in a really bad cloudburst. We had a quiet evening, but of course gossiped on late again, and I was dug out of bed by the phone about half an hour ago and didn't feel that it was worth going back to bed, hence this second effort at writing to you. Here comes my tea and the paper. I see that we had 2.9 inches of rain in Highlands on Saturday and Sunday. I guessed three inches, so I wasn't far out!

27 January 1962

I often say to myself in this post that nothing can ever be so hectic again as a spell I have just been through, but time and time again I have been proved wrong by subsequent events. This last fortnight has been one of the many periods of chaos and complete obliteration of anything approaching a private life. Now I have a few minutes without interruption – I hope – on Saturday afternoon. The phone has gone on and off for the last hour, but I am desperately hoping that there will be a small lull. For I hope to put this letter in Geoffrey Lawrence's hand to take back to London with him on the Boeing tonight and to post to you tomorrow. I have missed all bags and want to get something to you in double quick time.

This has been such a full and fascinating fortnight that I am afraid that I shall forget some of the best titbits. My main preoccupation of course has been with the Hammarskjöld Enquiry. Talk about intrigue and wheels within wheels! Slap in the middle of it I had to go off to Bindura some sixty miles out of Salisbury, to address an African Cultural and Social Club. I was taken by the Chief Information Officer of the S.R. Government, and a fascinating woman farmer, who is interested in developing multi-racial relationships, came with us. We stayed the night with the bachelor Native Commissioner in a typically uncomfortable bachelor establishment. It was a steaming hot night and I was very tired by the time I had given my talk and answered questions for the best part of an hour. Back home the Native Commissioner, who is crazy on the clarinet, treated us to a long session of his records. By the time we were allowed to go to bed I had had it – and to crown everything the mosquitoes kept me awake all night. I do mean *all* night. I don't ever remember having such a wholly wakeful night.

We came back the next morning through one of the Reserves, and had a long natter to an old chief, and sat down and drank some native beer with him. This was quite a story in itself, but I won't stop now to tell you of it. Suffice to say that by the time I got home after lunch I was more than ready for some sleep – and I found that my car battery had gone flat while I had been away. Seize in cleaning the inside had managed to switch something on which had taken all the juice out of the battery. Did I curse, particularly as I had to go to the airport that night at midnight to meet all our four British Hammerskjöld boys coming back from Ndola. I left the car on the hilly part of my drive, hoping that I could start it on the slope, set the alarm and snuggled down into my sofa for a hour or two. All went according to plan, except that it was pouring with rain as I went to get the car started, and daren't put on windscreen wipers or lights until the engine was running. So I did my perilous letting in of the clutch on the move in blinding rain and no lights, and found myself, when I could put my lights on, about one inch from the wall!

My dear boys came back from Ndola incredibly weary, but we had to set to and do some business there and then. That meant getting back home at 1.30 a.m. The Commission has sat all this week in Salisbury and I have been happily in and out of the intrigues throughout. The HC invited the four of them and me to dinner on Wednesday night, so I asked them here for drinks first so that we could all go along together. Dear G. Lawrence insisted on squashing into my little car instead of the office Jaguar, which pleased me – and we proceeded to have the most interesting dinner. I had a feeling that I connected Geoffrey Lawrence's name with the John Bodkin Adams case, and at dinner I plucked up courage to ask him if he had not indeed been involved. He had – he was his defence counsel, and he got him off. I then asked all sorts of improper questions which he answered with delightful frankness. He is the most enchanting little morsel you could wish to meet and we have all fallen for him a big way! If I ever get had up for murder I shall go straight to him to defend me! Anyway, to proceed. When the dinner party broke up the other three got into the Jaguar and G.L. back into my car. Back to the hotel I took him and he then invited me in for a last drink. How we laughed! The Ambassador hotel has housed all the people to do with the Enquiry – the Commissioners, our British Counsel, all the witnesses, the UN Representative, the Swedes involved – the lot. And of course during the course of the trial none of these groups has dared to be seen talking to any of the others in case somebody should say that somebody had been got at by some interested party. When G.L. and I went into the lounge, there were some of the witnesses in one corner and there were we – the wicked British – in another. G.L. then proceeded to let me into some of the interesting behind-the-scenes happenings of the Enquiry and had me in gales of laughter throughout. Besides being a brilliant man, he has the most splendid, giggly sense of humour. I can't tell you how thrilled I have been to meet him. He is obviously one of the great Counsel of our time, and I shall chalk him up as one of the most interesting people it has been my fortune to meet in this remarkable post. He and two of his companions go off tonight, and I see them off – hence my writing this letter now to put into their hands. The fourth man stays until further instructed.

I will save up for another letter the other interesting encounter of the week – my going to meet Dr Linner, the Chief of the UN in Léopoldville, who came down – very reluctantly – as a witness. I needed all my diplomatic nous to deal with him. But I will save that up for later.

I still haven't answered your last letters – including one that came yesterday – but I will in my next letter. And while I remember, the parcel of clothes has at last arrived. Do let me know what I owe for postage. Most of the stamps had come off. I wish you could have seen Sixpence's face. You would have been rewarded for all your trouble. He had the lion's share of the clothes, but Seize had some also. The old suit which I remember well is Sixpence's pride and joy and it fits him exactly. His figure is identical with Leslie's before Leslie put on a bit of weight round the middle! Must fly now and get ready to go to the airport. Sorry to be writing yet again against the clock.

1 February 1962

Just a quarter of an hour to go to the end of the lunch hour and then back to the fray. My, this has been a week. I always seem to say that and only hope that it is a convincing sounding excuse for not writing! Now to questions in your last three letters, for which as usual multitudinous thanks.

You ask about Bill McIndoe. He is also a First Secretary, and then we have the third one, Paul Thirsk, who is on loan to us from the Northern Rhod. Govt. It now looks quite definite that I shall be on my own without either of them and with no replacement for Bill for two months from May to July. Heaven help me. But at least I am almost certain to get my leave. The HC pulls my leg every day about stopping it, but short of a major catastrophe I am sure he doesn't mean it. But I shan't feel really safe until I am on my way and beyond recall by telephone. On present form Roger and I leave Salisbury for Bulawayo on Saturday, 10 Feb., pick up Tim and leave for the south, either on the Sunday or the Monday. I shall spend a week with them in the Cape, and then make my way back up the Garden Route. I don't yet know which way I will go and therefore what the chances are of calling on Helen. I haven't had time to breathe let alone start thinking about my holiday! I don't think that there will be a lot of point in writing to me on my journey, for although I shall be in the Windsor Hotel Fish Hoek for a week, it might be a little tricky hitting the right time. So just give your wee self a holiday and write an enormous letter to await my arrival back on 28th Feb!

Now, where am I? I think the last time I wrote was in time to pop a letter into Geoffrey Lawrence's hand. I went to see three of them off, and again G.L. insisted on coming in my car. I was immensely bucked when he said that he sometimes hated the way he met people on his travels and then never saw them again. And as he saw no prospect of coming back to the Federation he very much hoped that I would look him up when I got back to London. I really believe that he meant it, and I *shall* look him up. Since I saw them off I have been hard at it preparing for the arrival of the UN Commission. I had a long session with the Commissioners this morning. But before I tell you about them I must boast about the note which I had from the Secretary of the Federal Commission. He is a young lawyer in the Ministry of Law, and I think that he found it a terrible headache coping with lots of practical arrangements, such as getting witnesses together from all parts of the world. Anyway, I really did do a tremendous lot to help him, and had to be practical for the two of us. He sent me two dozen roses and a little note to say that without me the Commission would have been a failure! All nonsense of course, but I was very pleased.

Last night went to a party of 60 men and me!! More about all this anon.

8 February 1962

Sandys has arrived but I haven't seen him as he hasn't yet been into the office. He has brought for me a whole lot of his spare transparencies of the Falls, because he remembered my camera had gone wrong for some of the time. Unfortunately, they are not 35 mm. so I can't put them in my projector. But I am thrilled at the gesture.

No time for much news but one rather reassuring thing. I've been having trouble with numbness in my left leg, particularly bad when wakened suddenly in the night by the phone. Kept on finding it wouldn't work at all for a minute or two. Plucked up courage to go to a doctor, who said it was only a nerve that was a bit squashed. He wrenched my legs in all directions and said I must get as much exercise as possible and I probably wouldn't have any more trouble. I was doubly reassured when after all the contortions he said I was very supple (he didn't add 'not bad for forty' but that was what he implied!!).

Will write next from South Africa.

Windsor Hotel
Fish Hoek, Cape

16 February 1962

Here I am, safely at the end of my 1,700 plus mile journey. Everything went splendidly. After a mad scramble to get ready, Roger and I left Salisbury last Saturday morning and wandered quietly down to Bulawayo in time for tea. His parents have the most lovely Cape Dutch house. Mrs West is a mad keen gardener, but is very badly crippled with osteo-arthritis and can only get about on crutches. It is sad to see, for she is only in her early sixties and is still as energetic as her lameness will allow her to be. Pa West is immense – nearly six foot five. Tim is a bit smaller and Roger a mere six foot one. Quite an overpowering trio.

We pottered on Sunday. I summoned up courage to go with Roger to see his god-daughter, who is a mongol child of two. The mother can't bring herself to visit the child and Roger does some admirable work keeping an eye on the poor little thing. The home is run by Catholic nuns, and you certainly have to take your hat off to them. We saw a number of the children, of all ages, and I think it was about the saddest sight I have ever seen.

But to more cheerful topics. We were on our way on Monday morning, plugging steadily south. Roger's Volkswagen was always put in front to set the pace as the slower car. Both lads are very careful drivers, and we all took it in turns to drive both cars. I had my hood down all the way except for one short showery spell, and we are all colours from puce to near black as a result. Both Roger and Tim are fair and therefore suffered more than me, but we are all now happily peeling and no longer sore.

We had three night stops on the way, driving between 350 and 450 miles daily according to how we felt. Then yesterday we had a short 200 miles only to go to reach Cape Town, so that we were here long before lunch. First bathe in the splendid Cape rollers after lunch, when the boys left me at the hotel and proceeded to their friends. I am sitting out in the sun now this morning waiting for them to appear.

It is wonderful to be down at sea level again. I only wish I had more than a week before having to turn north again, but I shall make the most of it while I have the chance. One of the best things is that this is the time of the grape harvest. I've just bought what must be at least a pound of best white grapes for 5 cents – i.e. 6*d*!

Will write again before I start once more on my travels.

Fish Hoek

20 February 1962

Holiday still going splendidly. Roger and I played 18 holes of golf yesterday amid magnificent scenery, and we have explored accessible parts of the Cape. But most of the time we are content to swim and sprawl on the beach.

Kokstad

26 February 1962

High time you heard what I was up to. I eventually tore myself away from the beach on Saturday. It had been a wonderful nine days of just what I wanted – some golf, lots of swimming and lots of lying in the sun doing nothing. I feel completely rejuvenated. I made good friends of several of the elderly residents of the hotel (darlings they were) and they all came out to the car park to watch me pack and see me off and order me to let them know as soon as I got safely back to Salisbury!

I left just before nine and drove out along the Garden Route (i.e. the coast road from Cape Town to Durban). I had always heard that this was one of the most beautiful roads in the world, and it is. It is quite breathtaking. With two thousand miles to do in five and a half driving days I thought I had better try to get a good chunk done the first two days to get a bit ahead of schedule. So on Saturday I pressed on to Port Elizabeth – 482 miles in all for the day. I wasn't a bit tired. It is only my coccyx that begins to protest! P.E. itself is a pretty ugly town, and I had a noisy Saturday night of roisterers to contend with at a central hotel. But off again after breakfast on a 430 mile drive that brought me to this enchanting little place in the mountains, having driven right through the Transkei. I was completely captivated and spellbound by the Transkei – countless miles of undulating green pasture lands with native kraals neatly dotted about on them, and splendid deep blue mountains as a backcloth. I've had a wonderful, undisturbed night in a wild west type of hotel here and am writing this over my morning tea. Must breakfast and away.

Salisbury

2 March 1962

In exactly one hour the office car comes to collect me to take me to the airport to meet the Aikmans. Once they are here I shall have no time to write – and I still have to dress and make a few more preparations. So this is a hurried scribble just to let you know that I am safely back. I had my fair share of excitements in the 2,200 miles between Fish Hoek and Klokkespel, including hitting a boulder in a deviation and carving chunks out of my underneath; not being able to get out of overdrive and watching the car bang in front of me collect a cow on its roof. But I got patched up enough to get home and here I am. I popped into the office to collect my mail and draw gasps from everyone. The HC said he was glad he could boast an African on his staff at last! I'm the colour of mahogany and feeling terribly fit. I'll tell you all the tale soon. I was enchanted with your long letter, it was one of 39 communications that awaited my pleasure.

Much of the day shopping, washing and ironing, while Sixpence has been house-cleaning. I was thankful to see him back from his holiday I can tell you and very grateful to have such a reliable servant.

Klokkespel
Highlands

4 March 1962

It is Sunday evening and Colin is sitting beside me reading the Southern Rhodesia Constitution. Betty is battling away on my sewing machine and I'm snatching the opportunity to scratch out a quick note to you. I'm still not answering your last two letters since they are through in the bedroom.

8 March 1962

Quite hopeless There the two Aikmans started gossiping again, and I haven't had a second to get on with this since. I have packed them off to Northern Rhodesia for a few days, then they return to me on Saturday for a week. You know what it's like with visitors – planning meals etc. And Tuesday night I gave a farewell cocktail party for Irene and Bill, and all my lights fused in the middle of it! Couldn't repair them until the following morning.

Bill has now left the office and I have some of his work. It is a nightmare trying to catch up on what happened while I was away, and getting settled in again. Will try hard to write sanely at the weekend – Aikmans allowing.

Salisbury

8 March 1962

My leg seems to be completely better, as the doctor said it probably would be. The bit of vigorous manipulation, followed by so much swimming and golf, must have done the trick. I only felt it once – soon after I went to see the doctor – but have not had so much as a twinge since. It was given a good test too when I was wakened by the phone at an ungodly hour last night. Not a suspicion of a stumble. I can tell you I am jolly relieved. I don't quite know what I feared, but I think that I always have a sneaking dread of disseminated sclerosis from my various encounters with it. Anyway, all is well and I really am feeling just like my old self. It should have been a tiring holiday, but the very fact of having a break and getting down to sea level has done miracles for me. I shall never leave a trip to the sea so long again. I can always nip down for a long weekend to Beira if I begin to feel the effects of altitude again.

I handed the balance of the money personally to Rusike. He was enormously grateful. I will ask him for that picture when next I see him. Meanwhile I will look up the transparency I took of them all when I went with Lady Alport. When next you are having any prints of transparencies done, would you please have one of this done for me to give to Rusike? I think that I have met Jack Sims, but I know I haven't met Sir A. James.* Salisbury is getting such an enormous place that it is easy not to know people.

9/3/62 *Odd coincidence. Saw strange hat in reception room today and asked who the owner was. Sir Archibald James was the answer! Put it on my head just for fun!! He was seeing HC.

Linner. It really was rather amusing. He had been extremely reluctant to come to Salisbury to give his evidence, as he was pretty anti-Federation and very upset anyway because Hammarskjöld had been a very close personal friend. When his arm was finally twisted by our Ambassador in Léopoldville to come here, we expected that it might be rather tense. So the HC detailed me off to go and meet him as he knew he couldn't be beastly to a woman. The Federal authorities did just the same thing and sent their assistant Protocol Officer who is a woman. And the UN liaison chap who was attending the Federal Enquiry couldn't get out of court, so sent his Secretary. Linner was therefore confronted on arrival by three women and no men. The UN Secretary was horrified when she discovered this, and said to me, 'I at least expected Sir Roy Welensky to be present.' This gives a pretty good insight into just what the UN people think of themselves – very much Lord God Almighty. But the scheme worked out well. Linner had perforce to be polite, and in the end after a rather frigid beginning, I got him laughing heartily.

There is no doubt about it, it is very useful to have at least one woman in a post like this, and the HC never hesitates to make use of my sex when he thinks it expedient. Needless to say, I do not grumble.

Now that brings me to your last letter of 3 March. What a lot you seem to see of the Federation on your TV. Since you wrote, of course, we have had yet more excitements and Welensky's decision to go to the country. I suppose that this will mean a lot more touring by us to try to find out what the country is thinking – just as before the Referendum on the Southern Rhod. constitution. We don't have much of a pause between crises, do we?

Your atlas sounds a very good one if you were able to follow my wanderings in South Africa. Yes, from Kokstad I went towards Pietermaritzberg, then branched off for Durban, and redoubled my tracks, coming back up from Durban, through P'berg, and on up the main road to Standerton, where I left the main road and made my way up through Bethal, Middelburg and Marble Hall, rejoining the main road just south of Potgeitersroos. This is a very abbreviated account of my wanderings. As I may have hinted to you, the journey was not without its excitements. On leaving Kokstad, I found that I couldn't get out of overdrive. I therefore had no proper climbing gear, i.e. proper third, and the country is very hilly. So when I got to the turn off for Durban I stopped to deliberate whether I would go to the bother of the extra hundred miles or so just to see Durban. I decided against it. But when I started up after the pause, I discovered that my third and fourth gears had returned. So nothing daunted I about-turned and made for Durban after all. Then I discovered that when going downhill I started to free-wheel, though I was still in gear! I got down to Durban and had a quick look-see, but it was boilingly hot, so I turned inland for Pietersburg, where I decided to stop and get people to look at my peculiar gears. This took a precious three hours, and nobody could find the trouble without stripping down the gearbox – a one and a half day job. On being reassured that I couldn't do any harm and would probably get back safely to Salisbury, I decided to press on and not to worry. I got as far as Fort Mistake that night, halfway between Ladysmith and Newcastle, and stayed at a very modern motel. The next day was one of the happiest of the tour, when I left the main road and struck out across good provincial roads, with some shopping deviations and some dirt thrown in – but all quite navigable. It was good to find nothing on the roads. For miles on end I saw not a soul and I loved it. I got back to the enchanting motel at Pietersburg where Roger and Tim and I had stayed on our first night out of Bulawayo. There I had a swim and an entertaining evening with two commercial travellers, one of whom had been a next-door neighbour in Cape Town of a very good friend of mine in the CRO. The next day, when I was not more than ten miles on my way, I was the third car to strike a boulder in the middle of a deviation. Only I was damaged; and I spent the next four hours being patched up by a garage in Pietersburg. They were very good. All the mechanics downed tools to concentrate on my car. At last I was on my way again just after one o'clock, with some 350 miles to go and the border at Beit Bridge to negotiate, and Bulawayo to reach preferably in the daylight, as I wasn't sure of my way to the Wests, that is about 6.30. One wheel had gone out of balance, to add to my worries, and I had no comfortable speed between 45 and 85. Needless to say, I did not go at 45! I got through Beit Bridge and left at a quarter to four. I was in Bulawayo 210 miles away at half past six. I had a superb road almost entirely to myself – miles and miles of emptiness, and how I prayed that my patchings-up would hold, which thank heaven they did – for the chances of getting aid were slight. It was really too fast for comfort, but not in the least dangerous on that road. I was glad all the same to sink into a West hot bath and eat a West hot dinner. My last excitement came on the last leg of the journey, but only by proxy. Driving behind an Austin Healey I was horrified to see a herd of cattle stream across the road. The Healey's brakes were not very good and it collected a cow on the roof. I'm sure I have told you this already, so I won't repeat it. I would not have worried if I hadn't had the prospect of the Aikmans panting on my doorstep.

As it was I had just twenty-four hours to prepare for them, and I needed every minute of them.

As all my visitors seem to do, they simply collapsed when they got to my home, and were only too glad to be lazy. Not that they were allowed to be for long, for I had various things laid on for them. I shot them off to N.R. on Tuesday and they return to me tomorrow night for another week before proceeding to Nyasaland, and then on out of the Federation to Dar es Salaam.

I've come back to chaos in the office of course. Bill has now left, and Paul Thirsk and I have inherited half of his work each. I find it quite a job catching up on what has been going on during my absence in the Republic, let alone battling with the current work. But one becomes accustomed to chaos in this post. The great thing is that I'm feeling so wonderfully well after my holiday, and am therefore not dismayed by work.

As the Aikmans will be with me all next week I don't suppose I shall have a lot of time for writing. But once they have gone I'll do my best.

25 March 1962

I don't know whether I ever told you that my Bhili vanished off the scene some months ago. He just never turned up one day and that was the end of that. Despite his uncertain end the McIndoes asked me if I would give a home to their Willie-Willie. I have dearly loved W.W. since I stayed with the McIndoes, and am enchanted to have him. He is a fluffy, peach-coloured neuter and is adorable. He settled down within hours, and is a most affectionate companion. He has never had a very strong back and the vet says he might become paralysed at any moment. But he hasn't done in his two years of life so I am hoping for the best. He has the funniest of mews – it is more of a squeak than anything – and we hold long and interesting squeaky conversations together.

No, I wasn't at that meeting on Sir Roy's return. It was a press conference, which is covered by our information chaps. Roy is in very chastened mood at the moment. He has made a number of tactical errors recently and I think that he is just waking up to the fact. Things are getting increasingly interesting with our new big boss (no more Sandys visitations, for which we are all profoundly thankful), the HC and the Governors being summoned to London; Todd causing consternation in the UN, the Federal election coming up and then the S.R. one in October. I have never known the Europeans in S.R. so depressed as they are at the moment, and houses are going up for sale all over the place. (Selfishly, I don't mind about this, as it reduces the chances of my own house being sold!) You ask if the election etc. will mean more work for us. I don't think so at the moment. Nothing very much can burst on us in the Federal field until the election is over. But of course we never know what else will hit us. The United Nations business for instance has kept me personally very busy this last week and is likely to be a continuing bore. If it's not one damn thing it's another here.

Yes, I am indeed not smoking at the moment as it is Lent, and I shall try hard not to start again. There is a terrific to-do going on here too about smoking and lung cancer. In view of the fact that a large part of the wealth of the Federation comes from tobacco it is an enormously live issue. Evan Campbell indeed must be worried. He gave a broadcast talk the other day and I can't wait to tell him what I think of him. He virtually said that the doctors don't know what they are talking about, which coming from a layman and tobacco grower struck me as being just about as irresponsible as it could be. He wrapped it up, but that was the general impression left with me. Whenever he bumps into me he always pulls my leg about the bloody British Government, so I am jolly well going to get my own back!

Norman's book should be out any time now. It is to be called *Return to the Wild* and it is to be published by whoever published *Elsa* – Collins I think, but you can check that from your copy of *Elsa*. Ron (can't remember his surname for the moment, the man who helped Norman with the safari) popped into the office the other day on his way south to get himself engaged. He told us that Norman has indeed returned his lions to the wilds. He took them up to a very remote part of Northern Rhodesia miles away from everybody. He has heard nothing of them since, which he feels is a good sign. So it looks as if I was only just in time to be introduced. People going to Luangwa this year won't have that particular thrill. I have now shown my transparencies to the last person who wanted to see them – a girl who came to dinner last week. So I will now get down seriously to sending them off to you in dribs and drabs. Would you be an angel and get negatives made of the one of Big Boy and the one of the two of us laughing? Isn't the one of Big Boy an absolute winner? I can hardly bear to let him out of my sight. In fact if you agree, I think it would be a good idea to have a duplicate of this one made so that I can have the precious original back. If Norman's book is a success it should (I mean all my photographs of the lions) have special interest.

Betty Aikman told me that she had written to you, which was very sweet of her. It was fun having them. After a very hectic round of parties for them and with them they were due to leave for Nyasaland on last Saturday morning. Away they went and I got home at lunch time to breathe quietly again. Sixpence had stripped their beds and polished up their room. Just after lunch the phone went and it was Betty to say that the plane had been delayed until the next day because of the effects of the cyclone which had hit us and could they come back. I said that they would have to sleep in their sheets which were bundled up in the clothes basket as I simply hadn't any others to give them, and that there was nothing in the fridge. Their sheets were as crumpled as could be, but they were quite undismayed. I had to go out to a dinner party, so I left them to fend for themselves, which I must say they did with very good grace. The next day, last Sunday, broke cloudy and wet and I was quite certain that the plane again would not take off. But it did, and I was really able to relax – until the afternoon when Roger got back from his long return journey, to tell me all had befallen him and Tim. They too had had car trouble, but nothing like as bad as mine. What was really worse was that they had a lot of rain and cloudy skies, and they hadn't seen anything like the wonderful scenery that I had. I was lucky to strike a good patch of weather in the middle of what had been an unprecedentedly bad summer. Most unusual for me!

Well now, what other news for you? Nothing much. Despite the fact that I don't seem to have had much sleep since I came back from my leave, what with the Aikmans and a round of parties last week, I am still feeling wonderfully well and refreshed from my holiday. My leg continues not to bother me and I am religiously doing exercises every morning. I need to anyway in view of the fact that I am over nine stone again! Next week is going to be hectic too. Parties on Monday and Tuesday – the one on Tuesday is given by the Malawi party – Banda's party in Nyasaland which is opening up a branch in S.R. No doubt I shall be looked on with the gravest suspicion by the security forces of S.R. as a result, but the High Commissioner said before he left that it was a very good thing that I had been invited and I must certainly go and report back what happened. Then on Thursday I go down to Que Que for a couple of days to give a speech to another group of Africans, and to tour some African women's clubs. It will be a bit tiring but should be interesting too. And now, damn it, I have to go to a Sunday morning do given by the Japanese Consul-General. He and his wife have asked me at least half a dozen times, and I have dodged them. But they finally pinned me down. I loathe getting togged up on a Sunday but must do it. I am due there in five minutes time, and here I am still in my cotton sun suit, nattering away to you. I shall arrive half an hour late and leave half an hour early (I'm going to lunch with Ben and Roger anyway, which is a good excuse), and so I suppose I shall endure it. Heavens yes, look at the time. I really must fly.

Office
Near bag time

2 April 1962

Safely back from my trip to Que Que. Most interesting, particularly going deep into the African reserves. I gave a long talk to a group of African school teachers and was delighted to be subjected to a barrage of questions on the Common Market, British policy in general and particularly in Africa, the problems of South Africa and so on. Very bright boys they were.

HC has just come back and we're dying to hear what happened during his London talks. This is only a pot-boiler as there is a bag going.

4 April 1962

Now for a little account of my trip to Que Que. I was driven by a very pleasant young woman from the Native Affairs Department who had taken a social science degree in South Africa, and had done one form or other of social work ever since. Married with two small daughters and a wonderful mother-in-law who encourages her to keep up with her work while she looks after the brats. Hilary took me in her car so I was able to get mine into dock for a real go at that blessed differential. On the way we stopped to help the occupants of a car that had seized up – a new Government-owned Vauxhall, which the African driver had gone on driving for miles after the fan belt had come off – the clot! It contained a mental patient on her way to Bulawayo, with a nursing sister. We took the driver on into Que Que some twenty miles away, as the sister thought that she ought not to move the patient into her car. We then set about arranging a rescue operation before reporting to the Native Commissioner, in whose charge we were to be. The NC is a bachelor, and Hilary warned me that she found him incredibly difficult to talk to, with long periods of silence. Right, I thought, none of that nonsense – and I duly tamed the brute and had him roaring with happy laughter.

But back to my story. I was to give a talk to an African discussion group on the work of the CRO and the Commonwealth today. The group turned out to consist of some forty odd African teachers and Purchase Area farmers – in other words representatives of a growing class of responsible Africans, together with a few out-and-out nationalists with whom I subsequently had some terrific arguments. The evening went down very well. I had had a very strong whisky just before and really was in talking form, and we all ended up having a hilarious session, with lots of laughter and some very meaty questions thrown in. Tea afterwards and lots more questions and arguments. Hilary and I were far too late to get dinner in our hotel, so the NC named Ayling invited us back to his bachelor establishment, and there I began the thawing process! The next day Ayling, his African clerk, Hilary and I went for a great tour through Ayling's reserve to meet a number of African women's clubs. These are quite an innovation and one of Hilary's main jobs is to encourage them and give them advice. They meet to teach each other sewing and home craft and hygiene and child care and so forth, the more knowledgeable teaching the less. I did so enjoy the day. African women have a wonderful sense of humour, and wherever we went we were laughing our heads off *with* them. The roads in the reserves are of course only dust tracks, and we were very hot and grimy by the time we got back to Que Que. We then invited Ayling back to the hotel to have dinner with us, and were early in bed.

We both wanted to be back in Salisbury well before lunch, I to collect my car before the garage shut at 11.30 a.m. But it was not to be. At just about the spot where we had picked up the driver of the broken-down car we ourselves broke down – the accelerator cable had bust. We flagged down an old Vauxhall, the twin of my New Zealand one, and cadged a lift into the nearest town twenty-five miles away. Believe it or not, the driver of the car was the ambulance driver from Que Que hospital who had given his ambulance to the African driver of the broken-down car to go and collect his stranded patient. Wasn't that the oddest coincidence? Anyway Hilary got somebody to take her back to her car with a spare cable and I tried to get through to Salisbury about my car. We both accomplished our missions in due course, and Hilary was back with me in an hour and a half when we continued our journey. The other funny coincidence concerns the young man who had that cow on his roof when I was driving back from the Cape. The other day he went into Roger's office to seek advice about an accumulation of debts. In the course of conversation he mentioned to Roger, who of course hadn't a clue that he was the same young man, that to add to his troubles he had hit a cow near Hartley recently. Roger struck him somewhat dumb by saying, 'Yes, and I can complete the story, for it was a woman in a Sunbeam Alpine who picked you up and took you into Hartley!'

The period of peace in the office seems to be over. I started this letter this morning, and am now back home after a very busy day. The bag goes tomorrow and tomorrow is going to be an awful day anyway. Paul Thirsk, the other First Secretary, is in bed with a shocking cold and is sensibly being kept there by his wife, since he has suffered from TB and must be careful with any cold bugs. I myself go to the doctor to have that wretched sebaceous cyst cut out of the top of my head again. If you remember St Thomas's warned me that it might grow again and it has. It hasn't worried me much, but did get a bit sore when I got so sunburnt on holiday. I don't want to have another bald patch. And when I saw the doctor about my leg I mentioned the cyst and he said he might as well chop it out when I had a minute. Tomorrow is about the worst day from the work point of view, but I don't want to put off the date having once got round to arranging it.

12 April 1962

What a *whacking* great letter from you and bursting with bounce and energy! And chalk it up my girl. You had to acknowledge no fewer than *four* letters of mine, all in one go. I had in fact got to the stage where I had accused the Registry of keeping my mail from me, so long was it since I had heard from you. I won't say 'Take a row', because you are in fact the most wonderful correspondent. But I *was* relieved to hear, I can tell you. Won't stop now to answer it, but thought I must put something in today's bag.

This last week has been a bit of a b—. I think I told you that I was having that bump cut out. Well, the doctor did it very satisfactorily, though the dope wore off before he had finished, which wasn't too good, and he had great difficulty getting his needle through my scalp to stitch me up as he said that the sun had baked it hard! I had an hour at home, then back to the office where I promptly fell carrying a huge tray of files. The boys were washing the lino and my feet just went from under me. Very cleverly I fell in a tiny space between two metal filing cabinets and didn't burst my stitches open. But I still have a badly bruised thigh and it shook me up, happening just after my little op. Then yesterday I began to get awful aches all over and went terribly cold. Even in a hot bath I was shivering with all the hairs – even on my tummy I could feel them – standing up on end. I went to bed with a hot water bottle at six – and my dear neighbours the Campbells decided at that moment to bring round the enclosed photograph taken some time ago in their garden. What is more, Roger popped round on a social call – and before we knew where we were we were having quite a party in my bedroom! They gave me some strong tots of whisky and I downed anti-malaria pills and aspirin and succeeded in raising my temperature from 97 degrees to nearly 102 degrees in an hour. But I had a mighty sweat and was back to normal this morning. A bit weak at the knees, but otherwise better. Don't know what hit me all of a sudden.

Some interesting dates recently. Graduation ceremony at the University College. Dinner at the Scotts where I met the architect for the new medical school and teaching hospital, who is also one of the Piccadilly Circus architects (charming man and *so* modest, though one of the most eminent in his profession). Dinner with the HC where guest of honour was Sir Roger Stevens, ex-Ambassador at a number of posts and now very high in the FO (again a poppet!). And we all played roulette afterwards. HC is a most polished banker.

Time to return to work.

19 April 1962

This won't reach you for Easter but it is nevertheless to wish you a very happy holiday. We are hoping to close down this evening until Tuesday. I am on call all day on Sunday, but in any case I wasn't proposing to go anywhere but to sleep and garden. I had to send Seize to hospital today because his eyes were streaming so I may be without a gardener for the weekend anyway.

I may have told you about my queer temperature. Whatever bug I was fighting has only just left me – but I won the battle and nothing awful developed.

I see in today's paper that Norman Carr is off to England in time for the publication of his book and the release of a film of the lions. The latter will certainly be on television, so watch out for it.

I did see lots of baboons in the Cape but not in the reserve. I have some transparencies which will find their way to you in due course. The baboons came clambering all over the car and you had to keep your windows up or they would have been right inside.

Really must get back to work and then four days away from it, I hope. Hurrah! Butler will be upon us all too soon, so better make the most of this quieter spell.

26 April 1962

Now about my bug. No, it certainly wasn't malaria, thank heaven. You can't be injected against malaria: you have to take pills regularly if there is any danger, and that cuts the ten day life cycle of the malaria bug in the blood. I had a horrible suspicion that it might be malaria – there is very little in Salisbury, so we don't automatically take pills as we used to in India – so I gave myself a good dose of pills just in case. I still don't know what it was. I imagine some sort of flu bug that wasn't strong enough to get me down properly. I still get fits of not feeling quite up to scratch, but there is nothing bad enough to send me to the doctor. I had a very restful Easter holiday, only leaving the precincts of my house once to go round the corner and have lunch with Roger. I told all sort of lies, but was determined to have a really lazy time. It wasn't in fact, as Seize was ill and I had to do a lot of extra gardening, but at least I didn't have to go racing out to some dismal social do. I treated myself to a record player in the sales recently, and Roger has lent me a lot of his records (classical needless to say!), so I had a real feast of music too. One gets so little on the radio here and I do miss it.

The Hemmings arrive on Monday. Kay has to return the following Saturday. They are staying at first with Ben Gingell, but I have invited them to come on to me whenever they want to. According to Ben, James is going to be very busy, going up to Northern Rhodesia and possibly Nyasaland, so I don't expect that he will spend so much time in Salisbury as he did last time.

The office is still quiet, and I wasn't, as you will have gathered, called in once during the holiday. It is such a welcome change to lead a civilised life for a spell. Once Butler arrives it will be over, but meanwhile I am thankful for the respite.

Nearly forgot. Here is another cutting about Norman. I had a letter from him after the holiday saying he was coming to Salisbury on route for England and hoping he would have time to look me up. I had my telephone unplugged for most of the holiday when I knew the office didn't want me, so he may have tried and failed to get in touch. A pity. But he will be back and then I am determined to get him to autograph a copy of his book for me.

3 May 1962

James and Kay Hemming brought out for me the second *Sunday Telegraph* extract. I went and had a drink with them and Ben the day they arrived. Kay is a dear – full of good humour and spirits and fascinating tales about the children she teaches. Alas she has to go home on Saturday for the beginning of term. James stays on for another month and will spend a few days of it with me when he desperately needs quiet in which to write. He and Kay lunch with me on Saturday before Kay departs. They really are gems. Just before they came out they visited 215 Cavendish Road and found the Mein family busy playing some family game. They were shown all over and the house is evidently being well looked after. I do think it was so kind of them to go the trouble.

I had a little dinner party last night – the Secretary of the Federal Hammarskjöld crash enquiry (who was at Oxford with Roger) and his wife, Roger, and the woman who took me to Que Que and the Reserves there, and her husband. I told them it was your seventy-fifth birthday and we all drank your health at dinner.

13 May 1962

I am afraid there has been a very long pause between my hundredth letter and my hundred and first. What with preparations for Butler and a lot of work besides, James in the house and some additional entertaining, letters have been thrust into the background. Now it is Sunday evening, and James is busy writing letters on one table and I'm busy writing to you on another. I shall have to look up your last letter to me to see where you have got on your travels. I hope that you are having a wonderful time and that the car is taking good care of you.

I find it difficult to remember just what has happened since I last wrote. As I say, we have been flat out getting ready for the big man. Now he is here, but I haven't met him yet. He has gone to Umtali for the weekend to stay with his Courtauld relatives, who live in great splendour. By repute they had a Persian carpet about 100 feet by 80, and built their house around it; can you imagine what their drawing room must be like? I had a little lunch party yesterday for the man who is Butler's Private Secretary – a delightful quiet creature and not at all bumped-up because of his job. I had a couple from External Affairs and of course James was here and it was a very relaxed little party, with all of us getting out into the sun on the lawn after lunch and shedding our shoes. Tomorrow night I am bidden by the High Commissioner for dinner at

Mirimba, with the Butlers and three Southern Rhodesia Cabinet Ministers and their wives, so I shall have to be on my best behaviour. No kicking off my shoes then!

The other night I had quite a fright. James was away in Bulawayo and I was busy pottering around the garden after I got back from the office, when a car drew up. Out came a delightful family of father, mother and grown-up daughter. He is a professor at the University College and he had brought his family to see the house with a view to buying. They fell in love with it, though it is too small for them. I now wait in fear and trembling to see whether they decide to take it and to add on to it and make it big enough. The awful thing is that I like them so much that I can't feel hard about their interest in the house. But it will be sad if I have to go for my last year.

One little snippet of news that will interest you. Ann Sinnett is about to produce number three and they are due to leave Salisbury soon and to go to Germany. Though I haven't seen very much of them I have had quite a lot of official dealings with Richard who is a dear and intelligent, and I shall miss them. I asked James and Kay to try to find a silver thimble for me to give to Nicola, for whom I was proxy godmother at the christening. I didn't know what to give the child and then thought how much your thimble was used by me. I tried for months all over Salisbury to find one but without success, so turned in desperation to the Hemmings. They found that they are not being made any longer but they were able to find one in a secondhand shop. Your thimble is now all the more precious to me. Incidentally the Sinnetts were thrilled and thought it a splendid idea.

I am amused that you have at last heard from June. After months of silence I had three picture postcards from her in as many days, sent from the Continent, but I have still not had a letter, so I have not heard officially that she is going to break her journey with me. If she is not careful she will find that my spare bed is already occupied! James stays with me until 5 June, but will in fact be away on tour for a lot of that time. I do so enjoy having him. He is stimulating company and the most undemanding guest. I am sure that you will like him and Kay when you meet them. I have just asked James if he has a message for you and he has said, 'Of course, LOVE,' with much emphasis!! (I have just read that out to him and he has said with equal emphasis, 'GOOD.') And that reminds me – I really must go and get a spot of supper. I always send Sixpence away on Sunday to have a day off.

One last thing. James has treated me to a clock golf set, so we spent an hour or two this morning laying out the course on my top lawn. It is very nearly a pitch and putt effort, so long and rough are some of the holes, but it will be a splendid way of entertaining some of my more energetic guests.

I only hope that wretched University Professor will leave me in peace to enjoy it!

Monday in office

Bill McIndoe still not replaced. Paul Thirsk left last night for three months in England, Brian Unwin has gone sick, so it's only me out of four of us!

24 May 1962

It is Saturday evening and James is working away like mad at a revision to one of his courses. I am reluctant to disturb him with the clack of a typewriter – hence my hideous manuscript.

I have just thought. Of course it is *Thursday*, not Saturday. It *seems* like Saturday as it is a public holiday. Most of us had to work this morning, but I at least have had the afternoon off – and so I have been convinced that it was Saturday.

This has been another long silence. So much has been happening. I think that I may have been about to go to the dinner at Mirimba for Butler and his wife. It was pretty grand, and I found myself sandwiched at the dinner table between Mr Abrahamson, S.R. Minister of Labour, and Sir Hugh Beadle, Chief Justice. Mr A. is often tipped as a future S.R. Prime Minister. He is certainly the most able one of the bunch after Whitehead. We indulged in a most animated and entertaining discussion; and the sequel was that he rang me two days ago and asked me out to dinner – just him and a political correspondent here. In no time we were 'Abe' and 'Margaret' so I feel I am now 'ben' with the S.R. Cabinet! But back to the party. Butler is quite a man. I missed the original introduction to him when he and his wife came down the stairs from above, as I had only been in Mirimba for a minute or two when I was called to the phone. It was our Security Officer to say that he had just heard that three Africans had died of shot wounds inflicted by the Police during the strike (later it turned out to be two). Sir E. Whitehead was at the dinner, and we had the nasty task of passing on this unsavoury news to him. Anyway later I spoke to both the Butlers. She is a darling – very gay and a good balance to his inevitable pomposity. Butler himself in the course of conversation said that the problem of Central Africa was the most exacting intellectual exercise in which he had been engaged. Being Deputy PM, he would never have taken it on if it *hadn't* been!

25 May 1962

Fatal. Dinner intervened, then we started gossiping afterwards and I never got this finished.Now I am back in the office and the bag closes shortly. More gossip anon.

At lunchtime today Norman Carr is appearing at the main bookshop. I shall dash along and see him.

Many thanks for your last two long letters – both read out in full to James who marvels at your energy and enterprise and sends more LOVE. He roared over your fears at meeting him. He is in fact, despite his brain, one of the quietest people I have ever met.

27 May 1962

Sorry about this awful bumph. I seem to have left all my air mail paper in the office. It's a glorious sunny Sunday morning, and while James has decided that the garden is too distracting for work and is in the study, I'm out in the sun with the typewriter on my old string mora and my bottom on the very lowest stool in the house.

Now to try to fill in some of the gaps in my last letter. I think I forgot to tell you that James and I did get away in the end for our quick dash up to Inyanga. We went back to the place we went to last time because it is such a friendly hotel. It is only 150 miles of very good road most of the way, so you can do the journey comfortably in three hours. We took the hard top off the car and donned layers of woollies against the cold morning air, and arrived easily in time for lunch. The weather couldn't have been more perfect – cloudless skies but quite a nip in the air. We didn't do much on the Saturday except go for a short walk and play innumerable games of clock golf, deck quoits, croquet; for we were determined to save our energies for the next day and an assault on the Crusader. The Crusader is a group of rocks that look just like a prostrate crusader with his shield on his chest. Off we set after breakfast on Sunday to scale the prostrate giant. What fun we had – fighting through dry knife-sharp bracken, wriggling up chimneys of rock, solving after much thought three or four tricky problems of ascent and descent when we thought that we were well and truly stuck. We thought that we were going to be denied the pleasure of standing on the crusader's belly, but at last I found a tiny cranny up which we were able to ease ourselves; and leaving signs behind us so that we could find it again on the return journey, we eventually arrived triumphant at the top. We took photographs to prove it, which I shall send on to you in due course, if they come out. Our legs were in tatters by the time we got back home, and I was a bit stiff in the shoulders for a day or two, but otherwise we were none the worse – in fact far from it – we both felt fine after such a good muscle stretch. James is a very reassuring person to go climbing with – very competent himself but very careful and non-frightening with lesser mortals like me!

Who do you think we met at the hotel? Noni Campbell and two of her sisters, the one from Marlborough and the other from Aden with her husband. They were on a Cook's tour driven by Noni's son Colin, to show the Aden lot something of the country. There were whoops of recognition when the two sisters discovered who I was, and of course long discussions about Hereford and you and Pat – or Patience as they always call her. Wasn't it fun to meet them like that? I asked Colin whether he was married (you may remember that he introduced me to a girl he had got engaged to and of whom I didn't approve!). Much to my delight Noni said at once, 'Thank goodness, no. They agreed mutually to part.' I bet Mum had something to do with that and a good job too. Noni said they were all trying like mad to find him a wife but that she never approved of any that Colin found himself.

Next bit of excitement was seeing Norman Carr again. I spotted in the paper that he was to be in one of the best bookshops on Friday to sign copies of his book, so along I dashed. I told him that I had three copies on order from home but that I couldn't wait and was determined to buy another and get him to sign it. I handed a copy over to the salesman but Norman immediately whisked it out of his hand and said he wouldn't hear of it. It would save him the trouble of sending me a complimentary copy if he could give it to me then! So I have a free copy with an inscription, 'Memories of Luangwa, Norman Carr.' Norman said that he hoped my friends would not misinterpret this inscription and of course I retorted that I hoped that they would! He is off today to his family in Jo'berg, but says he will try to ring me on his way back in the hope that we can fit in a meal together. Just in case he does, could you send back the three or four best transparencies of the lions if they are back from the shop? The one of Big Boy with his paws crossed is still to my way of thinking the best I have ever seen of him – better than the ones in the book. And the other one I should particularly like to show Norman is the one of him bending down and hugging Little Boy with Big Boy lying alongside. That's the one with the light coming in from the left over Norman's shoulder. I also want to show them to James. I promise I will send them back again in double quick time.

We got rid of Butler last night. His visit seems to have gone down remarkably well, and we only hope that as a result some sort of sense will emerge from this chaotic land. If he can't solve the problems of the Federation, then I don't believe anybody can.

Did I tell you that Sixpence's wife has just had a second son? Of his other five children four are girls and he was desperately anxious to have another son. All is well and he is tremendously pleased. His elder son has just got into the lowest class of a secondary school. Sixpence will have to pay £30 a year for his fees. He is quite prepared to do so, for it really is something to get a child into a secondary school here, the competition is so great and the places so few. But I shall of course help him out. Not able to read or write himself, it is greatly to his credit that he has spared no effort or expense from his tiny income to get Bernard up to secondary school standard.

I was just boasting to James an hour or two ago that it is a long time since I was called into the office out of office hours, or indeed been telephoned out of office hours. So much for boasting. The phone has just gone and it looks as if I may have to do some work. The blessed United Nations again, blast them! Anyway, I had better stop this letter and go and prepare some lunch for James in case I have to nip out. The phone has just gone again and I have decided to risk doing nothing until tomorrow morning. Hope the risk pays off and that I won't be in the dog house.

I have just reread your last two letters. What a tremendous lot you packed into your trip. I was quite breathless at the end of it. I am so sorry to hear about Joyce's duodenal ulcer and even worse the arthritis in her feet. What a family we are for rheumatic conditions. Thank heaven all my spells in warm climates seem to have kept me free – so far. And when I read about all your contemporaries I am thankful that you put them all to shame by being so hearty. Tough lot we are – you and I! And don't worry about my occasional tiredness. It is truly only the altitude and I get over it by going to bed early whenever I can.

By the way, your parcel contained a very nice M and S cream blouse. Sixpence hasn't got that – I have! Many thanks to, I imagine, Dora! James and Sixpence and I all had a hearty laugh over the combinations. Haven't seen such garments for years. Sixpence was not a bit put out. He said that he would slit open the legs and turn them into shirts. 'Very good material, Madam,' was his delighted comment.

I have now had further dips into your *Lost Rivers of London*. It is a darling book and I am enchanted with it. Thank you so very much again. And of course I just sat down the evening I got Norman's book and read it at a stretch. James was out to dinner and I felt lazy. I had it instead of supper. I loved the bit where Norman describes why he really loves Little Boy best – sorry, the better of the two.

4 June 1962

I'm battling against the clock as usual. Not much news apart from work. James took eight of us on the razzle on Saturday night to Salisbury's nearest approach to a nightclub. And I had my first glimpse at striptease – very unmoved! And so were the men!! 'Not enough meat on her,' they unanimously declared. James and I ducked at 2 a.m. and Ben and his girl followed soon after. But the rest of the party kept going until 3.30 a.m. I don't know where they get their energy from.

Into the bag with this, and all my love with it.

8 June 1962

James is busy rattling round doing his packing and in half an hour we leave for the airport. He goes on the Boeing and I find it difficult to believe that he will be back home for lunch in Teddington tomorrow. Fantastic world we live in! He has promised to take a letter for you with him, so I must hurry up and write one.

We shall be quite a gang at the airport – James, Ben Gingell, Ben's fiancée (did I tell you he had got engaged to a girl who has been married twice to, and twice divorced from, the same man and has a small child? All very dubious in theory, but it may just work out), Diana Moon who works for Ben, and her husband. We all had a lunch party together today to celebrate Diana's birthday and yesterday I gave lunch at home to the Professor at the University College who is very tempted to buy my house, his wife, Ben and Eve and James. James and the Professor know each other of old, so it was a happy reunion. Unfortunately, the house was looking really lovely in the midday sun, so I am dreading the effect on the Professor! We shall just have to wait and see.

No more now. I have a fairly busy weekend ahead, though thank heaven it is Whit and therefore no official work on Monday. Did you hear my Mr Abrahamson on the radio by any chance?

Whit Monday

I am trying hard to catch up on a few chores now that James has gone. Half a dozen of us went off to the airport to speed him on his way. We all talked so much that he jolly nearly missed the plane, and had a special call all to himself. It was rather amusing watching James walking miles across the empty tarmac, keeping a whole great Boeing full of people waiting! To see a Boeing take off at night is an awe-inspiring sight – just like a train going up. I really do miss James. He is a wonderful person to have about the house – always seeing little jobs to do and quietly getting on with them. It is a long time since every bit of electrical equipment in the house worked perfectly, and good to have reluctant drains racing away in hearty fashion. He really was able to get a lot of work done in the peace of my establishment, and he is very pleased indeed with his whole trip.

Yesterday I had a blessedly quiet day of gardening and sleeping, but I had to go out to a party at night some twenty miles away. It was given by one of the Southern Rhod. MPs and his wife for the visiting Nigerian parliamentarians. There were some fifty of us in all, and buffet supper for the lot of us. What an effort! Thank heaven I haven't to go out anywhere today, so I have been ironing and letter writing, and will soon be out in the garden again. But after wonderfully warm days it is cold today, with an icy wind racing up from the south.

Did I tell you that I had had a letter from June? She hopes to call in on me on her way home, from about 8th July to 14th.

13 June 1962

Your letter of 6 June turned up yesterday just after I had put my last letter to you in the bag. I think that my letter in fact answered a number of questions in yours, but I must now look through and see.

I'm glad that you heard James' talk. He made it in a great hurry just before he left for Africa and was terribly disappointed with himself The BBC woman he made it for is a great friend, and he felt that he had rather let her down. He is such a perfectionist and so strongly self-critical, that unless something is perfect he is dissatisfied. Anyway, I'm glad that you enjoyed it.

How I laughed over Madge saying, And who is this James? I didn't know whether you had got round to telling her that James had come to stay with me, so out of sheer devilry, when I wrote to them the other day about the mortgage, I said something about 'my dear James Hemming having just gone back to England'! I was wicked enough to hope that they would be shocked to hear that I had had a MAN in the house and no chaperone! It is naughty of me, but it is quite incredible to me that anyone can stay so behind the times in 1962. I suppose it is the result of staying put in one place and having no brats. But even if you hadn't had us to bring you up, I am sure that unaided you would have kept up with the times!

Still not much news. Brian Unwin has come back to the office today and is going to work mornings only for a bit until he feels stronger. Thank heaven he will give me a bit of reinforcement. And Bill McIndoe's replacement definitely arrives at the end of June. But then David Scott is likely to be shot off on other work for three months, so we shall have to share his work between us. If it isn't one flaming thing it's another. London will seem like a rest cure after Salisbury.

Last night I went to a buffet supper at the Scotts. As luck would have it the nice Miltons – the couple who are interested in buying my house – were there. I said, 'Hey, what news?', and they replied that even now they haven't finally decided not to buy the house, but that it is much more difficult for them because they like me and don't want to turn me out! Good show! Long may they continue to like me. But I don't flatter myself that I am more than a passing hindrance; they will make their minds up on more important issues. I shan't breathe freely until I know that they have actually bought somewhere else.

Seize came back last night, thank heaven. I will say this for my servants, that they come back when they say, or I say, they will. So many slope off and come back days or weeks after they are expected. Sixpence's wife and new baby also turned up last night. She has not been at all well since the baby was born, so I suggested to Sixpence that he brought her to Salisbury where we can keep an eye on her and see that she gets proper medical attention. More worries for me! One of the women at the party last night is the Chairman of the Family Planning Association, so I asked her what advice I could reasonably give to an African woman about birth control. I am determined that now Sixpence has his second son and four girls it is time he stopped. One has to be jolly careful not to step on African religious and customs corns. Anyway, the woman popped some pamphlets into the post for me today, in English and Shona, and I shall have to do my best to encourage Mrs Sixpence to go along to the clinic and get fixed up and indoctrinated. What we get to do in this country. I am profoundly conscious of the fact that no fewer than thirteen lives now depend on me – my two servants and their respective families. I don't want fourteen plus!

I have so much work on today that I just had a sandwich in the office. But I thought that I would take these few minutes off to write to you and then I will go back not quite so stale to my labours. I have a blessed evening in this evening and am looking forward to it.

P.S. Only way to see the two Cape Point transparencies is by hand viewer held up to naked sun. Old New Zealand bought Australian made sun dress still going strong, you will see. Eight years old now.

21 June 1962

Not a lot of news again. I had a cable from June two days ago to say that she is arriving on 8 July, so I shall try to take a day or two of leave while she is with me. Mercifully Bill's successor will have been here about a week, so I think that I shall have deserved some leave. The second thing is that those friends of John Gartside's rang up the other day and they are coming to dinner on Tuesday: Checksfield is the name. The Miltons still haven't made up their minds not to buy my house, but every day they don't is a day nearer to my coming home. You can indeed now begin to count almost in months. I have got the office here to agree to my going any time from June next year onwards, without consulting CRO, and I am at this moment doing some planning. At the latest I should be home by August. More about this anon.

Bother – an interruption and I shall have to get back to work. I really haven't much more news anyway, so please regard this as a just a tiny pot-boiler. I don't want to miss another bag.

25 June 1962

News fairly light again – and for once I have no letter from you to answer. So I will simply take the opportunity at last to send you Joyce's letter as promised and a few more transparencies. Attempts to photograph Willy Willy on his own were hopeless – he just came and wound himself round me. So I commandeered Roger one day to hold him.

Sunday morning, 1 July

I must say I was jolly pleased to get your long letter of 24th June telling me all about your Nottingham trip. I was beginning seriously to think about sending out a search party for you! But I don't really mean this. I think our arrangement is a much better one than so many people have with their families – of always writing on a particular day, and then getting terribly het up if the expected letter doesn't arrive on the appointed day. What a lot of news you managed to cram into the letter.

That deep freeze sounds a bargain. Have you got it working now? I'm sorry you didn't manage to see Coventry Cathedral. I have seen such a lot of pictures of it and it really does look rather wonderful in the modern idiom. I should have been so interested to know what your reactions were to the reality. We must pay it a visit together when I get home.

Again not a very exciting week, but I did meet one very interesting character during it – a friend of Elizabeth's in Lagos. She is Argentinian and is married to a Pakistani, and speaks English, French, German and Spanish fluently. She is a freelance interpreter and was in Salisbury interpreting for a mapping conference. Her husband works in ILO in Lagos, and she buzzes off all over Africa interpreting and leaves him to get on with it. She was one of the most intelligent and cosmopolitan women I have met for a long time, and I don't think she could have been more than about thirty. And of course I have just remembered, since I wrote I have had John Gartside's friend and his wife to dinner. Not knowing what they were like or how they would fit in with other people, I asked as well only the young man in the office who has come to look after the HC while Brian Unwin is helping me, and Roger, who is always on to help out and get a free meal into the bargain. It was very funny, for Louise the wife took one look at Roger as I introduced them and said, 'Good heavens, I last saw you in Cambridge seven years ago.' They had moved around in the same set and Louise had often asked mutual friends if they had heard what had happened to Roger. Wasn't it an extraordinary coincidence that they should meet again under my roof in Salisbury? Of course they spent hours catching up on the fate of their old friends of college days. I liked Tony Checksfield immensely – such a cheery, intelligent young man. He has been responsible for installing and working a big electronic computer imported by the Southern Rhodesia Government – a mathematician by training.

This week coming up is hell. Tomorrow I meet Bill's successor and his wife who arrive in the early evening. I suppose I shall have to have them home for dinner and tell them the tale. Tuesday is a farewell party given by the brother of Evelyn Hone, the Governor of N.R. He and his wife live opposite me and have decided to chuck this country and go to England. On Wednesday I give a small dinner party, on Thursday I go to dinner with the Indian Commissioner and his wife, and on Friday I go to dinner with some people I met recently at a party. They have a daughter who is interested in joining our Foreign Service and she wants to meet me and get my advice. Saturday I am blissfully free of dates, and then June arrives on the Sunday for the best part of a week. As soon as she goes I get landed for another two nights with one of the Secretariat who are coming out to work with the Advisers appointed by Butler – and the rest of the time during the more-than-a-fortnight is my own – at the moment! Do you wonder that I rather look forward to the peace of Balham, Gateway to the South. (Have you heard that perfect Peter Sellars record? I reckon it has done more to put Balham on the map in a short year or two than several centuries of habitation!)

Talking about coming home, here is what I am planning. I shall either be on a British India ship that sails from Beira on 11 June, or on a Lloyd Tristino that sails on about 8 June. There is just a chance that James will be able to come home on one or other of these, and we are hoping to be able to synchronize our departure times. He will be out again anyway as usual next year and has decided that he must have a bit of rest, and a sea voyage is about the best way of getting one. It really would be a great joy to have a companion for the journey, and David Scott feels that is quite reasonable that I should pinch a month off the three years and present CRO with an ultimatum. I should certainly like to have as much of the summer as possible when I do get back, and if I get either of these sailings I should be back by early or mid July. I am almost certainly bringing the car back with me, as second hand prices are so low, but it just isn't high enough slung to battle with the bad African roads, so I think I shall just be prosaic after all and come home in prosaic fashion. I shan't mind anyway having a real restful holiday after another year in this mad house. So there we are – all being well and provided the office doesn't get bloody-minded and demand that I stay on, I shall be home in just about a year from now. Goody goody and hurrah.

Must go and make some lunch now as it is Sixpence's day off. He and his wife and little girl and the baby live in a *kia* down the garden. One room with a bathroom attached with flush lav., bath and hand basin, but only cold water, so that they have to carry hot water from the house. But they are better off than many, poor things. His other four children are either at school or in their home in the reserve in Inyanga. The new baby really is adorable, but so terribly small and feels so very light. But the doctor says he is a perfectly normal healthy baby so I am satisfied.

Klokkespel

10 July 1962

I am snatching a few minutes in the morning while June is in the bath. I got up at my unearthly hour as usual and have had my breakfast, and June has got up herself – at 8.30 (she says it is the earliest she has got up for ages except for getting up to catch planes!). This is mainly to thank you for your letter of 1 July. I was very interested to hear you refer to the plastic spray that they now use on wounds. I first heard about it when I had the bump cut out of my head. The sister sprayed me, and she told me then that it was being used more and more in surgery. Certainly it was a great boon for the sort of wound that I had, for it meant that very little hair had to be cut away, and of course it is difficult to put plasters on hair. I'm very thrilled to think that my birthday jumper is on

Klokkespel. With June Barnett and Sunbeam Alpine.

the way and can't now wait for my birthday! You ask about stamps. Actually I am quite well off at the moment. Please tell the family not to think of bothering about sending a present. They can give me an extra large rosy apple when I get home.

Now for news. June arrived safely at 11 a.m. yesterday morning on a SAA Boeing. As we are in the middle of Rhodes and Founders holiday I didn't have to go to the office yesterday and I am off as well today, which is very convenient. As the weather yesterday was rather chilly I was in my slacks and warm top. Imagine my astonishment when June emerged from the aircraft in a very pretty plum coloured suit, beautiful stockings and elegant high heeled black patent leather shoes! Before she left Ireland all her friends had said to her, 'Whatever happens you must change out of your slacks before you get to Salisbury, as you must not run the risk of embarrassing Margaret.' June had said that she would not commit herself but would see. And they all said, 'We know you, you wretch, you never will change.' Now she can't wait to tell them a) that she did change and b) that their hostess was herself in an aged pair of slacks to meet her! I took her for a little run to one of the local sights where there are old rock paintings, and then we spent the rest of the day round the fire nattering our heads off She is staying with me until Friday, when she goes to Jo'burg to catch the plane home. Today I am running her out to the tiny little game park that has been established about twenty-five miles out of Salisbury – no big cats, but quite a few other bits and pieces. That is if the day turns out good enough. We have been having marvellous weather, but the last two days have been cloudy and very windy, with great cold gusts blowing up from South Africa.

I can't remember whether I told you in my last letter that I am now quite definitely booked on the *Europa* sailing from Beira on 8 June 1963 and landing in Venice seventeen days later. I have also booked on the same ship for James, just in case he is able to spare the time to come back by sea. He is keen to do so and so is Kay, though it will mean that James is away that much longer. But she says that once he is in Britain he is never allowed a moment's peace – so many people are after him for advice and for lectures and to attend conferences and to write books. She can't get away from school long enough to go on a sea voyage herself but she very much wants James to have this rest. It will be fun if it works out. But of course there is always the danger the office may delay me at the last minute. If they try to I'm going to deliver an ultimatum, and if necessary I shall plead my aged Mamma as the reason for wanting to get home – concealing the fact that my Mamma is about as frisky as a twenty year old!!

I owe you lots of money. Do please let me know how much. Three copies of Norman's book and various sums for transparencies and black and white negatives.

Must go now and get on with a few more chores before June emerges from the bath and breakfast.

June sends her love and says you are going to get a big surprise. She is going to write to you from here!!

14 July 1963

Another great long letter from you written last Sunday. I read large chunks of it out to June, particularly about Wimbledon and her fellow Australians, and we both had a jolly good laugh together. Hearing me read, with emphasis, what you said, made June say that she could just hear *you* saying it! I even heard some of the final between Mrs Susman and the Czech, on my little transistor radio in the garden, pruning my roses. What does interest me very much also in the field of sport is the news in my paper this morning, which Sixpence has just put on my desk (6 a.m.), that Bob Charles of New Zealand came fifth in the British Open. Do you remember my watching him win the N.Z. Open at the age of seventeen? I rather think you may have watched him too but I can't quite remember. I do remember thinking that one day he might make a great name for himself, and it looks as if he is on the way. He can only be about twenty-five so there is time for him.

Now to questions in your letter. No, the Hone family are the brother and sister-in-law of the Gov. of N.R. The family with the children are the Campbells. The Campbell parents are in Europe at the moment, having left the four children with a housekeeper. I have frequent visits from the children, and they seem to be bearing up quite well without their Ma and Pa. They really are darlings and I am very fond of them. They have acquired since their parents went away, but with their consent, a puppy – a cross between an Alsatian and a Rhodesian Ridgeback. He is the most enchanting thing – almost pure Alsatian, but much heavier in build and with the ridge down his fat little back. I am sure he will be immense, for he has gigantic paws. Bobby Campbell is an Edinburgh man, and Shirley is very keen on pottery, so I gave them the address of the pottery in Portobello and told them if they had a minute to look up Gordon and Eric.

Well now, once more I am without visitors – but only for two nights, for I have to put up a girl coming out from home with the Advisers to Butler. I shall only have her for one night, and then as far as I can see no more for a bit. June left yesterday, and in very much better shape than she arrived. I gather that she wrote to you yesterday so you will no doubt by now have had her version of her visit. I told her firmly on arrival that I simply couldn't do my job and beat it up and that she was therefore in for a comparatively quiet time with not much drinking and early to bed! We went out to the Scotts for an introductory party they were giving to three new people in our office, came home after a quick cup of coffee with the Australian Trade Commissioner and his wife, and went to bed after a very quick snack. On Thursday I gave a small cocktail party, and shot her off to bed very soon after the last guests had gone. Result, she was having tea at 6.30 a.m. for the first time in her life and having breakfast with me at 7.30 and enjoying it. What is more, as we are so busy still in the office there was no hope of my taking any time off; so I just left her at home and bullied her into getting on with her letters. She worked like mad, and may have told you that she wrote seventeen postcards, four air letters and a long letter in the short time she was with me. She really is a funny girl. We had a long heart to heart about her letter writing. Obviously she is suffering from some very strange psychological quirk over it, which I think I have sorted out but can't be sure! Anyway, it was great fun having her, and she went off looking ten years younger than when she arrived. You will be amused to know that she is not nearly so addicted to her slacks, and has taken to wearing pretty coloured clothes and very high heels. So much for the influence of Europe!

There on Saturday morning I must have leapt into the bath, and I haven't had another minute all the weekend. It is once more just after 6 a.m. but this time on Monday morning, and I want to get this finished to take in for the bag. I have spent large chunks of the weekend trying to sort out my accounts. You may remember when we were in New Zealand we had to prepare the most detailed arithmetic sums of what we spent so that the office could judge whether our allowances were all right. As you know, I have never been one for keeping detailed accounts. I am just as reasonably economical as I can be and as long as I never get overdrawn I don't bother. And with the incredibly busy life we live here there has been even less time to keep track of every penny. I have been putting off the ghastly exercise as long as I could, but the Inspector arrives this week and we have to send in our returns today. So it has been a horrid weekend of arithmetic. I still haven't quite finished it, but will sneak half an hour at lunch time to do final battle.

Since starting this letter, I have heard that I don't after all have to put up that girl. We have discovered that she already knows one of the women in the office and will be staying with her. Praise the Lord. It's going to be a stinking week of social engagements anyway, so I am glad not to have this additional chore. Ah ha, there comes the sun at last over the horizon and I'm sitting in a pool of golden light. Lovely! But I mustn't be tempted to linger. Hard work ahead.

19 July 1962

Your finished-on-Sunday letter arrived on my desk this morning, while the HC was having a long chat. It hustled him on his way, for he said a) he must leave me to read my letters and b) he must go and see if anyone had written to *him*!

We are of course *fascinated* by all the Government changes – the Conservatives' last desperate fling to stave off defeat. Am thrilled to think I should be home for the next election. It should be an exciting one. How enthralling Telstar must have been. I've just had a letter from James saying that he had watched too. '*Wonderful* world,' says he, with his vast delight in life.

Awful turmoil these last few days. The Advisers thick in our midst, before leaving for Nyasaland, and tomorrow the Inspector arrives. On top of everything, the banging in the office has reached a crescendo; there is dust everywhere. I have moved. I now have a better view, some sun, less tramping of feet outside, and charming grey walls, Wedgwood blue door and white paintwork – very artistic after the universal dirty cream of my last office.

This cutting appeared in today's paper. Very bad of Noni but thought you might like to see. Did I tell you Evan has never been to see his married daughter in her farm home? Her husband is evidently delightful and a good farmer, but Evan has never forgiven her for not marrying somebody more 'nob'. Isn't he a b—! Other interesting snippet. Was talking to Richard Sinnett the other day and asking about John. He told me that his father was worried that the Duke would make him retire next year and he doesn't know whether he will get a pension. But the odd thing is his mother hasn't a clue how well-off or badly off they will be. Never in all their married life has he ever revealed to Sybil *one* fact about his financial position, and she has never liked to enquire. Can you imagine anything more stupidly Victorian?

It is pretty chilly at present and oddly enough the skies are very grey. But my sweet peas are wonderful, and roses I planted three weeks ago already have two or three inch long shoots on them. Incredible growing country, if you can keep the pests down.

Back to work again now. Shall be pretty busy this coming week with no David Scott and the HC on tour for a week, so don't be too hopeful about letters.

By the way, the children's enchanting birthday card took two weeks and five days only from Leominster to my desk by sea-mail. That's a record. I am delighted with it and will be writing to them soon.

27 July 1962

Guess what? For the first time in thirty-five years (about that I should think but you probably remember better than I), I've had 'flu! A really good, devastating attack that has had me in bed for the best part of a week, with the only food inside me for five days, a tiny bit of cauliflower cheese and a bit of steamed fish! Today is my first day up, and though a bit shaky at the knees, I have decided I shall live after all. In many ways it has been heaven to have an enforced rest from the office. There is quite an epidemic around, and I think I must have been in just the right frame of mind to pick up the bug. No need to worry – I'm fine now and will be back in the office I am sure by Monday. My dear South African doctor filled me full of some antibiotic, and that plus Sixpence's tender care and a lot of rest and sleep has done the trick. So, as you can imagine, I haven't much in the way of news.

Now my return journey. The ship only goes as far as Venice as it is an Italian ship, so I shall disembark there and drive home. It will in fact be quicker doing that than going on a ship all the way. It is a slow business wandering through the Med. and up the coast of Spain and France. If James has the time he will come with me. If not, he will fly from Venice. I have taken a picture of the Alsatian Ridge cross as a wee puppy, but the film is still in the camera. I will take some more when he is fully grown.

The inspectors arrived and I had my long inquisition, the very first of the whole office. That meant that I had to give them a lot of background information about life here in general. It was as well that they saw me when they did as I went sick the next day. And of course I had to cancel the little dinner party I had arranged for them yesterday. With a bit of luck I shan't have to entertain them at all now as I think that they go on 1 August.

I've just had a long letter from Irene McIndoe. To my great joy they have bought a house in Dulwich, so we shall be quite close when I get home, and I expect that Bill will join the golf club. Bill is working terribly hard as Sandys' Private Secretary and doesn't get home most days until after nine o'clock. But he seems to be enjoying it. Irene says that he was fined £18 and had to pay costs and doesn't think much of British justice. I can only assume that she is referring to the outcome of his smash on the way up to Scotland, when he went into the back of a stationary lorry. I hadn't heard that he was being charged, but suppose he must have been had up for negligent or dangerous driving. Poor lad. I must say though that I am not surprised. I was always terrified driving with him. He was one of those absent-minded drivers who rushes up to things and then suddenly realises something is in the way and puts his brakes on at the very last minute! I'm sure only the comparative lack of any real weight of traffic in Salisbury saved him from disaster here.

2 August 1962

I'm just beginning to feel a bit more like my old self again. 'Flu really does knock the stuffing out of you and I have been very glad to get to bed early. Except for Monday. I had Rusike and his wife and daughter all to dinner on Monday night, and then took them along to the first play put on by the High Commission. I flatly refused to take any part in it as I feel I have quite enough to battle with, but the proceeds were to go to Rusike's home, so I thought I must make an effort to get along and to take the Rusikes with me. I wondered how they would like European food, but they tucked in like mad, very carefully watching me out of the corners of their eyes to see that they took the right irons, which I thought rather sweet. What is more they had huge second helpings so they must have enjoyed it. The play itself went down very well for a first effort, but we are yet to hear how much profit was made. To go back a day, I had my first trip out on Sunday, to go to the airport to meet one of the men from the Central African Office who had about four hours between planes, going back to London from a conference in Nyasaland. He was Ken Neale, who had spent a few days with me in my other house when he was out here two years ago. I gave him my last letter to you to post in London on arrival on Monday morning. I hope he remembered. He is a very reliable type, so I thought it worth risking to save about forty-eight hours.

Great excitement when I got home from the office two nights ago. Sixpence's youngest brother had turned up. Sixpence hadn't seen him for twenty years, though neither of them has ever been out of Southern Rhodesia. It really was a red letter day for them both, so I gave Sixpence the rest of the day off to spend with his brother. I had a long talk with his brother, named Julius, and asked him how many children he had. 'Two Madam, and one in the stomach,' was the delightful, uninhibited answer. Salisbury is having a great oral vaccination drive against polio at the moment, so I am lugging along all my lot in ones and twos to be done. I had one myself as well, as we are advised to even if we have had the Salk vaccine. Nothing like being doubly sure.

I always like to try to explain to my African staff just why things are done, and I had a hilarious session with Sixpence trying to get across the principles of establishing antibodies in the blood. The nearest I could get was to refer to making soldiers in the blood who were always there afterwards on guard to fight any further attacks by a bug. I think that this just made sense to him!

I'm glad you are so excited too at the thought that I actually have my passage booked. Now I really have a target I can hardly wait for the months to pass. But I know the time will go very quickly. One's last year in a place always does, and then I shall be back with you before you have time to put the kettle on.

Back to work again now. Just for the moment life is a little easier in the office, but these spells never last long enough for us to take more than one or two deep breaths.

Have just been to the dentist for the first time in a year. Absolutely nothing to be done, so I am very cock-a-hoop.

12 August 1962

Sunday morning, and time to answer your letter of 3 August with its interesting enclosures. First of all, don't be too put out by what the Opposition in Westminster says about the dangers of violence from the Africans here. An opposition is always out to embarrass the Government, and in fact the chances of widespread violence are pretty remote. The Africans in Southern Rhodesia simply are not sufficiently well organised. There may well be isolated instances of trouble, but I am not likely to see anything of them where I live. So not to worry, love. The little snippet about career prospects amused me a lot. It is a very sore point among the senior officers in the CRO that so many of the High Commissioner posts are going to outsiders. But I don't think there is any alternative. With so many new Commonwealth countries being formed, we simply don't have enough men of the right calibre at the top to fill all the new posts. But of course there are grumbles from those who feel they are worthy, even when in fact they are not. It won't affect me anyway for I know that I shall never reach the elevated height of a High Commissioner.

Now to your letter. Yes, thank you. I really have shed the last effects of my 'flu. I am full of vitamin pills, and these really have helped. Bill McIndoe. I imagine that he will remain Sandy's private sec. for about two years – if the Conservatives haven't been chucked out by then. Then Bill will probably be sent overseas again. But they have wakened up to the fact that it is a good thing to have a house anyway, as I did, to save the awful bother of looking for somewhere every time you get back from overseas, and also to give you a small income from rent while you are away. Incidentally did I tell you that I had an income tax demand for £165 a week or two ago – on my rent for twenty-one months. I knew I should get it some time, but it was a nasty shock when it did arrive – particularly as I now pay nearly £40 a month in tax anyway. No, we haven't heard anything about Freda Smith, Sandy's special female. Young Brian Unwin is going to the UK for three weeks shortly to see his brother married, and he has a special task to find out what has happened to Freda.

My news – not much again. We got Ben safely married yesterday. It was a very quiet little ceremony in the house, with about fifteen people there. Cold buffet lunch, and then bride and groom left by car at three o'clock on their way to Nyasaland. Eve's parents were the nicest people. Her mother really was the sweetest little woman. I bet they are holding thumbs like mad that this marriage will be a success after the fiasco of the last two.

Kay Hemming has sent me two colour photographs taken in my garden. One, taken by James, is a complete failure as he must have shaken the camera, but the one taken by Kay is very good. She says that she has a spare one for you, she may have sent it on to you by now. She and James are on holiday in Greece at present, lucky devils.

Must go and move the hose pipe in the garden now, so this seems a suitable opportunity to shut down. By the way, I saw in *The Times* the other day the death of a Kate Bedale, of the Downs, Bowdon, wife I think it said of Frederick. Is this any relative of our old doctor?

Hose pipe, here I come.

Office

16 August 1962

I had meant to dash back from lunch early and bash out a long letter. But I bumped into a friend just back from England and she kept me talking, so this will be a note only, mainly to send on enclosed letters.

But I must quickly acknowledge your marathon effort of 8 August, for which many thanks. Will answer it properly at the weekend.

Am just getting over giving a dinner party I gave last night. It included an ardent British Israelite who expounded at length. Had to use all my tact in keeping the party from coming to blows.

Spell of quiet over for the moment. V.V. busy again!

19 August 1962

How I laughed when you wrote and said that you recognised the teapot and cosy and rug. I showed the photograph to Roger a little while ago and said that as soon as Kay sent a copy to you I knew you would write and say that you recognised the teapot and the cosy and the rug! He roared with laughter when I read that bit of your letter out to him. The rug you don't recognise is the Irish one that June gave me before I came out here. It is a small travelling rug and very soft and cuddly.

On Friday night I went out to dinner with Tony and Louise Checksfield, John Gartside's friend and his wife. They had a delightful young couple there also, the husband of whom had also been at Cambridge with John. His name is David Hughes, and he is married to a Canadian girl, who I thought was one of the most attractive young women I have met for many a long day – attractive in every way. I still find dinner parties rather wearing though, since I had that wretched attack of 'flu. I seem to get so tired, and all I want to do is go to bed at the first possible moment every night. It is nothing to worry about, for everyone has the same reaction for about a month after getting rid of the bug. I am stuffing myself full of vitamin pills and am really perfectly well again, but just get tired easily. Roll on next June!

And of course as luck would have it the office is seething with activity again. Yesterday morning, Saturday, was one of the maddest I have known, and we have had some pretty mad ones, and I just came home and slept all the afternoon to prepare for going out to dinner again last night – a fascinating dinner with a Rhodesian woman friend and a woman whose name has been well-known to me for years from the Colonial Office who is an adviser on Education. She is out here with a Commission of Enquiry into education in

Southern Rhodesia. She must be getting on for sixty, and still spends most of her life dashing about the world and going into remote jungle areas in the Pacific and Asia and Africa. A really wonderful woman.

Today, thank heaven, no dates, and I have written letters solidly all morning, resisting the temptation to go out into the heavenly sunshine and garden. I really have been monstrously good over letters these last few weeks, as you may have gathered from the ones that I have sent on to you marked 'answered' – and there are a whole lot I haven't sent on as well. I suddenly couldn't bear the enormous pile of unanswered letters any longer, and have had a continuing onslaught over a period of weeks. My great ambition is not to owe one single letter. It will never be fulfilled, but if I can only reduce arrears to about ten I shall be moderately happy. I'm going to count this minute and see how near my target I am. Wait a second! It's seventeen. Not bad, eh! (All right, I know – simply frightful by your impossibly high standards!)

Soon it will be lunch, so I think I will cut this chatter short and get into the kitchen. Not much more news anyway. Foul week coming up, including giving a dinner party myself, and already I'm longing for next weekend.

26 August 1962

This has been a hectic week. The dinner party I gave on Tuesday night went on until after midnight. Then on Wednesday I was invited out to dinner again by Abe Abrahamson. I was a little bit dumbfounded to find that it was *à deux*. I wasn't quite sure whether he wanted to pump for information, or whether he wanted to get something across that I would obviously pass on to the HC. In the event I decided it was a bit of both, plus a genuine liking for my company! His family live in Bulawayo, where he dashes away every weekend, and I think that he gets fed up with the endless round of Parliament. I must be about the only 'safe' woman he can take out in the circumstances! He took me to one of the so-called night clubs here, with a strip-tease act – got home at 1.30 a.m. But I got quite a lot of interesting dope out of the man. Incidentally, as I may have told you, he is tipped for Prime Minister of Southern Rhodesia if anything should happen to Whitehead. He is certainly the only one in the Southern Rhodesian Cabinet, apart from Whitehead, who has anything like a first-class brain, and an appreciation of the real facts of life in this country at this time. The two hours before he came to pick me up were fraught with excitement. I ran a bath at about six o'clock and got into it at 7.35! All the business of the release of those three Rhodesian airmen blew up. This has been one of my babies, and a hell of a lot of work it has caused too. By the time Abe arrived to collect me I was still waiting to get a long distance call through to our Consulate in Elisabethville. The call at last came through at 6.25, and then I was able to escape. At midnight I discovered later that another emergency telegram had come through, but I was still out watching the stripper, so the poor old HC had to be dragged out of bed himself. He was very forgiving about it, particularly when I told him who I had been with.

By Thursday evening I really was very tired, after two late nights. One is usually enough to knock me up in Salisbury. Anyway, I only had a cocktail party. I escaped from this early and took myself off home. I made a lovely mug of Ovaltine for my supper and was just about to drink it when the ruddy phone went. It was the office. I could have wept. In the end it meant a trip up to the High Commissioner, and I got to bed well after ten instead of eight as I had hoped. Another cocktail party on Friday, but straight to bed, thank heaven, after it.

Yesterday I was to have for lunch a friend of Madge Martin, a woman professor of Education from New York, who is in Africa with fifty-two other Yanks looking at the education set-up in various territories of Africa. In the event she had to cancel lunch, but I collected her from her hotel and brought her back here for a couple of hours for tea. She was a typical very smart and very attractive American career woman. You have to hand it to the Yanks. She has been all over the world studying comparative education, and has even been to Soviet Russia and many other countries behind the Iron Curtain. As soon as I had taken her back I curled up with a book in my chair and was in bed by eight p.m. There I stayed for eleven hours, and really feel back to normal again. I didn't let on to the woman that I had a free evening, I am ashamed to say. I felt I just couldn't battle with another late night. Naughty of me, but there are limits. As it was the wretched office rang just as I was about to leap into bed. Luckily I decided that it was something that could wait (hope I was right), so I got to bed after all and was not disturbed again. But that was three nights out of four being disturbed in one way or another by the bally office. Thought those days were over. Next week is very much quieter, thank goodness. Hope to have at least two free evenings!

I must get round to writing to Margaret Lonsdale, now Hamilton, the woman I went to Spain with. Two days ago our Registrar decided to have a spring clean of the strongroom. In the dust in a remote corner he found a private letter addressed to me and with a postmark July 1961! It was from Margaret, telling me about her forthcoming marriage. I had always wondered a little why she had never got round to writing to me, as we were very good friends. What had happened to the letter nobody knows. It probably arrived while I was on leave in Luangwa, and got thrown into my tray in the strongroom, only to miss the tray and fall into a corner. Margaret must be wondering why on earth I have never replied, or mentioned the letter even in my Christmas card to her. A long letter of explanation is clearly demanded.

Office

Monday lunch hour

Well, there was a bit of fun after I finished writing to you yesterday. I got home from my lunch party and the fire seemed to be out, so I settled down to a little sleep in the sun on my lawn. Half an hour later I smelt burning again. This time it was far nearer, in fact the whole of the bottom of the Honeys' garden was ablaze. It had started on the other side of the dirt road that runs down between our two plots, and as the wind was in the right direction for me, it didn't jump the road. If it had done it would have burnt my borehole and probably Seize's *kia* as well. The Honeys had quite a struggle keeping the fire from their borehole but they succeeded, with the help of every available person around, including Seize, who as usual on a Sunday was happily oiled with beer. At the end of the excitement I had a long talk with the young Honey son who had had a shot at the buck. He confirmed that they are duiker. He said that as his mother was cooking lunch yesterday his father, a very eminent surgeon here, looked out of the drawing room window and saw one of the buck calmly sitting in the middle of their lawn, not ten yards away from their old boxer dog. He let out such a wild shriek of astonishment that the buck was off before anybody could get a shot at him. The cheek of the thing! Anyway, I said to young Honey that if he did shoot one would he please let me have a look at it so that I could swear that I had seen one in my garden. I only wish that I hadn't been out when they saw the one on their lawn, for I could easily have peeped through from my garden. But now that such a large patch of their garden has been burnt, there won't be anything like so much cover for buck to hide in, so we may not have any more visitations.

I am of course so scared now of the part of my garden that hasn't burnt off, that I am going to muster all the staff around one day this week and have a controlled fire. Obviously it will go if it isn't hastened on its way, and I want to be around when it does go up. What fun we do have.

Now back to work. Neil is back, and I have had the greatest joy in palming off nearly all the day's telegrams either to him or to Paul.

2 September 1962

Well, I have been having a mild dose of domestic crisis this week. Three days ago when Sixpence had served my breakfast he asked if he wanted me for a few minutes. I said No, why, and he replied that two buck were fast asleep in my garden, that they had eaten all his tomatoes, and all my next door neighbours' vegetables in the night, and could he go to my neighbours' and ask them to come with their gun to try to shoot them. Bob Taylor has always sworn that buck have come into his garden, and as we have no fence between us in theory they should also have been in mine. But I always treated this story with reserve, until now. The Honeys' son was duly summoned, but I had to leave for the office before the fun began. When I got home that night rather to my relief I heard that they had both got away. One only has three legs, but is as nippy on his three as the other is on his four! I haven't seen young Honey yet to ask him what kind of buck they are, but at least they have been seen in my garden. The next night they came back and finished off nearly all the rest of Sixpence's and Seize's vegetables. My vegetable garden, which is fairly near the house, has remained untouched so far, but oddly enough a new rose tree which I put in about six weeks ago, and which was covered in lovely shoots with the beginnings of buds on them, has been neatly cropped down, so that I doubt if I shall have many flowers on it after all. But nothing else in the garden appears to have been touched. It is very maddening for the two boys, and infuriating for the Honeys who have lost absolutely everything, but I can't help feeling just a little bit smug to be able to say that I have buck on my estate.

Then this morning I have just come in from investigating a very bad bush fire. I was in the garden and suddenly smelt smoke and heard the crackle of flames. The fire had sprung up in a second in the valley below my house, and the wind was blowing in my direction. When bits of ash started floating in my garden air I thought I had better investigate in case there was any danger of its reaching me, or rather the Taylors. The Taylors are away and I thought I ought to act *in loco parentis* so to speak. I shot off down the road on my flat feet and found a terrific fire raging in the *vlei*. Quite a lot of people were fighting it, and at least trying to keep it out of their gardens. I could see that the wind was going to take it below our two houses, but at one time I thought that my lovely row of gums at the bottom of my land might go up. There is still a lot of smoke coming from that direction, but I think that I am now in the clear. The trouble is that there is a real gale blowing, and everything at this time of the year is tinder dry. Never a dull moment. Knowing that I had such a lot to do today, I dragged myself away and returned to my chores.

This is a bad weekend, in terms of social engagements. As you know, I do my best to dodge weekend dates, but it isn't always possible. Yesterday I had to go to a very posh wedding – the wedding of the daughter of the Comptroller at

Government House. The wedding was held at noon in the Cathedral Church. I had a hell of a morning in the office, as I was battling with one of our Congo crises, I had to find a minute to dash out and buy a hat, as I hadn't a suitable one for a very superior wedding and one can't let the side down; and then I had to appear calm and collected at the wedding! The reception was held at Government House, and the Gov. Gen. and Lady Dalhousie were very much in evidence. I drove from the Church to G.H. in my open car, and had to borrow David Scott's son to come with me and hold my hat for me, as it would certainly have blown away otherwise. It really was a bit of a bun fight. There was plenty of champagne, but the food ran out before I got anywhere near it. And as I hadn't had a second to do any shopping for food, I had relied on a good wedding spread to tide me over. No such luck. I was very tired and very hungry by the time I got home. Then I am due out to drinks and lunch today – in fact I ought to be there in ten minutes from now, and I'm still in a sun dress. I shall just be late and to hell with them. Actually they are people I like immensely from just one look at them. I met them at a drinks party, and they have now invited me back to them. They both lived in India for many years, so we talk India solid.

Paul Thirsk arrived back yesterday, and Neil Ritchie comes back from short leave on Monday, so I hope to have a quieter time. I am sick of doing three people's work, particularly when one of the subjects is the Congo. Actually I shall be rather sorry to hand the Congo back to Neil. It is an absorbing position for us to be in, acting as we do as go-between between so many people – the UN, HMG, Welensky and Tshombe. Really must go and get ready. Will leave this open in case I have another minute or two before the bag closes tomorrow.

9 September 1962

I'm sitting out in the hot sun at the front of the house, that being the only place where the wind isn't too fierce. Have you ever tried typing in a wind? It is the most infuriating occupation, as the paper keeps on blowing over the keys and getting bashed on the other side. But I just can't stay indoors. In many ways this is the best time of the year. The sun is getting pleasantly hot, but not so baking that you must seek the shade.

To return to the saga of my buck. One has at last been shot, in the bottom of my garden. I didn't see it, and I haven't seen my next door neighbour who shot it to hear the full story. But Sixpence and Seize are delighted, as they hope that the other one will be too scared to come anywhere near. We certainly haven't had any more night raids since it was shot.

The office is pretty busy again. Roger Barltrop and his wife have gone off to Beira to pick up their new car. Brian Unwin doesn't return until next Sunday. The Second Secretary is away on a fortnight's leave, and of course David Scott has returned to being an adviser to Butler again, and will return with the other advisers to London when they go back for the last time shortly. As the High Commissioner said, Well Margaret, it seems to be you and me again! This isn't quite true as Paul Thirsk is back from his long leave. I'm hoping my chance to get away will come at the end of September. Thank heaven I really am feeling very well again. It took ages to throw off the residual effects of 'flu, but I have taken vast quantities of vitamin pills, and at last they seem to have done the trick. The last week too was one of the quietest ever socially (after much lying by me), and I had four quiet evenings out of five, and went to bed very early. Of course, you know me. If I go to bed early I can't stay asleep in the morning, and I have been having a spell of getting up at 5.30, making my tea, and dressmaking while I have watched the sun rise. I have got too fat for so many of my clothes that were just about right when I came out here, and in any case all my summer dresses seem to have died together. So I have been having a dressmaking onslaught. I resent having to pay so much for shop-bought clothes as one has to in Salisbury. Next week I start off with a ghastly round of entertainments again, but at least I am feeling fit now again to cope.

Office

13 September 1962

I was very tickled to hear that you had seen Stephen on TV.* Do tell me what he looks like now. Has he lost his hair?! I often see articles by him in the weekly magazines like the *Spectator*. He must have carved quite a career out for himself. I'm not surprised. He had an outstandingly good brain.

We had a public holiday yesterday, Pioneer Day, and for once I got the day off and wasn't even on call. I have stood by for so many public holidays I simply put my foot down and said somebody else could do this one for a change. Roger and I played eighteen holes of golf in glorious sunshine and I felt much better for the exercise and fresh air. Now I face a solid fortnight of engagements and will be glad when they are all over. But I am still feeling so much better that I'm not too appalled.

The High Commissioner has given me a new job to do – to court the Right Wing and find out what they are up to. I had a long talk with their new Secretary the other day – a retired Naval Commander. He was quite incredibly

*Stephen Toulmin, an early boyfriend from TRE days, who has since had a pretty spectacular career according to *Who's Who*.

indiscreet and the HC whooped for joy at some of the things I was able to extract. It is astonishing what a man will reveal to a woman. Subconsciously I think that they rather like to show off to a woman and will say things that they would never say to a man. The HC is well aware of this and exploits my sex to the full. The idiot child ignorant little woman touch can work marvels. What I had discovered was soon winging its way to London over the wires, and I hope to press on with this particular form of quiet espionage. Huge fun. What idiots some men are. They do underestimate women!

19 September 1962

We get reports that the British papers are full of panic stories about Southern Rhodesia, particularly the *Daily Mail*, which I hope you don't see! Don't take any notice. There has been a bit more trouble than usual, but it is nothing to worry about. The papers just love to blow things up into sensations, the beastly things.

We have been having freak weather for Salisbury at this time of the year. Two mornings ago we woke up to white frost, and today is so hot we are all going around panting. I have to go out later today to the laying of a foundation stone for a new adult education centre, and I only hope that it will have cooled down a bit by then for it will be very hot if we have to sit in the sun. Needless to say I love it, particularly when I can take off most of my clothes and flop about in the garden.

Not much news really – a lot of blessed parties, but none very interesting. I'm giving a cocktail party tomorrow night, just for about thirty people, and I hope to have it in the garden if I can muster enough light.

I am almost certainly going down to Bulawayo the weekend after next to try to poke my nose into the inaugural Congress of the Rhodesian Front, the right wing party I have been ordered to court. If I do go I shall take Roger down with me a) because I shall be happier not travelling alone and b) because it will give him a free trip to see his parents and c) it will give me free lodging with Roger's parents! It will be good to get away from Salisbury if only for a short break. The Umtali trip I was going on will have to be postponed. A pity as I should have gone on for a few days' holiday to Inyanga, but perhaps I shall get that one in later in October, when it can be pretty nasty in Salisbury.

24 September 1962

I'm very interested to hear that you have seen something of our exhibition on TV. Yes, indeed, I have been to the exhibition, and wonderful it is too. It is the first of its kind ever to be held, and caused quite a stir, though the people of Salisbury were pretty slow in supporting it. They are still rather barbarian in their attitude to African art.

David Scott has gone back to London as he is one of Butler's advisers, and has had to go back with the other ones to prepare their report. He will probably be in London for at least a month. His wife Vera has just been in to see me, feeling rather glum at being without her husband for so long. Roger Barltrop is Bill McIndoe's successor.

I don't suppose you usually see the *Sunday Times*, but if you can get hold of a copy for 16 September I think that you will be interested in the colour supplement. There is a long chunk of conversation between James and a woman and another man on the use of leisure, including two camera shots of James. I feel quite vicariously important knowing James. The *Sunday Times* must have a circulation up in the millions.

We really are in the thick of another crisis, with the banning of ZAPU. It does not affect me so much on my side, but the office as a whole is fairly preoccupied. Lots of my neighbours are in the Police reserve and keep on popping round to see how I am. I in turn tell them to go away again as I am not in the least bit scared. In fact our area is as quiet as the grave and there is nothing at all to worry about. I am sure that you get a very garbled version from TV and the British press of what is going on, as it is only the sensational things that hit the headlines. Whitehead made a very good broadcast last night, in which he referred to some correspondence about a Fort Victoria African, which appeared in yesterday's paper. He, the African, is a moderate who has had bad treatment from European and African alike, but has stood out staunchly for peaceful co-operation. I met him when I was at Fort Victoria, and I also know several of the Europeans who wrote the letter praising the African, that Whitehead quoted in his broadcast.

The Rhodesian Front Congress in Bulawayo has now been brought forward a day, to avoid having a meeting at the weekend. This means that I shall have to go down on Thursday instead of Friday. I only hope that Roger will be able to get the time off to come with me. I have rung him but he hasn't yet rung back.

I'm dashing out now to take the car to have safety belts fitted. Have been meaning to for ages and am determined to get them put on before we go to Bulawayo.

Office of the High Commissioner for the United Kingdom
P.O. Box 1482
Salisbury
Southern Rhodesia

1 October 1962

Very wicked of me, but this is the only paper that I can lay my hands on at the moment, and the bag goes this afternoon. There is about five minutes of the lunch hour left. This is really just to let you know that we got back safely from Bulawayo last night. It was a pretty hectic few days. We got away after lunch on Thursday and reached the Wests just after seven. Lots of nattering then an early bed. It was breathless in Bulawayo – far hotter than Salisbury, and I had difficulty in getting to sleep.

Next day, off to the Rhodesian Front Congress. I ran straight into friends of mine from Salisbury who I was astonished to discover were firm supporters of the Right Wing, but I was glad to find some friends to sit beside. The Congress went on all that day, and most of Saturday. An awful lot of hot air, both in the hall and in the speeches, but it was well worth while my going and it was anything but dull. I ran into several people that I had met at one time or another in my travels round the country.

The Wests were very kind and had two small drinks parties for me on the Friday and Saturday evenings, so that I could meet some of the leading industrialists in Bulawayo, and find out what they were thinking of things in general. This was all most helpful. Then they had more friends in for lunch yesterday, and Roger and I turned homewards at about half past two, getting home at 7.30 p.m. I did most of the driving both ways, but Roger gave me a rest in the middle of each journey. Oddly enough he is happier when I drive than when he does. He says he is always dead scared of doing something to somebody else's car, and he gratifyingly thinks I am the best driver he has ever come across! The car was going very well and we were firmly tied in with our belts, and we had the hood down of course all the time, so altogether we enjoyed the journey.

The HC is up in Northern Rhodesia until tomorrow, so the office is reasonably quiet today. I don't suppose that it will last. I am catching up on being away from the office for two days.

Our receptionist has just returned to the reception office where I am typing, to claim her typewriter, so I had better stop. Will try to write more fully for the next bag.

4 October 1962

Are you in a fit and proper state to take a row, for I am about to deliver one! I can assure you that I have more respect for your intelligence than to try to fob you off with reassuring nonsenses if there really were any danger for me here. If there were I should tell you, for it would not be fair to lull you into a sense of false security. You can either believe the papers and the BBC who don't live in Salisbury or you can believe your daughter who does. Now which is it to be? Of course there are isolated instances of violence and arson, but these go on all the time and only hit the headlines at a time like this when S.R. is more in the public eye. What few incidents there are are either in the townships, which Europeans aren't *allowed* into anyway without permission, or in remote rural areas where it is impossible for the police to be behind every tree. In the European areas, such as where our office is or where I live in Highlands, there is not the slightest sign of any trouble, nor do I expect there to be. In fact the banning of ZAPU has evoked far less reaction from the Africans than did the banning of the NDP nine months ago. What is more, you don't want to listen to what the Labour Party is saying. I can't repeat often enough that any opposition tries to make life as embarrassing as possible for the Government in power, and that is what Denis Healey has been up to. To the best of my knowledge he has never been out here to see for himself, or has probably only spent a few days, and now sets himself up as an authority. So, my girl, all you are likely to read between the lines of my letter is a great big chunk of make-believe. And I'm not saying this to reassure you. If we took at its face value what appears in the press here about Britain and its strikes and its racial troubles in Notting Hill, and its resurgence of Fascist parties and the awful pictures of people being dragged along by arms and legs by the police, I should not be able to sleep quietly at night for worrying about you in that strife-torn country of Britain. This is not exaggeration. I just happen to know what the press is like and so take its outpourings with large dollops of salt. Now perhaps you will shut up! Very sweet of you to be so concerned, but a *waste* of *good concern*.

I must say that is a splendid idea of Barbara's about coming to Venice, if only I had some more seats. If by any chance James has to change his plans, which is always possible if not probable with him, then would you be prepared to race across on your own? Have a think about it. What I was proposing to do anyway was to take you off somewhere as soon as I get back, for a holiday. I should still have quite a bit of leave to come as it has been so difficult to get any here, and I'm damn well not going to forfeit any after working in the madhouse of Salisbury. Have a little think about that too sometime in case you have any bright ideas on where you would like to go.

Curiously enough your letter coincided with a very short one from James written to say that he had been very pleased about your writing to him after his TV session on 'Tonight'. He seems to be a bit agitated too about the situation here, so I suppose I shall have to get down to giving him a wigging too! I do immensely look forward to introducing James and Kay to you. They really are splendid people.

I'm glad that the car passed its test all right – not that I would have expected anything else from a car so carefully run and maintained as yours! How many miles have you done on it now? I'm nearly up to 23,000 on mine in two and a half years. Terrifying how the miles mount up in this country.

I'm just beginning to think about the ghastly chore of Christmas cards. I have decided, as I may have told you, to make quite a number myself, of that picture of Big Boy and me, small size, stuck on to coloured stiff paper. They are not going to be very much trouble, and work out far cheaper either than office ones or the better and more interesting ones that you can buy out here. And, I like to think, more fun for the recipients.

Lunch hour nearly gone again. We are pretty busy with all the trouble boiling up again in the blessed United Nations, so I must hop back into my own office. Showed the first page of your letter to my shorthand writer just now. She laughed as much as I had done, and said that she had had a similar letter from *her* Ma! But she added, 'What absolutely wonderful writing your mother's is.' I agreed, and so obviously do Barbara and Eric. Here comes the receptionist for her seat and her typewriter again.

All my love from your *very safe*
Maggie

7 October 1962

I really have just about nothing to tell you since I wrote last Thursday, but I imagine you won't mind a nothingy little type. And also I must send the insurance cheque before I forget. Here it is.

Now what *have* I done in the last few days? Went to the cinema for the first time in months to see a most remarkable film called 'Wild Strawberries'. There is one very small cinema in Salisbury that puts on what I would call cultural films (!) – not the popular variety – and this was one of them. Salisbury is a pretty barbarian city, and I was disgusted to find only about seventy people in the audience. Then on Friday I went out to dinner with some people in External Affairs who have just come back from a tour in Lourenço Marques. A pleasant dinner party. A wild Saturday morning in the office – all sorts of intriguing things happening and the HC in bouncing spirits, then gardening, and today nine holes of golf with Roger and more gardening this afternoon. We are longing for rain now, though the garden is full of colour even without it. I've just been tidying up the carnations that I grew from seed. They have been in full bloom since the beginning of March, and far from showing signs of flagging, are simply covered in blossoms and buds. And now the dahlias are coming to life again – earlier than ever this year, and should be in bloom for another fortnight.

And that really is all for tonight. Not a very good threepenny worth I am afraid!

11 October 1962

Madly busy. Flew down to Bulawayo yesterday morning and flew back last night. Hectic day between flights. Lots happening all the time here and all interesting. I'm in fine fettle and fat as butter! Many thanks for huge long letter received this morning. Will reply at weekend.

14 October 1962

Sunday morning. I have just been across to the Campbells to see how they enjoyed their trip to Europe. They immensely enjoyed their visit to the Pottery. They ordered some egg cups with the children's names on and at the same time they had one done with my name on. I am very thrilled. Now I am back it is far too hot to be out in the garden, so I thought that I would begin this letter to you. I have started the battle of the Christmas cards and have earlier today finished most of them for New Zealand and Australia, a few for India and a few for the States. What a job it is. I try to do a few at a time, rather than battle with a whole lot together. When one has to write virtually a letter, it does take time.

My safety belts. Yes, they are attached to the floor. In an open car they can't be attached anywhere else. I wouldn't be without them for anything now. They really are wonderfully comfortable to wear and stop you swaying. I hate being in a car now that hasn't got them. Will you please be a good girl and get some fitted – if only one for your driver's seat. In view of the statistics on the saving of life by belts, I don't think that anyone has the right *not* to have them fitted. It is in the same category to me as being vaccinated or inoculated.

If you really want to find what I said about Geoffrey Lawrence I think you will find it in letters written in January of this year, for it was then that the Hammarskjöld enquiry was held. Yes, I did meet him at dinner, but I also had a lot of other dealings with him over the enquiry and we got on like a house on fire. It was he who said that I was to be sure to look him up when I got back to London. I certainly shall too, if I can muster up enough courage!

Now my news. Last week was one of the more exhausting ones. There is a lot of work around, and then I had to have that day off to race down to Bulawayo to interview three African women and choose one to send on a course to Britain. Dr West had produced these three for me but he flatly refused – and wisely – to be responsible for the final selection. One of the women came from one of the great royal Matebele families, and is married to a Chief, who came with her to the meeting. A second woman also came from the Reserves, and the third one worked as a welfare officer among the wives of railway workers. I had three hours with the women altogether, jointly and one by one, and we all had the happiest and most hilarious morning. They really were darlings, all of them, and bubbling over with humour as all Africans are if you give them half a chance. The railway woman endeared herself to me at once when I asked her how many children she had. She giggled into her hand, which is very common among African women, and then said, 'I am a Catholic,' at the same time demonstrating with her other hand six stages of growth from shoulder level almost down to the ground. One year interval growth! She knew that she didn't need to say any more and we both laughed our heads off together. It was agony choosing between them, for they were all obviously dying to go – it was the sort of opportunity that would never normally come their way. In the end I chose the wife of the Chief, mainly because I wanted one woman from the rural areas – the other two are both form the towns (Salisbury), and also because with her status she is most likely to be able to spread the knowledge gained from her trip when she gets back. I must say it is a wonderfully easy trip if you go by plane. It is less than an hour's flight in a most comfortable Viscount. Dr West took me home to lunch, and then ran me out to a Coloured school to deliver some books that the office were presenting. Back to the Wests for tea, and then Mrs W. ran me to the airport. Although she is so terribly crippled with arthritis she can still drive the car without any difficulty, for which she is profoundly thankful. The Wests really are very kind to me. They think that I have had a very good influence on Roger (I'm known by the Wests one and all as Naggy Maggie as I bully Roger so much), and they seem to want somehow to repay me!

Yesterday afternoon I went to the official opening of the first African-conceived, built and run secondary school. I loathe having to do anything official at the weekend but I obviously couldn't refuse this. The school is some twenty miles out of Salisbury, and the last five miles of the way are on a very

African women.

bumpy and extremely dusty track. But over five hundred people made the effort, and it was a splendid multi-racial gathering, with a tremendous lot of good-natured chaff between the Africans and the Europeans on the platform. I wished that some of the critics in the UN and from some of the papers in Britain could have seen how happily the races can get on here, and how much mutual goodwill and respect there is. But this sort of thing is never news, and the critics of Southern Rhodesia don't want to know about it, for it spoils their preconceived ideas. The ceremony was held in the blazing sun, with only a few people lucky enough to get into the shade of the building. We sat for three hours very nearly. Of course it didn't worry me one bit. I had a big straw hat on, and you know anyway how much I like the sun. I was amused to see how uncomfortable most of the Europeans and even some of the Africans were by contrast. Must have been some mixed blood in me somewhere!

We are beginning now to long for rain: everywhere is arid and parched and the dust is horrid. We ought to be getting an odd shower any day, but we won't get any serious rain for the best part of a month yet. Poor old Willy Willy with his immense coat crawls about from patch of shade to patch of shade and only comes to life when the sun sinks. Then he comes to life with a vengeance and goes quite berserk. He presented me with a large and thank heaven very dead rat first thing this morning, which he had disdained to eat.

Now I think that I have earned a gin and tonic. Thirsty weather this and thirsty work writing letters. I won't stick the envelope down though in case I think of anything else to say before the bag closes tomorrow afternoon.

17 October 1962

As I have remarkably little news, and for once haven't a letter of yours to answer, I thought that I would send on this letter from Jean Grinstead, whom you may remember from Wellington days. I certainly wouldn't mind being posted to Port of Spain! Sounds good, doesn't it? I will also look out some transparencies for you before I close the letter.

I've got a pretty dreary fortnight coming up with far too many social engagements for my liking, and it is so very hot and stuffy that to have to get togged up and go out is a particular bore. Then next week I have to give a lecture to Lady Alport's group of International Women, so I must do some homework. Much to my amusement I also have to give a lecture next month to thirty African sergeants of Police. I happen to know socially one of the heads of the Police Force who is in charge of training and it is he who has roped me in for this – a talk about the Commonwealth in general. Lastly I have to address the Rotary Club in Umtali in a fortnight. My Umtali trip, which had to be put off in order to go to Bulawayo, is now to start on 1 November. I rang up the Town Clerk who organised my programme last time and asked if I could go back for a second dose. He actually sounded enthusiastic! The HC was down there recently as I may have told you, and was told firmly by the Umtali-ites that they didn't want to see *him*, a man, they wanted Miss Archer back. The HC passed this on with great relish. So back I am to go. They really are the jolliest lot and I know that I shall enjoy myself enormously. I am also going to spend a day or two in the Melsetter area and see what I can find out about them while I am in the area. Last odd thing to fall to my lot. I bumped into Lady Cumings at the cinema recently (the wife of Sir Charles who has been quite a power in the land), and she asked me if I would take over from her a chore that she felt she could not cope with – testing a Girl Guide for her badge on the Commonwealth. She rang me up today to tell me what the child has to know before she can pass her test, and I realise that I shall have to do some serious homework if I am to know as much as the child I am testing! Ah well, all in a day's work.

Now I must get ready to dash out to a beastly cocktail party.

21 October 1962

Your letter of 13 October arrived on my desk just after I had put my last letter in the bag for you. How I laughed over your opening words 'All right, all right, all right'! I really *am* all right! And don't take any notice of the fact that the Police Reserve come and visit me. They adore playing soldiers, and do it without any real provocation.

I am so glad that you seem to have been having better weather, and it was fun to hear all about harvest festivals; it has such a wonderfully English sound to it! That heating scheme sounds very good, and I shall certainly look into it when I get home. I'm sure that I'm going to feel the cold like mad again as I did when I got back from India. I'm enormously enjoying the present weather. We had the hottest day ever recorded in Salisbury on Thursday, but it seems to have passed its peak. Yesterday a great storm blew up and I could see torrential rain falling in the distance. I rushed round and shut all the windows and Sixpence and I got very excited, thinking that our respective bits of the garden were going to have rain at last. But not a bit of it. Rain fell all around, and we didn't have a drop. Terrible disappointment! Today however there is a lot of cloud, and we may even get a wee drop after all.

I must say, it is good to have a quiet Sunday in which to relax, after last week. Thursday turned out to be very hectic, apart from being the hottest day ever. I went out to a large formal dinner given by the Belgian Consul-General and his wife. I rather dreaded finding nobody but continentals there and the conversation all in French! But it wasn't as bad as I expected. One of my fellow guests was my dear Abe Abrahamson, so of course we got into a corner and talked and talked. As he only lived round the corner he asked me if I would run him home so that he could send his own driver away and let him have an early night. I was dying for an early bed myself but of course couldn't say no. We got away eventually at about 11.30. I ran Abe round to his flat and he asked me very particularly to come in and go on talking to him. He promised me lots of black coffee to keep me awake! I sensed that he had a lot more that he wanted to get off his chest, so putting duty before my desire for bed I agreed. I often think that being a Jew he has a peculiar sympathy for the African, being here the subject race. It turned out to be a remarkable two hours which followed. He has just about reached the end of his tether, battling with his reactionary colleagues, both Federal and Southern Rhodesian, and he was talking about clearing out of politics and giving up the struggle. I felt it imperative to pitch into him and tell him that on no account should he contemplate doing anything of the sort. I don't flatter myself for one minute that anything I could say would make a blind bit of difference to him; but I think that he was glad anyway to have had a sympathetic audience for his woes. Strange the jobs that fall to one if one is a female diplomat. I don't think that he would ever have got round to saying what he did to one of my male colleagues. Needless to say the whole conversation was reported to the High Commissioner the next day, and he was very pleased with me. Heigh-ho, what fun we do have to be sure!

David Scott is back, much to our relief. This means that for the first time in months we are right up to strength. It won't last long. The HC is off to London in a week's time for consultations, but is only going to be away for a week. But as I think I may have told you, we are all to go on tour in the next month or two, so there won't be many days when we are all in the office together.

I have had to shut the stoep door to stop this letter from blowing about too madly in the typewriter. I really do think that we may get rain. My gum trees are bent nearly double with the force of the gale. Willy Willy will be jolly pleased too if we get rain. The poor little sausage has been flopping about from one bit of shade to another in his great fluffy coat, trying to keep cool.

Sorry, my typewriter seems to be getting more and more tired but it's still just more legible than my fist.

26 October 1962

The top of the morning to you! I've been up since 5.15 a.m. in a desperate bid to get some letters ready for today's bag. The bag now goes on Friday instead of Thursday. This has been such a completely exhausting week that I haven't had a second in which to think of letters. But I actually had a quiet night last night, went to bed early, and was therefore fit for an early start this morning.

Now love, thank you for your letter of 20th. I simply adore Boothby as a TV character, and look forward immensely to getting the book. Thank you so very much. I wonder what that film will turn out to be like. Do keep an eye open for the Epworth Mission, where Rusike has his little home. Talking of films, have you yet seen 'Return to the Wild'? I gather that it runs for twenty minutes and is going to be shown all over the world. I haven't yet seen it myself. I could have gone to a private showing earlier this week, but as I was giving that talk to Lady Alport's international women I felt that I had to stay in that night and do my homework. It was the only chance I had had of really getting down to thinking about what I was going to say. Incidentally again, here is a cutting from the *Rhodesia Herald* reporting on said talk. Though I says it meself, I think that it was one of my better efforts. I gather that the group had had a string of pretty dull speakers, so I didn't have much competition!; but nevertheless I just felt in a talking mood and their ears were receptive, so all was well.

The evening of my talk was the Sinnetts' farewell party. They are off very soon now, expect to have a few months at home, and are then to be posted to Germany. Although I haven't seen an awful lot of them I shall be sorry to see them go. Richard really is the nicest creature. Then yesterday I gave lunch at home to the three women we are sending to London, including the Chief's wife that I chose in Bulawayo. The Chief was up in Salisbury attending a meeting of Chiefs, so he brought his wife up with him in order that she could meet the other two. I also had along a women from External Affairs. We had a very happy lunch hour. The African woman from Salisbury is going to be a terrific character, and had us in hoots of laughter over how she had pinched her husband from under the nose of her best friend. She is so fascinating that I'm quite sure Best Friend never had a look in after she had appeared on the scene! I think it quite possible that they may appear for a flash on TV or on radio newsreel or something like that, but we are very unlikely to know here when this might be. Anyway, their names are Miss Thomson, the European, and Mrs Moyo and Mrs Msimuni (the latter from Bulawayo). Neither of the African women has flown before, let alone seen the sea, and they are just about beside themselves with excitement.

Tonight I'm giving a farewell dinner party to one of my colleagues and his wife. Then I have no date at all for Saturday or Sunday (much lying to achieve this happy state of affairs)!! Monday is Federation Day and therefore a public holiday, but I shan't get much holiday out of it as there is the big official reception given by Welensky (before lunch this year), and a drinks party given by the Deputy Secretary of External Affairs in the evening, neither of which I can properly dodge. What a public holiday! Never mind. I'm off on my tour on Thursday morning, and although it will be hard work it is always a break to get away from Salisbury.

30 October 1962

I know I'm not going to have time to write for a week or so, so I thought that I had better warn you!

The holiday weekend was devoted to Christmas mail, punctuated by phone calls on Cuba, Welensky's big reception and a cocktail party. Now I am struggling like mad to get everything under control for my crack of dawn start on Thursday morning for Melsetter. I'm hoping to have Roger as a passenger. I shall dump him on the mountains and collect him again. He wants to try out his new walk. I may have told you that he is a spastic and I have been encouraging him to try to correct a decided limp. He seems to take things from me that he doesn't from anyone else and he has been working very hard on correcting the irregularity. It has been agony for him as he has been using muscles he didn't know he possessed, and after three weeks he is nearly walking normally, and the stiffness is wearing off. I don't know which of us is the more pleased! This has encouraged him without prodding to tackle the problem of his shaky right hand. He never dared lift a cup with it and now he is drinking regularly with it and scarcely ever a catastrophe. Anyway, to see whether his 'new' leg will stand the strain of the mountains. I have such a devastatingly full programme that I reckon I shan't even have time to spend a penny!

7 November 1962

Safely back from my trip to Melsetter and Umtali. Roger and I got away early on Thursday morning It was a lovely morning and we took the journey very gently, reaching Melsetter just before lunch. I found that I didn't have quite such a hectic programme as I had expected. I may have told you about Heather Stelp, the woman I met when I went on one of my tours round the Reserves. She lives in Melsetter but was in Salisbury last week and said that she had heard that I was coming to Melsetter and would I go and spend at least one night with her. She said that a fierce programme was being laid on, and I asked her to get in touch with the people doing my programme and plead with them to give me at least one day free. She had obviously done her stuff. Anyway, I had a number of talks with various individuals, a meeting with the Women's Institute, talks with the Native Commissioner and so on. I had heard that Heather had built a fabulous house in the wilds – and that she was going to be delayed in Salisbury. So on the first afternoon when I was left free I drove round to find her house. It is right out in the blue down a very rough dirt road. The bridge which took the track up to her house was washed away in the rains last year, and she is busy building a permanent bridge. As a result you now have to clamber over a river on a very shaky foot bridge and then scramble up some hundred feet of rough rock. The house and garden when you get there are worth all the effort. I have tried to get a few photographs but I don't think that they will give any real impression of her courage in building where she has. Of course the house was all shut up, but from peeps through the windows it looks out of this world. Heather is reputedly an ex-Windmill girl. She was engaged seven times without ever getting as far as the altar. Then at last she met somebody she *was* prepared to marry and he was drowned in a boating accident. She evidently never got over it, and when an old flame who had been wanting to marry her for years contracted cancer, she agreed to marry him to make him happy at the end of his life. He only lived a year. You will gather from all this that she is quite a woman (middle fifties now I should

My favourite picture of Roger.

say). She is also one of the most highly qualified musicians in the country and took a grand piano all the way up into her mountain fastness. It must have been a herculean task.

On the Saturday I was left free, so Roger and I set off up the Chimanimani Mountains to the hut where you can sleep – if you take all your own bedding and food! Needless to say, soft old Maggie wasn't going to cart all that stuff up, so we simply went up to the hut, stayed there for a couple of hours and then made our way down again. The mountains are splendid and completely deserted. But was I stiff after that little lot – in fact I am only now getting my calves back to normal. I was jolly glad too to have Roger with me for I don't think that I would have gone on my own. Saturday evening I gave a dinner party at the hotel for the Native Commissioner and his wife and two farmers and their wives.

On Sunday we drove back to Umtali along what is known as the scenic route. It is most beautiful, but you have to drive along forty miles of unspeakable roads. When I tell you that it took us over two and a half hours to do forty miles you will guess what it was like! Everything inside the car and the boot, including ourselves, was coated with fine red dust. I wanted to see a hotel in the Vumba, some twenty miles out of Umtali, which had a very good reputation and where Roger and his mother had stayed some four years ago, so we went to see if we could get in. It is quite small and we were lucky and got the last two rooms. It is absolutely enchanting – thatched, furnished in exquisite taste and with the most splendid views imaginable. Down below in the valley you can see Sir Edgar Whitehead's farm. We left early the next morning so that I could get myself well sorted out for what was to prove the most gruelling twenty-four hours. I gave my talk to Rotary at midday, then meetings at 2.30, 3.30 and 4.30, the last going on until 5.45. Mad dash back to the hotel to change and back to the Civic Centre by 6.15 for the Mayor's reception for me. That went on until 8.30, when I was asked to join two of the Councillors and their wives for dinner. I was driven out to the border of P.E.A. where there is a new and very smart restaurant being run by a funny little Geordie. I got back to my hotel well after eleven and pretty dead as you can imagine. The next morning, first meeting at 9 a.m., then off to meet about sixty women at 10.15, back to the Civic Centre for another meeting at 11.30, which went on until 1 o'clock! Back to the hotel to collect Roger and then home to Salisbury. On the way the heavens opened for the first time in months and we had hurriedly to put up the hood and drive through torrential downpours. Were we glad though to see the rain at last, after all the torrid heat of the last few weeks. Roger had to dash straight off to see some friends from South Africa. I was supposed to go to a cocktail party, but by then I really had had it. Sixpence gave me a quick supper and I was in bed by 8.30. Quite a busy time. Although it was hard work at Umtali it was fun to meet a number of people again that I had met before and I had some quite hilarious sessions. The Rotary talk seemed to go down well. They had invited wives to be present, and one of the wives told me afterwards that the men had not only enjoyed listening to me but also looking at me! I've bought a really rather super blue hat for such occasions, and I'm sure that it's the hat and not the face that does the trick!

No bag for a couple of days so will send this airmail. Mustn't start another page as I'm trying to catch up on a lot of things.

11 November 1962

I am being terribly strong-willed and not letting myself get out into the garden until I have written at least three letters. I have just completed one to the Meins, now a short one to you and then perhaps one to June or Elizabeth, to both of whom I am in debt. I did briefly thank you for your Hallowe'en letter finished on 1 Nov. I am so sorry about this blessed stamp business. I can only think that it is something to do with this particular lot of paper. It is made locally and is therefore a bit cheaper than the terribly expensive imported stuff. I will try running a rubber over the surface of the envelope to roughen it up a bit and see if that will make any difference. I only hope that none of the other recipients of letters from me has had to suffer in silence and tip up sixpence. Never mind, I like to think that they will think my letters worth it! (I see on re-reading your last letter but one that you expressed these sentiments so far as you are concerned. Jolly good show!)

This last week has been one of trying to catch up on being away for a week. As soon as I got back, Roger Barltrop went away to Bulawayo to cover the UFP Congress, as I had covered the Rhodesian Front one. So I have had his work as well as my own. But that is nothing compared to what the HC and David Scott have been up to. For your private ear we have been having one of our major crises behind the scenes, and my bosses have been up until 2 a.m. this morning, and late night nearly every night of the week. We are breathing again, but are not sure how long the lull will last. But then we have had so many days like this that we get quite blasé about them. Out to a late dinner party last night, given by one of my colleagues for Viscount and Lady Dunrossil, i.e. John Morrison as was, son of the late Speaker in the Commons. He is the last remaining CRO man in our Embassy in South Africa. All the best have been replaced now by Foreign Office types, and John says there is about a tenth of the work that there was when S.A. was in the Commonwealth, but the FO have about five times more people than we ever had. There is no doubt about it, unless you happen to be in one of the really hot Embassies, such as Moscow or Washington or Paris, life in the FO is a hell of a sight easier than it is in the CRO!

Apropos nothing, but it has just come into my mind – true story told me by one of the Umtali Councillors at the Mayoral Reception. Three Africans filling in their form for claiming the vote were replying to the question, 'What is your sex?' First one answered, 'Male,' the second, 'Not prepared to disclose,' and third, 'Three times a week.' Thought you might like that one, knowing you!

I've been invited to see Norman's film on Tuesday. I had invited the son of people I met on the ship and his fiancée to come to dinner that night, but my would-be hostess has invited the lot of us. I hope that the young people won't think it very odd to find themselves not having dinner with me but with the Parliamentary Secretary for Home Affairs and his wife! I have warned the Foots that I have never met these young people so can't give an idea of what they are like, but Enid Foot doesn't seem to be in the least perturbed. This is very typical of the open-heartedness of Rhodesian hospitality – very much like New Zealand.

I posted your Christmas parcels – what am I talking about – I finished wrapping your Christmas parcels in the office yesterday and will post them tomorrow. The silly thing is that I have had the presents for ages, got as far as inner wrappings and then simply couldn't find a second to get them finally wrapped and posted before leaving for my tour. The post offices don't open until after I have gone to the office and I rarely get away until after they have closed, so it isn't always easy to get things off when you want. I only hope that they won't be too late. It is difficult finding out a last posting date. The last date for cards is about 27 November, much to my surprise, but I am sure that parcels must be earlier. There are two parcels. The smaller one is yours, and the larger one for the rest of the family.

Have you got your safety belt yet??? I shall be on at you as you were on at me some time ago over polio injections – and the chances of having a road accident are enormously much greater, alas, than catching polio!! *You have been warned.* And that I think really is the lot just for the moment.

16 November 1962

Now what news? Most important, I have seen Norman Carr's film, 'Return to the Wild'. It was rather funny how this came about. Do you remember my telling you of a South African couple who were at the Captain's table with me on the ship coming out, named Downing? They were dears and had all the right ideas about South African policy. Well, Edie wrote about a year ago to say that her young son was coming up to Salisbury and she had given him my address. It dawned on me some months ago when writing to Edie that son Trevor had never in fact looked me up so I asked if he had indeed come to Salisbury. Edie had then evidently bombarded him with letters saying 'have you looked up Margaret Archer?', and at last after repeated bullying he finally plucked up courage the other day and rang me. I discovered that he had got engaged, so I asked him and his fiancée to dinner. No sooner was this done than I was asked by the Parliamentary Secretary to Home Affairs and his wife to go to a private showing of the film and a finger supper. I told the wife the story of young Trevor and his girl and said that I was very sorry but I wouldn't be able to come as I had invited them to dinner that night, as a result of which dear Enid Foot invited us all along to the film and supper. So off we went and joined about sixty other guests. The Foots had laid everything out in the garden – chairs for the film show, drink and all the food. About half an hour before we were all due to arrive, a terrific storm broke, and they had to whisk everything indoors as quickly as possible. Poor things, I felt so sorry for them, though in fact the evening went very well despite this chaotic beginning.

The film is absolutely enchanting – and of course enormously interesting to me, since so much of it was filmed round the little camp where I met the lions. Have you seen any sign of its being shown in Britain? If you have only seen it on television you *must* see it in a cinema, for half the charm of the film is the colouring.

Trevor and his girl are getting married in early December, and I have written to the Downings asking them to come and stay with me while they are up for the wedding. They are such dears and I shall love to have them. But before then I have another visitor, Tim West, Roger's younger brother. I told him that there would always be a bed for him if he wanted to come up to Salisbury, and he rang me yesterday and asked if he could doss down for a couple of nights next weekend. So Sixpence and I are going to be busy.

Watch out around Christmas for a little extra something which will be coming your way, probably with a formal little note in saying, from Miss M. Archer. Don't be deterred by the formality. It wasn't until I had filled in the form that I discovered it said that the name and address of the sender would be included in the parcel. And as I had given my name and address as Miss M. etc., that is presumably what the parcel will say. This is a bit of an experiment, which I have also tried on Eva, Kate, Madge and Noel and the Hemmings. If you follow the instructions carefully – which you at least will!! you should have 'them' for up to two months. I shall be very interested to hear if they are in fact a success.

Got up at five twenty-five this morning to get letters written. Simply haven't had a minute at any other time this week. Oh, by the way, we got our three women off to Britain on Wednesday night. The 'plane was very late, and the two African women were getting more and more nervous about flying; but in the end they went off bravely. I don't think that the chances of their being seen on television are very great, but you may like to keep an eye open just in case.

Now I must stop gossiping to you and get one more letter written for the bag today before I dive into the bath.

Sixpence for you if you can guess what 'them' be!

18 November 1962

Just a very quick Sunday note to bring you up to date, and to answer that letter of yours of 8 November which I failed to answer in my last letter. Now let me see. What Evan Campbell said. I bumped into him as I often do, since we are in the same building, and he suddenly shouted out, 'What's all this I hear from my wife about you? She says you are the best public speaker she has ever heard – better than Churchill. Eh, eh, what's all this?' That was the sort of line, in Evan's big, beefy voice. Arrant nonsense, but very gratifying, particularly as Evan always goes out of his way to be as rude to me as he can about the bloody British Government. But that little story is only for your ears – sounds like boasting unless you happen to know Evan Campbell, then you see the story in perspective.

I'm sure you'll get a shock when you see me, I look so ruddy well! Fair, fat and forty, that's me. Fair as I have decided not to give in just yet to the onslaught of grey hairs, and so have given myself a corn gold rinse. This simply turns the white hairs into gold, without affecting the brown hairs – what are left of them. I flatter myself that the result is natural and rejuvenating. Anyway, you will see soon, if I haven't let it grow out by then.

This is my last peaceful weekend for some time. I think I may have told you about all my visitors – Tim West, Roger's brother, coming up for next weekend, the following one probably in Fort Victoria, and the third one putting up the Downings from South Africa who are coming up for their son's wedding. Then there will be all the mad rush of festivities over Christmas. Did I tell you that Mrs West has invited me down for Christmas? I'm hoping that the office will let me be out of Salisbury. It would be fun to spend Christmas in a family again. I'm not very keen on Christmas on my own . . .

Lots and lots of lovely rain last night, and the garden is suddenly green once more. Any minute now if it doesn't rain again I shall be out in it. Have cut a picture out of the paper of our three women. It is in the office, but I will enclose it before I shut up this letter.

Very early, Tuesday morning, 20th

Just as well that I didn't seal this letter on Sunday, for your thunderstriking letter about Trafford Park arrived yesterday, and the bag goes today. If Leslie and Dora nearly fainted, I'm still flat on the floor with astonishment and delight. You really are the most *wonderful and generous* Ma imaginable, and I don't know where to begin to thank you. We are the luckiest two children. Now, in no circumstance are you to run yourself into a bigger overdraft in order to give me my whacking great chunk of munificence. I have planned to pay off my mortgage in January, when I should have saved just enough money to do so. But that will leave me pretty low. This won't matter at all. When a little extra cash may come in very handy will be when I get home, for I expect that I shall have to spend some money on the house. The Meins say that they had some trouble with the roof, which has made a mess of the ceilings. Ceilings are such brutes to do that I would like to get a professional chap in to do them. Then I would like to look into this business of having some form of central heating, for I know that I shall feel the cold terribly when I get home this time. So my darling little Ma, please don't give me my wonderful present until I get home. That is when I know I shall want it most. Good old Trafford Park. Have they ever dished out a free issue of shares before?*

Your weather sounds very depressing, and I see in the papers yesterday that you have had widespread snow – pretty early for that. On the news it said that the temperature in London had been at freezing for the first time in a number of years at this time of the year. I couldn't help thinking of our three women from Central Africa, who were terrified of what they had heard of the British weather, but whom we had reassured, saying that it was never very cold in November!

By the way, I meant to tell you that I have decided to pass on a little of my wonderful good fortune by buying Sixpence a transistor radio for his Christmas present. I sometimes put mine on on the African service for him and he is wide-eyed with delight. And as he spends so much time alone in his rather dreary *kia*, I thought it would be a good form of entertainment and instruction for him. He really has served me so well and faithfully that he deserves a little extra treatment. I shall tell him that the money for it really comes from you.

Busy week ahead. I did have a quiet night last night, but celebrated by going to bed immediately after dinner. It is the last free night I shall have for the best part of a fortnight. And I simply can't write letters at night – far better for me to go to bed early and then get stuck into my letters early in the morning. Bath time now.

The very biggest hug for your wonderful generosity. Bless you and a thousand and one thanks.

23 November 1962

This isn't going to be a letter – just a quick note to let you know that I shall be so busy this next week that I shan't be able to write. Mad week of late dinner parties nearly over and I'm dying for some good long sleep. But Tim West arrives this afternoon, and almost as soon as he is gone I have to set off on my Fort Victoria tour. Sanity should return again after the Downings have been and gone – I hope gone by 9 December.

I had some of the junior staff in for dinner last night and then took them to see a local production of 'Heartbreak House'. I reckon it is fifteen years since I appeared in it, but I found that whole chunks of the script came back verbatim to me. It was an excellent production and we all enjoyed it. I have inadvertently grown a huge crop of mushrooms in my garden, and decided to

*The Company in which my grandfather bought shares 'for his pension' as he put it, and which stood not only him, but subsequent Archers, in good stead; alas recently bought over.

make mushroom soup. An Italian recipe. It was absolutely gorgeous, but it took me one hour and twenty minutes to prepare. Never again. I'm giving the mushrooms away first!

Must get back to work again now. I'm not sure when I shall get round to writing. I'll try to pop a wee note in next Tuesday's bag, just before I go off on tour, but won't promise. What bliss England will be after this – but how I shall probably miss it all when it comes to the point.

I enclose an extract from the *Rhodesia Herald* which will interest you.

Rhodesia Herald

Epworth Mission plans revealed

CHILDREN'S HOME IS TO BE EXTENDED

The Epworth Mission children's home near Salisbury the Federation's first African orphanage, is to be extended at a cost of £10,000. The home is run by the Rev M. Rusike, a 65-year-old retired African Methodist minister, who holds the MBE for his work in child welfare.

It cost £6,500 to build and was opened in July 1961, to care for children living a hand-to-mouth existence on the streets.

Now it is planned to build a second block of dormitories, dining and recreation rooms, a house for Mr Rusike, another for an assistant warden, and a row of workers' cottages.

The mission superintendent, the Rev H. Buckley, said yesterday: 'The plan has been approved by the Children's Home Committee, and it goes to the Methodist Synod in January.

APPEAL

We have only £1,000 so far, but shall be appealing for more with the aid of brochures.

And if the money starts coming in after January we shall start building next year.'

There are now 40 unwanted children at the home. It will house 80 with the new block to be built on the same modern lines as the existing building.

'Although we plan to get bigger, we don't want to get too big,' said Mr Buckley. 'We don't want to get like an institution. We try to give the children a form of "family" life.'

Enkeldoorn

28 November 1962

I never got that note in the bag after all, but as I have half-an-hour to spare in this cockeyed little dorp, i.e. one-horse town, I will make up for the deficiency.

Yesterday was the usual scramble in the office to get clear enough to go away for a few days. Up at 5 a.m. this morning to wash hair and pack and on my way by 9 a.m. Enkeldoorn is only a hundred miles and therefore a comfortable two hour journey. I travelled all the way from Salisbury right to this hotel behind a new Wolseley. The occupants drew up in front of me outside the hotel and I suddenly realised that I knew the man – a relative by marriage of Eve Gingell, whom I had met at Eve's wedding. He had his mother-in-law with him. She looked so young I thought she was his wife. She has just lost her husband in his ninetieth year. They had been forty-seven years married and in those forty-seven years had never been apart for one single day. Isn't that a fantastic record? No wonder she is feeling desperately lonely.

In twenty minutes I am to meet the Native Commissioner. I stay the night here – the hotel is about Dannevirke standard! Then go on to Fort Victoria tomorrow. Wild thunderstorms last night but so far today dry, thank heaven.

2 December 1962

Safely back again, after an extremely exhausting little trip, but an interesting one all the same. I dived into the office on my way back yesterday and collected my mail – quite a batch, including half a dozen Christmas cards and your letter of 24 November. A wonderful effort. You talk about my writing, but it never ceases to amaze me how much fascinating news you manage to pack into your letters. And you always seem to lead such a busy life yourself that I *am* truly most grateful to *you* in return for sparing the time to write such long letters to *me*!

Yes, I did go through Paarl when I was down in South Africa – but of course the chances of being dragged out of bed and hacked to death are far, far slimmer than having a car accident and being polished off that way!

Now for a short account of my trip. When I last wrote I was in Enkeldoorn. I spent the day under the wings of the Native Commissioner and his wife. This meant meeting a number of people around the district, which is a great Afrikaans stronghold, being taken to the Club in the evening and then having to face the crowd in the bar at the hotel after dinner. This of course is where one picks up most of one's bits of information, so although I was longing for bed I did my duty, spurred on by mine host and two of the men who had been at the Club. Two burly Afrikaaners who were travelling up from the Republic to go fishing at Kariba joined us. One was drinking and was very merry and wanted to flirt madly with me, while the other one was driving and drinking tomato juice and was trying equally wildly to persuade his companion to continue the journey! Having got rid of them we were then joined by a very earnest Conservation Officer, who wasn't happy until he had regaled me with the full story of where he thought the S.R. Government had failed in its land policy. I finally escaped the lot of them at 11.30, having been up since soon after five a.m.

Mine host was a very civilized man with a delightful wife, a beard and dark brown shorts that covered his knees. He had had no opportunity of a long crack with me so he asked me to join him while he had his breakfast – I had had mine. He sat down to pawpaw, a kipper, a chop, two fried eggs, bacon and fried potatoes, brown bread and butter and a glass of wine! As you can imagine my eyes nearly popped out of my head, until he explained that this was his one meal of the day. He had so often missed lunch because he was serving in the bar, and had so often missed dinner for the same reason, that he had established this custom of a huge breakfast to last him for the rest of the day. Not a bad idea. I left Enkeldoorn in time to drive the hundred miles on to Fort Victoria in time for lunch. There I was given a great welcome back by the people I had met a year and a half ago, and of course I had the usual round of meetings and Mayor's reception and lunch parties. The first evening that I was there was the evening of the Mayor's reception, and I asked to be allowed to go back quietly to the hotel after it, have dinner and go to bed. My wish was granted and back I went. I had my dinner and made straight for my room. But was I going to be allowed to go to bed? Not on your life! I was accosted by three men – two commercial travellers and one J. Arthur Rank chap who was wandering around the Federation on a look-see visit. They had eyed me at the dinner table and had decided that as I was alone they weren't going to miss the chance of a talk. One of the travellers had an unmistakable Lancashire voice and of course that did it. I relented! How I laughed. He said, 'You're a representative, aren't you?' 'Quite right,' I replied. 'What in?' Long pause and scrutiny of me, admittedly looking my best as I had been all dolled up for the Mayor.

'Cosmetics,' he said at last. Complete explosion of me as you can imagine. 'No, the British Government.' Complete explosion of him! They were a very jolly lot, but of course this meant another late night.

Next day a run round the African township and then a further bout of meetings, including one with the Executive Committee of the UFP, the Chairman of which is an African named Gondo, who was one of the men who went to the UN as a petitioner. He is a butcher, and one of the few really moderate Africans who believes that white and black can not only get on with each other but need each other. Because he won't join an African nationalist party he has been subjected to all sorts of intimidation, but he doesn't take a blind bit of notice. And he has a terrific sense of humour. He was saying how frightened he was of travelling so far by plane. He had only ever been in a small one before. He said that he didn't mind taking off, but that he hated coming down, leaving his stomach behind. 'Never mind,' said he, 'I just fastened my seat belt as tight as I could and so kept my bowels down.' The things that impressed him most in Britain on his way back from the UN were the orderly queues and the kindness and politeness of the police. The police here are often the worst type of young arrogant white, and they can be beastly to Africans. It is one of the things that desperately needs reforming. In the afternoon – sorry, forgot, lunch with the Town Clerk and his wife, and then on in the afternoon for a long session with about twenty women of the WI and Loyal Women's Guild. They were such pleasant women.

When I had my meeting with the UFP they asked me if I was doing anything in the evening. Since my programme finished with the women I answered 'No.' 'Then come to our first election meeting,' they said. I really longed for an early night but of course couldn't refuse, and in any case I thought that I might be able to pick up quite a bit about the feeling in the place from such a meeting. 'Who is speaking?' I asked, and roared with laughter when I discovered that not only were the two UFP candidates, one of them being Gondo, both on the platform, but also Abe Abrahamson. That clinched it. Imagine my astonishment when just as I was about to go in to an early dinner at my hotel in order to be sure of getting a place at the meeting, in walks Abe and asks me to dine with him at his hotel. He had in turn heard from the Committee that I was in Fort Vic. and he wanted to know what I had discovered about the place before he embarked on his electioneering speech that night. I must say I do feel a little bit smug when Cabinet Ministers, albeit of a funny place like S.R., seek me out to hear my views! We had a quiet little dinner, and then one of the candidates came to collect us and cart us off to the meeting. It was an extremely lively one, with quite a bit of barracking from Rhodesian Front supporters at the back. But it was also remarkably good tempered, and Gondo spoke extraordinarily well – far better than the European candidate for the other constituency. It was the first time that I had heard Abe speak, except in Parliament, and he produced some splendid rabble-rousing stuff. As I may have said before, he is the most liberal and enlightened towards the African of all the S.R. Cabinet, and therefore of course I thoroughly approve of him! The meeting ended soon after ten, when about twenty of us repaired to Abe's suite, and there we quenched our thirst with beer and went on talking as hard as we could go. I ducked at about 11.30, but the party was still going strong. I bet Abe was dying to get rid of them by then. He had flown down in the middle of the afternoon, and was dashing off again early the next day for more meetings. It is a desperately busy time for Ministers, when they still have to go on with the affairs of state, canvass in their own constituency and rush around all the other constituencies in support of lesser known candidates. I'd far rather be a civil servant, thank you very much!

With such a hectic week ahead of me, I decided to make tracks straight back to Salisbury on Saturday, instead of going down to Zimbabwe and Kyle, as I had originally intended. So I left at 7.45 a.m. and had done the two hundred mile journey by 11.15, which gave me time to collect my mail and do some weekend shopping. I had arranged to borrow one of the office motor mowers, as my hand machine has gone wrong again, and the grass was getting meadow-like. In any case I have so much lawn now that it is really beyond a hand mower. Roger popped in from canvassing to see if I had got back safely, stayed to help me mow and returned again on Sunday to finish the job. Even with a motor mower there is about seven hours of mowing to get all my lawns cut. Anyway, I hope that they will now last for a week or so and certainly until after the Downings have been and gone.

I started this letter yesterday, Sunday, but from the middle of the second page has been written early on Monday morning. I went to bed early last night, but couldn't sleep very well as I slipped on one of my little mats yesterday and landed on my elbow. Only superficial damage, but the elbow is rather uncomfortable to lie on. So I thought, more typing to my Mamma. Now it must be into the bath, off to the office, and start planning for my eleven guests for buffet supper tomorrow. Golly, I must be wicked judging by the lack of rest!!

10 December 1962

I was up at 4.50 a.m. today to make tea for Ken and Edie Downing and ensure that they had an early start on their way back to Nigel. My alarm clock, which I haven't used for ages, had, I discovered in the middle of the night, gone wrong, so I had to rely on my internal alarm which as you know never lets me down. It didn't, so all was well. It has been fun having the Downings to stay. They really are the nicest pair and so grateful to have a home to relax in. instead of having to live in a hotel. They gave me a beautiful copper jug as a thank you present. The wedding was on Saturday afternoon, and although we had rain on and off for days, it actually managed to keep dry when we were popping in and out of the church and the reception. Now I can take a quick deep breath before all the Christmas festivities begin.

Let me see what I have to thank you for. We had to wait ages for mail last week as no planes took off from London Airport because of the fog. But I had a wonderfully large clutch of letters when at last it arrived, on Saturday morning. This included your letter of 1 December, for which many thanks. Don't listen too carefully to what Neil Bruce says. He isn't nearly as good a reporter as Dicky Williams was. And it is absolute nonsense what he says about violence against the Europeans. The Rhodesian Front, which is the reactionary party, is, we are convinced, not going to win, and even if it did we doubt whether there would be more than the odd incident. Africans are far more prone to acts of violence against their own kind than they are against the European.

We can't wait to have the election on Friday – the country is in a wild pre-election fever, with political meetings all over the place. Thank heaven it will all be over well before Christmas. I'm trying hard to find a moment to leap out of the office and go and see the doctor. I slipped on a rug on a polished floor and fell on my elbow. This was ten days ago and I still can't rest it on anything and am wondering if I have chipped a bit of bone. There isn't any swelling so doubt if there is a fracture, but it seems a bit odd that it doesn't feel a tiny bit better since it happened. Silly how easily these accidents can happen.

Christmas mail is beginning to pour in now from all over the world. I will send on in due course the more interesting letters that come my way.

14 December 1962

I'm still rather in the throes, and have about five minutes in which to whip off a short note to you. I've got to examine two Girl Guides for their Commonwealth badge immediately after lunch, and the bag will have closed before I get back. I am therefore wickedly typing this in a spot of office time just before lunch.

Today is election day and everyone is rushing around being excited. I hope to be awake enough to sit up and listen to the results tonight, but I have a horrid feeling that I shall go to bed. For last night I went out to dinner with a woman I met when I saw Norman Carr's film. She is an incredible widow of about seventy. I thought she was remarkable when I met her, but after an evening in her company I am more convinced than ever. She is an ardent and practising spiritualist, and tells you all about her experiences in the most racy and matter-of-fact way. I was absolutely thunderstruck. Mustn't stop to give you details now, but will try in a later letter if I have time.

One fascinating occurrence the day before last. Norman Carr suddenly appeared in my office. He is setting out by jeep for England and is then going on to America. He had been enquiring in the passport office about visas, and of course looked me up while he was about it. He is hoping to run some really tough safaris next year, where you vanish off into the bush for a week and live quite rough. He wanted me to be a guinea pig, but unfortunately I shall be on my way home before he gets back and has a chance to organise these new holidays. Actually he will be back before I go and I hope to see him once more on his return, but I will be gone before he starts his safaris. A great pity, but there you are. He was thrilled to have seen the lions again, but was very sad that he just didn't have time to stay with them.

This is an inadequate note, and I must go this very minute. More later.

20 December 1962

Your two letters dated 12 and 15 December arrived by the same bag, and together with one from Dora and Leslie. Thank you all – a marathon effort all round.

My elbow. Still a bit dicky. There was no bone broken but I have bruised the bone and have to go every day for physiotherapy. It is an awful bore sparing the time, but I am hoping it will do the trick. I've had five treatments and I think it is showing signs of improving at last. I'm being an awful baby over it. It isn't really too bad, but I just don't want it to get to the stage where it doesn't get better, or begins to get stiff or something.

I'm so glad the chincherinchees have arrived. The Hemmings's have as well, and when they wrote they were going through the same processes as you. By the way, do you know how to pronounce the word – it is chinkerinchee, with slight accents on the first and third syllables. Do let me know how long they last.

So much is happening on the political front here that I can't even begin to tell you about it. My lips are certainly not sealed, but I could go on for about ten days! Suffice it to say that we were completely shattered by Whitehead's defeat. We had never thought it possible. Now we have to start thinking all over again. There may be certain blessings in disguise, as it may make the Africans and Whitehead's party get together in opposition, which would be a good thing, and something that Whitehead was never able to achieve when he was in power. Abe Abrahamson rang me up a couple of days ago to ask me to have a word with him before he finally packed up as Minister and went back to Bulawayo. He has got his seat back all right, but of course is no longer Minister. He was remarkably cheerful, and is convinced that the UFP will get back in two or three years, either with himself or Whitehead as PM. Nothing like having confidence in yourself! I shan't half laugh if he does eventually become PM. I shall be able to boast that I know at least one PM on the personal level!

Then yesterday came the Nyasaland announcement and Welensky's great attack on the British Government. The HC came back out of the Legislative Assembly where he had been listening to the speech absolutely purple with rage, and trying to make up his mind what to say in reply. This meant wild telephone calls to London. I left the office some time after seven, as nobody could help the HC much on what was essentially his own responsibility. David Scott and Brian Unwin got away round about ten p.m. We almost wondered whether we would all be declared *persona non grata* after what W. had said! But I had a phone call this morning from one of the big industrialists in Bulawayo whom I know quite well, to say that most of his friends think that W. must be stark staring mad, and that they for their part fully understand and appreciate what the British Government is up to. It is encouraging to have a few boosts like this when we are so wildly unpopular with most of the whites.

Despite all the excitements I am sure that I shall get away to the Wests all right for Christmas. Poor Roger had a very unfortunate accident to his car the other night. His father was up for the day and the two of them were at a party which they left too late for Dr West to catch his night train back to Bulawayo. They arrived at the station to find the train drawing out. Dr West asked Roger to drive quickly up the line to see if they could catch it at the next stop, on the other side of Salisbury. They got alongside the line and took a dirt road which appeared to go to the station. It was a filthy night, black as anything and pouring with rain, and suddenly they pitched at about 35 m.p.h. into a three foot wide and three foot deep drain right across the road. The windscreen shattered and a lot of superficial damage was done to the front of the car. Thank heaven VWs are so tough though, for with the aid of planks they managed to get it out and to drive it away. Forty pounds of damage has been done, but the garage think nothing structural. You can imagine how popular Pa West is with his elder son, particularly when they discovered afterwards that the train didn't stop at that station after all. And Pa West worked as a doctor on the railways for years! But this is typical of Salisbury, to have a ruddy great drain across a road without a word of warning.

This evening I am having to stay, a woman I used to know in Delhi – Dollie Byrne. I may have mentioned her to you before. Her husband died here a few days after I arrived so I never saw him. Dollie has been left very badly off and I feel terribly sorry for her and have her to stay once in a while. Then out to dinner tomorrow night and I hope off to Bulawayo early on Saturday morning. We are going very slowly and are not attempting to get there until the afternoon. Roger is very tired too and we both hope to have a very lazy family Christmas. Roger did a tremendous amount of canvassing for Whitehead's party, and his candidate was roundly beaten, so he is feeling pretty down in the mouth. His brother Tim had been doing the same thing in Bulawayo, and Dr West said that he came home in the early hours of the morning on which it was certain that the UFP had lost, literally in tears. Tim is the last person I can ever imagine having a weep, but this gives some indication of how deeply distressed the really liberal and go-ahead Europeans are at the result. They feel that the rest of the world will judge the lot of them by those who have got into power.

I see everybody trooping back into the office after lunch, so I think I had better scoot. This won't reach you before Christmas, but I shall of course be thinking of you all.

27 December 1962

As I seem to have a monstrous pile of letters to write, please may I send you an omnibus to thank you all for all your Christmas greetings, presents, cards and letters. What bounty all round. First of all, Mother, I can't wait to get my nose into Boothby's book. I have always thought him one of the great characters of our generation. I was very strong-willed and didn't open the parcels until Roger and I were just about to leave for Bulawayo on Saturday. And thank you, Rest of the Family, for the lovely cheque, which will be devoted to a gramophone record. I am beginning to assemble quite a nice nucleus of a record library, and hope from it when I get home to convert some of the younger members of the family to the lasting joy and satisfaction of the world's great music! In fact, warm thanks all round.

Now a very brief account of Christmas. Roger and I got away just before eleven o'clock on Saturday morning. I had a lot of chores to do, sorting out the servants and the house and so forth. Sixpence's son Bernard turned up the night before, so of course I had to have a long chat with him too. Sixpence was absolutely thrilled with his transistor radio and couldn't believe his eyes. I told him about my good fortune from you and that I wanted to share some of it with him. And he laughed and laughed over the picture of himself that you sent to him. He can't wait to show it to his wife and will probably send it via hand of Bernard when he goes back home. Sixpence thanks you very much indeed for it. By the time Roger and I got away I was feeling pretty tired. It had been such a harassing week before. So I got Roger to do most of the driving, curled up in my seat belt and slept for large chunks of the way. We went *very* slowly. I become a slower and slower driver as more and more people that I know get killed on the road, the latest being the wife and mother-in-law of James' collaborator, Bill Miller, who retired to the Cape a few months ago because of ill health. Roger is very co-operative and feels just as I do, so we hardly went above sixty, which is crawling by Rhodesian standards. The Wests had organised very little, knowing that I would probably not want to do very much, and this of course suited me admirably. Odd people popped in for a drink, and we had a party on Christmas night and that was about the lot so far as social engagements went, praise the Lord. On the Monday Roger and I did some last-minute shopping in Bulawayo and then went on to spend the day in the Matopos. The day started in pouring rain, but we were very lucky and had some sunshine while we were making a pilgrimage to Rhodes' grave. I had been there once before, but wanted to go back once more, for it is such an impressive place. On Christmas morning we went to that home to see the poor little mongol child, of whom Roger is godfather and guardian, having had dinner the night before we left with the parents. The mother still cannot bring herself to see the child. The wee thing is much more mongoloid than she appeared to be when I saw her a year ago, but she is very sweet and is able now to walk quite well. One of the presents we were asked to take to her was a little pram, and this she simply adored, pushing it up and down the corridor of the home as hard as she could go. But of course she has to be watched every second at the moment. After we left the home we went to church for the morning service, then on to a very quick pre-lunch drinks party, and back to White Gables for traditional Christmas lunch – things on our knee and coffee, so as not to use the table or make too much washing up! A sleep in the afternoon, last minute preparations, and then ten of us for dinner – four Wests, two couples with whom the Wests have had Christmas dinner *every* year for *twenty-one* years, the son of one of the couples and me. It was a very jolly party, and we all ate far too much of course. But it was very gay, with lots of crackers and jollity. Bed I suppose round about midnight. I thought of you all at midday, and again in the early evening at drinks time – I mean I thought of you particularly then, but throughout the day I kept on imagining what you would be up to, taking into account the time lag of two hours. Now I'm waiting to hear all about it.

Tim took me round yesterday morning to see Colonel Prentice, with whom I used to have many dealings in Rhodesia House. He is now fifth in line in the Federal Army. I always liked him immensely, and didn't want to go back to Britain without seeing him again. We had a hilarious hour with him and his wife and son, then back for a very early lunch, so that R. and I could turn back to Salisbury in time to reach home before the daylight failed. Again we travelled very slowly – in fact we didn't have any alternative most of the way, for we drove through blinding rain for well over half the way. This is quite the wettest of wet seasons and we are fed up with it. It rained nearly all the time we were in Bulawayo, except for our Matopos trip, which was lucky. Anyway, we made it with the last of the daylight. Because the weather was so beastly there was very little traffic on the roads, so it was, apart from the rain, a pleasant journey.

I have today and tomorrow off as leave. I am supposed to ring the office on my return just to see whether they want me to come in, but I haven't let on yet that I am back. I have so many things to do at home that I want to get at least some of them done before I run the risk of getting dragged back.

1963

3 January 1963

I must say I was relieved to get your two letters today. We have all been wondering like mad how our folks have been getting on at home, for the British weather has been headline news after the Congo! Badly though you seem to have fared, it sounds as if once more you have got off considerably more lightly than a lot of other people. I had a letter from James yesterday to say that he and Kay had had a nightmare time having gone down to Sussex for Christmas. They had just managed to stagger into some remote little pub which was overflowing by the time they arrived. They were taken in and the next day they all had to help dig each other out and give each other push starts. I'm quite glad I'm in Salisbury, even if we are fed up to the back teeth with heavy rain. Now for other points in your letters. After a week of physiotherapy my elbow seemed worse than ever, but it must have had a long term effect, for at last it is much better. Dr West said that I had probably got a blood blister under the skin of the bone, which could take a good month to disperse. It is about five weeks now since I did it, so it is due to get completely better any minute.

I was delighted to hear that my parcels reached you in time. It shows how wrong the post office is in telling you the last posting dates for Christmas. All my cards seem to have arrived before the end of November, and the parcels, which were sent off in theory about three weeks too late, were just in time!

Right – I will duly address the girls of the school. I feel able to tackle any audience now, and after my hundred sixth form boys here, a lot of girls should be chicken feed! I may have told you that while I was in Bulawayo I was asked by the Rotary Club to go down and address them later m January. The HC has agreed, so I shall fly down for the day on 25th, give my talk and fly back again the same day. They want me to stay the night, but I shall be glad to get back for the weekend.

Now about the film. I think I am right in saying that both of them were made by the Central African Film Unit. 'Call from the Wild' is one on wild life generally in Central Africa, and I haven't yet seen it. 'Return to the Wild' is a twenty minute film entirely on Norman Carr and his two lions. This is the one that I *have* seen. Whether Norman's film will be on general release in England or not I don't know. I know that America have bought the rights of it, and I dare say somebody in England will too, but I haven't yet heard. I will try to find out more about this. But I rather suspect that the only one which will be available at the moment is 'Call From'. I believe it is wonderful, so don't feel too fed up that it isn't the lion film. I am sure that it will be well worth seeing.

I don't think I have any startling news. I dodged all noisy New Year's Eve parties, and dear quiet gentle Roger came round instead, and we had a session of my gramophone records, and brought the New Year in in very staid and prosaic fashion. I am really not good in this country at beating it up: I get too jolly tired. The next day I had some sort of tummy upset and was thankful that it was a holiday. After breakfast I had nothing for the rest of the day but a cup of Oxo, as a result of which I was fighting fit again yesterday. Just as well to have a day of starvation anyway, with my girth!

Yesterday evening I had all the Lawley family to dinner, son John who I picked up in Pretoria and brought up to Salisbury, and his parents. They are all dears and we had a very happy evening. They didn't budge until nearly midnight, but they are so nice I didn't mind in the least. Tonight I go to dinner with Ben and Eve Gingell. It will be interesting to see how the marriage is working out.

The office has returned to a state of comparative normality – though we have already had over seventy telegrams in in the first two days of the New Year. But you may be amused to see the enclosed note which the HC sent round the other day to pep us up a bit. He himself is in splendid heart after all his battles of the last fortnight and bumbled into my office yesterday for a long chat. He loves nothing more than to be at full stretch.

10 January 1963

Life has gone a bit quieter this last few days. The Congo is still causing some work, but not very much of it falls my way. You will have seen now that Rab Butler is coming out again next week, and that of course will cause us a lot more trouble. But we are hoping to stay quietish until he arrives. I have just been warned by the High Commissioner to stand by to help out at a dinner party which he and Lady Alport are proposing to give. The other guests will include the Butlers, the Welenskys and Sir Malcolm and Lady Barrow (Deputy Federal Prime Minister). Shan't be able to eat peas on my knife on that occasion! I expect that there will be one odd man present – hence the need for an odd-very-woman to balance things up.

On the social side I have been to a very good stage show of the London musical 'Oliver', and an amusing dinner party given for a visiting Brigadier, who turned out to have got a First at Cambridge in Engineering, and then went into the Army. He was highly intelligent and I am invited to have lunch with him at the Oxford and Cambridge Club when I get back to London. Another no-peas-on-the-knife occasion! Now I have the blissful prospect of several free evenings in a row. *What* bliss.

I've just dictated a letter to a Mrs Elizabeth Cumming. It came back from the typist addressed to Mrs Elisabethville Cumming. The poor girl has typed Elisabethville so many hundreds of times in telegrams in the last few weeks, that her fingers just automatically typed it again!

While I remember, the next time you are in the post office would you be a dear and ask for a driving licence application form. My licence is out of date, and I may as well get it renewed before I come home so that there is no difficulty about driving back from whatever port I land at. Isn't it exciting! In less than five months now I shall actually have sailed.

I have written to James to ask him how long he thinks we shall spend on the drive across Europe, and what port he suggests we should make for on the Continent, so that I can arrange to book the car on a suitable ferry. I want to be able to let you know where and when I shall be landing again on my native shores. I don't know whether you will feel you can bear to drive down and meet us, or whether you would prefer me just to drive to Hereford as hard as I can go after landing. But there is still a little bit of time to think about all this.

You may be amused by the enclosed press notice. There is a terrific row going on here as a £10 per lb. tax has been imposed on imported hops. The home brewers are absolutely livid and the papers are full of their protests. I could make quite a lot of money smuggling in good Herefordshire hops at a cut rate. Just imagine though having to pay £10 a lb. in tax, for an article that costs about five bob a pound – or whatever the price is.

Must go out now and buy some fruit for my lunch. I got a terrible fright at the dinner party the other night. I weighed myself on the bathroom scales and found that I had gone up to 10 stone. I thereupon decided to diet. I weighed myself again today to make sure, on the proper chemist's scales, and discovered that after all I was only 9 stone 6, clothed! Vast relief, but I am still too fat round the middle and am fed up with letting out clothes. So I'm going to try for a bit to cut down on food. I don't eat an awful lot at the best of times, but of course I don't get nearly enough exercise, and I don't want to get to the stage where it becomes difficult to get it off again.

15 January 1963

Please thank all the family for their Christmas letters. The thought of my forty-three year old brother sledging from the top of Upper Hill fills me with glee. I only wish that his forty-one year old sister could have been there too. If there is any snow left, for goodness sake tell them all to get my skis out of the loft and have a go. It seems awful that they are there and not being used. I have arranged to send to Leslie a book, a Year Book of the Zoological Society. There were extracts from it in the paper here, and it sounded to me absolutely enthralling. So I have taken pot luck and ordered it from Smith's in Leominster. It may turn out to have lots and lots of dreary technical details which are of no interest to anyone except zoo keepers, but I hope that he – and the rest of the family – will enjoy some of it. It is so difficult to think of things to send men when you are overseas.

Yes, I have met the Duke of Montrose, at that Rhodesian Front Congress in Bulawayo. He calls himself very humbly here just Lord Graham. I very nearly was to have dinner with Winston Field. The High Commissioner asked me to swop from the Butler/Welensky dinner to another one the next day for the Southern Rhod. big-wigs. Having agreed, he then asked me to switch back again. So it is after all still next Monday with the lot I listed in my last letter.

I started this at home this morning, and then brought the typewriter into the office for an overhaul. I've got a new ribbon out of it, thank heaven. I've just had a quick glass of milk and a sandwich, and am now back in the office to finish this before the bag goes in the afternoon.

I have been spending a lot of my free time in the last few days battling with one of the office motor mowers that I have been able to borrow. It arrived completely useless, with the throttle cable adrift from the carburettor. I have had huge fun taking it all to bits and wandering round motor cycle shops to get bits soldered on here and there. Even then I couldn't get it to go, so decided to try a new plug. Still no luck, so I had the whole thing to pieces and cleared out all the muck and at last got it going at the weekend. Then I left the office early last night to do a bit more mowing and it started being temperamental again. After two and a half hours of dismantling and putting together again at last once more it went. But there was only then ten minutes of daylight left! But it is all a great education, and what I don't know about motor mowers and their foibles now isn't really worth knowing!

I've got a visiting British Council woman foisted on me for a couple of nights on Sunday and Monday, which will rather wreck my weekend. But all my colleagues are busy putting up Butler and retainers, so it is only fair that I should do my share.

After several glorious days in which we had to start watering the garden again, it is raining once more. I think we are cursing the rain as much as you are cursing the snow.

I had a letter from Irene McIndoe a few days ago. They had all gone up to Brechin for Christmas when Bill got an SOS to tear back to London as all their pipes had broken. So he had to take two days off from his holiday and travel all the way back to London to cope with the deluge and then go back again to Brechin for the rest of his holiday. I only hope that I haven't had any bursts in Balham. The Meins certainly haven't told me of any such troubles, so I am hoping for the best. At least if I do have a break it will all be confined to the ground floor.

18 January 1963

I am simply appalled by the latest saga of your winter in your letter posted on 14 January, which reached me yesterday. Jolly quick in view of the weather. 31 degrees of frost is something that I didn't think Britain could ever run to. What has happened to the Gulf Stream? Gone to sleep, it strikes me. Every day I wait to see in the papers that the thaw has set in at last, but each day's carries just as dreary news as ever. You poor, poor, things. I am so terribly sorry for you.

Life has had its moderate excitements since I last wrote. Perhaps the most entertaining session was lunch yesterday. There are two senior BOAC men here at present doing some work. I had been invited to a cocktail party two nights ago to meet them, and then in addition I was invited by Central African Airways to meet them all over again for a very posh lunch yesterday. I suspected that I might be the only woman, and indeed I was. There were twenty-one men, including Sir Albert Robinson, the Federal High Commissioner in London who has come back to Salisbury for consultations, the Federal Minister of Transport, the Director of Civil Aviation, Bob Taylor as Chairman of CAA, and so on. I was put at the right of the guest of honour – the more senior of the two BOAC men, since I was the only woman, so of course was in a strategic place to hear all the most interesting table talk. They all pulled my leg like mad, but were extremely chivalrous to me all the same – nay, gallant is the word! After lunch Bob proposed the toast of the visitors and the other airline representatives present, so all the Government officials got to their feet. Then the chief guest got to his feet and proposed the toast of the Government officials. And then somebody said in a stage whisper, 'Hey, how about Miss Archer?' whereupon forty-two eyes turned to me and 'Speech' was demanded. It was the shortest of my career. 'I give you a toast – the men, God bless 'em,' and drank on my own, to whoops of laughter and clapping.

My other short session among the elevated was much more private. Dear Abe rang me to say he was up in Salisbury for a night, he had had most of the day with Whitehead and could not face dinner with him as well, so would I go along and keep him company. I shot off round to his hotel after the cocktail party and had a tremendous chinwag over a quiet supper. I can't help feeling just a little bit flattered to be preferred to an ex PM!

Last night I gave a small dinner party and took some colleagues after to the film of 'West Side Story'. I know that you didn't much enjoy the stage show, but I thought it wonderful, and the film even better. But it meant bed long after midnight. What with the lunch and that it was quite an exhausting day.

Tonight I go to the other extreme from my aviation larks by attending a cocktail party given by an Indian I know, to say goodbye to Dr Terence Ranger, who is a lecturer at the University College and who has been declared a prohibited immigrant. You may just have seen something about this in your papers. Three of us from the office have been invited. The HC was a bit dubious about letting us go, but we were determined, and he has reluctantly agreed. We don't agree in principle with the deportation (I mean the British Government), and I don't see why we should not make this known by attending the party. But of course there are bound to be security chaps around who will know we are there, and we shall be down in their bad books. We get quite used to this, however.

Roger's landlady comes to lunch on Saturday. She is a splendid old woman in her very late seventies, and is wonderfully on the ball. Her hearing is not very good, though she can hear me perfectly well, and poor soul, she has just been told that she has a type of inoperable cataract and will go blind fairly soon. She still drives a car, but knows that she won't be able to do so much longer. She lived for years in India, so I always love talking to her – and even at her age we argue like mad about the politics of this part of the world. I'm on duty over the weekend, which means I have to spend most of Saturday night meeting the Queen's Messenger at the airport, coming in to the office and opening up, which means mastering umpteen safe combinations, and depositing the bags, and then repeat the whole business on Sunday morning, which wrecks most of the morning. On Sunday afternoon my British Council woman arrives to stay for two days. So I shan't have much of a weekend. Monday night is of course 'may daining' with the 'farst Secretary of Staaat'!

24 January 1963

Life has been so scatty this week that I just haven't had a second to get down to a letter to you. Now I have at least part of a lunch hour and I want to get something ready for the bag which goes tomorrow.

So much news since I last wrote that I shall have to write it in shorthand! Duty weekend last weekend, which meant four trips down to the office and back. Then the British Council woman arrived on Sunday afternoon and I had to collect her from the airport. She turned out to be a pleasant and interesting woman – about my age and the daughter of an Eton master. I had her until Tuesday morning. Monday evening was of course *the* dinner. I had already been up at Mirimba an hour or two before to hear Butler give his initial press conference. Then back home to put on glad rags and away back for dinner. Lady Welensky didn't turn up. Since she had a heart attack a month or two ago she is having to take life very gently and she had to duck. Mrs Butler was absolutely marvellous. As you know, B. and W. are at daggers drawn; and as W. entered the drawing room, Mrs B. flung her arms round him and said, 'Roy, are we on kissing terms still?' Of course what could Roy do after that but embrace her. She is superb at coping with tricky situations and did much throughout the rest of the evening to reduce tension. But it wasn't the happiest of parties – there was too much underlying strain, and I think that we were all glad when it was over. I had a happy time at table anyway, sitting between Sir John Clayden, Chief Justice and Deputy Gov. General, and the official who is the head of the Central African Office. Sir J. is very informal and relaxed and we prattled merrily throughout. B. and W. were as far removed from each other as the table allowed!

Yesterday I had been invited to lunch by one of the biggest industrialists from Bulawayo. I met him two years ago at the Bulawayo Trade Fair and we had not seen each other since. Having accepted the lunch date, I was intrigued to learn that just before the lunch he and four other leading industrialists were due to see Butler. When I eventually met de Haas he was bubbling over after their interview. They had put forward a quite startling idea for the future of this country which Butler had obviously been much intrigued by. They had come from the meeting and had a further meeting among themselves, as a result of which they had decided to ask Mr Butler for his sanction to go ahead and take a particular course of action. As I was lunching with de Haas, it had been agreed that he should make me their emissary. So over lunch he unfolded their further scheme, which I subsequently got to the S of S through David Scott, and was able to let the little man know before the day was out what Butler's reactions were. All rather fun. De Haas has invited me when I fly down to Bulawayo tomorrow to talk to Rotary to spend an hour or two going round his factory – the biggest textile factory in the Federation. This should be interesting. I seem to do rather well with my Jews from Bulawayo – first Abe and now de Haas!

Tomorrow will be pretty hectic. I get up at some ungodly hour and fly off at about 7 a.m. I don't get back until nearly twelve hours later. But it's all in the day's work.

Last night Brian Unwin gave a small dinner party for Butler's Private Secretary – a very smooth young man who has got very far in a very short time. It was very entertaining hearing some of the personal side of Butler from him. I had the job of collecting him from the house where he was staying and taking him back again, and it was on these occasions that he let his hair down. It is *not* all beer and skittles working for a man like Butler!

27 January 1963

I see from this morning's paper that it is actually thawing in Britain. I do hope that this really is so and that it is not a false hope to be followed by hard frost again. I was very tickled to see on the front page of yesterday's Salisbury morning paper a picture of a real Dobbin, being driven across the Thames at Oxford by a student. It did my heart good to see the brave little chap, over thirty years old now I reckon!

What do I wear to a party such as the one given for the Butlers? Long evening dresses are usually only worn at Government House functions, though occasionally older women wear long ones. At this party Lady Alport asked me to be sure to wear a short dress, as Mrs Butler and Lady Clayden were going to be in long ones, but she and Lady Barrow in short. She wanted me to keep her company in a short one. I was delighted to do so. Driving in a long dress is an awful bother, and a few months ago I treated myself to a new short dress that has been nicknamed 'The Firefly'. It is chiffon with fly away panels and is in a misy-mosy pinkish, bluish mauvish pattern that looks a bit like rising flames. It really is rather pretty, and I also have a smashing pair of blue suede evening shoes with buckles of brilliants that go with it. My wardrobe is in a rather dreary state, as I don't want to buy anything more than I can help when I shall so soon be home to a country where clothes are so much cheaper. So I just have one or two respectable rigs that I can trot out on state occasions. The Firefly will have to be worn again next Thursday, when I am bidden to dinner with Sir Humphrey and Lady Gibbs at Governor's Lodge. (He is Governor of Southern Rhodesia.) The Gibbs are completely natural and disarming, and I know that I shall enjoy the evening. They are very old friends of the Wests, and to Roger and Tim they are Uncle Humph and Aunt Mollie.

Now to my bits of news. The Bulawayo trip was hectic but most interesting and I thoroughly enjoyed my day. To my vast astonishment, just before I left the office on Thursday night a letter came from Bill Worth, saying that he was hoping to fly out to the Federation at the end of next week to do a big deal with the one and only really large radio manufacturers in the country, in Bulawayo. You can't fly direct to Bulawayo from Britain but have to stop in Salisbury. So he is hoping to arrive on Friday next, see our Trade Commissioner and then fly on to Bulawayo on Monday. He gave me the name of the man he will be seeing in Bulawayo, and he said that it would all depend on whether this man cabled to say that the dates would be all right.

I decided that I might just as well look up the man while I was in Bulawayo, and compare notes on dates, get a bit of lowdown for Bill and also tell the man something about Bill. This indeed I was able to do. But to go back. I was out of the house soon after half past six, on to the plane soon after seven and in Bulawayo by 8.30 a.m. There I was met by two Rotarians, both of whom I knew. I was able to ring Chassay, the radio man, and discovered that he would be coming to my Rotary talk, so we agreed to meet there. Then off to Joe de Haas, to see over his blanket factory. The factory turns out 10,000 blankets a *day*. It really was the most fascinating hour or so, and good to see what skilled jobs so many Africans were doing in the factory. It is about the only factory in Bulawayo that hasn't had one single strike through all the political upheavals of the last few years. On then to the home of one of the Rotarians whose wife was one of the very senior women in the ATS in the war – she ran all the ATS in East Africa. Cool drinks and washes and brushes-up, then on to Rotary for lunch. About a hundred people there, including the wives as a special treat for them. All went well, and I met Chassay afterwards and he took me back to his works and showed me all over. Again enormously fascinating, and again Africans doing wonderful work. He was very glad to have a bit of first-hand information about Bill, so now we sit back and wait for him to arrive. It will be fun to see him and hear all the Dulwich gossip. Amazing what a Clapham Junction Central Africa has become in recent years.

I was jolly tired when I clambered back on the plane in the evening. It had been sweltering in Bulawayo. Oh, I nearly forgot, after seeing Chassay I went round to Dr West's office, and then he drove me back to White Gables to see Mrs West. I had a quiet tea there, and then Mrs West ran me the eighteen miles to the airport. They haven't had any rain in B. since we were there at Christmas, but true to my tradition, as the plane took off, over came great rain clouds and I am sure that some of B. would have rain, even if it may have been a bit patchy. I discovered to my delight when I got back to Salisbury that it had been raining here most of the day. We needed it; for a week without rain means bringing out the hose pipe again, and we had already had to start watering. I was glad to take it a bit easy yesterday, though I had to get togged up and go out to the Australia Day party at one of the big hotels. In another hour I have to go round to a colleague's for a pre-lunch drinks party. I usually lie my way out of all Sunday dates, but these people only seem to give Sunday parties and I have refused so many times I felt that I had to give in once. What a bore getting out of my canvas shoes and my sun dress. Won't begin another page. Here are a few enclosures to see and destroy. Lall Singh was the Sikh accountant at Eastern House. I will also send on later a letter from Lalla Ram's wife. The poor old boy died about a year ago. I wondered why I had not heard from him.

4 February 1963

Thursday night was the dinner party at the Gibbs at Governor's Lodge. We were twenty altogether, and a very happy and unstarchy party it was too. After dinner we played a drawing parlour game, which went down with a bang, and got over that rather dreary time when the men rejoin the women and nobody knows quite what to say! Then at midday on Friday Bill arrived. He is very much older. He has been very ill – two completely different things, the worst being a back injury which reduced him to crutches for a very long time and which the doctors said would stop him from ever playing golf again. He got so depressed about this, that one night when he was hobbling on his crutches across one of the London bridges on his way to pick up his car, he decided to throw his crutches into the river so that he would have no alternative but to walk without aid. That was the beginning of his recovery. He had a long meeting with our Trade Commissioner, and of course I put him up for the weekend. We sat up until the most godforsaken hours nattering as hard as we could go and it was fun to catch up with so much gossip. Yesterday, Sunday, I took him out for the day to Ruwa Country Club, where we played eighteen holes of golf – his first for many weeks and my first for many months. His golf has lost all its old punch, though flashes of it reappear from time to time. Subconsciously he is obviously terrified of a recurrence of his back trouble. I put him on that early plane to Bulawayo this morning. He will spend two days there, then go on to South Africa, and sail home on a Union Castle ship. His co-Directors have insisted that he has this sea voyage to help to set him up again. Now with him off my chest I wonder who my next visitor will be. I don't get left in peace for very long.

On Saturday morning Butler gave his final press conference, which I went to, and at last we are shut of that little lot. But how long our official peace will last is another problematical question!

Like you with your winter, we are back to floods of rain. We had over four inches in twenty four hours three days ago, and I think that we have probably had another five in the last two days. We were very lucky when we played golf yesterday, for we started just after torrential rain; it then kept dry while we played, and proceeded to rain like mad again as soon as we got back. Today the skies are as grey as grey again, and when I drove Bill out to the airport this morning early we were driving through low cloud and drizzle, for all the world like England!

And that's all for the moment. This week should be a quieter one. I go out to dinner with people who lived opposite me in my first house, and on Friday the HC is giving a party for the man who is succeeding Hugh Foot at the United Nations, to which I am bidden. But apart from those two dates I am free. This sort of thing hasn't happened for months.

8 February 1963

Poor old Butler was hours late in leaving Salisbury. We have had some terrific storms and have had over six inches of rain in the last week. The last day or two have been a bit better, but judging from the skies there is still plenty of rain to come.

The HC has just announced that he is returning to Britain in June and is sailing from Beira on 11 June. This is the ship that I was originally booked on, but then I changed as I wanted to see Venice. One other of my colleagues is also on the 11th sailing, and he and his wife are seriously thinking of swopping it. Nobody really wants his boss around on board ship! You may be amused to know that your second licence application form is being used by Alport. He has come along to me for a lot of advice on shipping cars, I having just gone through all the preliminary palavers myself, and when I asked him if his licence was up to date he said he was sure that it wasn't. I then told him that I had a spare form if he wanted one, as I had such a sensible little Mamma, that she wouldn't dream of sending only one in case it got spoilt. He was delighted to have the second one.

This has been a fairly scatty week with three dinner parties in a row. Then tonight I am to go to two cocktail parties; one at Mirimba for Hugh Foot's successor, a man called C.E. King, who is out here for a week on a quick look-see tour – something Foot refused to do, which made us all the more wild that he resigned over British Government policy in a territory that he had no first-hand experience of; I shall probably cut the second party. One is enough for me in one night. Then the weekend is blissfully free. I have a lot of lawn mowing to do, but that is a pleasure with my motor mower and not too hard work.

I think that that's about all the news for the moment. I'm having a terrific onslaught on my mail, and try to write two each lunch hour that I don't have a lunch date. I want to be really up to date by the time I leave. Four months today I shall be on the High Seas. What a heavenly thought!

12 February 1963

There is very little news since I last wrote. I went to that cocktail party for King, Hugh Foot's successor, but I didn't see much of him. But I was also invited to a dinner party on Saturday night, where I had a much better opportunity of getting to know him. And I ran him back to Mirimba in my car afterwards (I seem to have had quite a number of VIPs squashed into my little bit of scrap iron from time to time!). At this dinner party were also a couple of Africans, I mean an African couple. The husband runs a school in Highfields, one of the African townships, for children who can't get into any of the government schools. The Government have been pretty beastly about his efforts, which makes us all very angry, as he is undoubtedly filling a big gap. His wife, who is very quiet-spoken, is nevertheless a rabid supporter of the banned party, ZAPU, and had some strong things to say about the day being long past when there was any hope of African and European women getting together. All rather frightening in its way.

After I wrote my last letter to you on Friday I had a very interesting visit from a youngish Tanganyika woman, who had got stuck in Salisbury trying to get back to Dar es Salaam. She was a junior Cabinet Minister in the Tanganyika Government, and a great character. Her main job is Community Development; and she says that as it is the women in the villages who have the main task of implementing community development schemes. She has a great say among her male Cabinet colleagues, as they know that she has such a monstrous army of women behind her. It is very interesting to see how some African women are beginning to emerge and play an important part in the life of their country. Southern Rhodesian African women are far behind the times in this respect.

Yesterday Ben and Eve Gingell dropped in a for a drink and told me that they are in the middle of writing a play, oddly enough on the very theme of race relations between women in Africa. They are hoping to get it put on in Salisbury and perhaps get it on the local television. I hope that they succeed, for I feel that it is very enterprising of them to embark on such an exercise.

Tonight the young son of those people who I met on the ship and who came up for their son's wedding, and his wife, are taking me out to dinner. I wish that they had suggested a quiet bite in their flat, but they must feel that they owe me something a bit grander, so they are taking me out to Salisbury's most expensive restaurant. I wish they wouldn't, but I can't offend them by saying that I should be just as happy, if not happier, to have a scrambled egg on my knee!

It is now over a year since I had any leave, and I feel that I must squeeze in a short one before I have to face the ghastly business of packing up and farewell parties. I'm not desperately keen on wandering around Africa on my own, and Roger has some leave, so we are thinking of having a quick flip to Paradise Island, off the coast of Mozambique. The real name is Santa Carolina, and it is two miles long and about half a mile wide, and all you can do there is to swim and fish and goggle-fish. Roger and I get on very well in our funny way, so I hope that we shall be able to arrange it. I've got to the stage where I am really fed up with work and am longing for a break. Rather greedy of me when I shall be having a sea trip so soon afterwards, but as I shall never be in this part of the world again it would be good to see just one peep more of a part I haven't seen.

I went to External Affairs this morning and got caught up with the formal opening of the Southern Rhodesia Legislative Assembly. I got great amusement out of the sixteen horses who were supposed to stand still for half an hour. There were two very naughty ones among them who did their best to upset all the others, just like naughty children. The Africans standing beside me loved it and were grinning all over their faces.

More torrential rain this lunch hour, which has kept me in the office bashing away at the typewriter. Thank the rain therefore for this letter!

17 February 1963

I'm absolutely bursting with virtue. I have just written three letters, including one to Uncle Lindsay, and yours is the fourth. As you may guess, it is pouring with rain outside, and has been with mighty little pause for the last seventy two hours. The garden is completely waterlogged and depressing, and it is no temptation to neglect letters and get out into it.

I gave a cocktail party on Thursday night, and half an hour before my guests were due to arrive we had a cloudburst. My drive went under water, and some of my guests virtually had to swim for it. Several of the women wearing sandals had to wash sandals and feet before they could appear in public. Just my luck. Sixpence and I always say that if we have a party it is sure to rain – and it usually does. Then next Tuesday night I give a buffet supper for twelve. This may well be quite a bun fight; for I have invited several Rhodesian Front supporters (the new right wing party that pushed out Whitehead) and at the other end of the scale a man who used to be an MP in Garfield Todd's government and who is as left wing as can be. This is quite deliberate on my part as I think it does people good to come in close touch with people with wildly different ideas. We shall see. I hope that the feathers don't fly too freely!

22 February 1963

5.45 a.m. on a wet and dripping morning. I actually managed to get in an early night last night, so I was awake early, listening to the steady downpour and getting madder and madder at the noisy drain outside my bedroom window. I've never known such a country as this for noisy drains. I can sleep through the row at the beginning of the night when I am tired, but not in the early morning when I have had a good night's rest. So I decided that I would get up and have a little date with my Mamma, in case I don't have too much time this lunch hour.

Two great long and fascinating letters from you to answer today. The first I briefly acknowledged receipt of in my last to you. The second, which arrived last night, is dated 16 Feb. It never ceases to amaze me how much news you seem to manage to find to pass on, when you are miles in the country and nearly snow-bound anyway. Shows an alert and vigorous mind! Now to your various questions. Yes, the HC said on his appointment that he would only come here for two years. He obviously didn't want to be too far out of the Conservative Party's eye for too long. Actually he had intended staying on until August and had actually booked passages then. But after Butler's visit he announced that he was going in June. We don't know whether this was his own choice or whether, for reasons unknown, Butler delivered an ultimatum saying he must come home then. From the office point of view I think it is a pity, for he really does know his stuff; but if by then Butler has really made up his mind about the future of the Federation in so far as the British Government is in a position to determine its future, they may both feel that it would be as well for him to skip at that stage.

Yes, the bathing at Paradise Island is wholly safe, you will be pleased to know. We are planning to go on 25 March for about ten days. You have to come back when the planes fly. There is no regular service. I really am looking forward to it after all these months of dreary rain and grey skies.

We have had our first minor bit of crime at Klokkespel. When I got home from the office last night Sixpence was in a terrible stew as the watch I gave him over a year ago had been stolen from the kitchen. He always takes it off when he does the housework and washing, and being a creature of habit, always puts in on a particular table in the kitchen. When he is in the house he never bothers to lock the back door. Somebody must know his habits and sneaked in when he was at the back of the house doing my bedroom. I phoned the police immediately, and Sixpence and I did some cunning detective work over tyre marks outside the kitchen door. But I doubt whether we shall have any success. We are going to watch out for anybody who comes to deliver things to the house and see if he has a bicycle wheel with a similar tread. Poor Sixpence was nearly in tears. He was so proud of his watch and took such great care of it. Luckily nothing else seems to have gone. The maddening thing is that I don't think that my personal insurance policy will cover this, but I shall try to find out at once. I got rid of the police just in time to rush down to town for a quick drink with a splendid woman out from England who is working on an education Commission here. And then it was back to bed and an early night, as I said at the beginning of my letter.

My dinner party, sorry, buffet supper party, on Tuesday passed off without any fur flying, but I was glad to see the back of them. By the way, I made for the first time for ages, as one of the puddings, your lemon soufflé, and it wasn't fluffy enough. I can't remember, but are you supposed to give it another beat when the gelatine has just begun to set a bit? This isn't in your written instructions and I may therefore be wrong. But it certainly wasn't as Mother makes it. Good old Ma!

Won't start another page but will leap into the bath and get cracking on the rest of the day's work.

27 February 1963

I had a few casual days' leave to come before the end of Feb., and was able to get two of them – yesterday and today. They came at an opportune moment as I am enjoying(!) my first cold in about four years. It hasn't been a bad one thank heaven and has only given me a smallish bark. But it is pleasant not to have to cope with it and the office at the same time. On top of everything I must have been bitten by a mosquito in the very corner of my eye yesterday, and my eye now looks just like Daddy's did when he had a bee sting. I don't look my most glamorous, I can tell you.

You are an indefatiguable creature – papering the walls of your kitchen now are you? Well, well! I'm afraid that my whole house will need freshening up, not only the kitchen! I haven't any illusions about the state I shall find it in. Many of the walls will have had nothing done to them for six years – the sitting room for instance – and six years of London is equal to about twenty elsewhere. But I'm not going to worry. I shall just get stuck into it with a vengeance, and if I find it too much I shall get some professional help. I shan't be anything like as broke as I was when I bought the house, so I needn't be quite so aggressively independent. The thing I want most of all is a front door that really does fit and doesn't let in all the draughts, as the present one does. I'm feeling cold now, with the temperature at about 65 degrees (terribly cold for Feb. here), so what I shall feel like when the temp. goes below freezing I dread to think.

I see from *The Times* that Bill's ship was thirty hours late. After engine trouble it got held up by fog! Poor old Bill. I bet he was hopping mad. All very well being held up in glorious sunshine, but not in Channel fog.

I'm supposed to be going out to a fairly high-powered lunch this lunch time, but I haven't made up my mind whether to duck or not. I ought to make the effort but what with cold and eye I think I should be a rather unsavoury companion! And I have to prepare anyway for Joe de Haas, the blanket man, coming to dinner tonight. He is on his way back from a trip to Northern Rhodesia, and wants to tell us about his reactions to what is going on up there. A bit of a bore, but one has to do one's duty.

More and more and more rain. Floods are getting serious now in some parts of the country, and most of the strip and dirt roads are impassable. I'm glad that I haven't got to go off on any tour that takes me off the main roads. How awful to think that you haven't had your car out all these weeks, nay months. But at least you have a garage for it. I wonder how all the motorists in London and other cities where garages are scarce have fared, leaving their vehicles to the mercy of the elements? My little car is going to miss its shelter and its *daily* bath – one of the joys of having a full-time gardener.

I missed a bag yesterday as I wasn't in the office – hence this air letter for a change. Must away now and start a few preparations for this evening.

1 March 1963

I had an early night last night and so am up early this morning and typing this letter over my morning tea, at six a.m. I have got the office motor mower again, but only for a very short time, so I dashed back from the office as soon as I could yesterday and got stuck into the mowing – in fact until the light failed. I may have told you that even with the motor mower I have about eight to ten hours of solid mowing to do. And it is by no means an easy job. On my sloping garden you have to do quite a bit of manual manoeuvring, and the machine is a ton weight. So I drip with sweat in the process, and am thankful to flop into a bath and go straight to bed after supper. With all the rain we are having this year the grass grows and grows at a terrific rate and it is a nightmare keeping it tidy. (Talking of nightmares, did you hear the pleasant little story of the man who took hay to bed with him to feed his nightmares?)

All of which is a prelude to saying thank you for your last letter of

23 February with the snippet of your kitchen wallpaper enclosed. It is so pretty and I can just imagine how fresh and clean the kitchen must look. You really do absolutely astound me. Not content with paper-hanging at the age of seventy-five you are now determined to 'have a shot' at painting the ceiling. Painting ceilings is one of the most exhausting and exacting of all decorating chores but are you deterred by the fact? Not on your flippin' life!

You ask how the buf sup. went. I can't remember whether in fact I have already told you anything of it in my last letter, but here goes in case I didn't. I think it went very well. I was a bit dismayed by the opening remarks of the Rhodesian Front Organising Secretary, an ex Naval Commander. He and his wife had both accepted but he arrived without his wife. (I had not met her before.) I said that I was very sorry his wife was not with him and hoped that she wasn't ill. 'Oh no,' says he, 'We've just separated. I've got rid of the old bag at last and life is bliss.' Now what in heaven's name does a diplomat answer to that one?! The curious thing about the party was that everyone was terribly polite and chatty to everyone else. I'm sure that my two Rhodesian Front guests had never sat down socially with an African and his wife before, but they rose to the occasion well, and so of course did my wonderful Zulu Economics Lecturer from the University College, who I think knew exactly what I was up to and had a rare twinkle in his eye. Perhaps because their political views were so diverse, they didn't want to embarrass me by becoming involved in a great wrangle, so on the whole the conversation was disappointingly amiable. You ask what I gave them to eat. My stock buf. sup. fodder – something easy, that can be kept hot and served without difficulty and eaten without difficulty on the knee with a fork and no need for a knife: i.e., chicken roasted for hours very slowly in tin foil, then all the meat taken off the bones and put into a white sauce, which I always make myself to my own recipe. This includes at least half a bottle of white wine, tabasco, mushrooms, butter, not marg., a tin of asparagus soup and anything else that catches my fancy. I think it is jolly good, and I shall make it for you when I come home! Then puddings according to the mood. This time it was strawberries and cream, fruit salad and your lemon soufflé, which I wrote to you about and which wasn't a howling success. Biscuits and cheese to follow. Oh I forgot, with the chicken, potatoes done in the oven in layers with onions, flour and milk, peas, and tomatoes also done in the oven, with their tops cut off and cheese sprinkled on them. This gives the table and the meal a bit of colour. That big black pot with the candle underneath has come right into its own here. I also have a Pyrex with a candle under. The chicken mess goes into these two pots on the table and so keeps piping hot, and I find that my guests always go back for a second helping!

Your last letter sounded as though there were some hope of an improvement in the weather, even if it had frozen up again. The Queen's Messenger who arrived yesterday said that he had left London the previous night in a snowstorm. So I suppose you are inundated once more.

I had a comic letter from Bill yesterday posted at Southampton. I had warned him what the clientele on the *Union Castle* was likely to be and how right I was. He said that he was the youngest male first class passenger (he must be fifty-one or two now!), danced with all the old dears very happily, and reserved the old-fashioned waltz for a five feet, seventeen-stone who was featherlike on the floor. How often immensely heavy people are very light dancers.

I found myself on Wednesday the only woman among eight men at lunch time! Great fun. Then I had Joe de Haas back for dinner, as I may have told you. He had just got back from talks with Banda and Kaunda and had some fascinating things to tell.

Bath time now. I enclose Mrs Lallaram's rather touching little note. I have replied and have sent her the charcoal and chalk sketch I once did of Lallaram. It is not a work of art, but it really was like him at the time. I don't suppose she has any photograph of him, so she may be pleased to have it.

5 March 1963

Office strangely empty today. The HC plus five of the staff have gone off to a meeting in Zomba. Roger Barltrop has gone to get his wife and new baby out of the nursing home, so only David Scott and I are around the place. There is plenty of *work* around the place as a result of our small numbers.

No exciting news. Too many parties this week for my liking. I had a man from Kenya to lunch at home yesterday – a publisher – and it was very interesting to hear his version of what is going on there. British Government policy in Kenya is always severely criticised in this part of the world; but when you hear from a European actually on the spot the whole situation is so much more encouraging than the papers make out.

Tomorrow night I have to dinner that incredible old woman who is a practising spiritualist. I've got one of the women from the office coming to keep us company. It should be fun!

13 March 1963

Yesterday I missed the bag as I was out of the office for the day talking to the WI at Enkeldoorn. I think I may have told you that I was going. First thing in the morning was to deliver a pile of books which the British Govt. had given to an African Secondary School for boys. I volunteered to do this for the Information people as I thought that the school was on the way to Enkeldoorn. Having volunteered I found it wasn't, so I had to do my delivery, make a little speech to the entire assembly of boys and masters, come right back into town and then take the Enkeldoorn road. Luckily it was a glorious day, the best one for ages and it was a real pleasure driving. I got to the funny hotel where I stayed last time, in time for lunch and was greeted like a long-lost friend, given a couple of gins and lunch, and ordered by mine hostess, who is also an official of the WI, to put my feet up for an hour in one of the bedrooms so that I could miss the dull business part of their meeting, and only put in an appearance when I had to give my talk. That suited me well, and I had a jolly good sleep. Then off to the meeting, where they kept me talking for an hour and a quarter. I kept on stopping and saying they had had quite enough and they kept on saying that they hadn't had their full money's worth and asking me to go on. It was all very informal with shrieks of laughter all round and I really thoroughly enjoyed myself. Of course it was late by the time I got away on the hundred mile journey back again, and I had to drive over half the way in the dark. But thank goodness the road is now passable again, after very heavy rains which have made the low level bridges virtually impassable. Altogether it was an interesting day and really much less exhausting than a day in the office. I came back to a mountain of files this morning as nobody bothers to do your work if you are only away for a day, but though it looks pretty awful it doesn't amount to all that much in practice, thank goodness.

Now I must dive out and spend the last bit of the lunch hour doing some shopping. The larder seems to be completely bare.

16 March 1963

I missed the blessed bag again yesterday, after having a late dinner party the night before, so that I didn't feel energetic enough to get up with the sun, then having a lunch date so that I couldn't write in my lunch hour and finally getting bogged down with an official visitor after lunch so that I couldn't even pinch a few minutes of official time before the bag closed at 3.30. So here I am instead early on Saturday morning, with the sun just peeping over the clouds in the valley below.

I've done jolly well this week – two letters dated 8 and 9 March which both arrived on the same day, the one in the morning and the other in the afternoon. So corn in Egypt to you too! Lovely. First there are one or two things in your letter of 6 March that I haven't answered. Yes, I did just know Terence Ranger and went to a highly subversive party given by an Indian friend of mine to say goodbye to him and his wife. I must have forgotten to tell you about it. It was at this party that I met and had quite a long talk to Joshua Nkomo. Two of my colleagues were also invited. The HC was a bit dubious at our accepting but we prevailed on him in the end. All rather fun. And I also knew Frank McEwan and his wife. They were very close friends of the last HC and his wife, the Metcalfs, as Dorrie Metcalf is very artistic and used to do beautiful ceramic work, which is also a speciality of Cecelia McEwan. Frank is an amusing customer, and is much scorned by many of the tough, barbarian Rhodesians. But he has done a wonderful job at the National Gallery and he doesn't care a damn what people think of him. The Kenwood mixer. Don't laugh – I still don't use it! The thing is that it is not the sort of machine that one would trust in the hands of an African servant, not even one as reliable as Sixpence, and I don't have time to do much cooking myself, except the odd complicated thing if I am giving a party. So I'm saving it up for us to experiment with when I get back to Balham.

You poor things – floods now. How thankful you must be to be on that bit of a rise. But the poor folk in Leominster. I hope they felt that there was some compensation in being on the TV map! Fame indeed. No, I don't know Mrs Stewart Moore, but I will make enquiries about her the next time I see Mr Ruseki. Incidentally he has been given funds by some people in America to go over to the States to talk about his orphanage. We are trying to get some friends from Britain to give him a few weeks there too. I will give him your address just in case he comes anywhere near you. We are all hoping that this trip will finally put the home on its feet. The Americans are so generous and have the money to spare, if only they hear about a good work.

I also know Neil Bruce – in fact he came to dinner with me very soon after he arrived here. I had invited his predecessor and his wife, and Neil was staying with them at the time so they asked if they could bring him along too. He is not far off the mark in what he said about this country.

I don't really seem to have left much room for any news. I can't remember where I was when I last wrote, but I must have been to Enkeldoorn since then. It was a good day, first of all delivering a whole pile of books which we were giving to an African secondary school – a new school being run on a shoe-string, with the white headmaster having to teach all day, one other European teacher, and three young Africans who themselves have only just passed their 'O' level. No, I'm sure I've told you about the trip in my last air letter, so shut up, Margaret! At lunch time today I have to go to Mirimba to a pre-lunch drinks party which the HC is giving for some of the Rhodesian Front MPs. He doesn't want to have them but must, and he came round cap in hand to my office a few days ago to ask if I would come and help him out! Then out to a buffet supper tonight, but tomorrow, praise the Lord, I have no dates whatsoever. Must begin to think soon about sorting out and prepacking exercises. Have done a very little bit but not nearly enough. And by the time I have had my little holiday James will very soon be descending upon me, and I shall want to be as well organised in advance of that as possible.

18 March 1963

A British MP who is out here at the moment – a man called Deer – is quite a dear. He was calling me 'luv' in no time when he discovered that I was a north country woman, and also had a house in Balham – he lives in Streatham when he is not in his constituency. I met him and five other MPs at that party which the HC gave on Saturday morning.

You ask what my address will be at Paradise Island. Quite frankly I don't know. I have left all arrangements to Roger. But there won't be the slightest hope of getting a letter to me there. I think that a boat only goes out once or twice a week. So please just send to the office as usual. So that you will know when you can have a bit of a rest, we leave Salisbury on Monday 25 March and return on Thursday 4 April, so you can have ten days off! If I discover that one can get mail away I shall of course write to you from the Island.

7 April 1963

Returning from a holiday sometimes makes one wonder whether holidays are worth it! Roger and I got back late on Thursday afternoon, and he then dashed off to Bulawayo to spend the last few days of his leave with his family. I have given Sixpence the whole fortnight off so of course he wasn't there. He has left Bernard, his son, behind to feed the cat and keep an eye on things, but he is more of a liability than a help, as I have since had to help with his arithmetic! Seize has been doing a lot of unimportant jobs instead of urgent ones, so the garden was looking pretty scruffy, and I came back to a mountain of mail and a talk to work up for yesterday at lunch time. So what with housework, cooking, shopping, redirecting Seize and doing a bit as well to encourage him, preparing my talk and so forth, this is the first moment I have had to get round to writing to you. I've cleaned the house, given the kitchen a good vimming all over (I always like to do this when Sixpence is out of the way as no African however good is a 'bottomer'), made my bed, done the washing and got it on the line, paid all my month's bills which were lined up for me on my return, and now it is 10 a.m. and I have a clear conscience to write to you. I hope anyway that you get the p.c. which I posted the day after we got back, to let you know that I was still in one piece.

No, I am not surprised that June didn't get invited to any of the do's when the Queen was out there. Just as I have no particular status when I go back to London, so she has none in her own country. It is only when you are away from your own country with diplomatic status that you get these perks.

Yes, David Scott will be pretty busy. We don't know who will replace the HC or when. Brian Unwin, the young man who was or rather is Alport's Private Sec., is going to do my job for a bit after I go, and until we know whether a HC will come out who will warrant a Private Sec. Brian is very able – I think he got a First at Oxford – and he is fed up with stooging for the HC. It will give him some good experience and will save the office the cost of sending anyone else out for a bit. If the Federation breaks up completely, as it is bound to, our office will inevitably become much smaller, and we shall open up offices in Lusaka and Zomba.

Now I don't seem to have left any room for news of our holiday. No bag goes until Tuesday, so I thought that I would get this air letter off to you to keep you quiet for a few days! I'll write and tell you all about the holiday in time for Tuesday's bag. Suffice to say that it was great fun and the most marvellous rest. I don't think that I have spent such a lazy ten days ever in all my life and it has done me a lot of good. We got enormously sunburnt, so much so that even I am peeling, something I rarely do as you know. I virtually lived in a bikini and now only the smallest patches of pure white are left to show my real colour!

Klokkespel

8 April 1963

Now for the promised letter on the holiday. I've just got back after a stinking day. A huge pile of files was awaiting me on my return but I have hardly had a minute to get stuck into them as I had to go first of all to the formal opening of the Federal Assembly this morning, and then this afternoon back again to hear Welensky giving his latest diatribe against the British Government. It was the most vitriolic one so far, and it made me squirm to sit there and not be able to get up and give our side of the story. Undoubtedly Butler has played his cards very sloppily, I think, but so much of what Welensky had to say was one-sided and disingenuous. I shall be glad now to get out of this country and back to the insanities of Europe just for a change. To crown everything, as I got into the lift this evening, very late in leaving the office, who should I bump into but Evan Campbell. He was his usual rude self and said that Britain had swopped the Tudor rose for a banana as its emblem. Explanation? Britain like the banana is soft, yellow, crooked and always turns black in the end! He can be a poisonous man!

But this was to be a holiday letter. Well now. We flew down in a Dove, which is an eight or ten seater. My first trip in one, and very intimate and comfortable, with the pilot's door open all the way so that we felt we were part of the machinery. We arrived at Vilancules well before lunch and came down on the landing strip there. You may find Vilancules on your map: it is in P.E.A. about two hundred miles south of Beira. It was gloriously hot and Roger and I split a bottle of cheap Portuguese wine to quench our thirst. We had a surprisingly good lunch at the cock-eyed little hotel, which boasted the smelliest lavatories I have been in for many a long day! After lunch a very bumpy mile or two journey down to the quay, me with a baby monkey perched on my shoulder – being taken to our island by a Portuguese who was quite happy for me to take over the wee thing for a spell. On to a paintless but efficient launch for a two and a half hour journey up the coast to our island. There are four islands in the group, the largest being Basarute, which you may well find also on your map. Our island is called Santa Carolina, and is the smallest in the group. After a lovely trip, in which I had a kip lying on the bare boards in the sun(!), we arrived in that wonderful golden light of late evening, the island and the holidaymakers there to watch us, looking pure south sea island. There are three blocks of bedrooms and bathrooms and a central dining room, bar and sports room. Our bedrooms were in the block right beside the central mess, so we didn't have far to go for our meals. The food was pretty ropey, but we had been warned about this before we went, so we were not put off. Virtually no green vegetables was the greatest deprivation for me, and when we got back the first thing I bought was a huge crisp lettuce and I scoffed the lot in one go! Every day the pattern of life was virtually the same – early morning swim, breakfast, back to the beach in bikini with books, suntan lotion, sunglasses, snorkel and mask, towels and my huge beach umbrella that I bought in Spain. We spent all morning lying about in the sun reading and flopping into the sea when we got too hot, and generally pottering. Lunch; then either a zizz or, if we weren't too sunbaked, a return to the beach. Tea, another swim, then down to the little harbour on the leeward side to watch the fishermen come in with their day's catch. Santa Carolina is a famous centre for deep sea fishing, and soon after we arrived the island was inundated with forty tough South African fishermen who had come for a fishing competition. They were a noisy lot, and one night a terrible fight broke out among them when they were tight, which resulted in two of them being laid out for days, one with his eye nearly knocked out – not pretty! But of course they were out fishing all day so we didn't have to put up with them for long. I had been warned that the bar was notoriously expensive, so I had popped a couple of bottles of diplomatic grog in my bag, and we just bought sodas and drank on one or other of our verandahs, away from the loud-mouthed fishermen.

It was fascinating though to see what the fishermen brought back with them – and rather sobering. One day they brought back two great shark, and also a hammerhead shark. These had been taken in the deep channel that runs right up the coast of Africa. Santa Carolina is supposed to be safe from sharks as it is surrounded by coral and shallow sandbanks, but it made one think when one saw some of these beasties that had been caught within sight of the island.

In fact I had only one minor alarm. The very first day I must have been stung by some marine creature. At first there was nothing to see, and then my finger began to come up in an agonising purple round blob that bit deep into the skin. I went to bed that night feeling a bit uncomfortable but nothing too bad, and then wakened an hour or two later with my finger much worse, and the whole of my body racked with quite frightening aches. Like a clot I hadn't even taken aspirin – I had all sorts of medicine for runny tummy and coral scratches, but nothing for aches. So I just didn't get any sleep whatsoever. An odd experience! In the morning I was able to get aspirin and I had an overdose which gradually killed the pain and restored me to normal. But my finger has taken a long time to heal, and as I type I keep on feeling it as I hit the keys. I'd be jolly interested to know what in fact had stung me. Luckily it was only temporary discomfort that hit me; but in those dark watches of the night I don't mind admitting that I wondered what on earth I would do if I were in for a serious bout of poisoning. There was no medical aid at all on the island, and not much hope of reaching any for the best part of twenty four hours. But as I say, all was well that ended well! As it happened, neither of us had the slightest sign of tummy trouble, nor did we graze ourselves on the coral – which can be a very painful business. So we did very well. The only other hazard I suppose was too much sunshine. But Roger had been so desperately burnt when we went down to the Cape last year that he had learnt his lesson with a vengeance and took great care for the first four days. I was careful too, but not quite so punctilious about it. Result? I am flaking away on arms and shoulders and positively peeling on my previously unburnt and recently bikini-exposed tummy. Roger, who popped in to see me last night on his return from Bulawayo, says he is not peeling anywhere, which makes me livid!

By the way, I really am feeling rather smug. Obviously I was cut out to teach people how to swim. I may have told you that to my great astonishment I discovered at the Cape last year that Roger could hardly swim a stroke. I gave him his first real lessons and he did quite well. But of course I wasn't there for long so couldn't keep him at it. Not so at Santa Carolina. I really put him through his paces and by the time we left he was swimming with great confidence and the beginnings of some style. In the process he screwed himself up into telling me the story of his non-swimming. As a child of seven, and desperately conscious anyway of his spastic condition, he was thrown into the deep end of a swimming bath at his prep school by the sports mistress, and left there until he had very nearly drowned. This gave him such a complex about water that he flatly refused ever to go into the baths again, either at his prep school or later at his public school. He evidently created such terrible scenes that in sheer desperation his masters gave way to him. It has taken him virtually a quarter of a century to get this terrible fear out of his system – but he has needed a lot of encouragement – like you at fifty!! Can you believe though how wickedly insensitive some teachers can be in their methods of dealing with a nervous and handicapped child, and what long-term results that insensitivity can have on such a child?

One day one of our fellow guests asked us if we would like to make up a party to sail across to the mainland at Inharrsaro, about one hour away by boat. About ten of us went in the end and it was great fun. We went in one of the funny little boats that the fishermen take out – again no paint or obvious forms of maintenance, but seaworthy and swift all the same. It was only a tiny boat and we were a bit overcrowded, so Roger and I and a Nottingham man got up fo'rard on the roof of the little cabin. This was fine going; but on the way back we ran into really heavy seas, and the waves were breaking over us every few seconds. It was most exhilarating and we really felt that we were very brave. I hope that all the photographs we took of this trip and indeed of the whole holiday will come out so that I can give you some impression of it all.

I must tell you the story of how Santa Carolina came to be developed as a holiday centre. Many years ago a young, uneducated and penniless Portuguese came to Mozambique and set up a small store, providing cheap goods for Africans. He met and began to live with a remarkable African woman who was herself illiterate but who had a splendid business head on her shoulders. Together they opened more and more stores. Then they bought an aged bus and began a transport business. From this he built up his business and leased Santa Carolina, which had been a penal settlement at the turn of the century but had been uninhabited for a long time, from the Portuguese Government. He leased it ten years ago and it has never looked back. Now he is in the

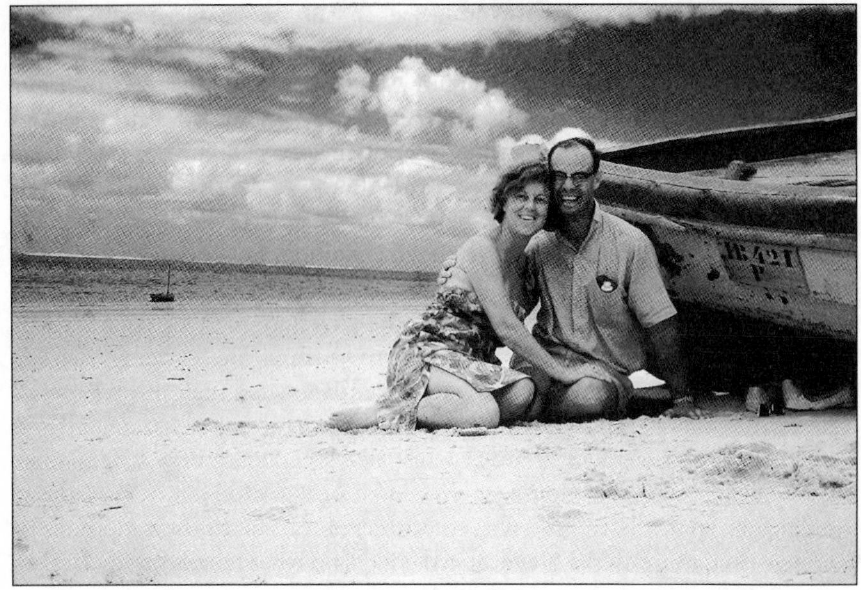

Roger and I at Inhassaro.

throes of developing the other three islands in the group. The story goes that for years he wanted the African woman to marry him, but she refused, saying that she was black and he white and that it would be wrong. A few months ago, after some forty years together, she at last agreed and they were married. They never had any children. I was fascinated by this story, which seemed to me pure Somerset Maugham. I was delighted therefore when the man himself, Joachim Alves, was on the boat with us when we finally returned to the mainland. He is now reputed to be a millionaire.

And that's about it. On the journey back there were many more of us so there was a Dakota waiting at the airstrip. We were back in Salisbury in the middle of the afternoon. It had really been a wonderfully relaxed holiday, with no telephone, no newspapers, no mail and no radio. It has taken me all my time since I got back to try to catch up on all the happenings that I missed in the ten short days that I was away.

Now I must go and see to a bit of supper. Sixpence arrived back this morning just as I was about to leave for the office. He had travelled through the night, so I sent him off to bed straight after tea this evening.

I sail two months today – not long now!

Easter Sunday

It is a most wonderful morning. The sun has just risen over the mists and the whole garden is flooded with golden light. This is a splendid time of year for sunrises. From my bed I can see the star of the morning, as wondrously bright as it was when we saw it in Switzerland, in the beginnings of a slight orange glow; then the glow increases and the star fades and I know it is time to leap out of bed and get started on my chores. First one today is to write to you, I can hear Sixpence just arrived in the kitchen, so soon tea will be along to encourage me.

I am having a wonderfully domestic sort of weekend. I've lied like mad out of a number of invitations and have only in fact accepted one, for drinks before lunch today. And I've actually started to pack. By the time the weekend is over I shall have washed all my blankets, underblankets and bedcovers. It is such good drying weather that even my thick Dormy blankets are dry in about three hours. Then I have been able to get one of the office mowing machines again, so I am doing all the lawns. I only got this last night and managed to do about an hour and a half of mowing before darkness fell, so to continue with that today will be my main job.

Yes, Welensky has been behaving in a most childish manner. I went to the official opening of Parliament on Monday after I got back, and then I went back into the Assembly in the afternoon to listen to his speech. It was the worst attack he had ever made on the British Government; and although some of his criticisms were just justified – but only just – most of them were over actions that the British Govt. had had to take in sheer desperation, as Welensky wouldn't face up to realities. He is now the major stumbling block in Central Africa. No progress will be made at all until he disappears from the scene. And poor man, he can't see this, and lingers on, even in the face of what we know to be the advice of his own Federal Civil Servants. In a way it is pathetic. Welensky is so nearly a great man; but he hasn't been quite great enough for the situation. Won't go on to another page this morning, but will see if there is any more news towards the end of the holiday. 'Bye for now.

Early Tuesday morning. Alas the holiday is over and in another two hours I shall be back at my office desk. Now to finish this letter.

I think that I have got most of the things done that I hoped to get done. The only thing I was thwarted over was mowing the lawns. I did get quite a bit done on Sunday and then about an hour's work done yesterday. After that up rolled the clouds and we had very heavy rain for the rest of the day, with lots of thunder and lightning thrown in. This really is the most extraordinary year for rain. Last year I think we had one shower only after I got back from the

Cape at the beginning of March. This year we have gone on having rain regularly throughout March and April. I could hear it raining again in the night, and this morning it is so dark I can hardly see to type. By now the sun should be up. Anyway, I shall have to try to do a bit of mowing each night this week when I get in from the office, in the hope that I can get through before I have to hand the machine on again. With all this rain the growing period is very much extended.

Believe it or not, my blessed finger is very sore again – the place where I got that sting on holiday. Every few days it comes up and I get some more pus out of it and then I think that it is really getting better finally at last. This morning I realise I am wrong again. I think that I shall have to take myself off to the quack after all. What a bloomin' nuisance. James sent me a little note in reply to my holiday letter to them giving me his latest plans (it doesn't look as if he will be staying with me at all this year as he will be out of Salisbury nearly all the time and feels he must spend the few days he is here with the Gingells), and he said that he thought it was probably a Portuguese man-of-war that stung me. He was once stung by one and had the same reactions. Good, here comes Sixpence and my tea, so off we go.

Salisbury

21 April 1963

I've just got back the first roll of films of Paradise Island and will enclose a few with this letter. It's a pity that the one of Roger sitting among the strange coral formations has a bit of light in at the side. The reason is that Roger had taken the shot before, and he is so completely unmechanical that he is a bit scared even of turning round the spool, and in his fear of breaking the thing, can't have turned the screw far enough, silly chump. The hat is one of mine which he commandeered and refused to return for the rest of the holiday. I think he rather fancied himself in it. How do you like the monkey? I'm afraid the transparency shows up all my many wrinkles, but I haven't a hope of concealing them any longer, so you may as well be prepared in advance! I was looking through my transparencies the other night, and I still have quite a good collection that you haven't yet seen. I think that I shall try to find a cranny for them in my sea luggage – I mean the luggage I take with me – so that we don't have to wait for all the heavy luggage to arrive. Did I tell you that some time ago I bought a screen? It makes a tremendous difference and is a vast improvement on a wall, however clean.

I don't think that I have any very interesting news today. On Friday night I went out to a dinner party given for a Brigadier Lloyd Owen, who ended up in the war commanding the Long Range Desert Group. Leslie may have heard of him. He looks as if he is only in his early forties now, so he must have been very young to be in command. Next week and the week after I get tied up with farewell parties for the Dalhousies. The High Commissioner is giving a pre-lunch drinks party next Saturday, and Welensky is giving an evening reception – can't remember which day off-hand. Hats and gloves at both functions I'm afraid, and I don't know whether I can run to two respectable hats!

I've been having a wonderful chucking-out session this morning. I started at Easter; and Lady Alport rang me up one day last week and asked me if I were having a good pre-departure clearout would I let her have the jetsam for a jumble sale. She wants it all for the day after tomorrow, so I thought I had better get cracking this morning. The longer I live the less sentimental I get over my possessions, and the more eager I am to be parted from all but outright necessities. And as I shall have to settle down in my tiny house after having so much space here, I must go back as light as possible. I've let out some of the good clothes that I don't really feel I can part with yet, but the others I feel I have a splendid excuse for being generous to charities over. I'm nine stone eight now, for the first time in about twenty years. The lightest I got in New Zealand was eight stone five!

Although I am at the moment sitting in the sun in a sun dress, we are beginning to feel the touch of winter in the evenings. Very soon now we shall be back to fires and I for one shall be delighted. Did I tell you that the owners of Klokkespel have decided to come back here to live when I go? They have despaired of selling it; and Rosemary the wife is fed up with living twenty miles out of Salisbury and being so far from all her friends. She has a small child, and Geoff her husband has to be away in Europe for three months of every year. During that time she is virtually a prisoner, for it is difficult to get babysitters, and in any case she is not very fond of going out on her own. So back they are coming. I expect they will keep on Seize, but I am still trying to find a good job for Sixpence.

26 April 1963

This really has been a terribly hectic week, both in and out of the office. Paul Thirsk is away and I am doing his work, and I also have more than enough of my own. I couldn't have battled if I hadn't worked through my lunch hours, with a sandwich and a glass of milk. But I am a bit clearer today. There is such a lot going on at the moment and it is all intensely interesting. I went out to dinner at the Scotts on Monday to meet the new man who will be in the Africa seat in the Foreign Office, Sir Geoffrey Hamson. He was great fun, and

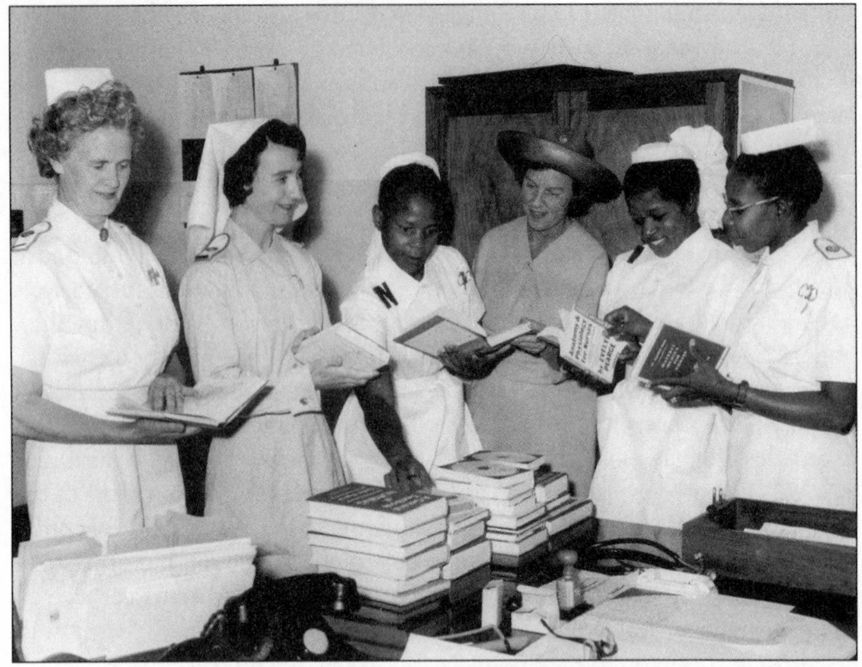

Presenting books to nurses at Harare hospital.

he and I pulled each other's legs like mad. On Wednesday I gave a farewell drinks party for one of the junior members of staff This involved getting up and making sausage rolls at 6 a.m.! I never dare leave Sixpence to make pastry. It is one thing that he is absolutely hopeless at. The morning of the party I went down to Harare hospital – a huge hospital for Africans in one of the townships – to present some books on behalf of the British Government. Somebody at home is writing a book on careers for women, and had asked the CRO for a picture of a woman diplomat in an obvious Commonwealth setting. So we got along a photographer to take my picture at the hospital with the books, surrounded by some African and European nurses. I haven't seen the results yet. I went on a conducted tour of the hospital after the presentation and it really was an eye-opener. The children's ward was quite heartbreaking, as children's wards so often are. But the place I liked the best was the maternity home. Rows and rows of little black babies – but of course they aren't very black. A new born African baby can be quite white, and takes several days to turn black. There were some tiny little things in incubators – very few premature; most of them have mothers who hadn't eaten the right food during pregnancy and therefore their babies were very underweight when born. The mothers come in regularly and feed their babies, but the babies have to stay in the hospital until they are up to 4 lbs. Then, provided they are healthy, they are allowed to go home with their mothers.

Tonight the Indian Commissioner and his wife are giving a farewell party for me. Tomorrow at lunch time I go to the drinks party given by the HC for the Dalhousies, and an hour or two later rush off to the wedding of one of my neighbours' daughters to the son of the grocer opposite our office. It is really the groom that I know. Three of us have been invited, and we are catty enough to think that we have been invited to lend a little tone to the groom's party. The girl he is marrying comes from an old and wealthy Rhodesian family! (Three of us from our office I mean.)

James arrives on Monday. I can't remember whether I told you or not, but Ben wants him to stay at Jerico Lodge with the man from S.A. who will also be up here. Eve Gingell's mother will be up at the same time and as there is no space for her at Jerico I am putting her up. It will only be for two nights. I am to go there to dinner on Monday night to join the Gs, Eve's mother and the two James. Then I shall bring Eve's mother back for the night to sleep. I'm planning to leave Klokkespel about 29 May when I shall get the packers in. I shall then sleep for the last few nights at Mrs Pigott's house, the woman in whose garden Roger has his little *pondoch*. I have got to know her quite well through Roger and she is a darling. She has just lost her tenant in the house and the one in the other *pondoch* and is feeling the financial draught. It will be very handy as she is only about half a mile away from me and I shall be able to slip back to Klokkespel and supervise the cleaning up after my goods have gone. I didn't want to go into a hotel and I don't particularly want to stay with a colleague as this means one is never away from 'office'. So this should be a happy arrangement. James will also be near at hand, so we can keep in touch over the final arrangements for departure.

Two o'clock is looming and it's back to the grind.

3 May 1963

Getting letters written at the moment is just about impossible. I've just got back from Welensky's farewell party for the Dalhousies. It is 1.15, and before I go out and get a spot of lunch I must at least get a tiny scribble on the way to you, since the bag goes this afternoon. I won't attempt to answer your letter of 26 April but will save this up for the weekend when I hope to have a little time to spare.

News in brief. I'm putting up James after all. There were mad last minute changes in the Gingell plans, as a result of which they asked me if I would cope with James for the whole week. So he came to me on Monday and leaves again on Sunday for Lusaka. Thank heaven he is such an easy guest, for I have literally seen him at breakfast only since he came on Monday. I had a solid week of evening engagements as I did not expect him to be staying with me, and I have just had to get on with them. Next week is a bit quieter and he will be away anyway, so I am hoping to get myself a bit better organised. There really is such a hell of a lot to do and to plan before I get away. I'm supposed to be having a vaccination and yellow fever inoculation at 2 p.m. this afternoon but I don't know whether I shall be able to make it or not. At least I have got all the arrangements made with the packers so that is one thing off my chest. Did I tell you that my landlord and landlady had a smash driving home some nights ago from what I suspect was a pretty drunken party? They turned the car over twice and Rosemary has a broken shoulder and Geoff a broken neck. It has rather upset their forward planning for getting back into Klokkespel again.

I'm just recovering from a buffet supper party which I gave for eight people last night. I then took them on to the theatre afterwards, and even after that they all trooped back to my house for last drinks. I don't know what time I got to bed and I am feeling pretty sleepy this afternoon. Tonight for the first night this week I have an evening on my own, so I intend to crawl into bed at the earliest moment.

Remind me to tell you if I forget about the HC's farewell party for the Dalhousies. Lady D. had the most fantastic tale to tell me of her experience of Paradise Island. But that must wait. Now for a quick spot of lunch.

5 May 1963

Now I can really get round to answering your letter of 26 April which I briefly acknowledged in my last letter to you. James and I are both sitting in the garden in the sun doing our clerking. In fact I think that he is at this very moment sending you a card. He is trying to banish the deadly pallor of his back before he has to appear on board ship. One forgets how incredibly pale people are whose skins have not seen the sun for months. Most of us here are some shade of brown rather than universal dead white.

Yes thank you, my finger is better at last. It has a little scar still and is still a bit red and tender but it is quite definitely recovered: it certainly took a long time. And that reminds me of Lady Dalhousie's story of her trip to Paradise Island. She and two of her children went there for one day and a night in the course of an official tour round P.E.A. The G.G. himself couldn't spare the time to go across to the island. She went to bed that night with her small son in the same room and her daughter next door. At about 1 a.m., in the middle of the wildest tropical storm a knock came at her door. Thunderstruck she flung on a dressing gown and found herself confronted by a young man in swimming trunks with the rain sheeting down on him. He asked her to take a message back to his father in Salisbury as he was just off to commit suicide. Playing for time she said that she couldn't possibly discuss such a matter in her dressing gown and he was to wait until she had some clothes on. She then returned to him and suggested that it was far too filthy a night in which to commit suicide and wouldn't it be better to wait until morning. He then said that he was going to swim across to the mainland and he would either drown or be eaten by sharks. At that moment he drew out of his trunks a large knife with which he was going to have a go at the sharks before they got him. The next moment her daughter wakened up and came to the door, to see her mother apparently about to be attacked by a man with a knife! To cut a long story short, Lady D. persuaded him to give up the attempt that night; and very early in the morning she got the island authorities organised to get him back to Salisbury in double quick time. He had had some pretty severe matrimonial troubles and was a bit round the bend. But before he was whisked away the next day he was going round saying how Lady D. had saved his life. That was her peaceful break on Paradise Island; I had a very tame time in comparison!

I'm getting on very gradually with all my preparations. James and I got round yesterday to fitting on the little rack that I have bought which goes on the boot of my car. This will give us a bit more luggage space for our journey back. I shall only be able to bring with me on the ship what I can carry in the car, and what is left over from James and his luggage. So I shall be living in the odd pair of slacks and aged cotton dresses until my heavy luggage arrives. Now I have the rack on I can take to town one of my aged tin trunks that had the locks and hasps wrenched off on the journey out here. All sorts of little jobs like this have to be remembered and seen to in time. I think I may have told you that the packers come in on 26 May, which will leave me free of any house worries for my last week. Then follows the Whit weekend when everything should be pretty quiet, so I am hoping to get away without a last-minute wild scramble. If James can get away, we shall leave Salisbury on 3 June and spend a day on the way down in the Gorongosa game park in P.E.A. We have to be in Beira by 6 June to get the car on the ship. I can hardly wait now to get away; but I shall need every scrap of time to get through everything.

10 May 1963

A *pondock* (or possibly *pondok*) is probably a Bantu word for a hut. In fact what Roger has is a square thatched cottage, which consists of a bed-sittingroom and a bathroom. Lots of houses here have these little *pondoks* or rondavels if they are round, so that people can have a bit of privacy if they want it.

No time to stop and tell you very much news. There is a lot going on and of course I am going out much more than I wish. But it will pass and it isn't long now. Only just over three weeks before I leave Salisbury. By the way, I met at lunch a few days ago a cousin of Winston Field, the PM. She is a Mrs Mellor, and she has a Field brother who farms just outside Tenbury Wells. I wonder if Leslie knows him. All the Fields, including Winston, were at Bromsgrove School, but they would all be after Daddy's time.

12 May 1963

Yes, I did manage to fit in my inoculations (the one word you are never able to spell, and thank heaven there is *one*!). They had not the slightest effect on me, but my vaccination did come up into the tiniest little itchy place which proved that it had taken. I think I have been jabbed so many times now that I have worked up a complete immunity to all the side effects. So that is one more thing done. In fact I think that I am terribly well organised! I have done everything I can think of before the actual final packing itself The only one remaining worry is a job for Sixpence. I had hoped to get him one through spreading the word around my friends, but everyone seems to be well suited at present, so I shall put an advertisement instead in the local daily paper. This always brings results evidently.

The parties are in full swing, but I have lied to such good effect that I have managed to keep a few nights free, and my weekends. This is sheer self-preservation and I'm sure that the good Lord will overlook my wickednesses of lying! I gave a small dinner party on Friday night – it should have been a biggish buffet supper, but six people I invited fell by the wayside for one reason or another and it was too late to ask anybody else without their realising that they were fills in!! Then on Tuesday I have all the locally engaged girls and their husbands and fiancés and boy friends to a quick supper and on to see a film of Cliff Richard. I thought I ought to give them a final bun fight, and as there isn't a good stage show on, we decided a film would be the next best thing. They are all young things, so ought to enjoy our Cliff! My last bit of planned entertainment is a beer party on my last Sunday morning in the house – I may have told you this already – open house for all and sundry.

It's early Sunday morning. I got up long before the sun and started typing this in almost total darkness. Now the sun is pouring in and I must get cracking on the other chores of the day. This will probably not go until Tuesday's bag, so I shan't close it down now in case I have anything world-shattering to add.

Tomorrow I have another farewell lunch date, so I shan't have time to type any more before the bag goes in the afternoon.

16 May 1963

Letters from now on will probably be pretty scrappy affairs, but I'm determined to try to keep up the record to the end.

News is all of the mad round of farewells. A very late dinner on Monday night, a lunch party on Tuesday, eleven people to buffet supper on Tuesday (all the local girls and their husbands and boy friends) then off to the cinema and home long after twelve. Yesterday another lunch party for me, this time an all hen do for fifteen women I know. Last night I don't mind admitting that, as I had no engagement I was in bed by 8.15 p.m.! Shall I be glad to get away now. Today I got from the AA all the papers about exporting the car and tickets for the trip across the Channel. I really feel now that I am on the way.

Off now to the next chore – not that writing to you is ever a chore.

28 May 1963

Things are getting organised, but only just, and I must not stop for more than a few minutes to write to you. So shorthand news.

I land at Venice on 25 June. Presumably a letter sent to me c/o *Europa*, Lloyd Triestino Line, Venice would find me.

Seventy people for my drinks party on Sunday. The morning was foul and I had terrible visions of trying to cram everyone into my small house. But just in time the sun came out and all was well. The packers came in this morning and all my chattels have gone, except what I am bringing back with me. Tonight I go and stay with Mrs Piggott, and in the next two days Sixpence and I will see that Klokkespel is clean and tidy. I've got Sixpence a job with a Yorkshire woman who sounds very nice on the phone, so I hope that will work out. But it was a long and complicated business getting this arranged.

James is away and comes back on Friday. We leave on Monday afternoon, spend the night just outside Umtali, go on the next night into the Gorongoza game reserve in P.E.A. and then trundle quietly on to Beira to get the car there on the Thursday morning before we sail. I doubt very much if I shall write again before we leave Salisbury, but I shall certainly write from Beira just to let you know that we have reached there. Now off again to the next chore. The Barltrops give me a farewell party tonight. I have dinner with Abe Abrahamson tomorrow and that is the end of my engagements.

Have remade my will. Top copy going to the Bank and copy for you will go by next bag. Very simply £100 to each of the children, £250 to Helen Broadbent and the rest to you. The other was so out of date I thought I had better scrap it.

Peplow Guest House

4 June 1963

Hurrah, hurrah, we're on our way. First night out of Salisbury over and in ten minutes it will be breakfast time.

Two letters from you arrived on my very last morning in the office – Saturday. One bag had got delayed, hence the coincidence of the 'two' letters. I had a terrific giggle over your reply to the Rotarians. Hope I can live up to the reputation you have given me!!

Won't stop to tell you much news in this letter. Its main purpose is to give you one or two addresses in case you feel like writing!!

Passenger, c/o *Europa*, Lloyd Triestino, Calle Larga XXII, Marzo No 2288, Venice. There on 25 June.

de Castro & Co, PO Box 262, Port Said. There on 21 June.

L. Savon & Ries, PO Box 1228, Aden. There on 17 June.

Must drop a little line now to Mrs Piggott to thank her for putting me up. James and I expect to leave here at about 9.30 this morning and get to Gorongoza after lunch for the afternoon game viewing. Next letter from Beira.

Beira

8 June 1963

This should have been a long and fascinating letter all about our adventures in Gorongoza and Beira. Instead it will be a short tale of woe, now happily told and all well again.

We made Gorongoza by late afternoon, having had to wait only one hour (marvellous) for the incredibly inefficient ferry. I felt perfectly all right that night but didn't want any breakfast the next morning. However up at dawn and three hours of driving round the reserve. By the time we got back I was feeling pretty ropey so straight to bed. Temperature of 103 degrees and aches and pains. James is terribly efficient and carries all sorts of medicines around with him. So he dosed me up and hoped that after a day in bed I would be well enough to beat it to Beira. There was no medical aid in the camp – not even hot water, so it wasn't a place to linger in for long.

The next morning I still felt wretched but temp. down to 101 degrees so off we set. The road between the park and the main road is thirty miles of hell plus the ferry. With such a heavy load I had about three inches of clearance. So we decided that despite fevers I had better drive as I know the exact limits of the car's abilities. You never saw such a funny sight as me in lovely warm weather with your huge apricot woolly on, a rug tucked behind my neck and all the windows closed – and shivering. James must have suffocated! Somehow we got to Beira and within five minutes I was in a hotel bed – with a temp. of 104 degrees! Life was looking a bit grim, I can tell you. Well we got the hotel to call a doctor – to my surprise this turned out to be a fat Portuguese woman. She prescribed various pills (this was Thursday midday) and all that day and night and Friday until I went to bed I alternately sweated till the bed was soaked (and moved over to the other bed – no single rooms in this hotel) and shivered and shivered, and my temp. refused to budge below 101 degrees and kept on bounding up to 103 degrees. We were all set to get another doctor in this morning to take a blood sample, as I dared not go aboard ship with an unspecified bug, but miracle of miracles, at about 4 a.m. I suddenly felt the fever break. I took my temp. and it was normal.

Now I am lying in bed on the morning of the day we sail. James has had to do everything and has been simply wonderful and I'm saving up my strength so that the ship doesn't think that it is embarking an alcoholic. I haven't had a bit of solid food for three days so I'm feeling a bit wobbly on my pins.

James has just returned this minute from paying the doctor's bill. She told him that she thinks I may have malaria. I personally don't believe this because I haven't been anywhere near a malarial area in the incubation period. My guess is tick fever. I found two on me about a week ago. Anyway, I'll have a blood test when I get home. The great thing is I'm normal and the sea voyage should set me up again no end. So *no need to worry*, Calamity!

Now I'm going to get up quietly and we shall go. The ship is in; all I have to do is walk!

And so ended my African venture. Little did I think when I was first appointed as a female labourer, temporary, that I would experience these three memorable years in Africa. I was indeed fortunate.

Postlude

In 1963 I returned to my little house in Balham and to the Commonwealth Relations Office in Downing Street. Eight months later Roger pursued me to London. On Saint Valentine's Day 1964, three days after his arrival, he finally caught his Old Bag.

We are still married.

Years later, on holiday in South Africa.

Appendices

I would not be human if I did not like the tone of these appendices. But looking back I have few illusions. There were not many women in diplomacy all those years ago: one did one's job to the best of one's ability, sometimes as good as the men, sometimes better and sometimes worse. But the men of those times, if not prejudiced against women, gave one extra credit for what one did, because one was a woman. These are the grains of salt that one should take when reading the appendices. I doubt if these would be the reactions nowadays.

Reference: CX 100/32B/90

TELEPHONE NO. 27005
TELEGRAPHIC ADDRESS "FEDPRIME"

OFFICE OF THE PRIME MINISTER
AND EXTERNAL AFFAIRS,
P. O. BOX 1403,
SALISBURY

21st August, 1962

Dear High Commissioner,

Now that he has virtually closed off his files on the subject of the Hammarskjoeld Commission of Inquiry and the Extradition Treaty with South Africa, O'Donovan, the Secretary for Law, has asked me to express to you his very great appreciation of the valuable assistance he received from Margaret Archer in both connections.

O'Donovan refers particularly to Margaret's great efficiency and cheerful co-operation at all hours of the day in arranging for the attendance of witnesses at the Hammarskjoeld Inquiry from all corners of the globe. Both Mr. Perry, the Commission's Secretary, and Mr. Cooke, who led the evidence for the Federal Government, have also expressed their appreciation of the assistance she gave. O'Donovan mentions in similar terms her most valuable assistance in keeping him informed of developments in connection with the negotiation of the Extradition Treaty with South Africa.

In passing on these expressions of gratitude I should like personally to be associated with them.

Yours Sincerely,

Hugh Parry

(H.N. Parry)

His Excellency The Rt. Hon. Lord Alport, T.D.,
High Commissioner for the United Kingdom,
R.T.A. House,
Baker Avenue,
SALISBURY

HNP/RH

IN CONFIDENCE

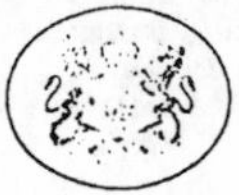

BRITISH HIGH COMMISSION
P.O.BOX 1482
SALISBURY
SOUTHERN RHODESIA

17th October, 1963.

Dear Kenneth,

I would just like to let you know what widespread praise and admiration has been expressed to me during my first months here for Margaret Archer's work during her posting in Salisbury.

I have rarely heard so many kind things said about a former officer in a post, by so many categories of people. The whole office (my Brigadier claims she knew more about defence than the whole of B.D.L.S.), Ministers, Federal and Southern Rhodesian Civil Servants, the top brass in business and industry, and many private individuals have all sung her praises and regretted her departure.

I have no doubt Alport reported on her in this sense: but it is now some months since she left here, and I thought the fact that so many people still speak to me so warmly of her abilities and representational qualities should not go unrecorded.

Yours ever,

Jack Johnston.

(J.B. JOHNSTON)

K.A. East, Esq.,
Commonwealth Relations Office,
LONDON, S.W.1.

The Sudden Assignment

As soon as Hare and his advisers had departed, the U.N. South-West Africa Committee arrived. It had a distinguished and articulate Latin-American professor as chairman, and gave promise of every sort of embarrassment for Welensky and myself. The committee had been refused by the British Government a visa to go to Bechuanaland since they had not given the required assurance that they would not try to enter S.W. Africa from the Protectorate without prior sanction of the South African authorities. As the committee was multi-racial and included an Egyptian who, we assumed, would be happy to become involved in a good juicy incident, everything was done to ensure that the visit passed off smoothly.

A week before their arrival, one of the leading hotels in Salisbury had turned multi-racial and the committee were installed there in comfortable suites under the wing of the efficient and hospitable Cypriot-Greek proprietor. The members, who had apparently suffered the discomforts of hotel accommodation elsewhere in Africa during the earlier stages of their tour, found that the luxury of the Ambassadors Hotel provided a striking contrast. Although both the Federal authorities and I kept as much as possible in the background, since this particular committee had no direct business with either the British or Federal Governments, things were arranged apparently very much to their satisfaction. I had on my staff a vivacious and attractive woman First Secretary. Up to that time I was guilty of the normal male prejudice against women diplomats. I gave this officer the task of maintaining liaison with the committee and her tact, combined with her willingness to transport the chairman and other members of the committee to see the sights of Salisbury in her white Sunbeam sports car, won her a convincing personal success. When she attended the committee at the airport five days later to bid them goodbye on my behalf, the chairman flung his arms round her neck and kissing her enthusiastically on both cheeks, exclaimed, 'You are ze only beautiful thing to happen to me in Africa.'

As the visit had gone off without incident and as I had been kept in close and friendly contact with the work of the committee, I came to two conclusions. First, that international diplomacy was not quite as serious a matter as I had anticipated and secondly, that women diplomats are of essential value, provided they have the expected attributes of their sex and equip themselves with appropriate means of personal transport.

I regret, though I am not surprised, that this officer has since left the service on marriage. It is neither realistic nor right that the State should expect an attractive and talented woman, except in very particular circumstances, to make diplomacy a career and forgo the fulfilment of marriage and family life. Yet on a short-service basis they can provide an important element of strength for a normal diplomatic staff. Special conditions should be available in the newly established Diplomatic Service for this type of official.

From *The Sudden Assignment* by the Right Honourable Lord Alport (Hodder & Stoughton 1965). Incidentally, Alport got it wrong. I did not go to the airport to see off the professor, as you will see from my letter of 17 July 1961.